PandoraHearts

Jun Mochizuki

D1545176

CONTENTS

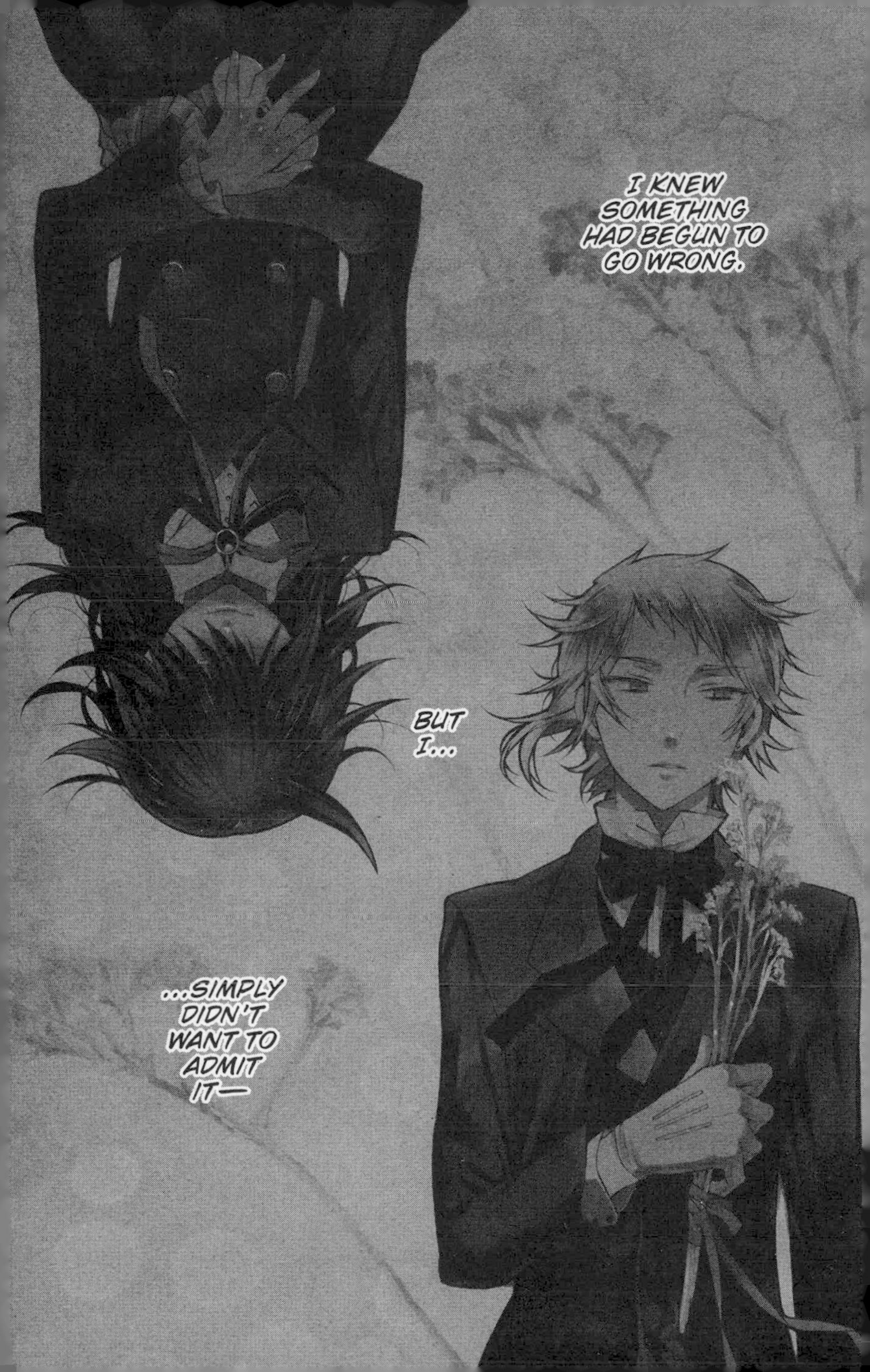
I KNEW SOMETHING HAD BEGUN TO GO WRONG.
BUT I...
...SIMPLY DIDN'T WANT TO ADMIT IT—

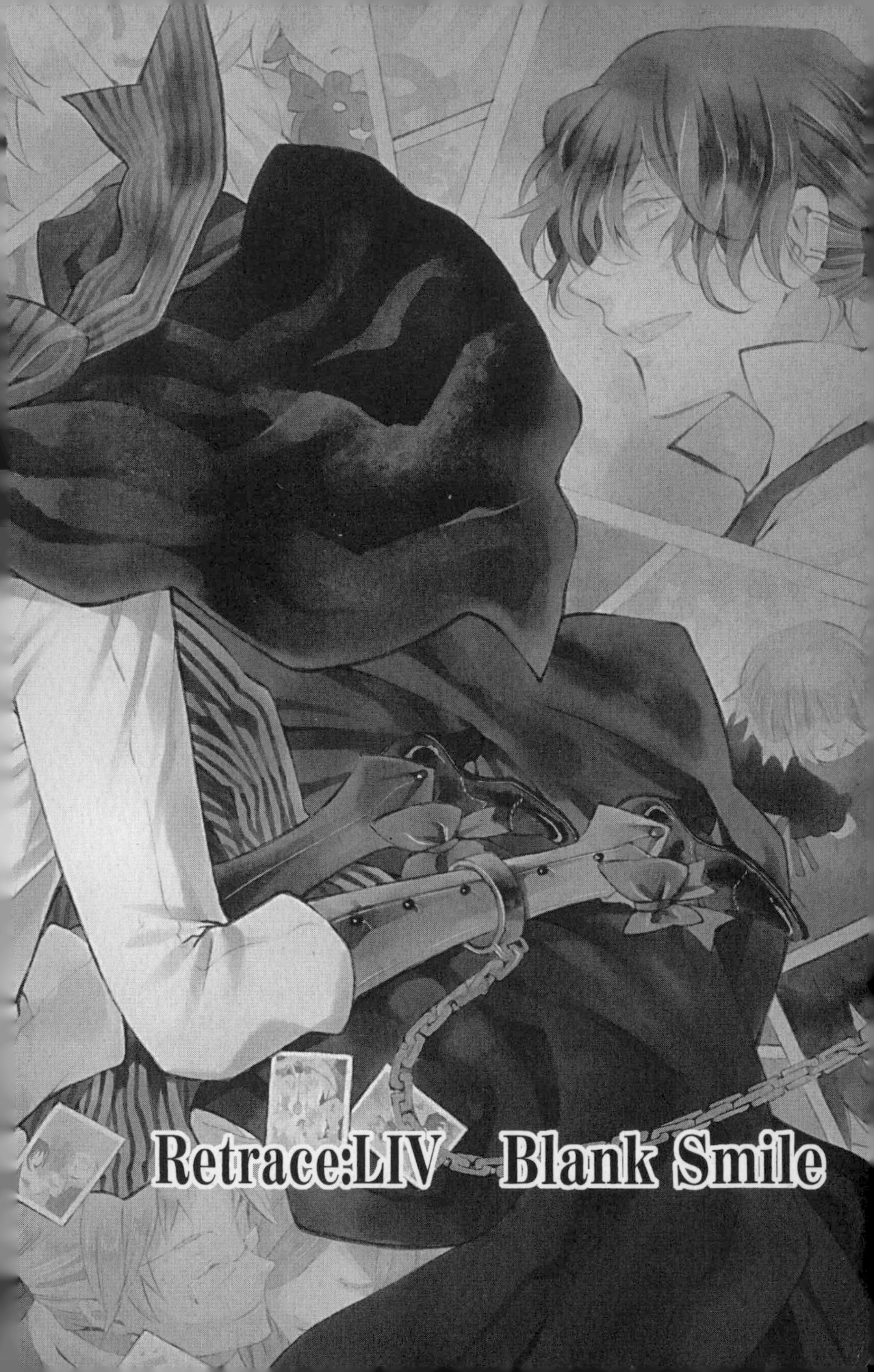
Retrace:LIV Blank Smile

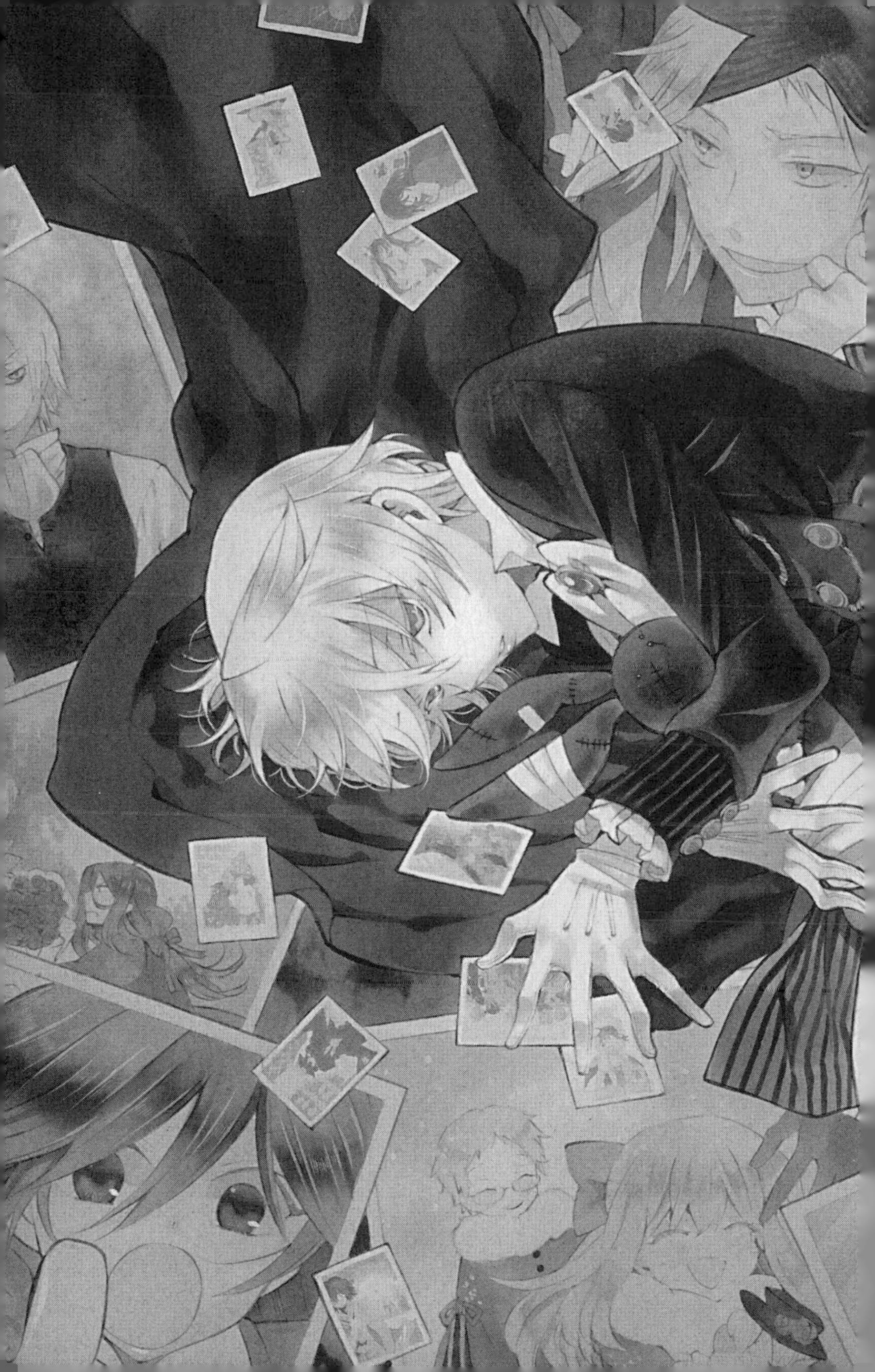

BONUS: WHICH DO YOU LIKE BETTER?

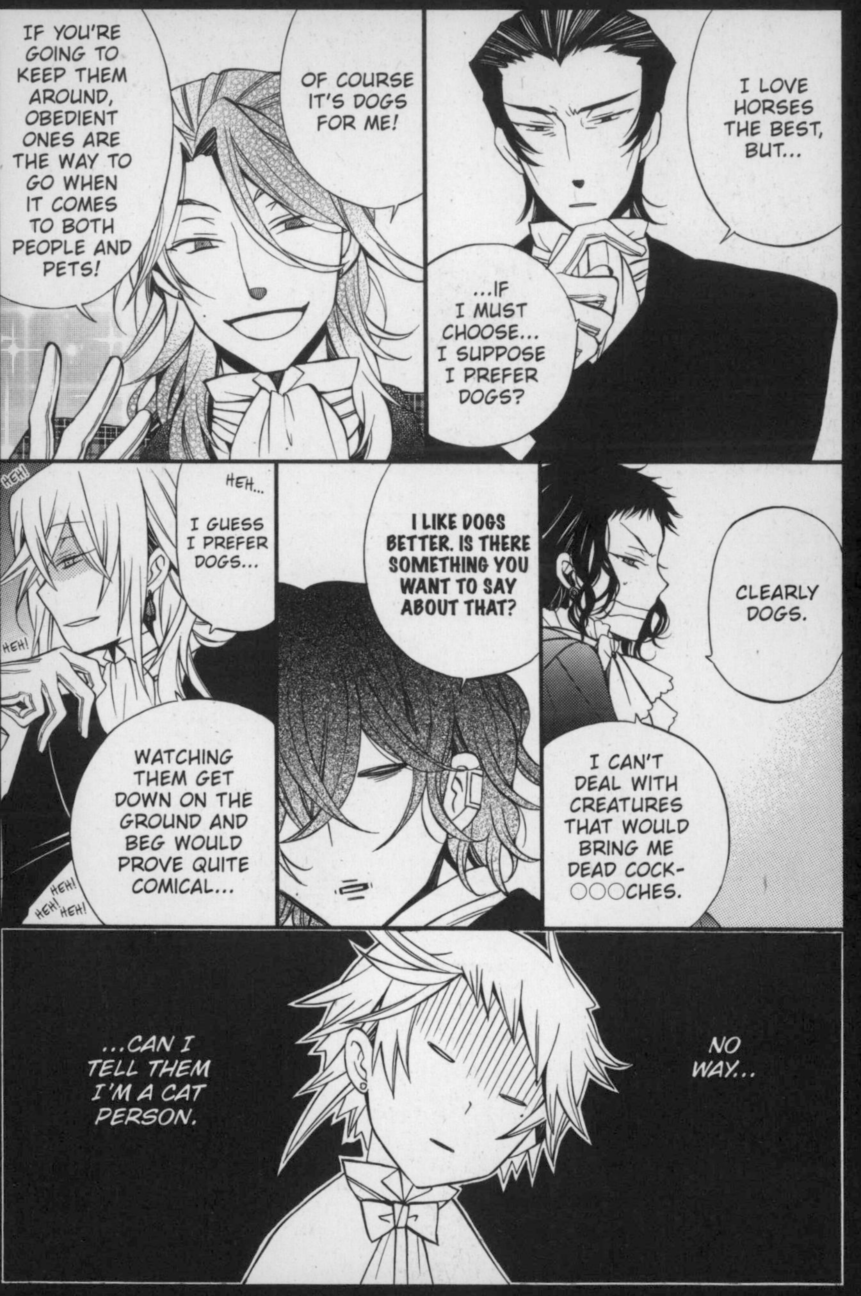
I LOVE HORSES THE BEST, BUT...
...IF I MUST CHOOSE... I SUPPOSE I PREFER DOGS?
OF COURSE IT'S DOGS FOR ME!
IF YOU'RE GOING TO KEEP THEM AROUND, OBEDIENT ONES ARE THE WAY TO GO WHEN IT COMES TO BOTH PEOPLE AND PETS!
CLEARLY DOGS.
I CAN'T DEAL WITH CREATURES THAT WOULD BRING ME DEAD COCK-○○○CHES.
I LIKE DOGS BETTER. IS THERE SOMETHING YOU WANT TO SAY ABOUT THAT?
HEH!
HEH...
I GUESS I PREFER DOGS...
HEH!
WATCHING THEM GET DOWN ON THE GROUND AND BEG WOULD PROVE QUITE COMICAL...
HEH! HEH! HEH!
NO WAY...
...CAN I TELL THEM I'M A CAT PERSON.

THE VESSALIUS FAMILY PREFERS CATS.

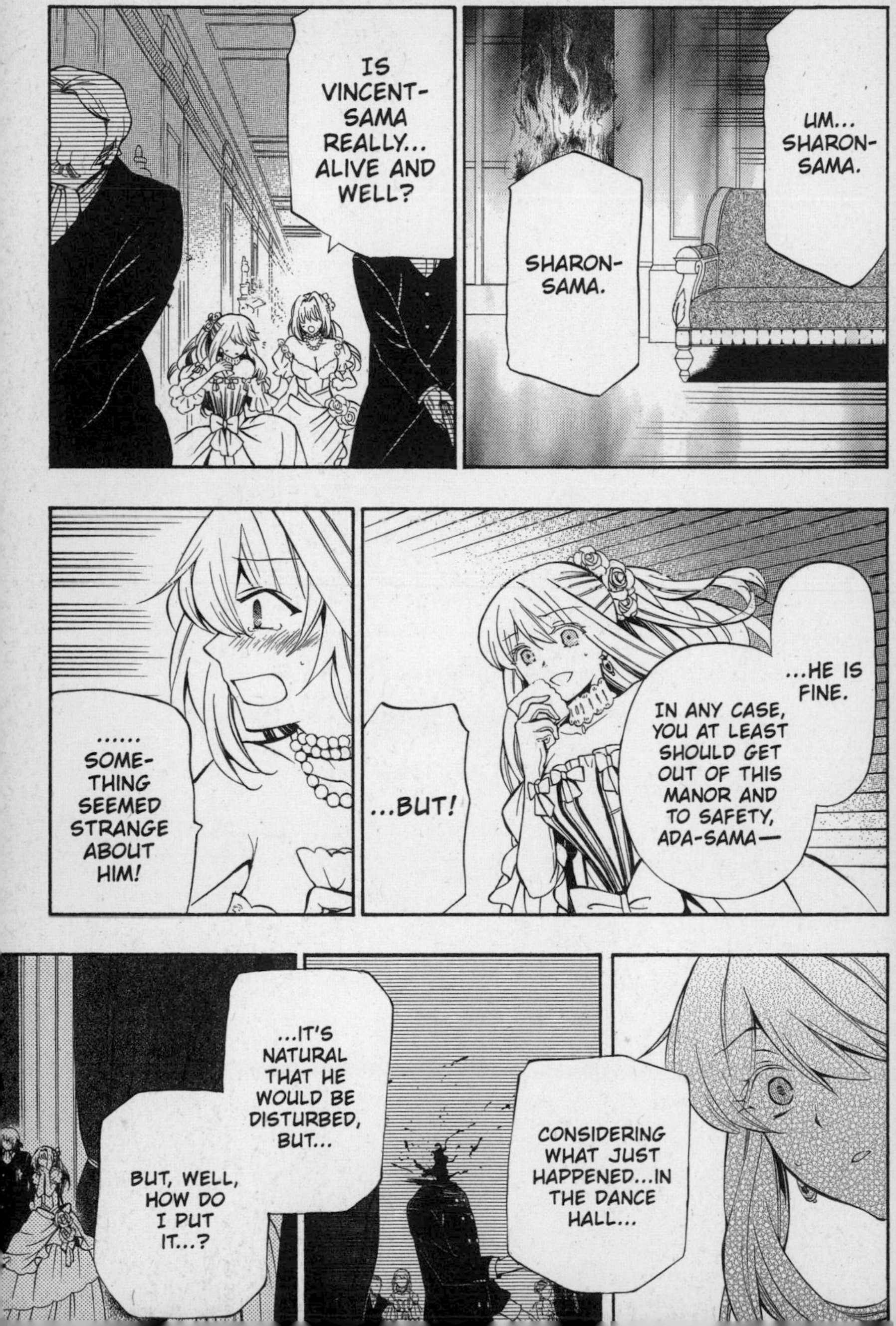
UM... SHARON-SAMA.
SHARON-SAMA.
IS VINCENT-SAMA REALLY... ALIVE AND WELL?
...HE IS FINE.
IN ANY CASE, YOU AT LEAST SHOULD GET OUT OF THIS MANOR AND TO SAFETY, ADA-SAMA—
...BUT!
...... SOME-THING SEEMED STRANGE ABOUT HIM!
CONSIDERING WHAT JUST HAPPENED...IN THE DANCE HALL...
...IT'S NATURAL THAT HE WOULD BE DISTURBED, BUT...
BUT, WELL, HOW DO I PUT IT...?

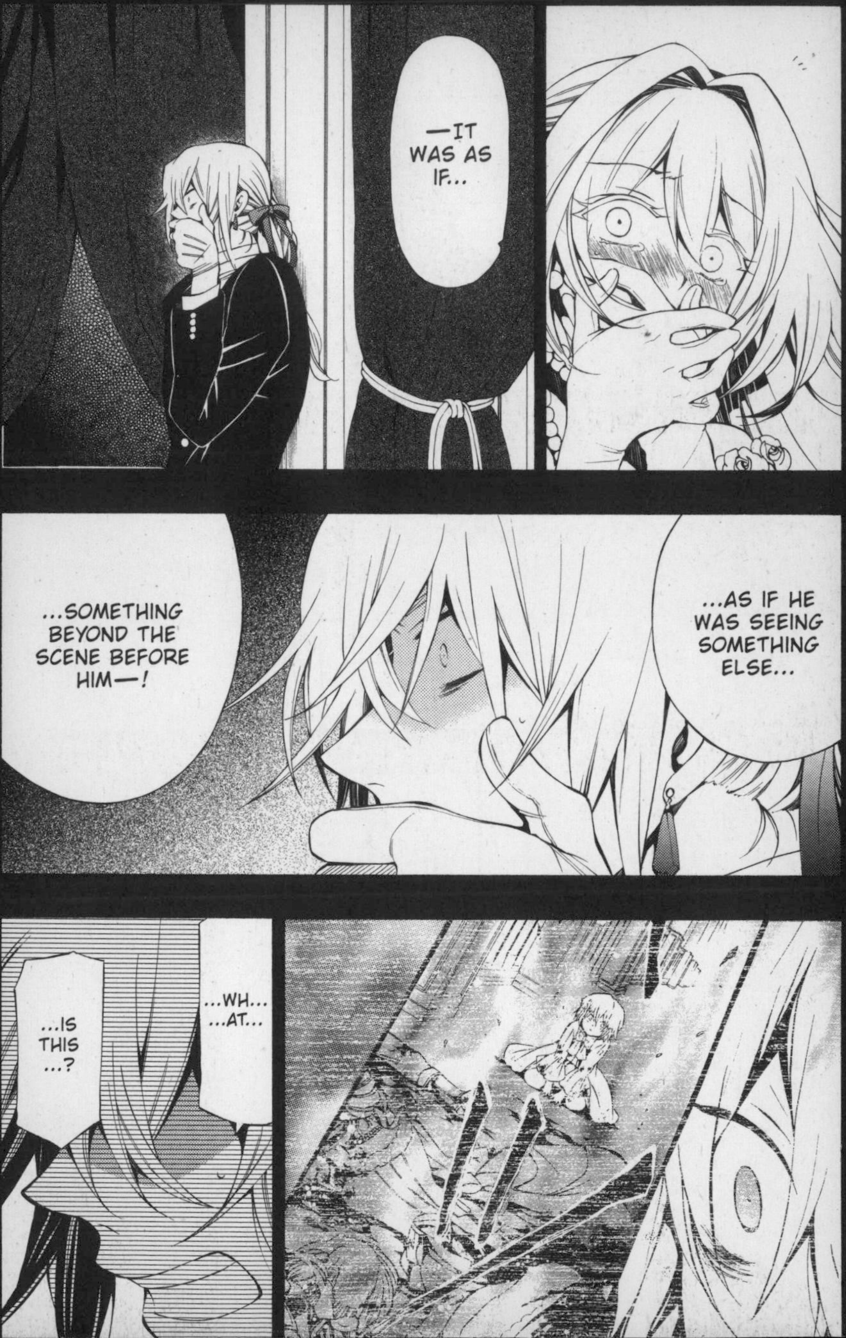
—IT WAS AS IF...
...AS IF HE WAS SEEING SOMETHING ELSE...
...SOMETHING BEYOND THE SCENE BEFORE HIM—!
...WH... ...AT...
...IS THIS ...?

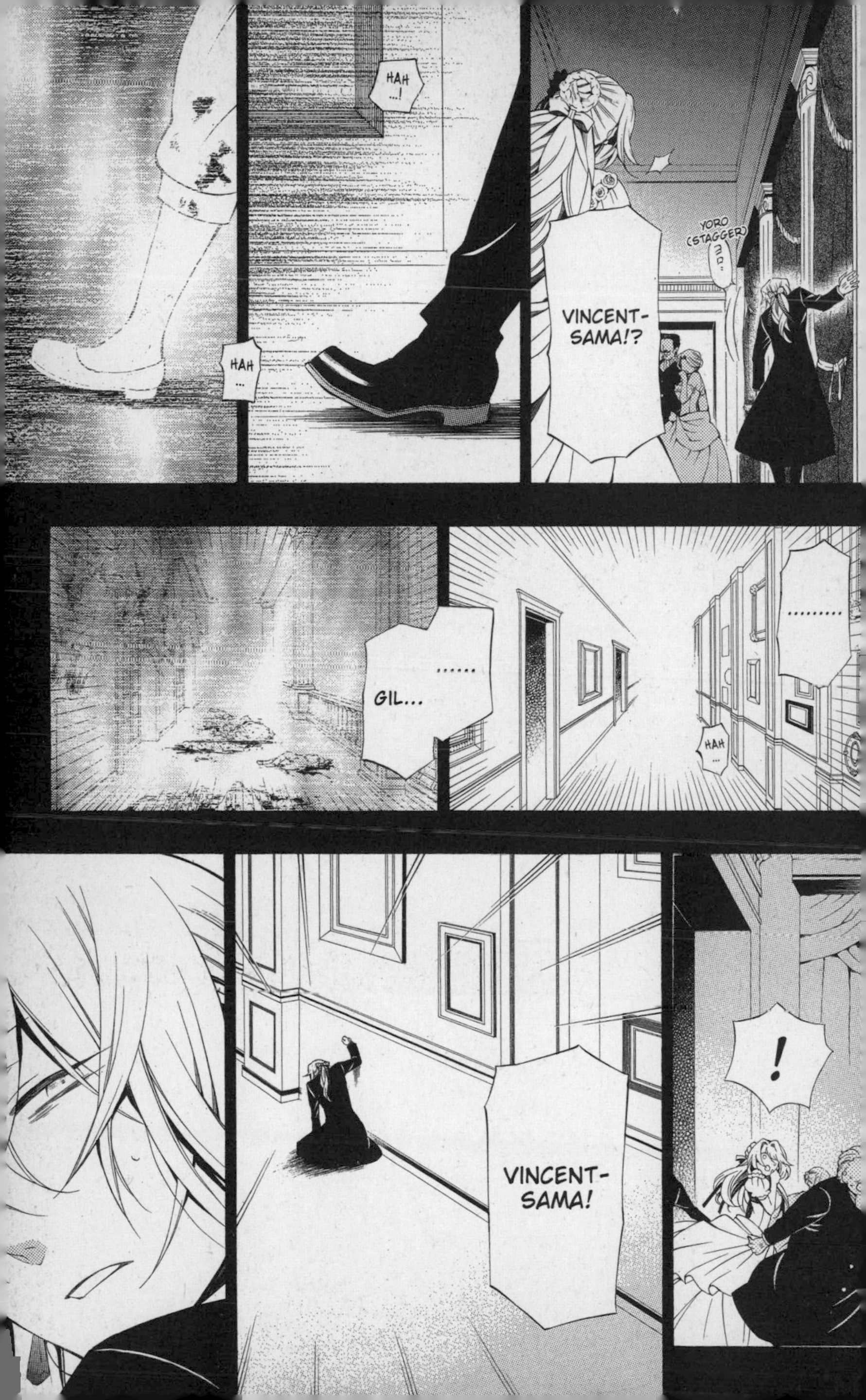
YORO (STAGGER)
ヨロ…
VINCENT-SAMA!?
HAH ...!
HAH ...
....
HAH ...
......
GIL...
!
VINCENT-SAMA!

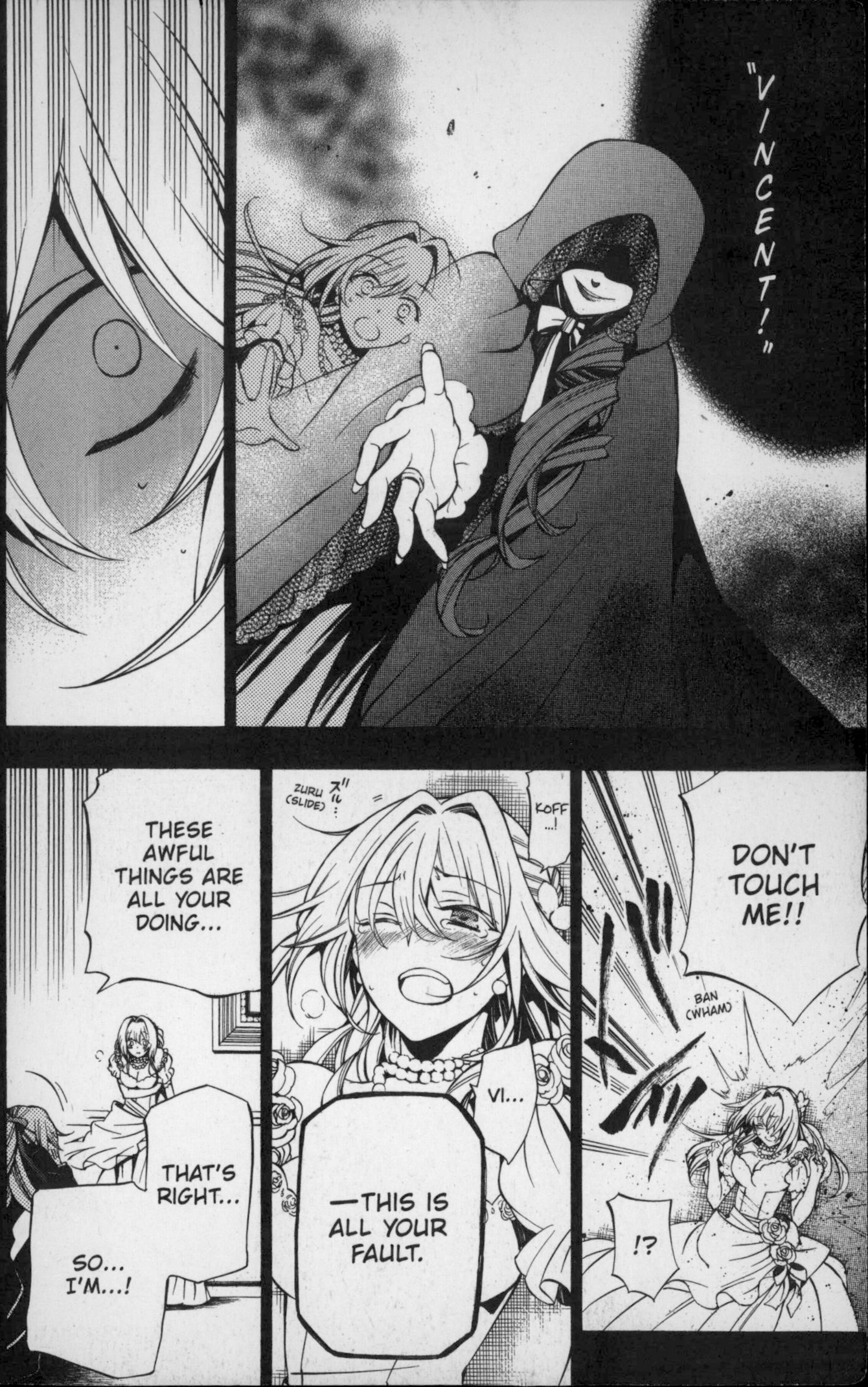
"VINCENT!"
DON'T TOUCH ME!!
BAN (WHAM)
!?
KOFF ...!
ZURU (SLIDE) ズル…
VI...
—THIS IS ALL YOUR FAULT.
THESE AWFUL THINGS ARE ALL YOUR DOING...
THAT'S RIGHT...
SO... I'M...!

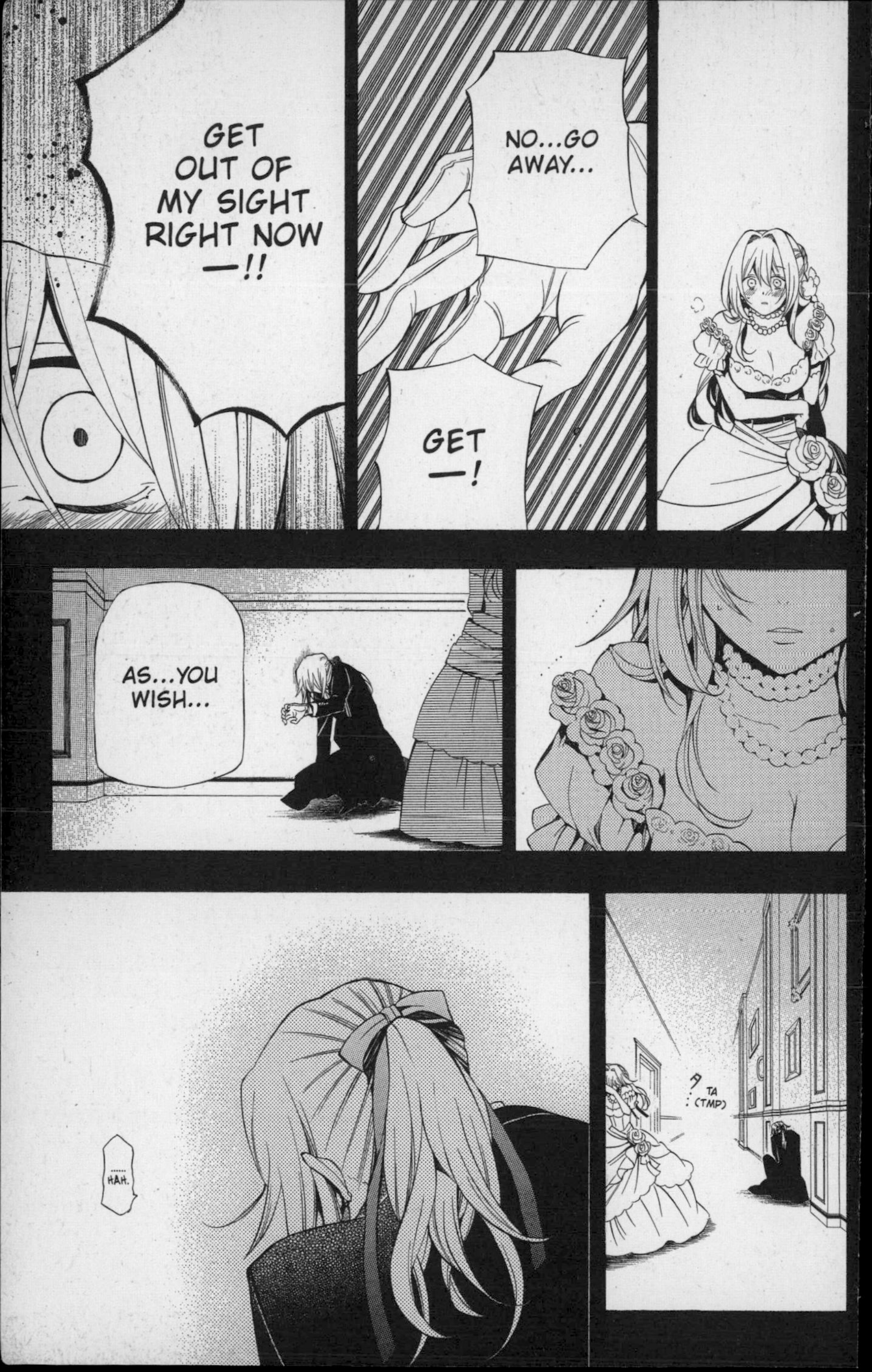
NO...GO AWAY...
GET—!
GET OUT OF MY SIGHT RIGHT NOW—!!
AS...YOU WISH...
タ
TA (TMP)
......HAH.

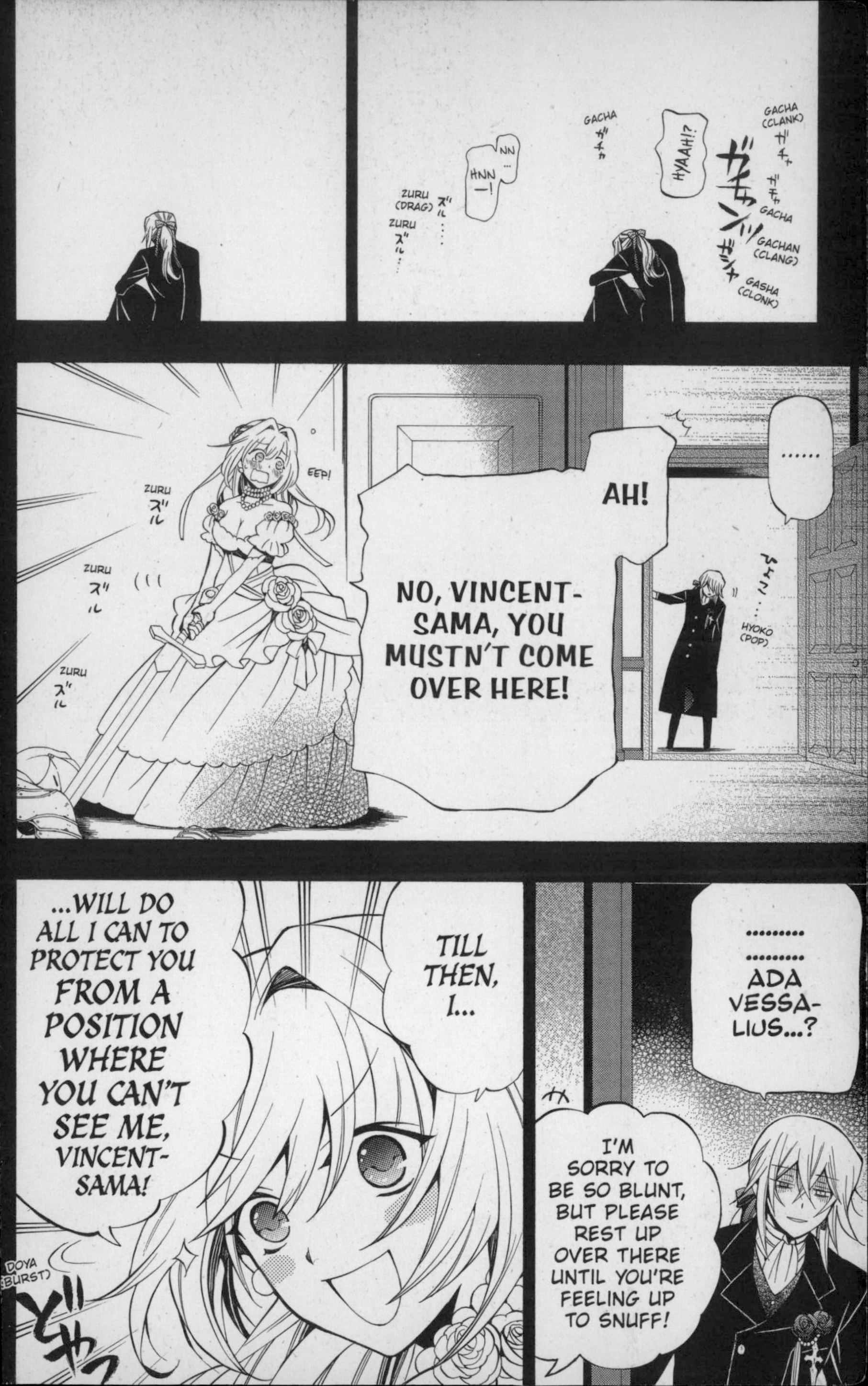
GACHA (CLANK)
HYAAH!?
GACHA
GACHA
GACHAN (CLANG)
GASHA (CLONK)
NN... HNN—!
ZURU (DRAG)
ZURU
......
HYOKO (POP)
AH!
NO, VINCENT-SAMA, YOU MUSTN'T COME OVER HERE!
EEP!
ZURU
ZURU
ZURU
.... ADA VESSALIUS...?
I'M SORRY TO BE SO BLUNT, BUT PLEASE REST UP OVER THERE UNTIL YOU'RE FEELING UP TO SNUFF!
TILL THEN, I...
...WILL DO ALL I CAN TO PROTECT YOU FROM A POSITION WHERE YOU CAN'T SEE ME, VINCENT-SAMA!
DOYA (BURST)

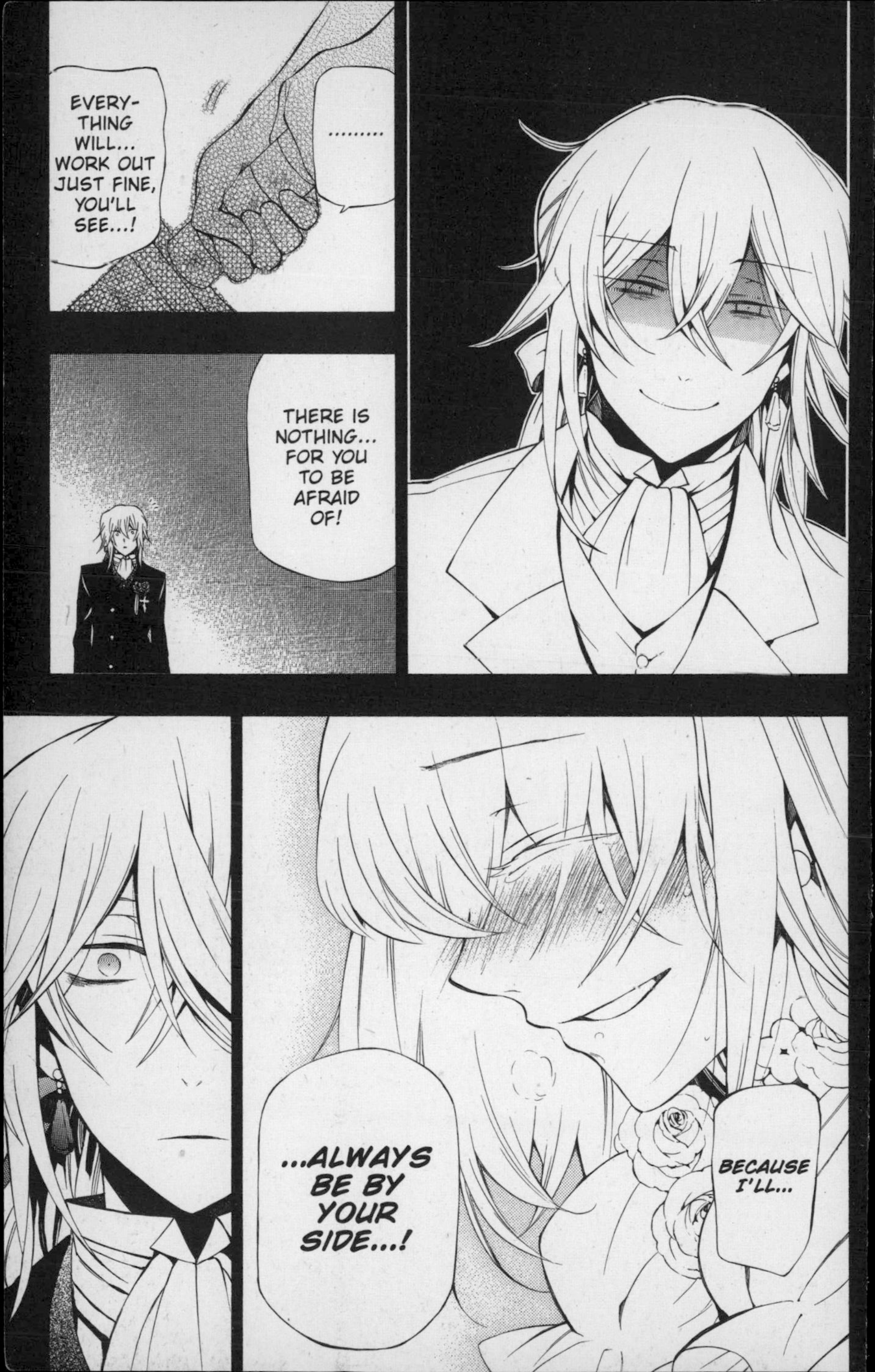
....
EVERY-THING WILL... WORK OUT JUST FINE, YOU'LL SEE...!
THERE IS NOTHING... FOR YOU TO BE AFRAID OF!
BECAUSE I'LL...
...ALWAYS BE BY YOUR SIDE...!

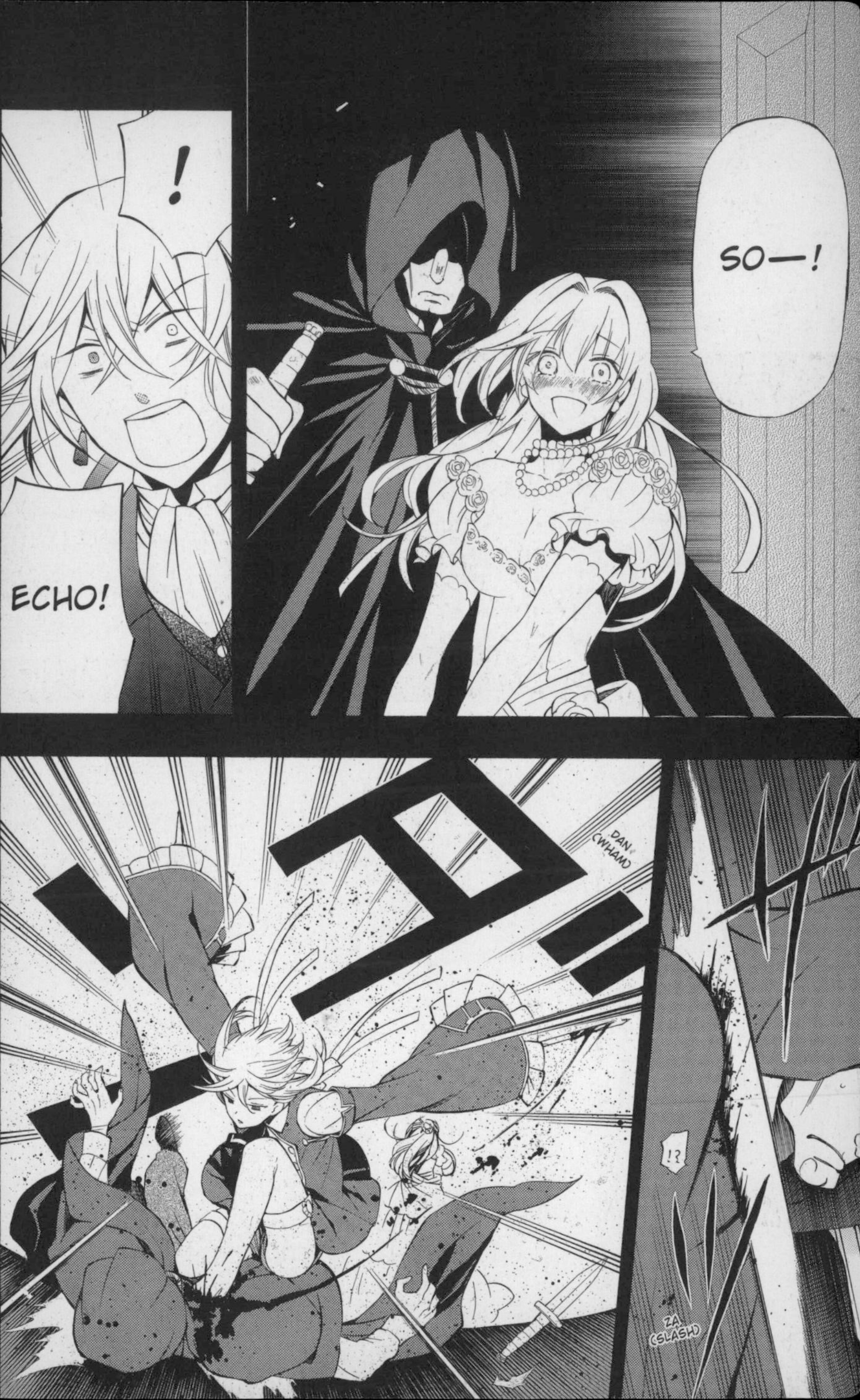
SO—!
!
ECHO!
!?
ZA (SLASH)
DAN (WHAM)

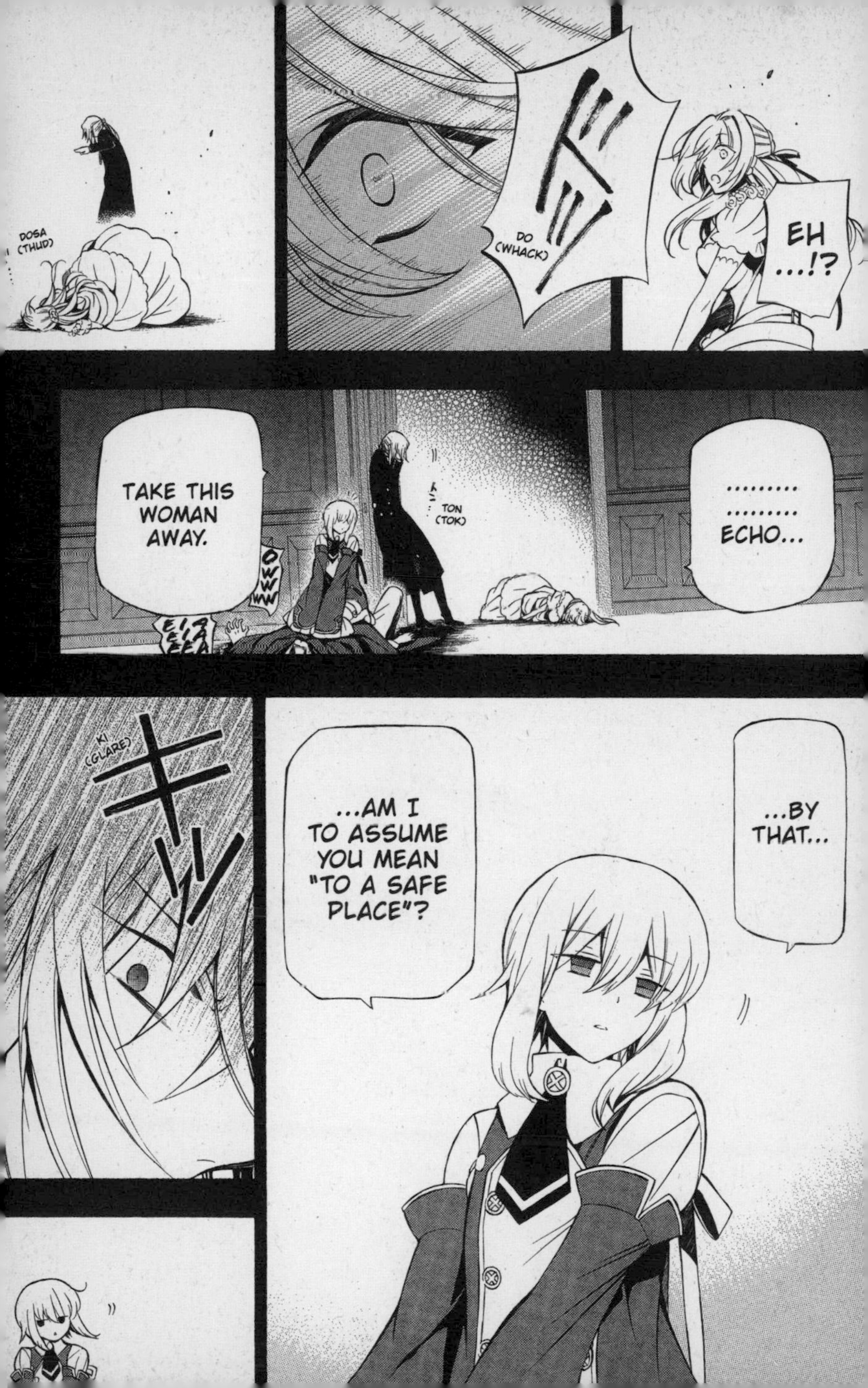
EH ...!?
DO (WHACK)
DOSA (THUD)
.... ECHO...
TON (TOK)
TAKE THIS WOMAN AWAY.
OWWWW
...BY THAT...
...AM I TO ASSUME YOU MEAN "TO A SAFE PLACE"?
KI (GLARE)

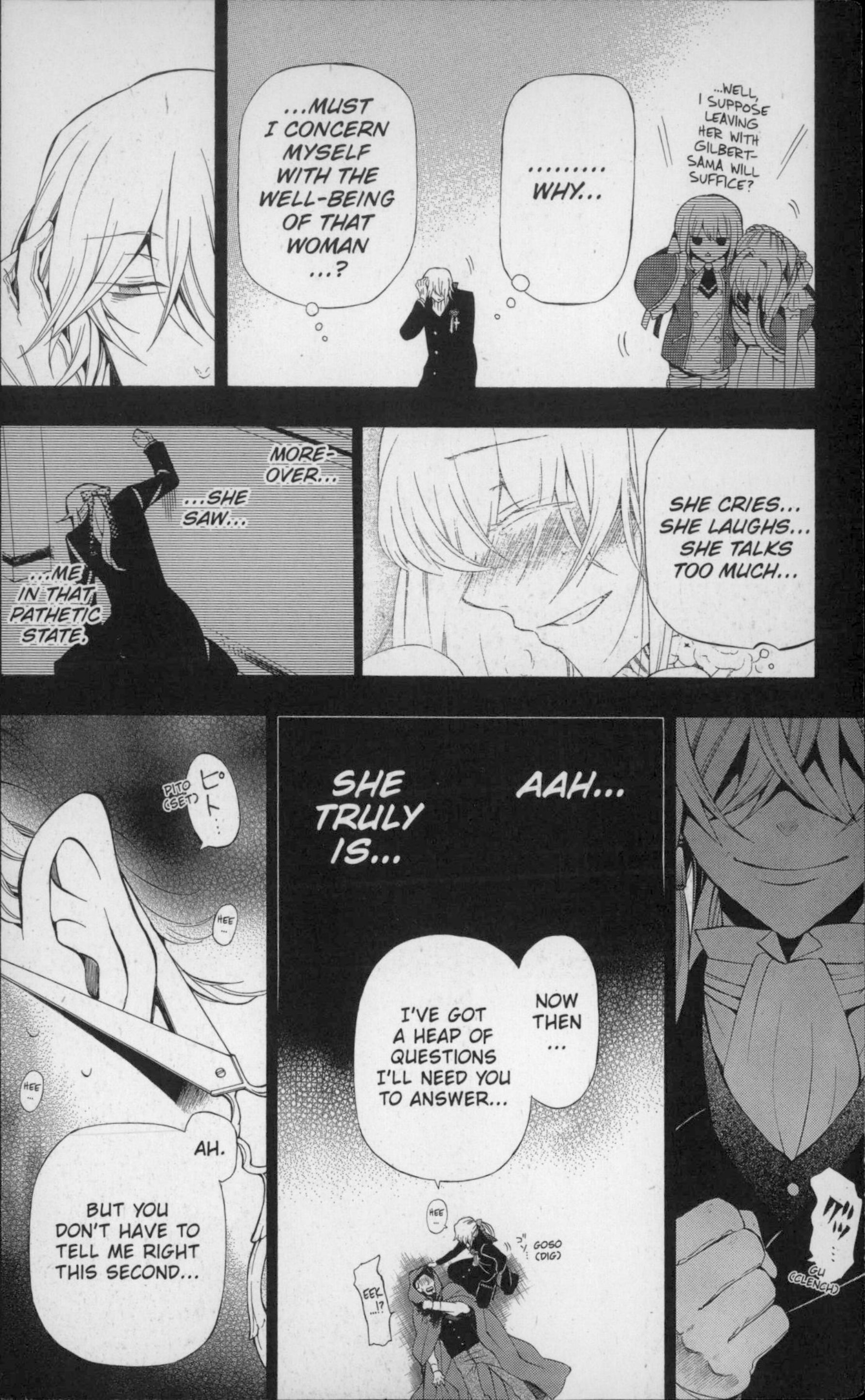
...WELL, I SUPPOSE LEAVING HER WITH GILBERT-SAMA WILL SUFFICE?
..........WHY...
...MUST I CONCERN MYSELF WITH THE WELL-BEING OF THAT WOMAN ...?
SHE CRIES... SHE LAUGHS... SHE TALKS TOO MUCH...
MORE-OVER...
...SHE SAW...
...ME IN THAT PATHETIC STATE.
GU (CLENCH)
AAH...
SHE TRULY IS...
NOW THEN ...
I'VE GOT A HEAP OF QUESTIONS I'LL NEED YOU TO ANSWER...
HEE ...
GOSO (DIG)
EEK ...!?
ピト…
PITO (SET)
HEE ...
HEE ...
AH.
BUT YOU DON'T HAVE TO TELL ME RIGHT THIS SECOND...

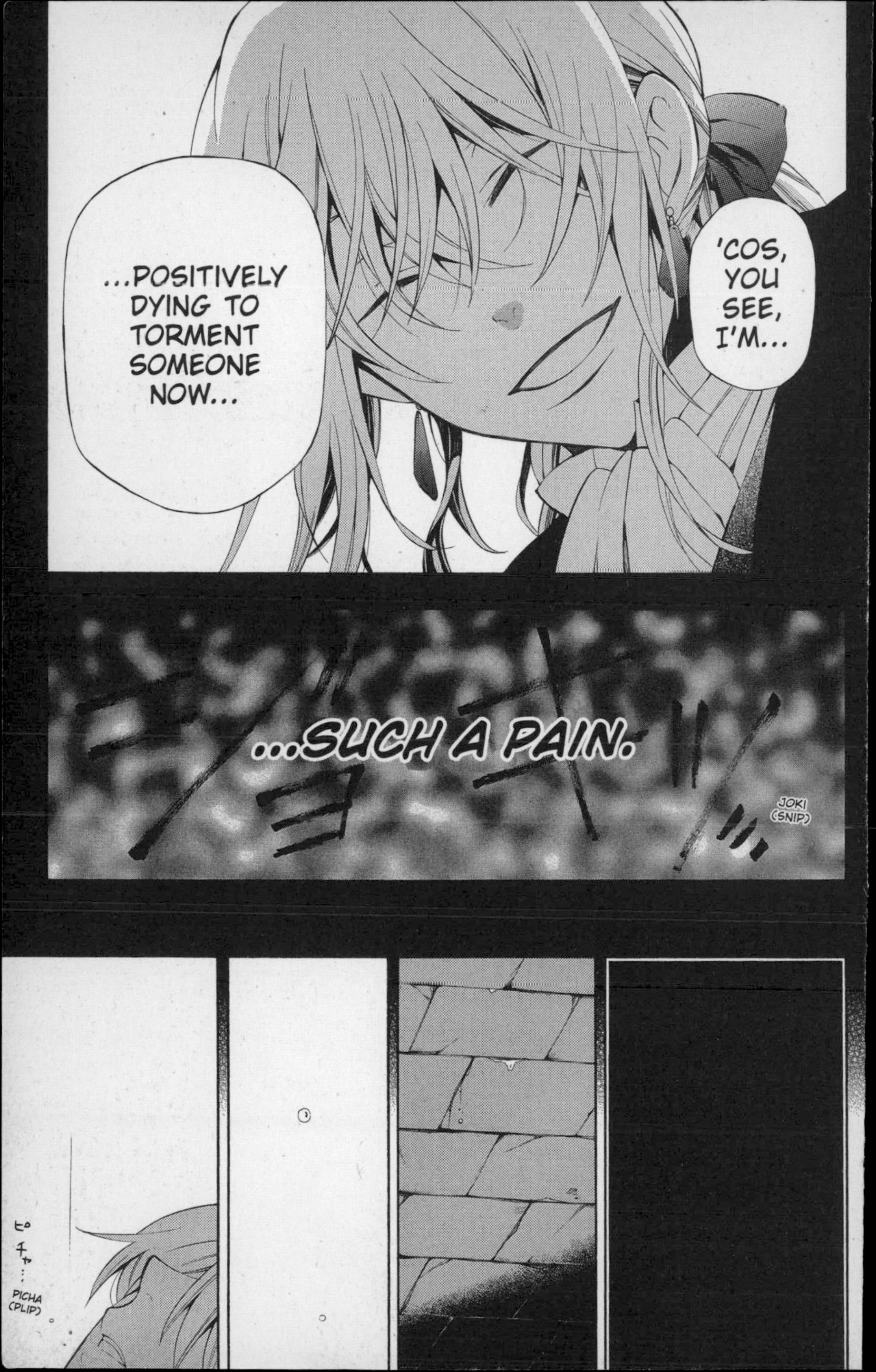
'COS, YOU SEE, I'M...
...POSITIVELY DYING TO TORMENT SOMEONE NOW...
...SUCH A PAIN.
JOKI (SNIP)
ピチャ…
PICHA (PLIP)

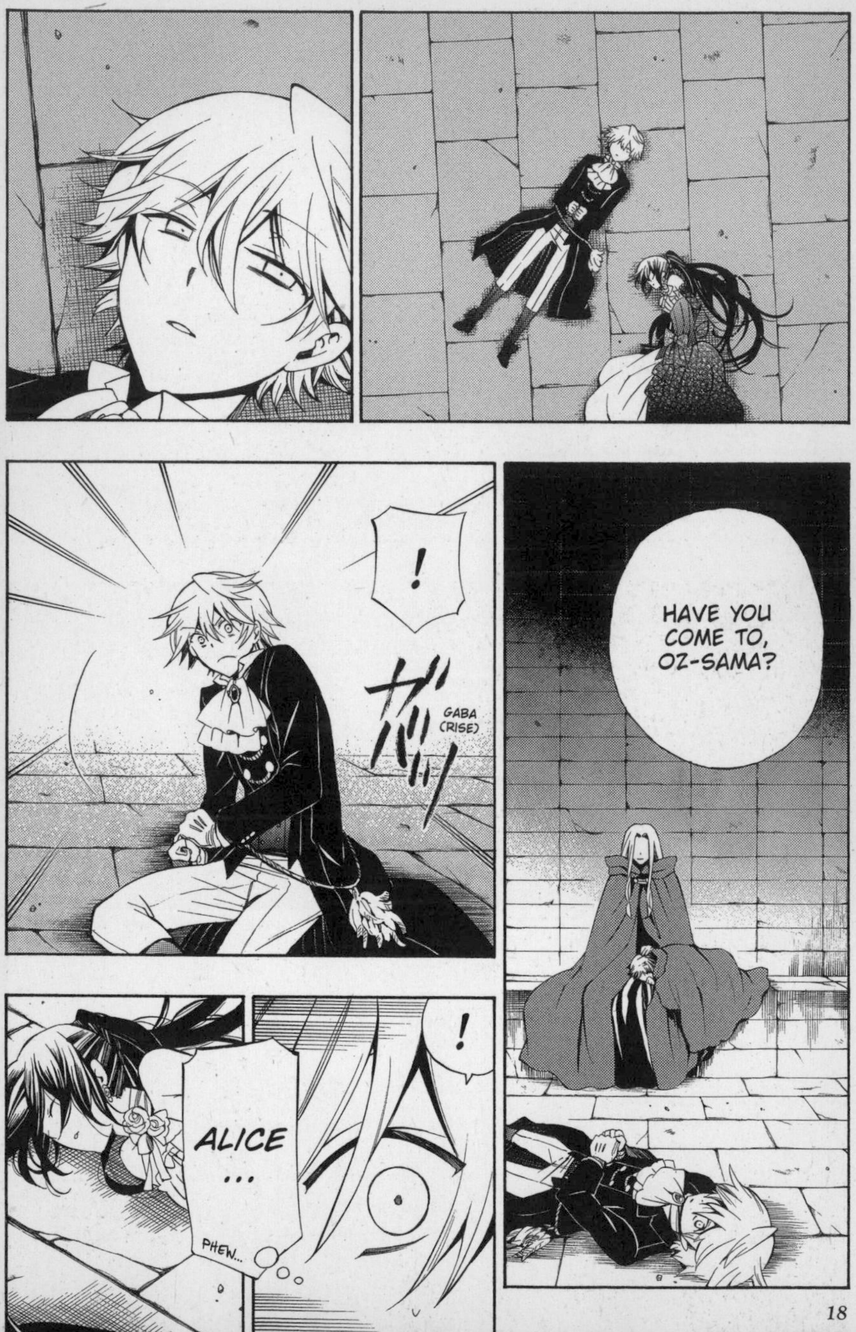
HAVE YOU COME TO, OZ-SAMA?
!
GABA (RISE)
!
ALICE ...
PHEW...

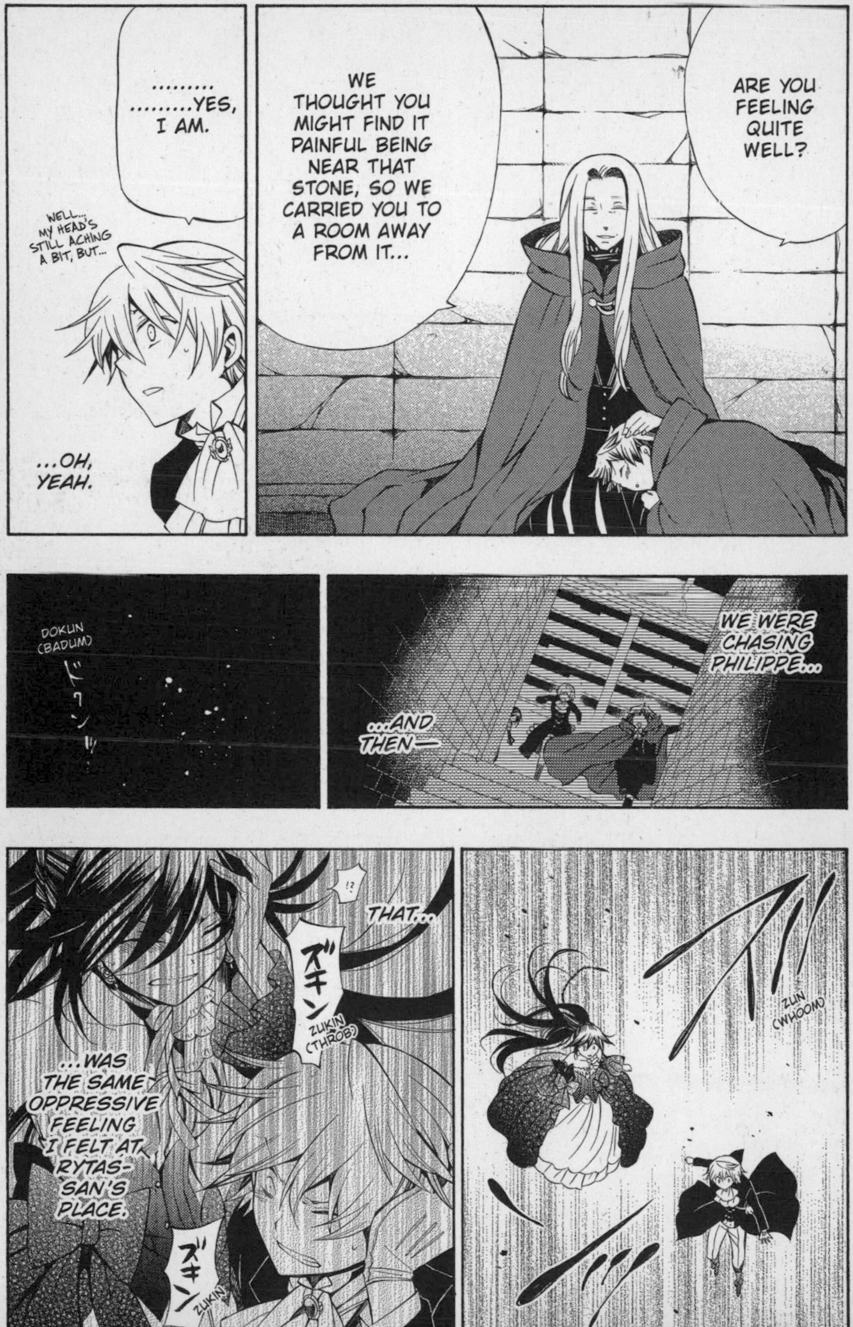
ARE YOU FEELING QUITE WELL?
WE THOUGHT YOU MIGHT FIND IT PAINFUL BEING NEAR THAT STONE, SO WE CARRIED YOU TO A ROOM AWAY FROM IT...
....
.........YES, I AM.
WELL... MY HEAD'S STILL ACHING A BIT, BUT...
...OH, YEAH.
WE WERE CHASING PHILIPPE...
...AND THEN—
DOKUN (BADUM)
ドクンッ
ZUN (WHOOM)
!?
THAT...
ズキン
ZUKIN (THROB)
...WAS THE SAME OPPRESSIVE FEELING I FELT AT RYTAS-SAN'S PLACE.
ズキン
ZUKIN

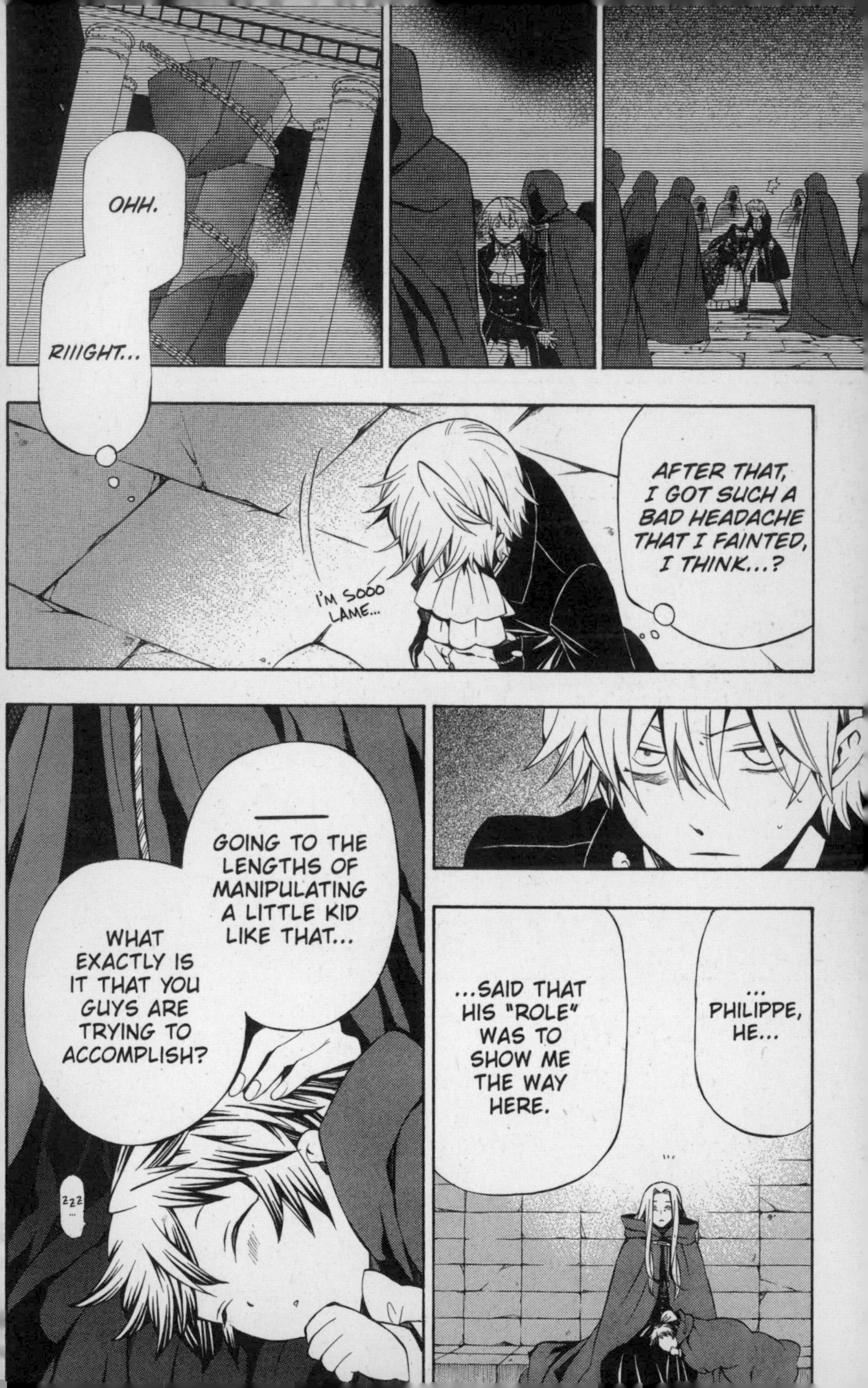
OHH.
RIIIGHT...
AFTER THAT, I GOT SUCH A BAD HEADACHE THAT I FAINTED, I THINK...?
I'M SOOO LAME...
... PHILIPPE, HE...
...SAID THAT HIS "ROLE" WAS TO SHOW ME THE WAY HERE.
—— GOING TO THE LENGTHS OF MANIPULATING A LITTLE KID LIKE THAT...
WHAT EXACTLY IS IT THAT YOU GUYS ARE TRYING TO ACCOMPLISH?
ZZZ...

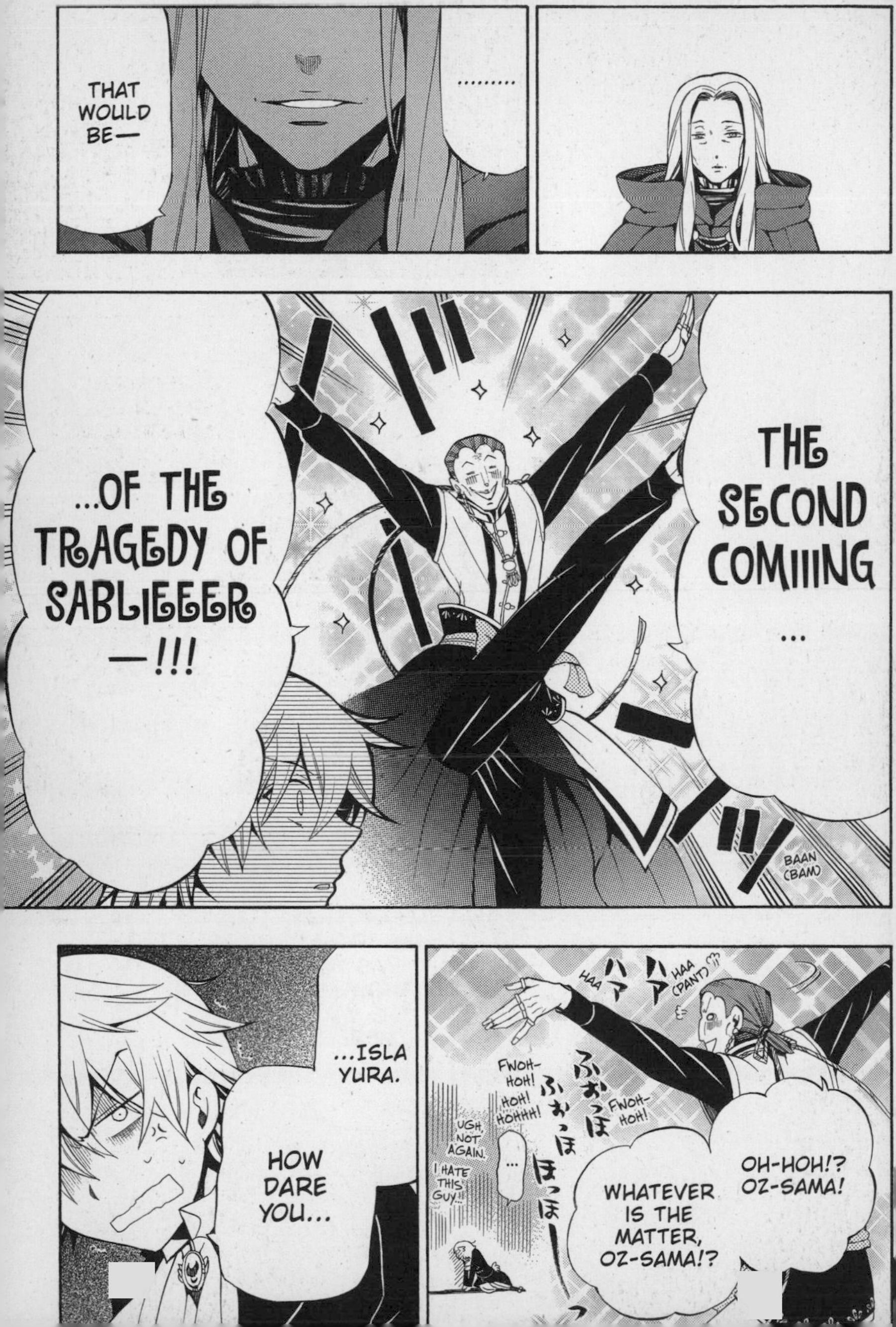
....
THAT WOULD BE—
THE SECOND COMIIING ...
...OF THE TRAGEDY OF SABLIEEER —!!!
BAAN (BAM)
ハァ ハァ
HAA (PANT)
HAA
OH-HOH!? OZ-SAMA!
FWOH-HOH!
ふぉっほ ふぉっほ ほっほー
FWOH-HOH! HOH! HOHHH!
WHATEVER IS THE MATTER, OZ-SAMA!?
...
UGH, NOT AGAIN.
I HATE THIS GUY!!
...ISLA YURA.
HOW DARE YOU...

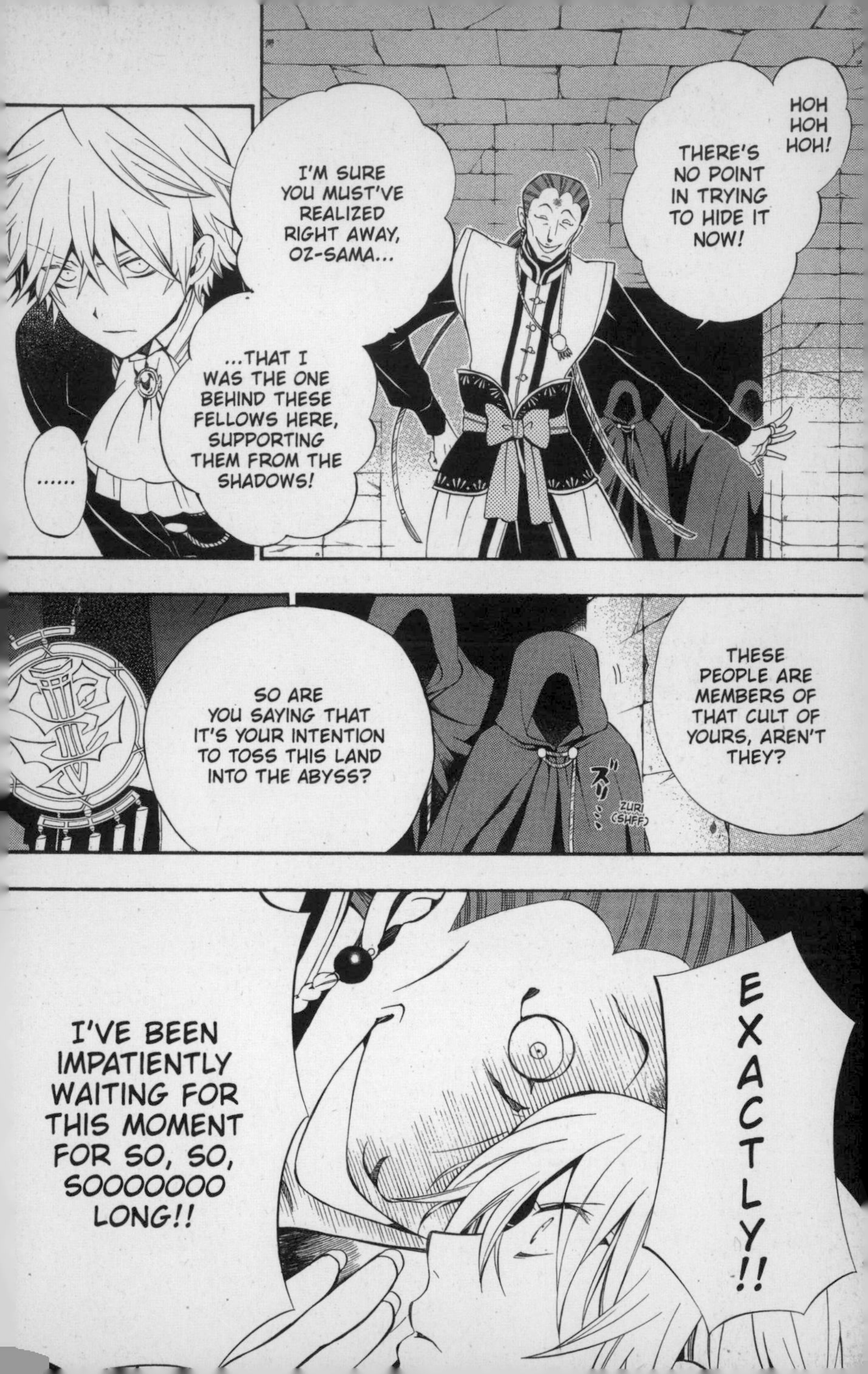
HOH HOH HOH!
THERE'S NO POINT IN TRYING TO HIDE IT NOW!
I'M SURE YOU MUST'VE REALIZED RIGHT AWAY, OZ-SAMA...
...THAT I WAS THE ONE BEHIND THESE FELLOWS HERE, SUPPORTING THEM FROM THE SHADOWS!
......
THESE PEOPLE ARE MEMBERS OF THAT CULT OF YOURS, AREN'T THEY?
ズリ…
ZURI (SHFF)
SO ARE YOU SAYING THAT IT'S YOUR INTENTION TO TOSS THIS LAND INTO THE ABYSS?
EXACTLY!!
I'VE BEEN IMPATIENTLY WAITING FOR THIS MOMENT FOR SO, SO, SOOOOOOO LONG!!

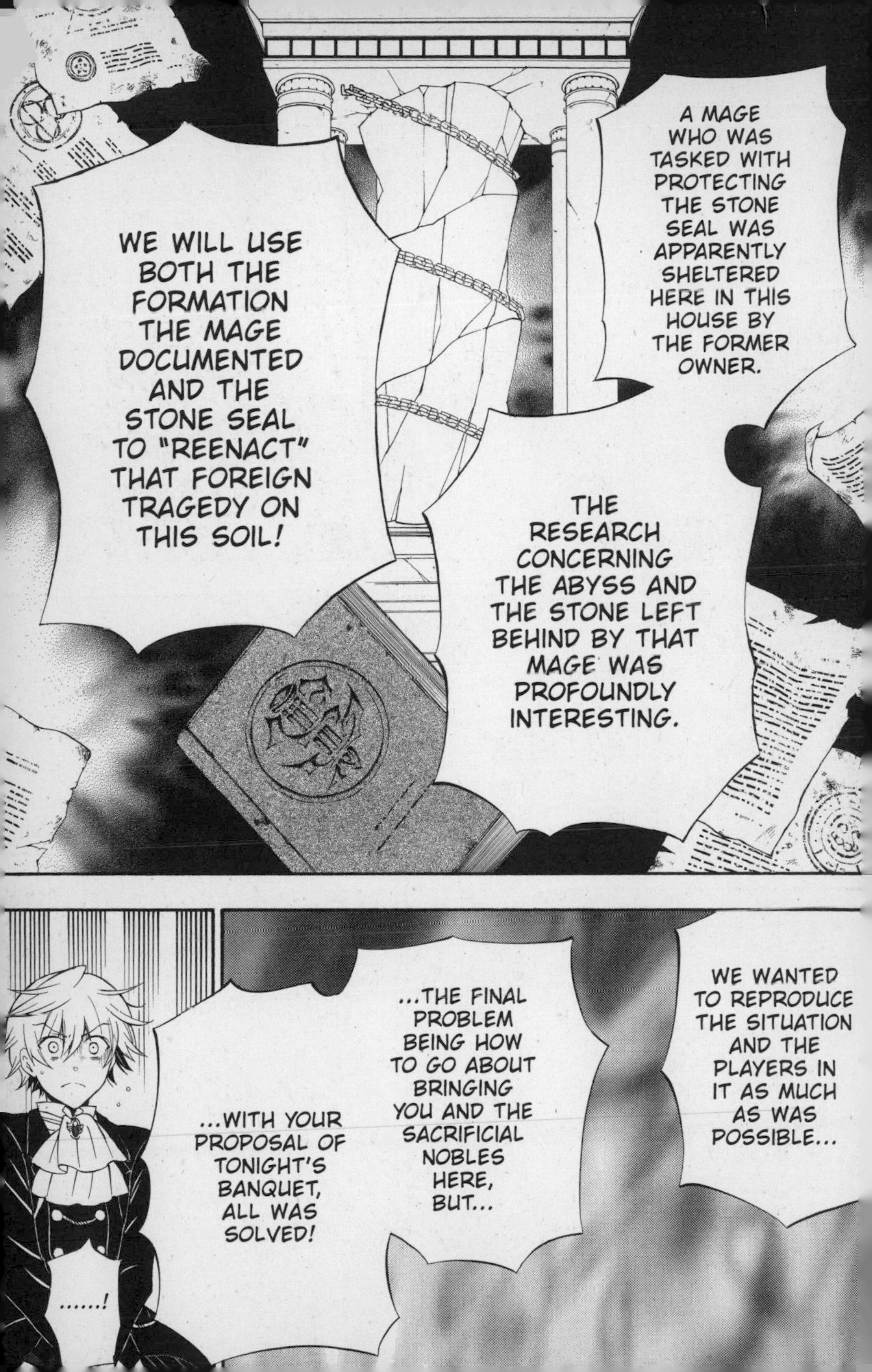
A MAGE WHO WAS TASKED WITH PROTECTING THE STONE SEAL WAS APPARENTLY SHELTERED HERE IN THIS HOUSE BY THE FORMER OWNER.
THE RESEARCH CONCERNING THE ABYSS AND THE STONE LEFT BEHIND BY THAT MAGE WAS PROFOUNDLY INTERESTING.
WE WILL USE BOTH THE FORMATION THE MAGE DOCUMENTED AND THE STONE SEAL TO "REENACT" THAT FOREIGN TRAGEDY ON THIS SOIL!
WE WANTED TO REPRODUCE THE SITUATION AND THE PLAYERS IN IT AS MUCH AS WAS POSSIBLE...
...THE FINAL PROBLEM BEING HOW TO GO ABOUT BRINGING YOU AND THE SACRIFICIAL NOBLES HERE, BUT...
...WITH YOUR PROPOSAL OF TONIGHT'S BANQUET, ALL WAS SOLVED!
......!

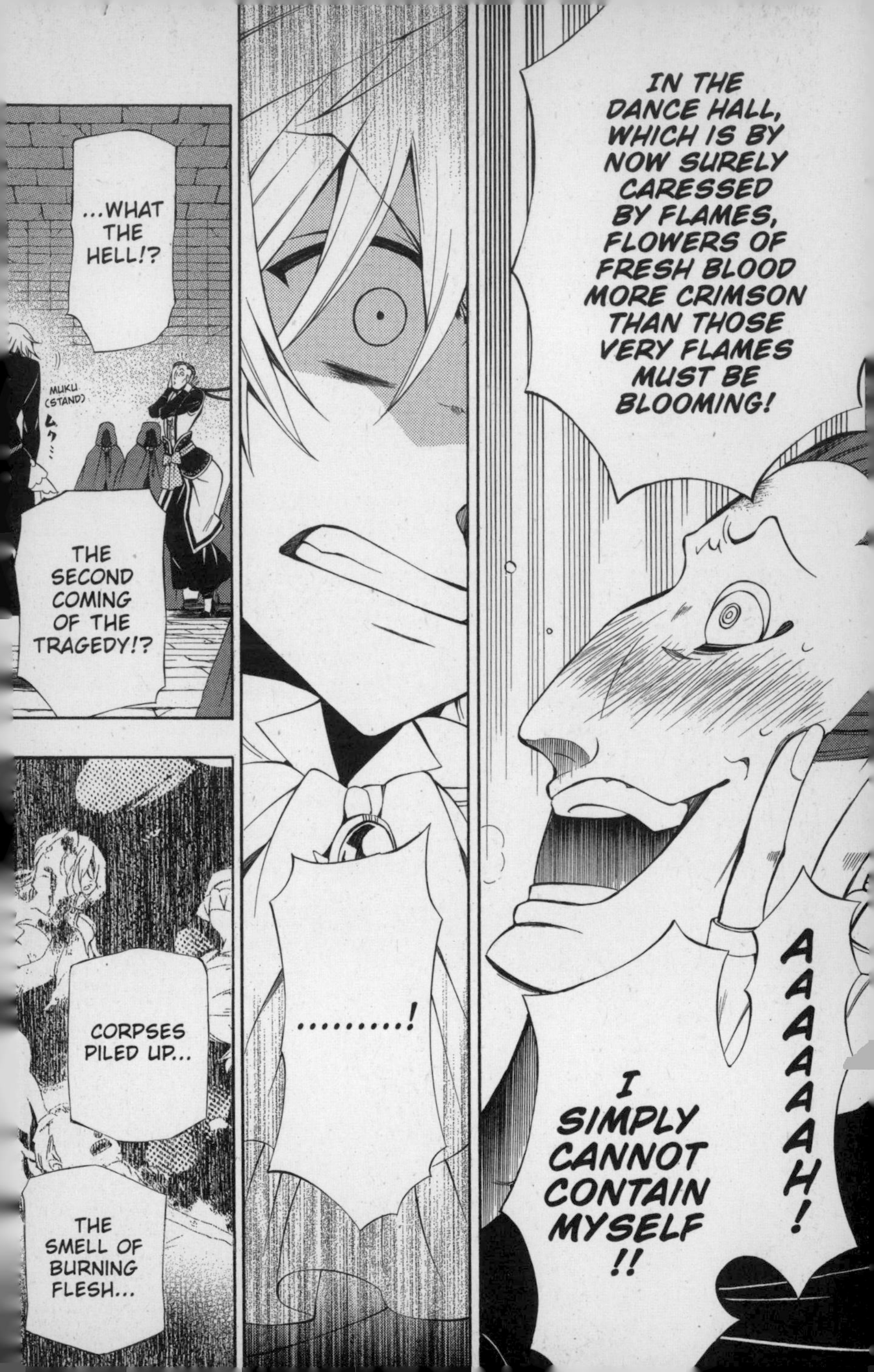
IN THE DANCE HALL, WHICH IS BY NOW SURELY CARESSED BY FLAMES, FLOWERS OF FRESH BLOOD MORE CRIMSON THAN THOSE VERY FLAMES MUST BE BLOOMING!
AAAAAAH!
I SIMPLY CANNOT CONTAIN MYSELF!!
.........!
...WHAT THE HELL!?
MUKU (STAND)
ムク
THE SECOND COMING OF THE TRAGEDY!?
CORPSES PILED UP...
THE SMELL OF BURNING FLESH...

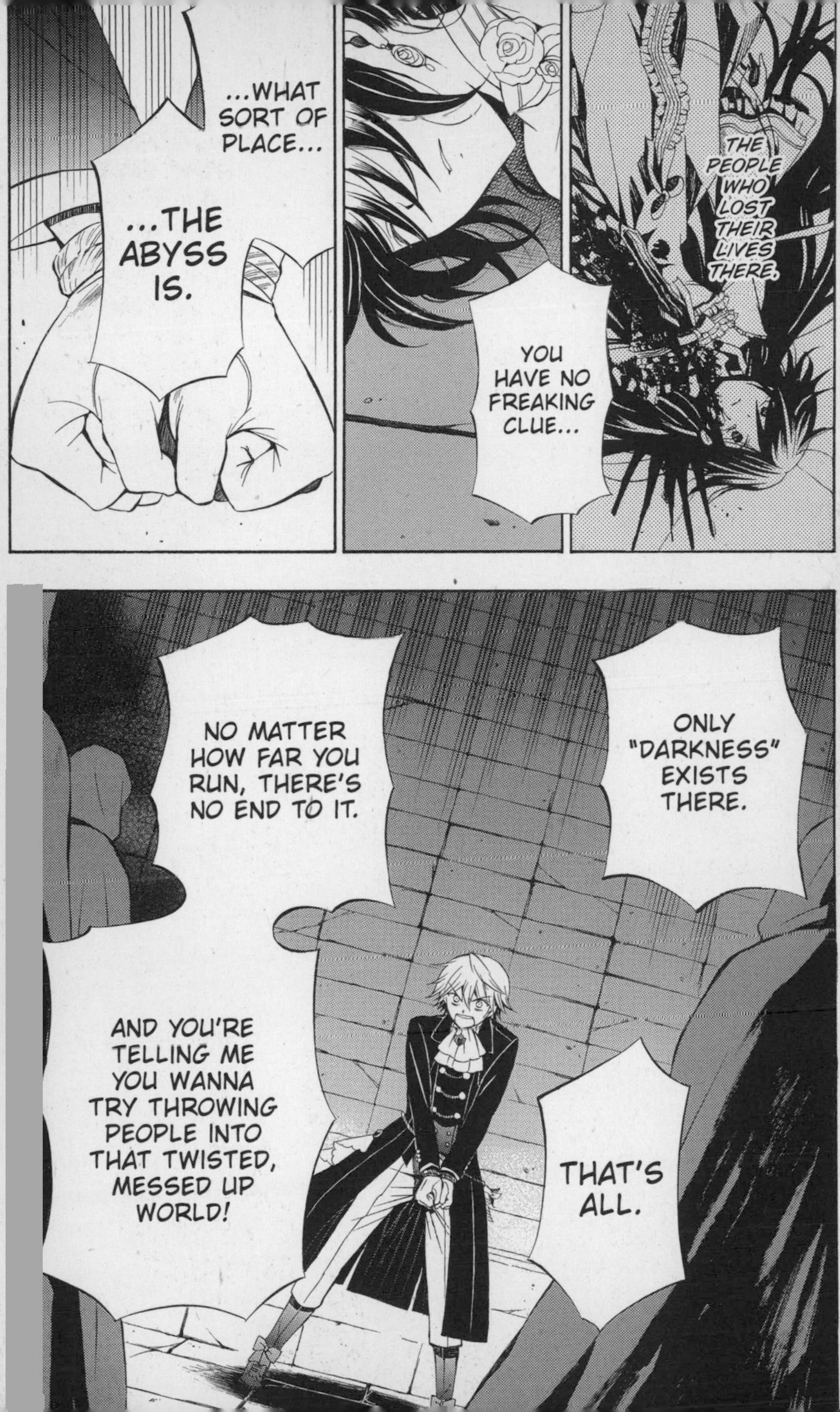
THE PEOPLE WHO LOST THEIR LIVES THERE.
YOU HAVE NO FREAKING CLUE...
...WHAT SORT OF PLACE...
...THE ABYSS IS.
ONLY "DARKNESS" EXISTS THERE.
NO MATTER HOW FAR YOU RUN, THERE'S NO END TO IT.
THAT'S ALL.
AND YOU'RE TELLING ME YOU WANNA TRY THROWING PEOPLE INTO THAT TWISTED, MESSED UP WORLD!

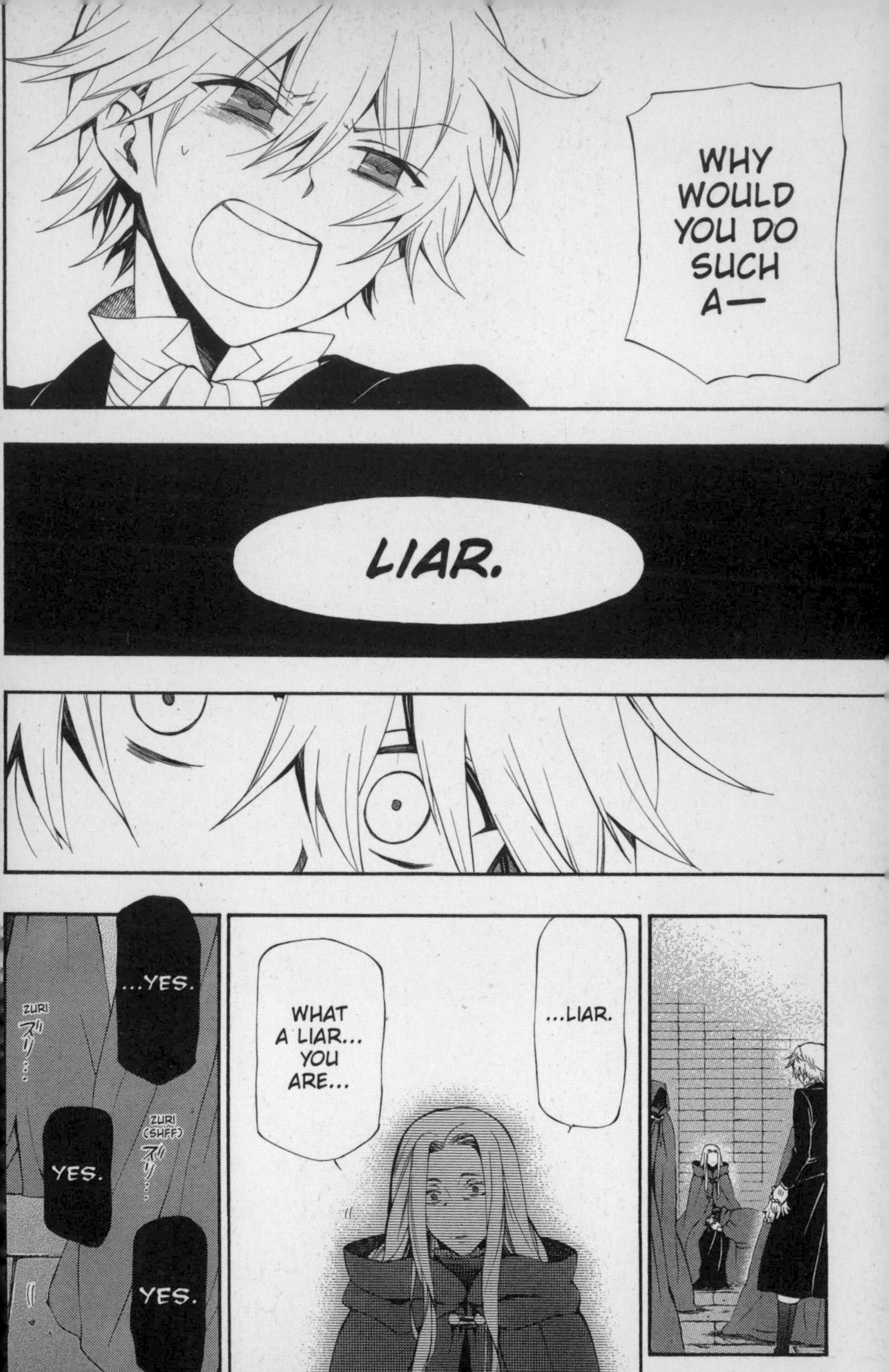
WHY WOULD YOU DO SUCH A—
LIAR.
...LIAR.
WHAT A LIAR... YOU ARE...
...YES.
ZURI
ズリ...
ZURI (SHFF)
ズリ...
YES.
YES.

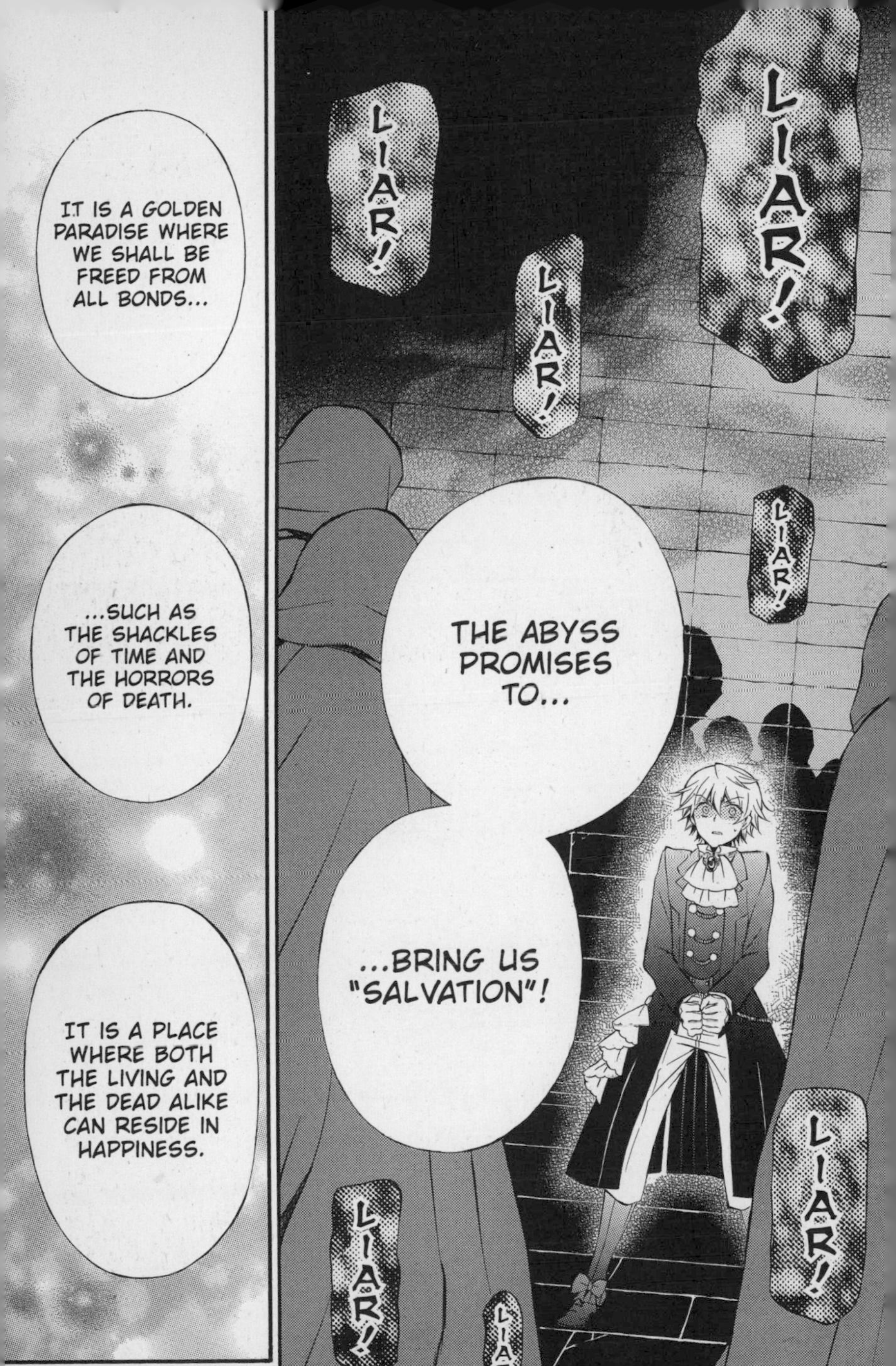
LIAR!
LIAR!
LIAR!
LIAR!
THE ABYSS PROMISES TO...
...BRING US "SALVATION"!
LIAR!
LIAR!
LIAR!
IT IS A GOLDEN PARADISE WHERE WE SHALL BE FREED FROM ALL BONDS...
...SUCH AS THE SHACKLES OF TIME AND THE HORRORS OF DEATH.
IT IS A PLACE WHERE BOTH THE LIVING AND THE DEAD ALIKE CAN RESIDE IN HAPPINESS.

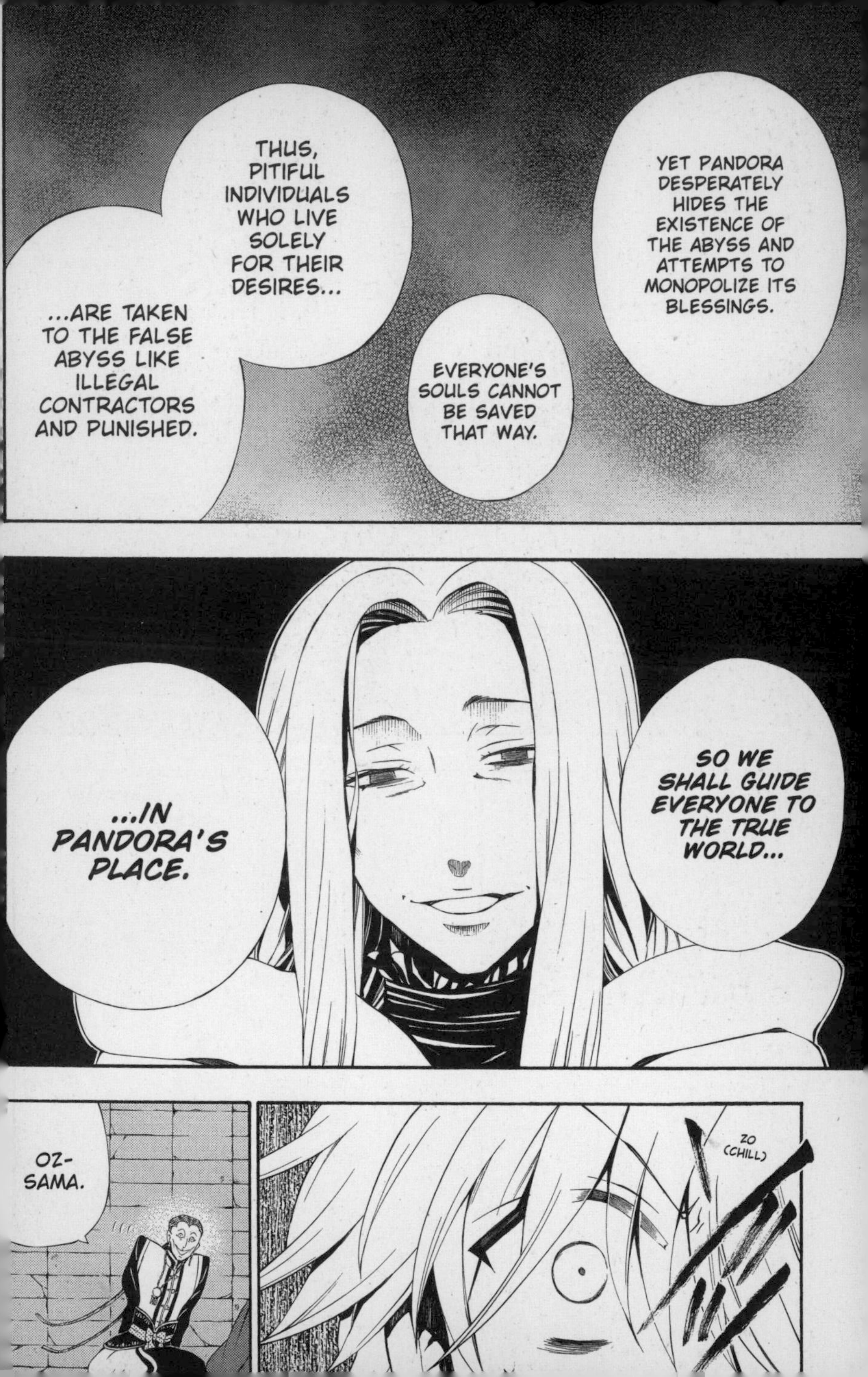
YET PANDORA DESPERATELY HIDES THE EXISTENCE OF THE ABYSS AND ATTEMPTS TO MONOPOLIZE ITS BLESSINGS.
EVERYONE'S SOULS CANNOT BE SAVED THAT WAY.
THUS, PITIFUL INDIVIDUALS WHO LIVE SOLELY FOR THEIR DESIRES...
...ARE TAKEN TO THE FALSE ABYSS LIKE ILLEGAL CONTRACTORS AND PUNISHED.
SO WE SHALL GUIDE EVERYONE TO THE TRUE WORLD...
...IN PANDORA'S PLACE.
ZO (CHILL)
OZ-SAMA.

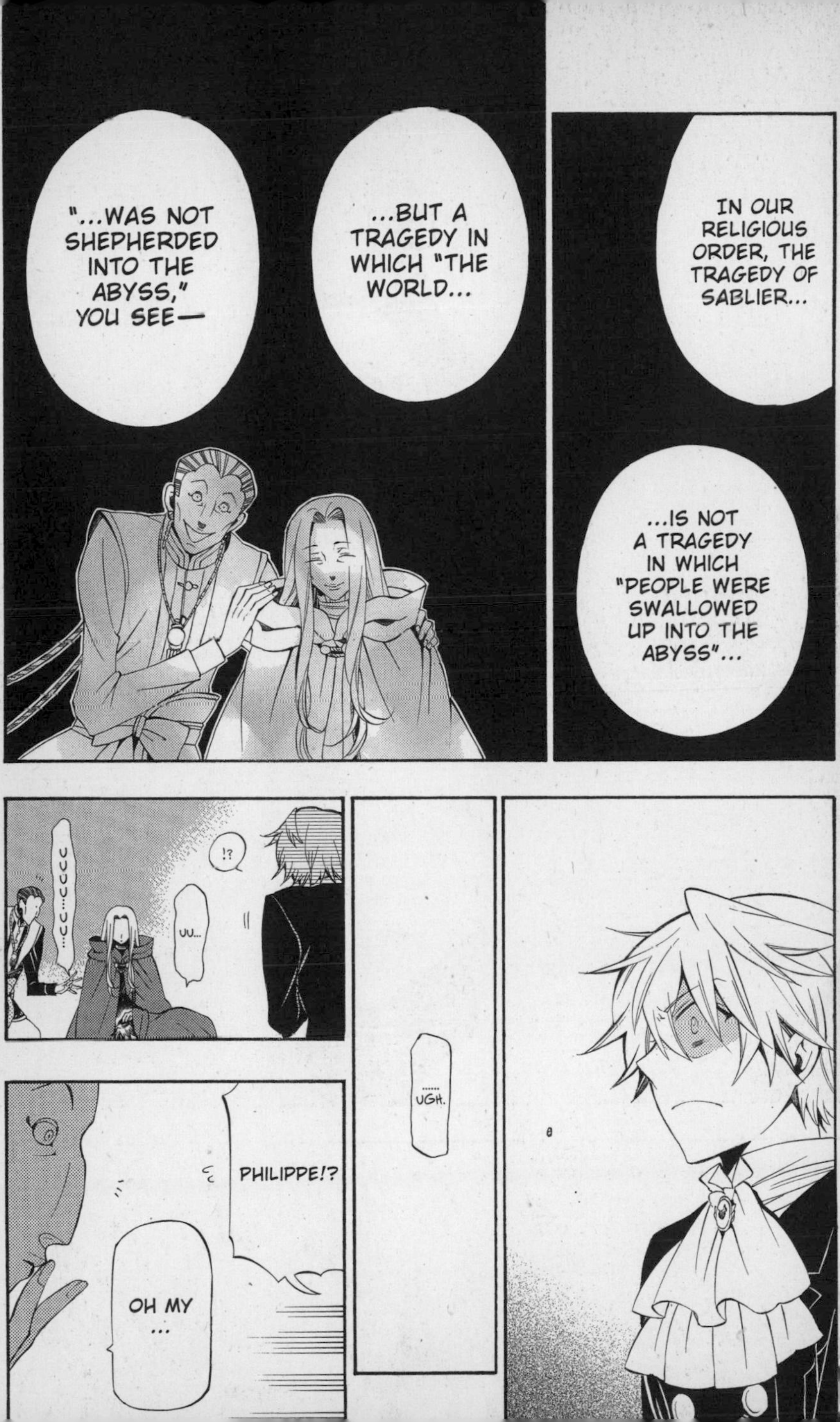
IN OUR RELIGIOUS ORDER, THE TRAGEDY OF SABLIER...
...IS NOT A TRAGEDY IN WHICH "PEOPLE WERE SWALLOWED UP INTO THE ABYSS"...
...BUT A TRAGEDY IN WHICH "THE WORLD...
"...WAS NOT SHEPHERDED INTO THE ABYSS," YOU SEE—
......UGH.
!?
UU...
UUUU...UU...
PHILIPPE!?
OH MY ...

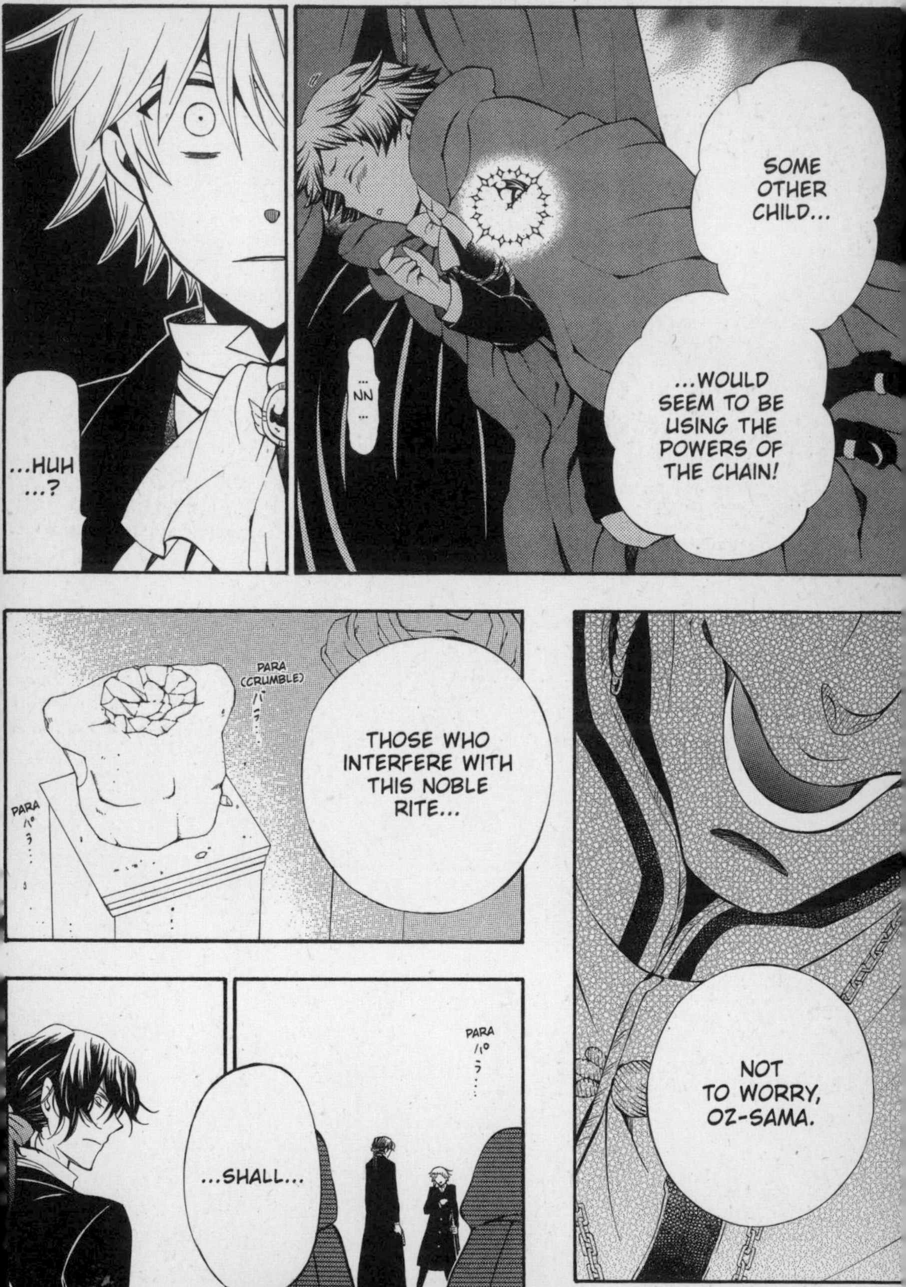
SOME OTHER CHILD...
...WOULD SEEM TO BE USING THE POWERS OF THE CHAIN!
...NN...
...HUH...?
NOT TO WORRY, OZ-SAMA.
PARA (CRUMBLE) パラ...
THOSE WHO INTERFERE WITH THIS NOBLE RITE...
PARA パラ...
PARA パラ...
...SHALL...

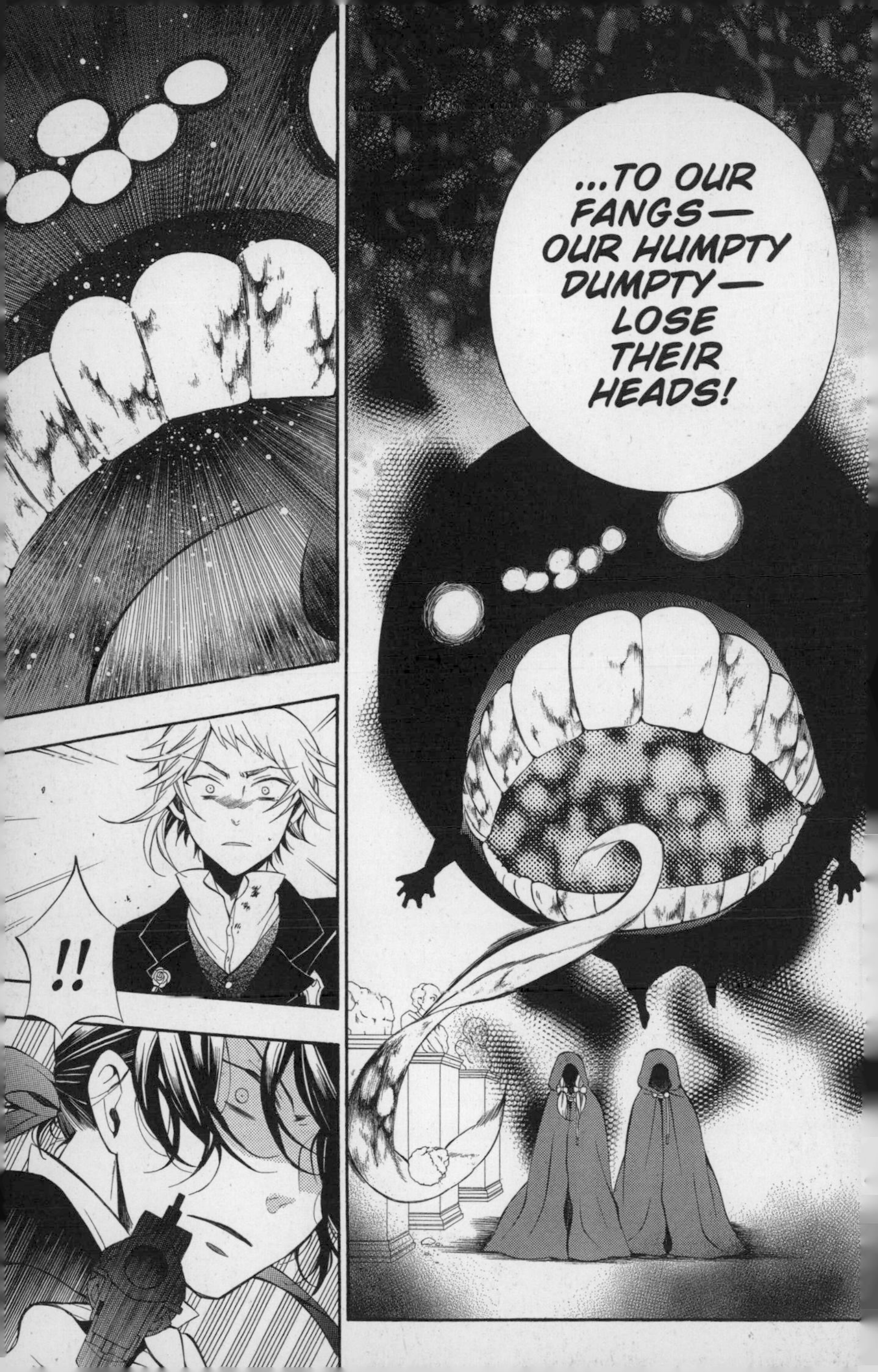
...TO OUR FANGS—OUR HUMPTY DUMPTY—LOSE THEIR HEADS!
!!

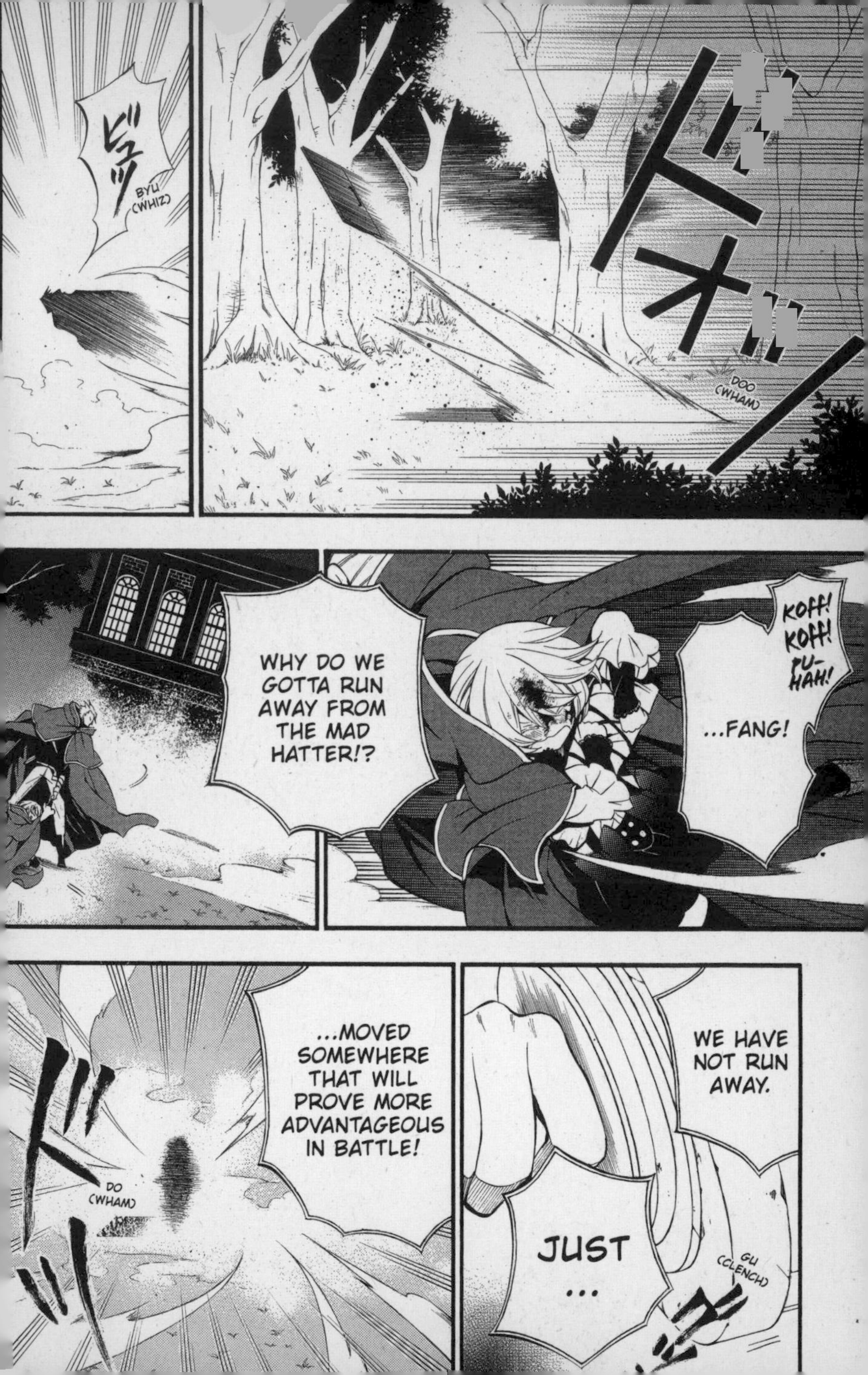
DOO (WHAM)
ビュッ
BYU (WHIZ)
KOFF! KOFF! PU-HAH!
...FANG!
WHY DO WE GOTTA RUN AWAY FROM THE MAD HATTER!?
WE HAVE NOT RUN AWAY.
JUST ...
GU (CLENCH)
...MOVED SOMEWHERE THAT WILL PROVE MORE ADVANTAGEOUS IN BATTLE!
DO (WHAM)

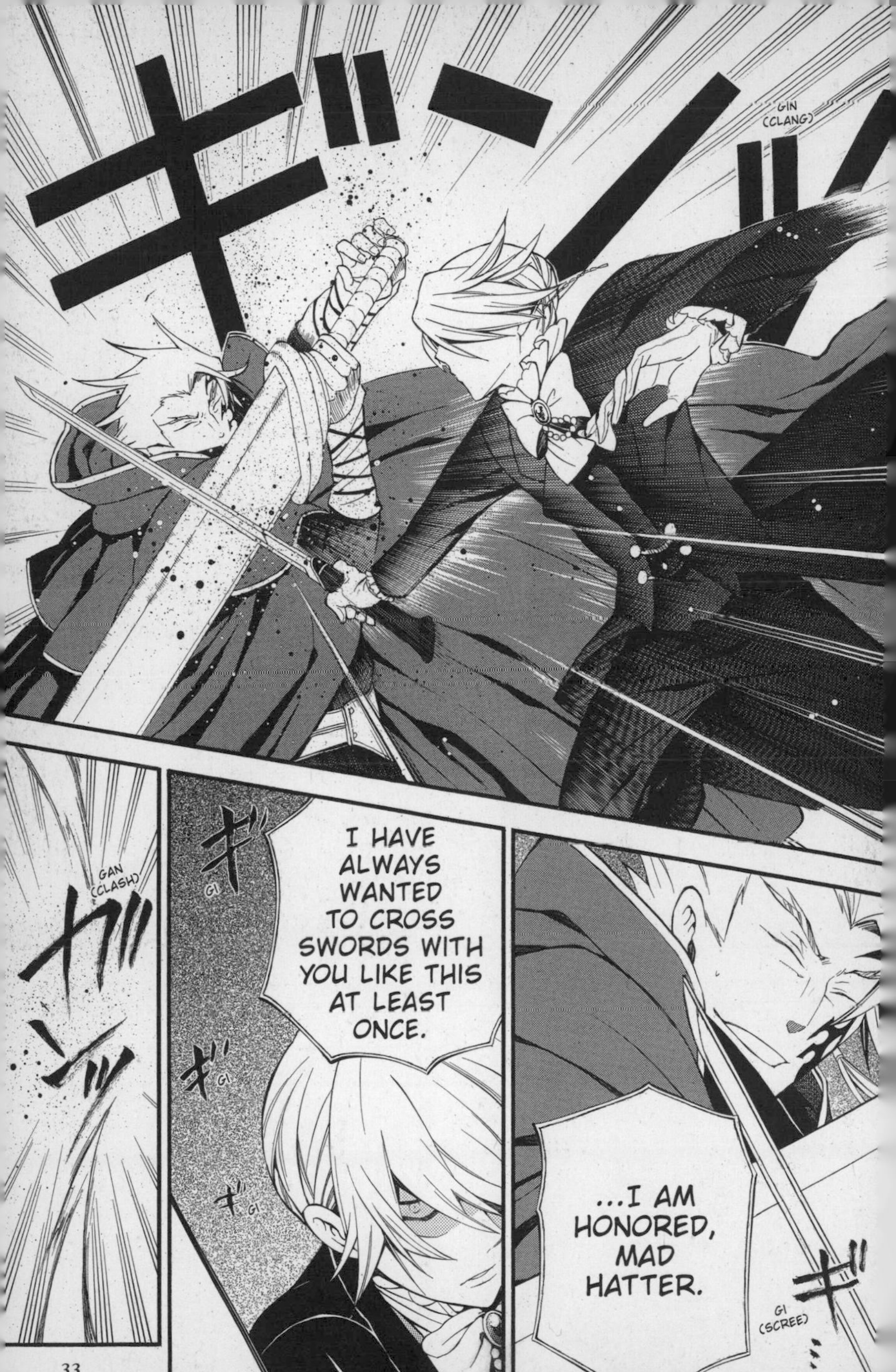
GIN (CLANG)
GAN (CLASH)
GI
I HAVE ALWAYS WANTED TO CROSS SWORDS WITH YOU LIKE THIS AT LEAST ONCE.
GI
GI
...I AM HONORED, MAD HATTER.
GI (SCREE)

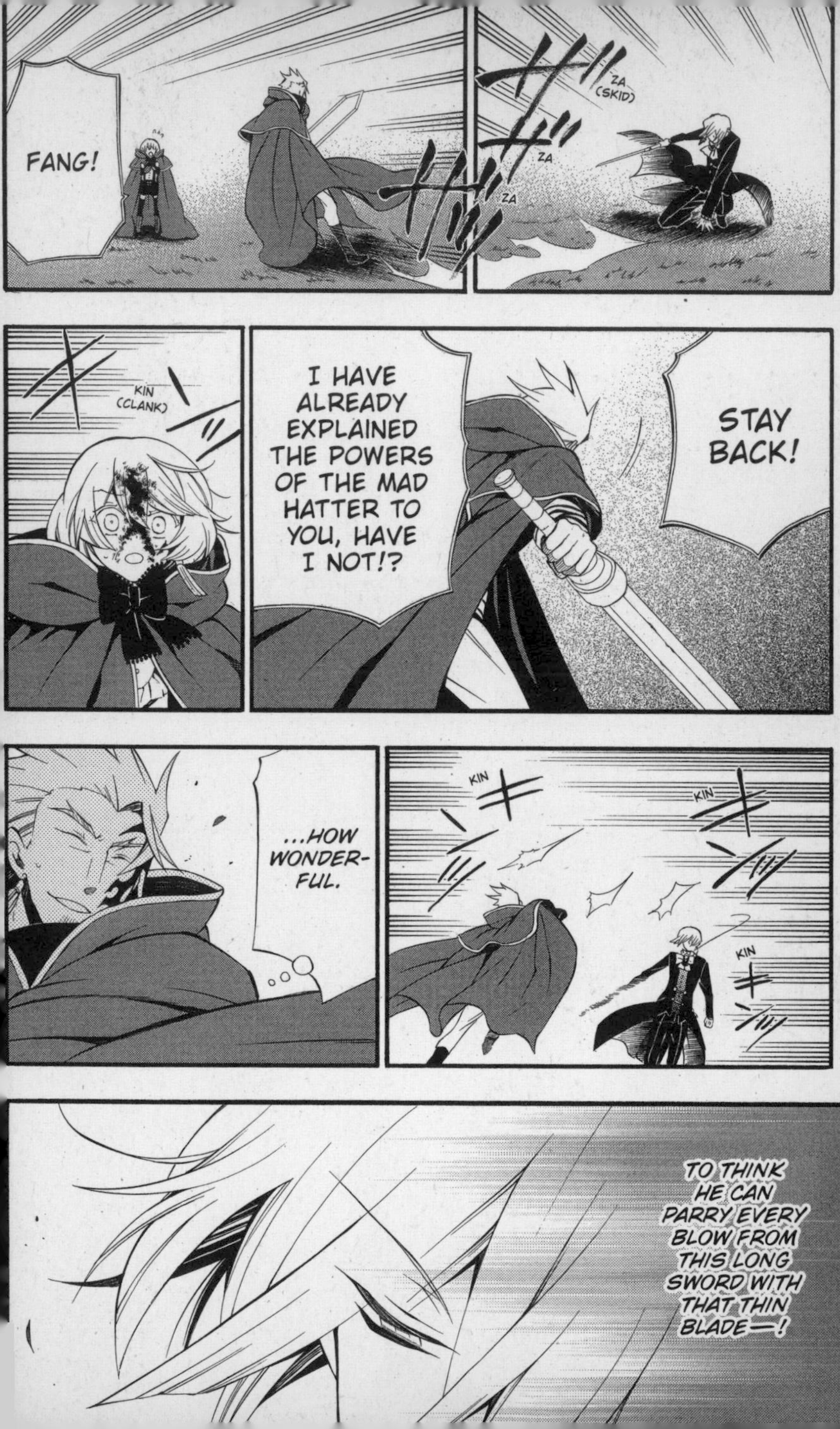
ZA
(SKID)
ZA
ZA
FANG!
STAY BACK!
I HAVE ALREADY EXPLAINED THE POWERS OF THE MAD HATTER TO YOU, HAVE I NOT!?
KIN
(CLANK)
KIN
KIN
KIN
...HOW WONDER-FUL.
TO THINK HE CAN PARRY EVERY BLOW FROM THIS LONG SWORD WITH THAT THIN BLADE—!

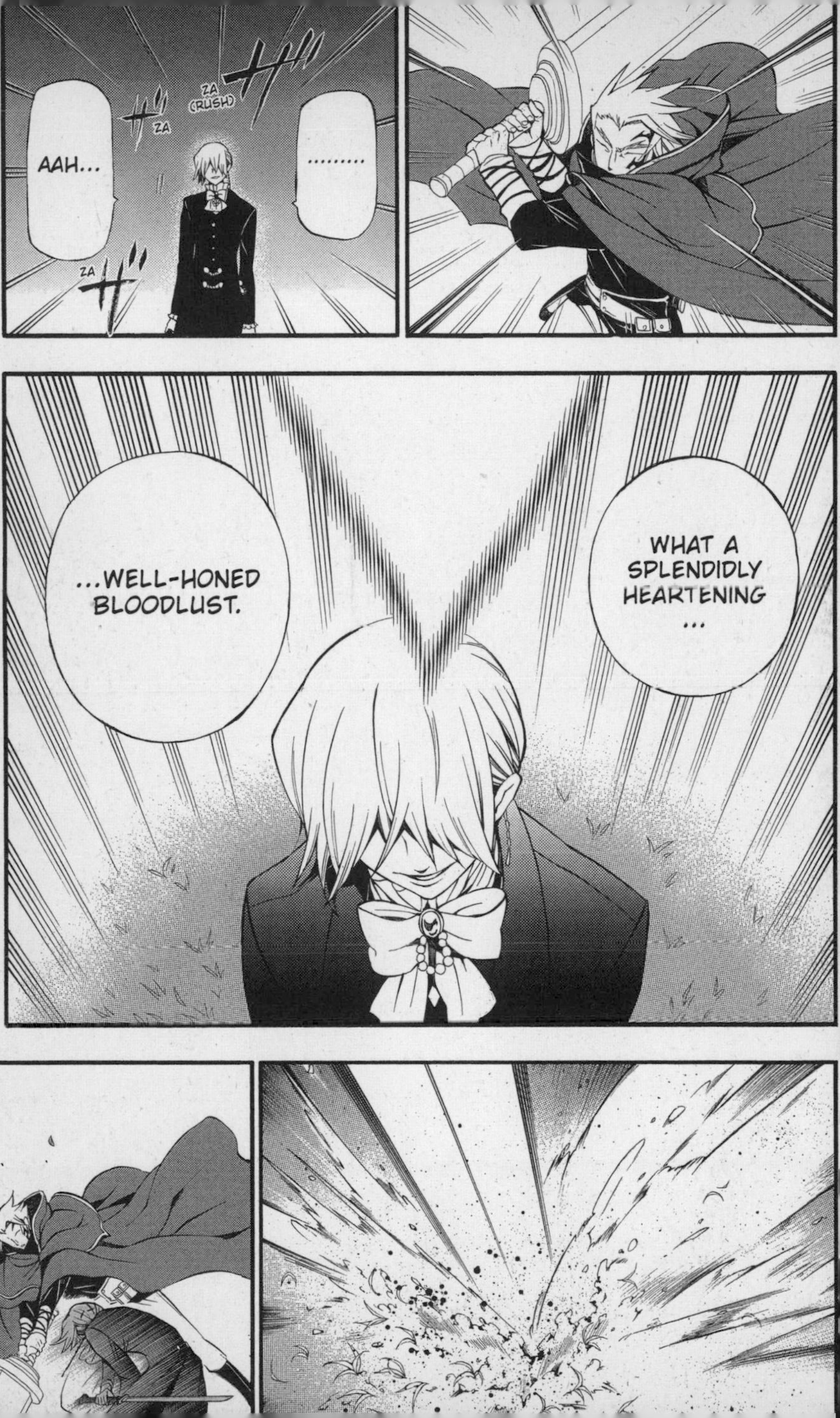
ZA (RUSH)
....
ZA
AAH...
ZA
WHAT A SPLENDIDLY HEARTENING ...
...WELL-HONED BLOODLUST.

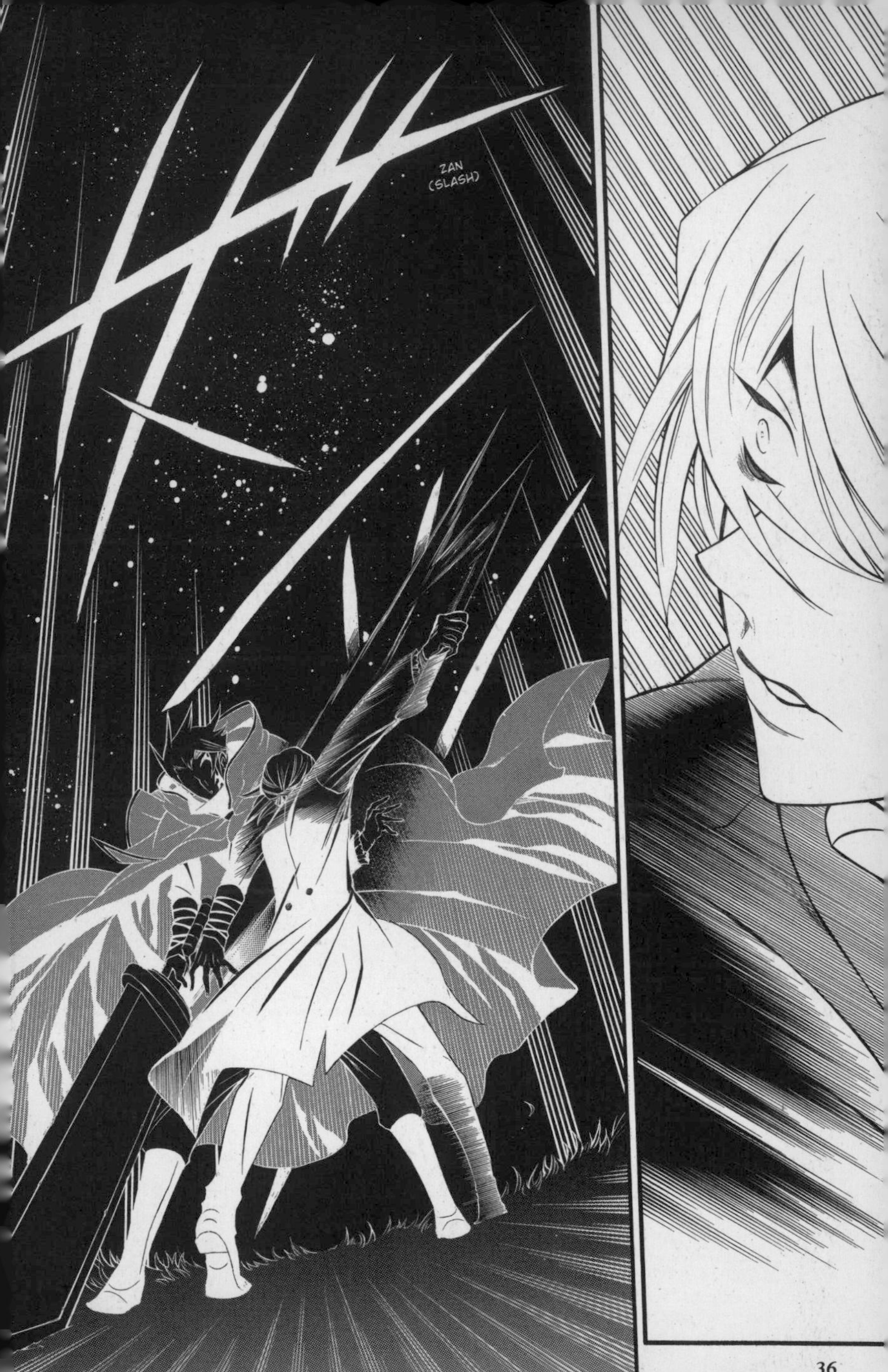
ZAN
(SLASH)

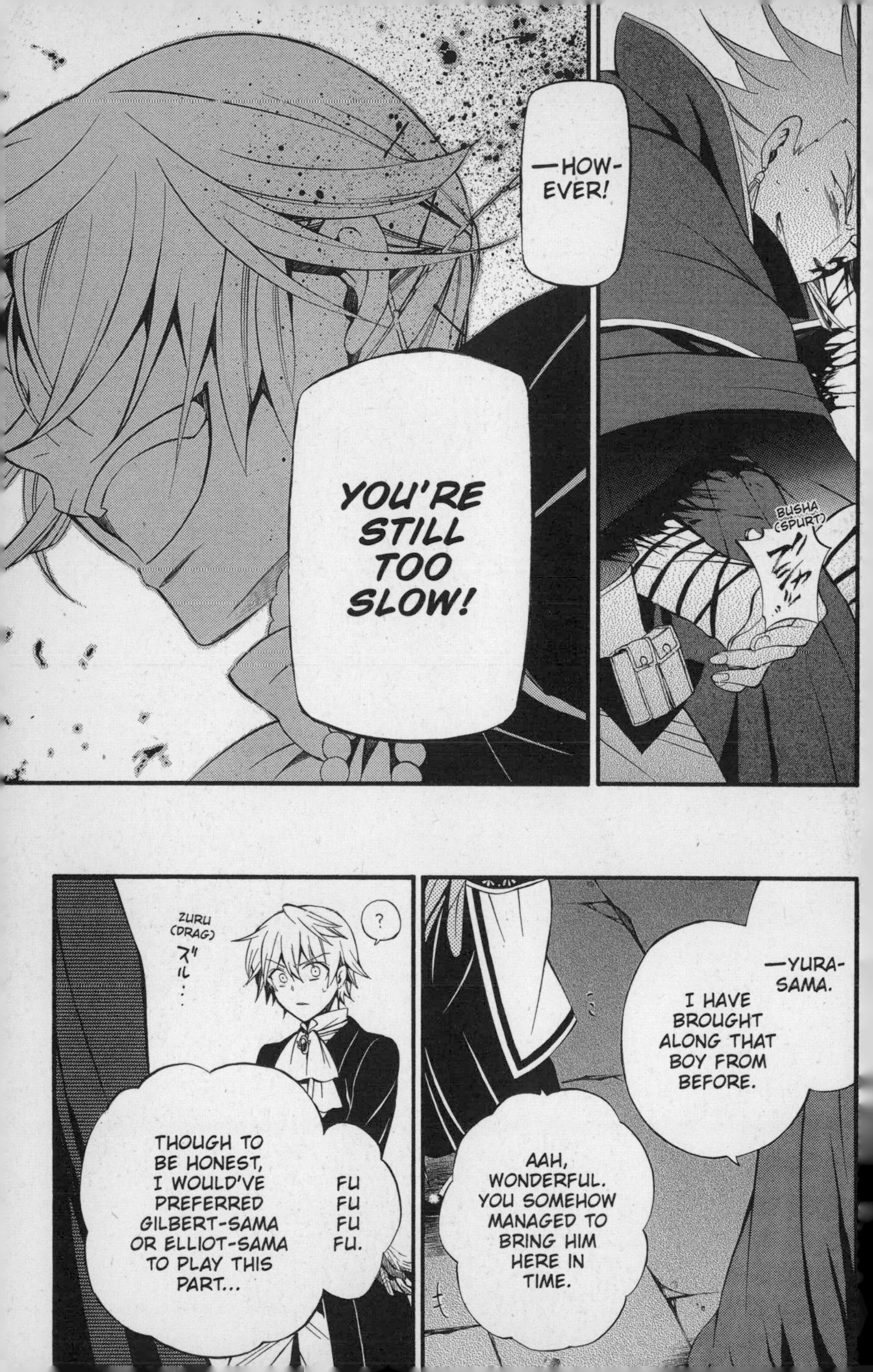
—HOW-EVER!
BUSHA (SPURT)
YOU'RE STILL TOO SLOW!
—YURA-SAMA. I HAVE BROUGHT ALONG THAT BOY FROM BEFORE.
AAH, WONDERFUL. YOU SOMEHOW MANAGED TO BRING HIM HERE IN TIME.
?
ZURU (DRAG)
FU FU FU FU.
THOUGH TO BE HONEST, I WOULD'VE PREFERRED GILBERT-SAMA OR ELLIOT-SAMA TO PLAY THIS PART...

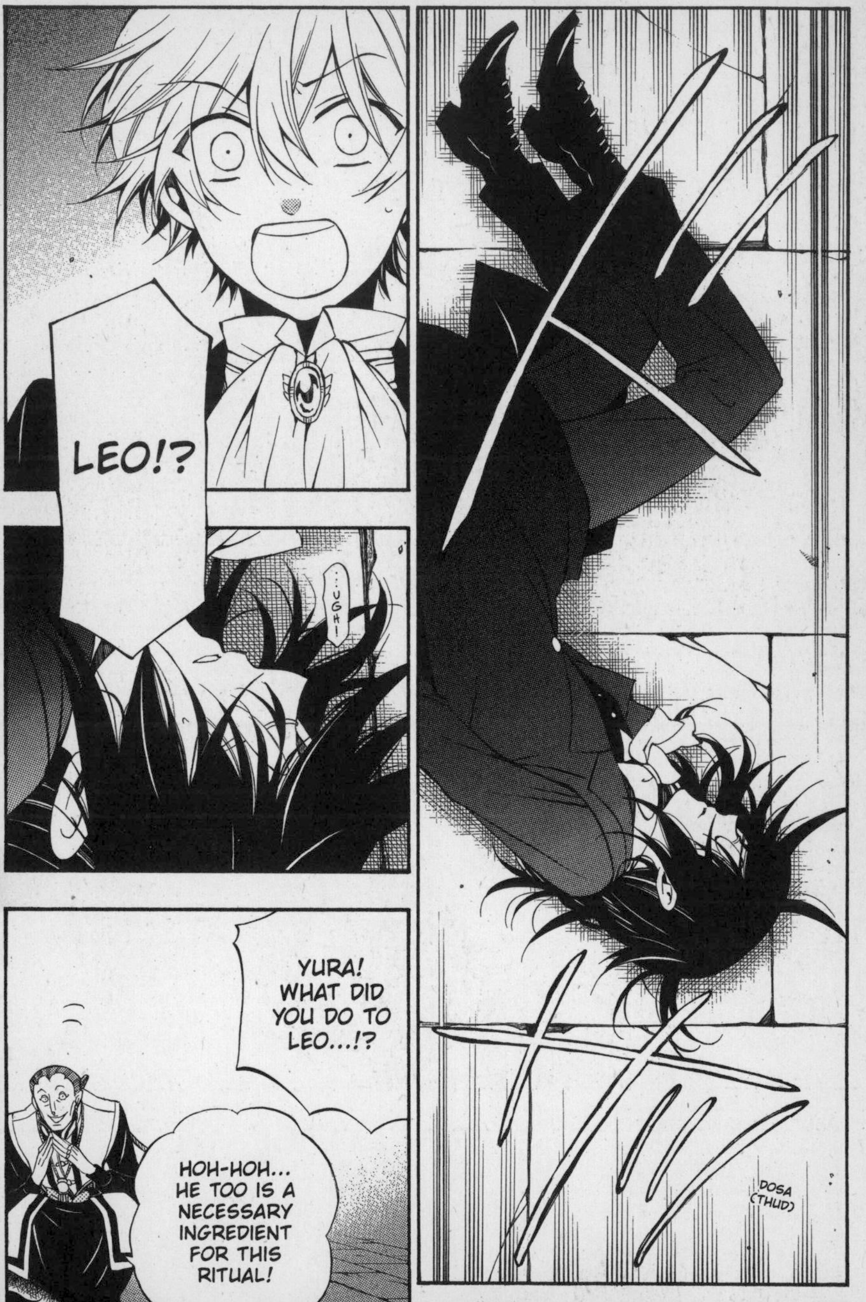
DOSA (THUD)
LEO!?
...UGH!
YURA! WHAT DID YOU DO TO LEO...!?
HOH-HOH... HE TOO IS A NECESSARY INGREDIENT FOR THIS RITUAL!

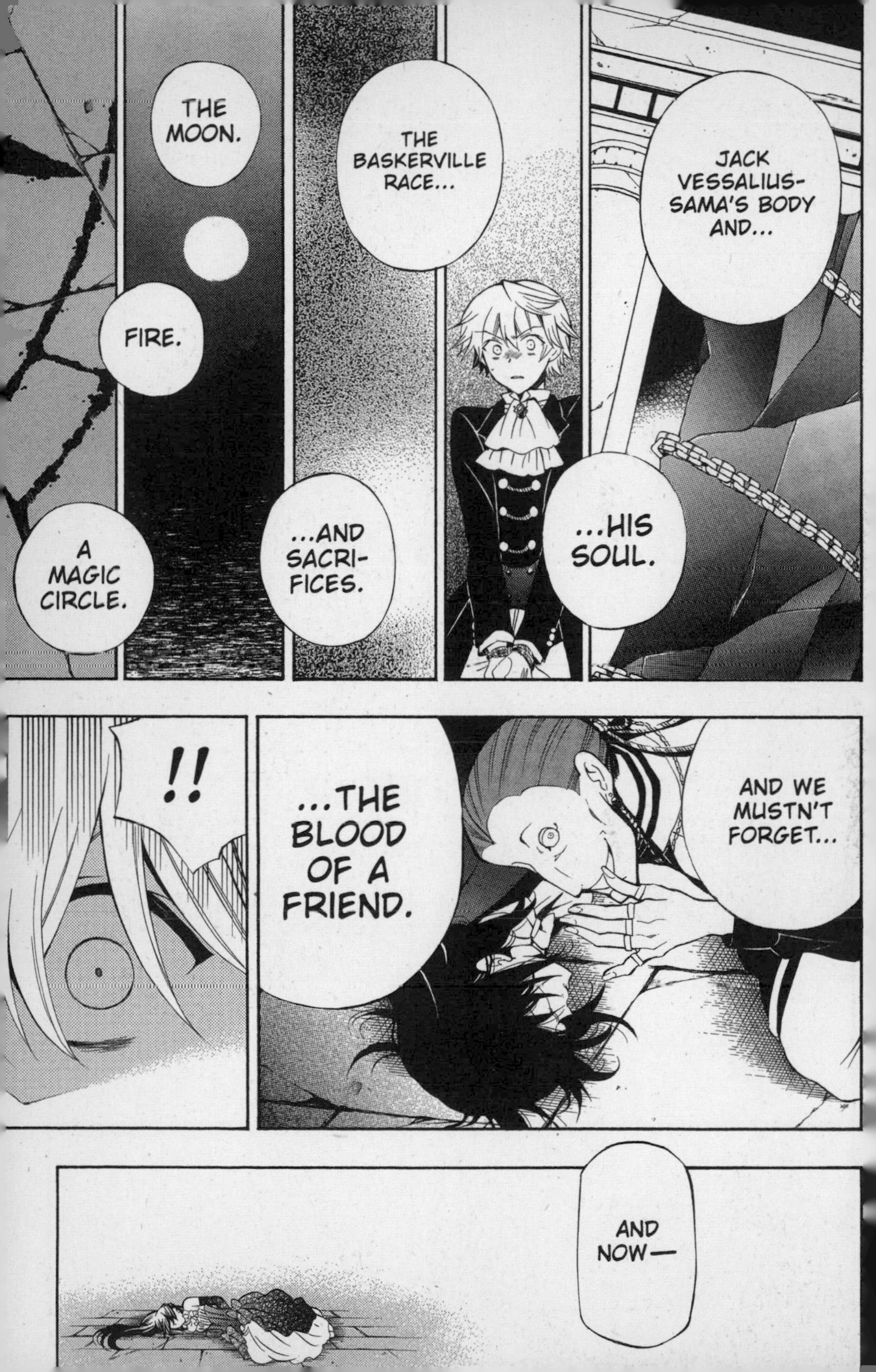
JACK VESSALIUS-SAMA'S BODY AND...
...HIS SOUL.
THE BASKERVILLE RACE...
...AND SACRIFICES.
THE MOON.
FIRE.
A MAGIC CIRCLE.
AND WE MUSTN'T FORGET...
...THE BLOOD OF A FRIEND.
!!
AND NOW—

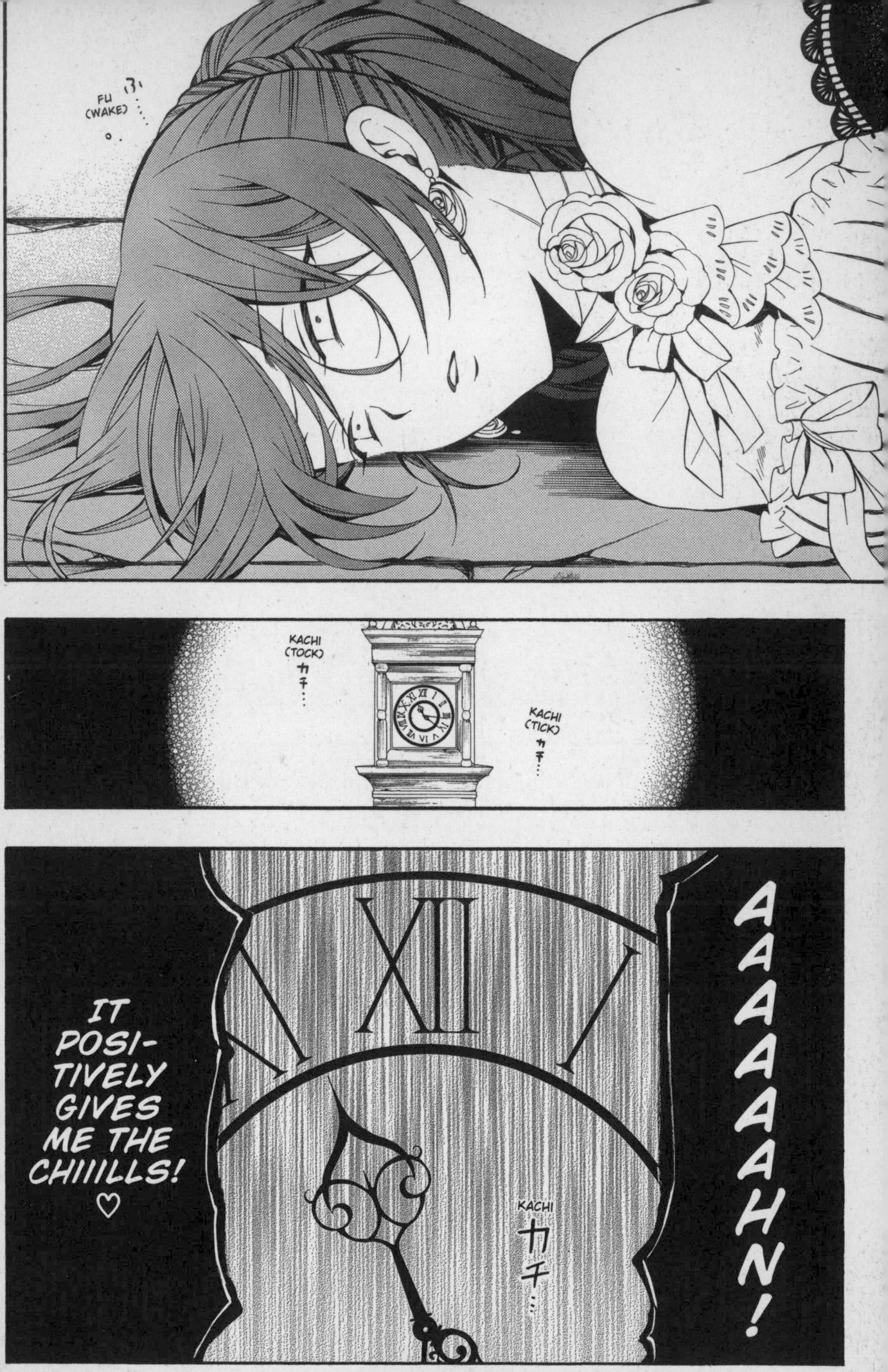
FU (WAKE) ふ…。
KACHI (TICK) カチ…
KACHI (TOCK) カチ…
AAAAAAAHN!
KACHI カチ…
IT POSITIVELY GIVES ME THE CHIIILLS! ♡

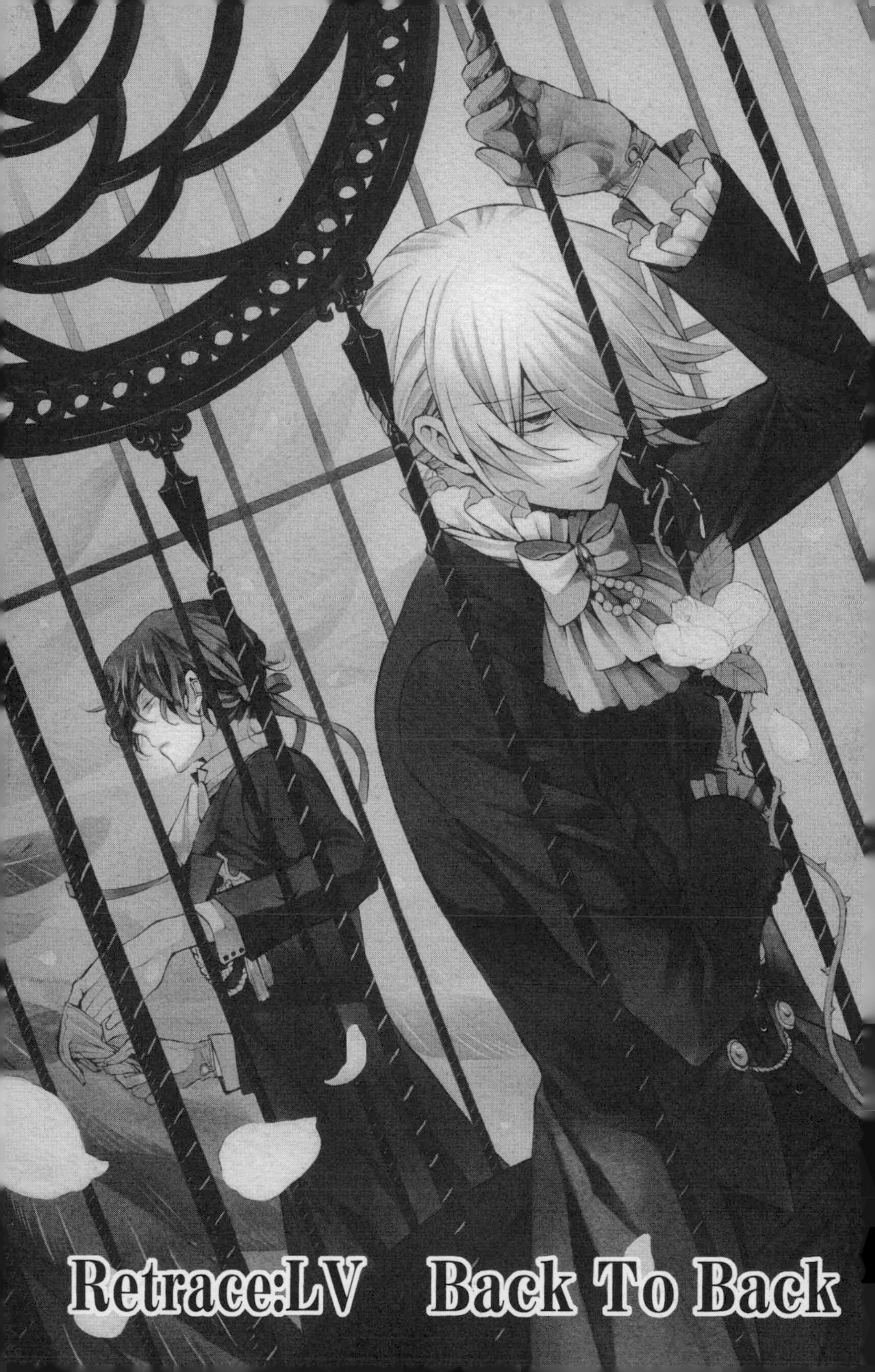
Retrace:LV Back To Back

MEOW, MEOW, MEOOOOW!

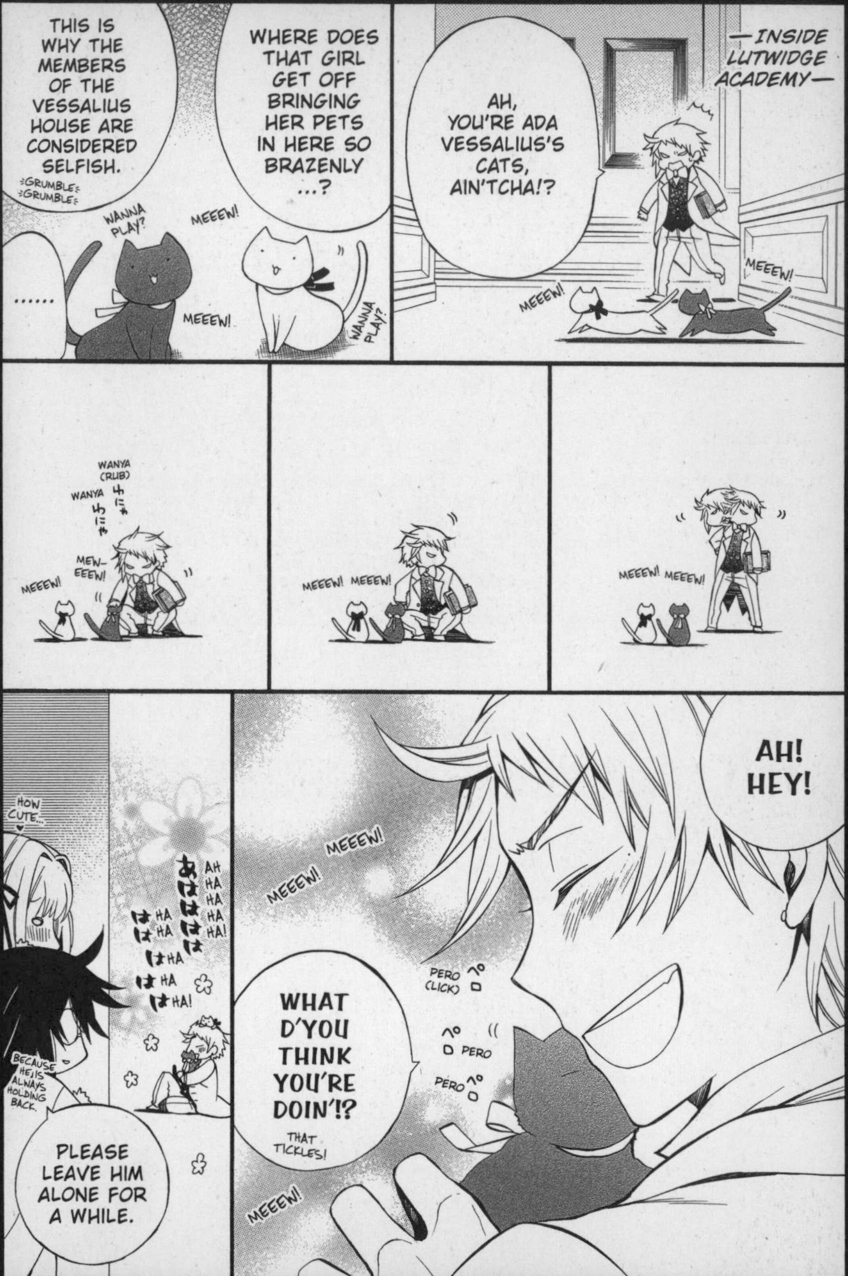

—INSIDE LUTWIDGE ACADEMY—
AH, YOU'RE ADA VESSALIUS'S CATS, AIN'TCHA!?
MEEEW!
MEEEW!
WHERE DOES THAT GIRL GET OFF BRINGING HER PETS IN HERE SO BRAZENLY ...?
MEEEW!
WANNA PLAY?
THIS IS WHY THE MEMBERS OF THE VESSALIUS HOUSE ARE CONSIDERED SELFISH.
GRUMBLE GRUMBLE
WANNA PLAY?
MEEEW!
......
MEEEW! MEEEW!
MEEEW! MEEEW!
WANYA (RUB) WANYA
わにゃ わにゃ
MEW—EEEW!
MEEEW!
AH! HEY!
MEEEW!
MEEEW!
PERO (LICK)
PERO
PERO
WHAT D'YOU THINK YOU'RE DOIN'!?
THAT TICKLES!
MEEEW!
あははははははは
AH HA HA HA HA HA! HA HA HA HA HA!
HOW CUTE...♥
BECAUSE HE IS ALWAYS HOLDING BACK.
PLEASE LEAVE HIM ALONE FOR A WHILE.

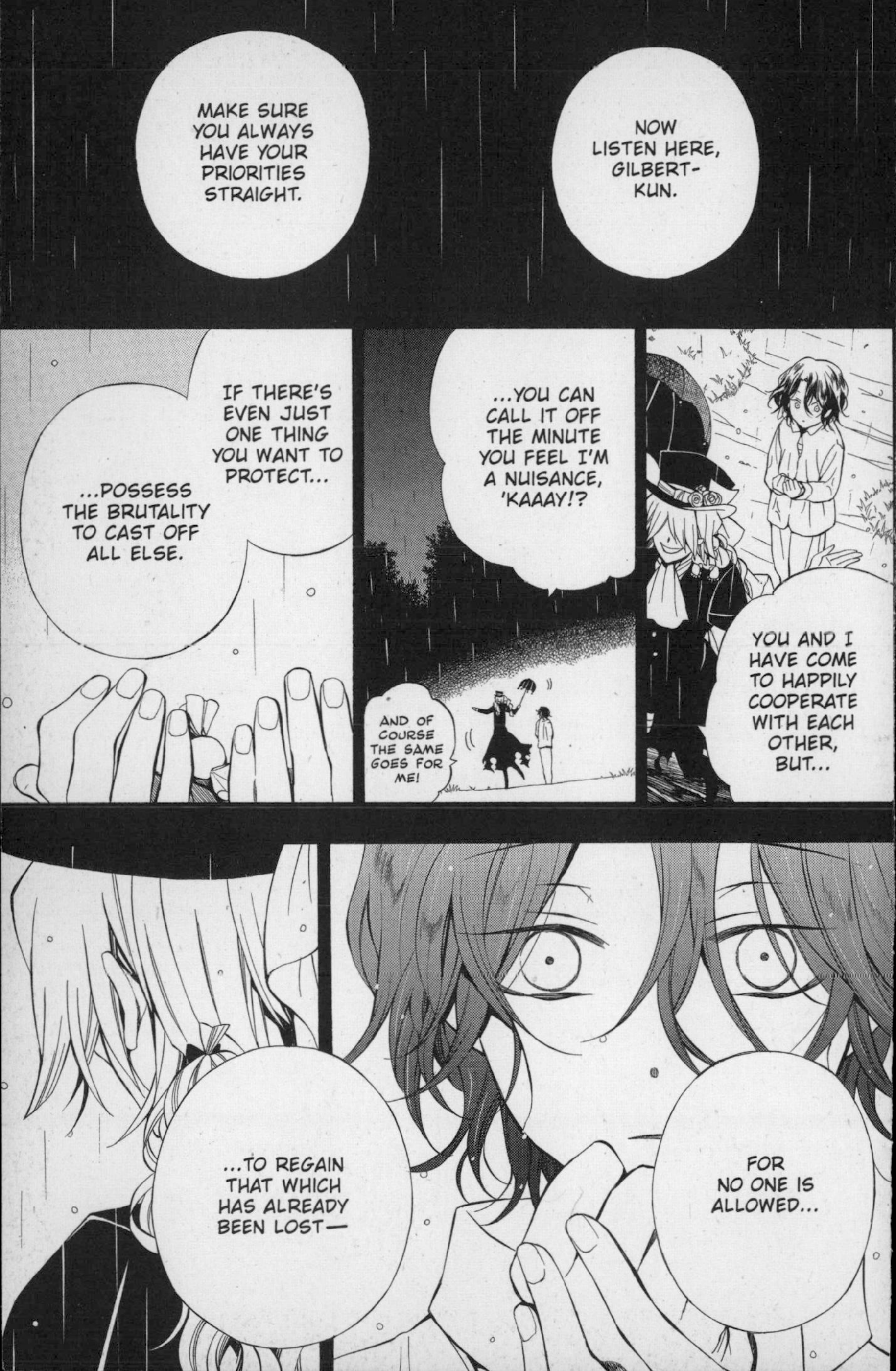
NOW LISTEN HERE, GILBERT-KUN.
MAKE SURE YOU ALWAYS HAVE YOUR PRIORITIES STRAIGHT.
YOU AND I HAVE COME TO HAPPILY COOPERATE WITH EACH OTHER, BUT...
...YOU CAN CALL IT OFF THE MINUTE YOU FEEL I'M A NUISANCE, 'KAAAY!?
AND OF COURSE THE SAME GOES FOR ME!
IF THERE'S EVEN JUST ONE THING YOU WANT TO PROTECT...
...POSSESS THE BRUTALITY TO CAST OFF ALL ELSE.
FOR NO ONE IS ALLOWED...
...TO REGAIN THAT WHICH HAS ALREADY BEEN LOST—

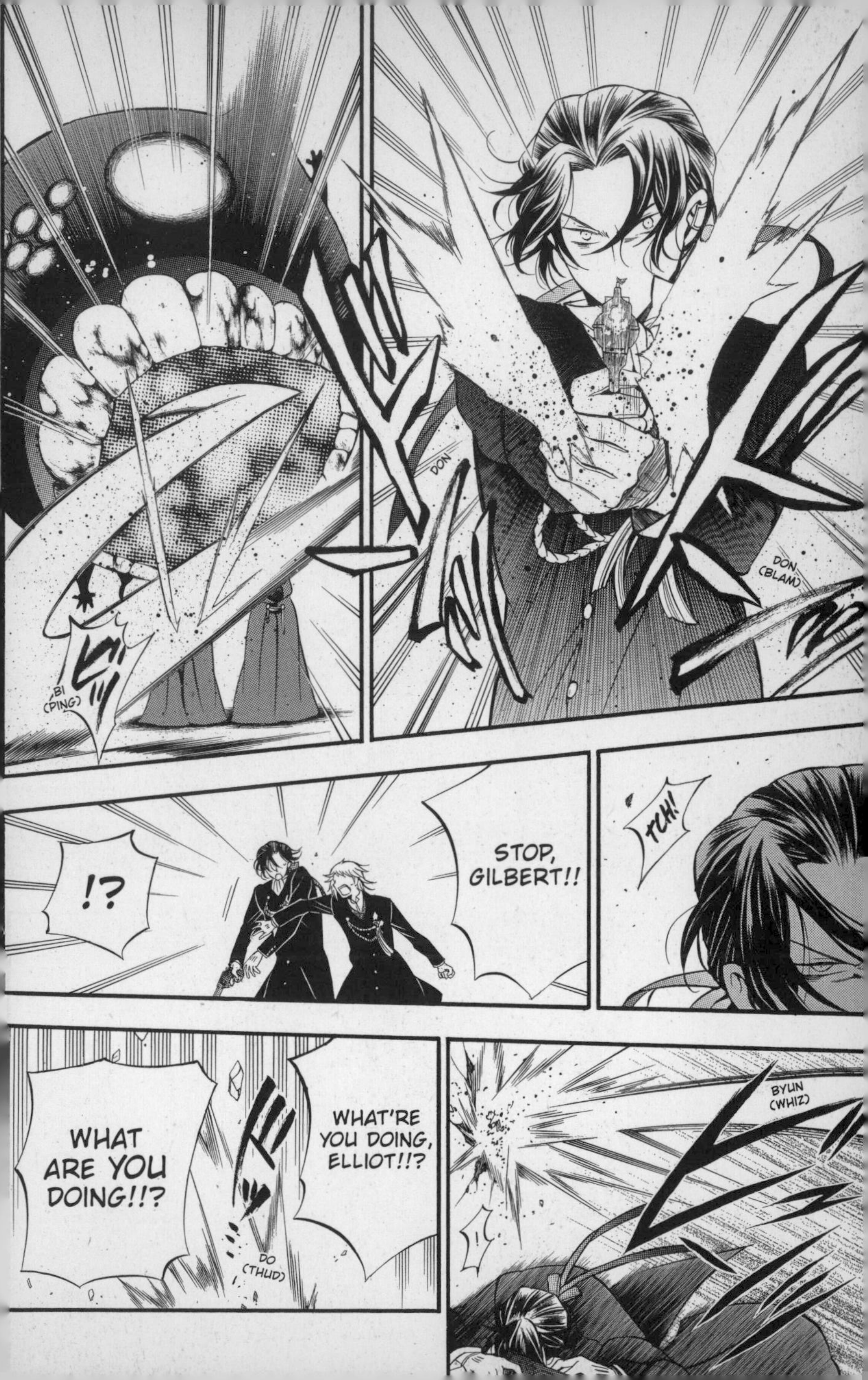
DON
DON (BLAM)
BI (PING)
TCH!
STOP, GILBERT!!
!?
BYUN (WHIZ)
!!
WHAT'RE YOU DOING, ELLIOT!!?
DO (THUD)
WHAT ARE YOU DOING!!?

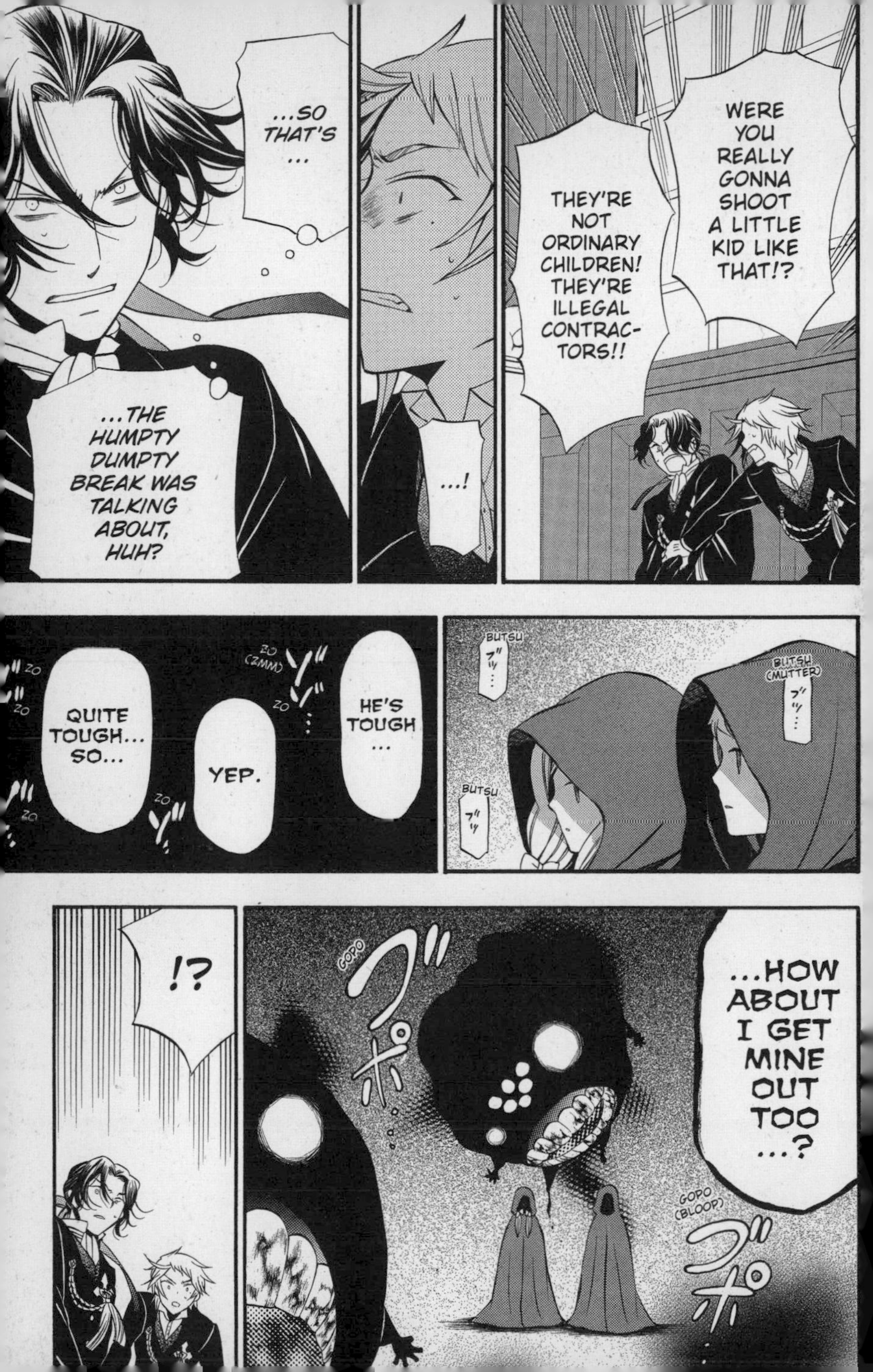
WERE YOU REALLY GONNA SHOOT A LITTLE KID LIKE THAT!?
THEY'RE NOT ORDINARY CHILDREN! THEY'RE ILLEGAL CONTRAC-TORS!!
...!
...SO THAT'S ...
...THE HUMPTY DUMPTY BREAK WAS TALKING ABOUT, HUH?
BUTSU (MUTTER)
ブツ...
BUTSU
ブツ...
BUTSU
ブツ
HE'S TOUGH ...
ZO (ZMM)
ZO
YEP.
ZO
QUITE TOUGH... SO...
ZO
ZO
ZO
...HOW ABOUT I GET MINE OUT TOO ...?
GOPO (BLOOP)
ゴポ
GOPO
ゴポ
!?

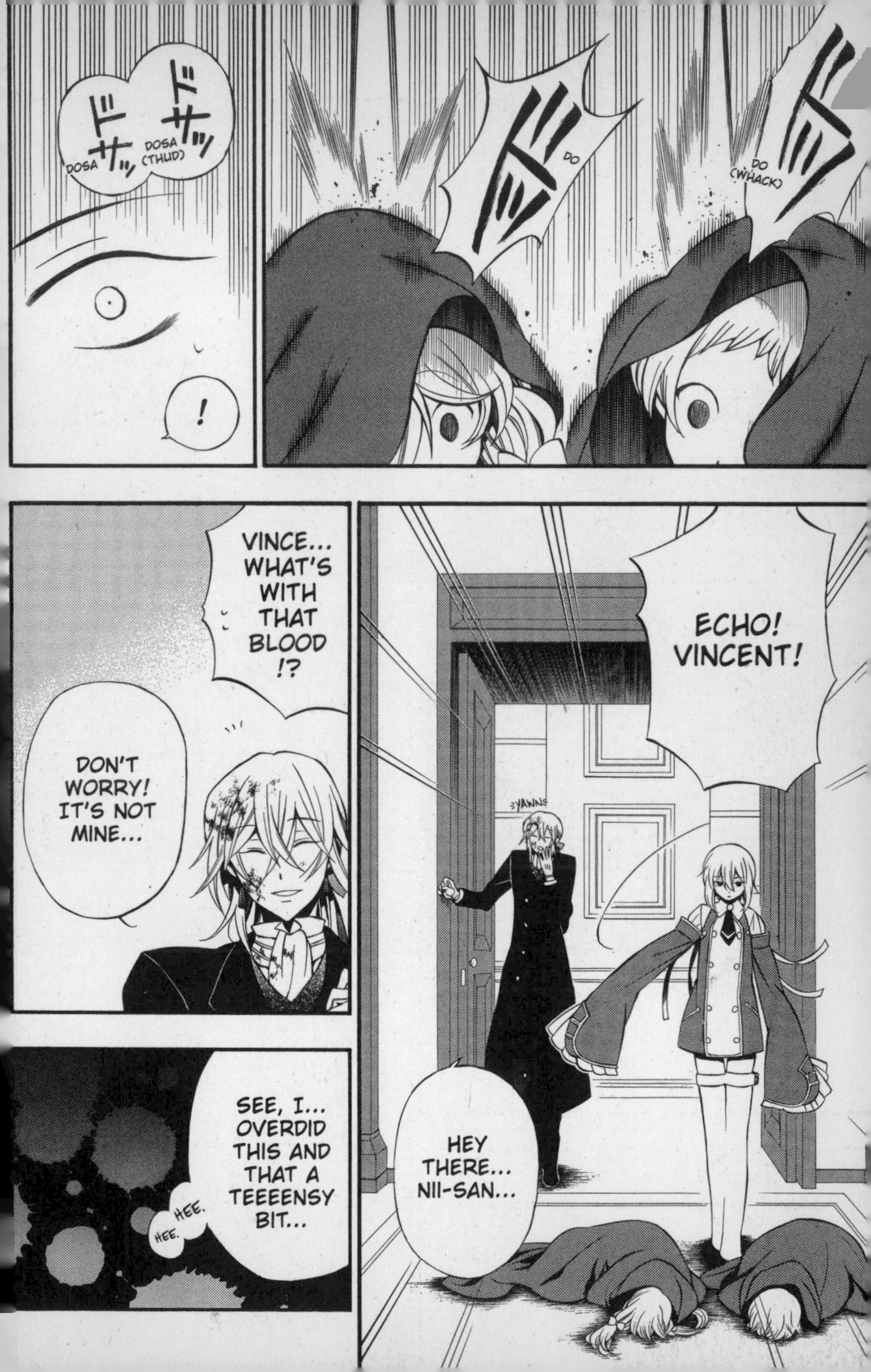
DO (WHACK)
DO
ドッ
ドッ
DOSA (THUD)
DOSA
ドサッ
ドサッ
!
ECHO! VINCENT!
YAWN
HEY THERE... NII-SAN...
VINCE... WHAT'S WITH THAT BLOOD !?
DON'T WORRY! IT'S NOT MINE...
SEE, I... OVERDID THIS AND THAT A TEEEENSY BIT...
HEE. HEE.

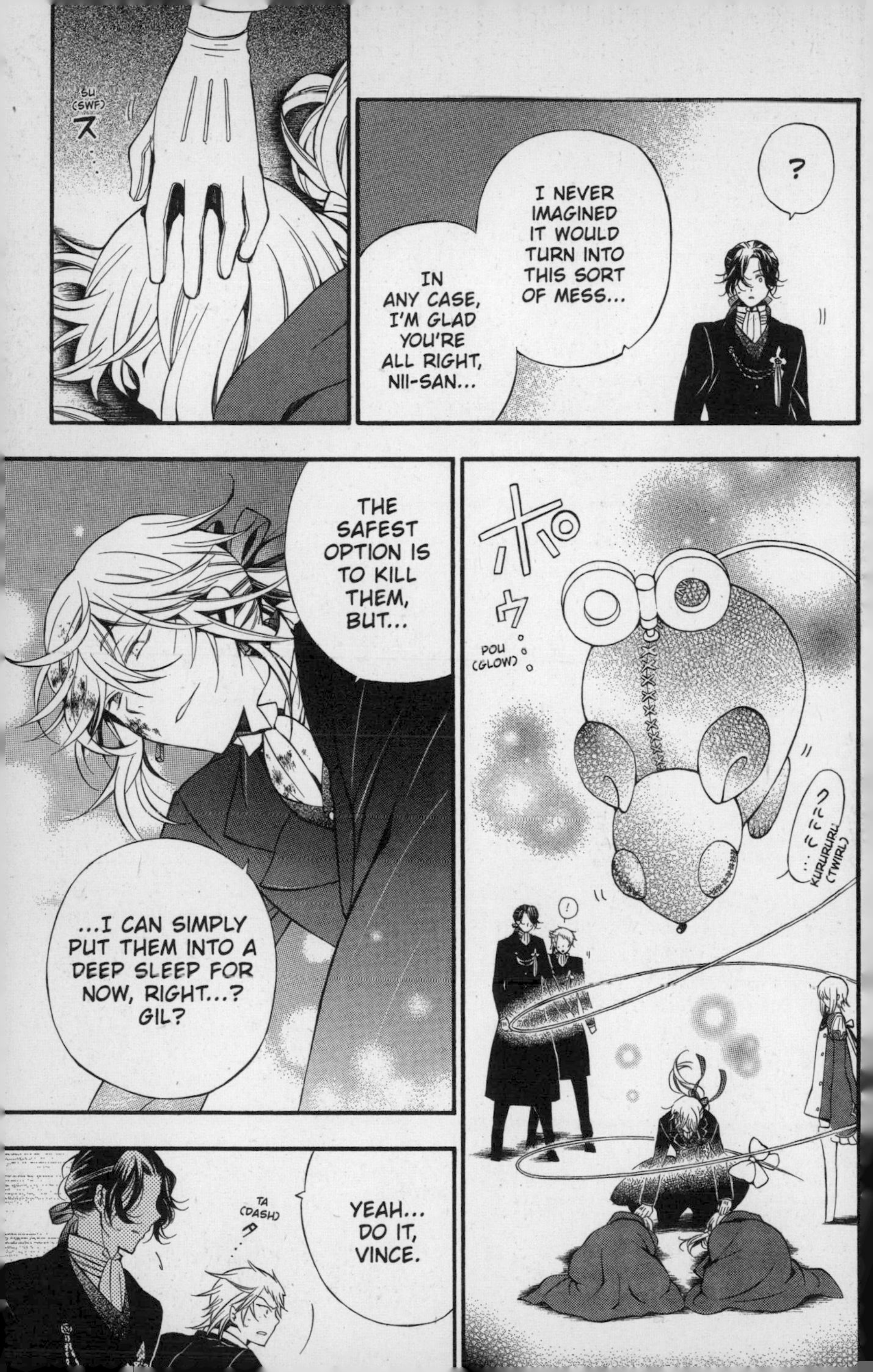
?
I NEVER IMAGINED IT WOULD TURN INTO THIS SORT OF MESS...
IN ANY CASE, I'M GLAD YOU'RE ALL RIGHT, NII-SAN...
SU (SWF)
ス
ポゥ
POU (GLOW)
クルル…
KURURURU (TWIRL)
!
THE SAFEST OPTION IS TO KILL THEM, BUT...
...I CAN SIMPLY PUT THEM INTO A DEEP SLEEP FOR NOW, RIGHT...? GIL?
TA (DASH)
YEAH... DO IT, VINCE.

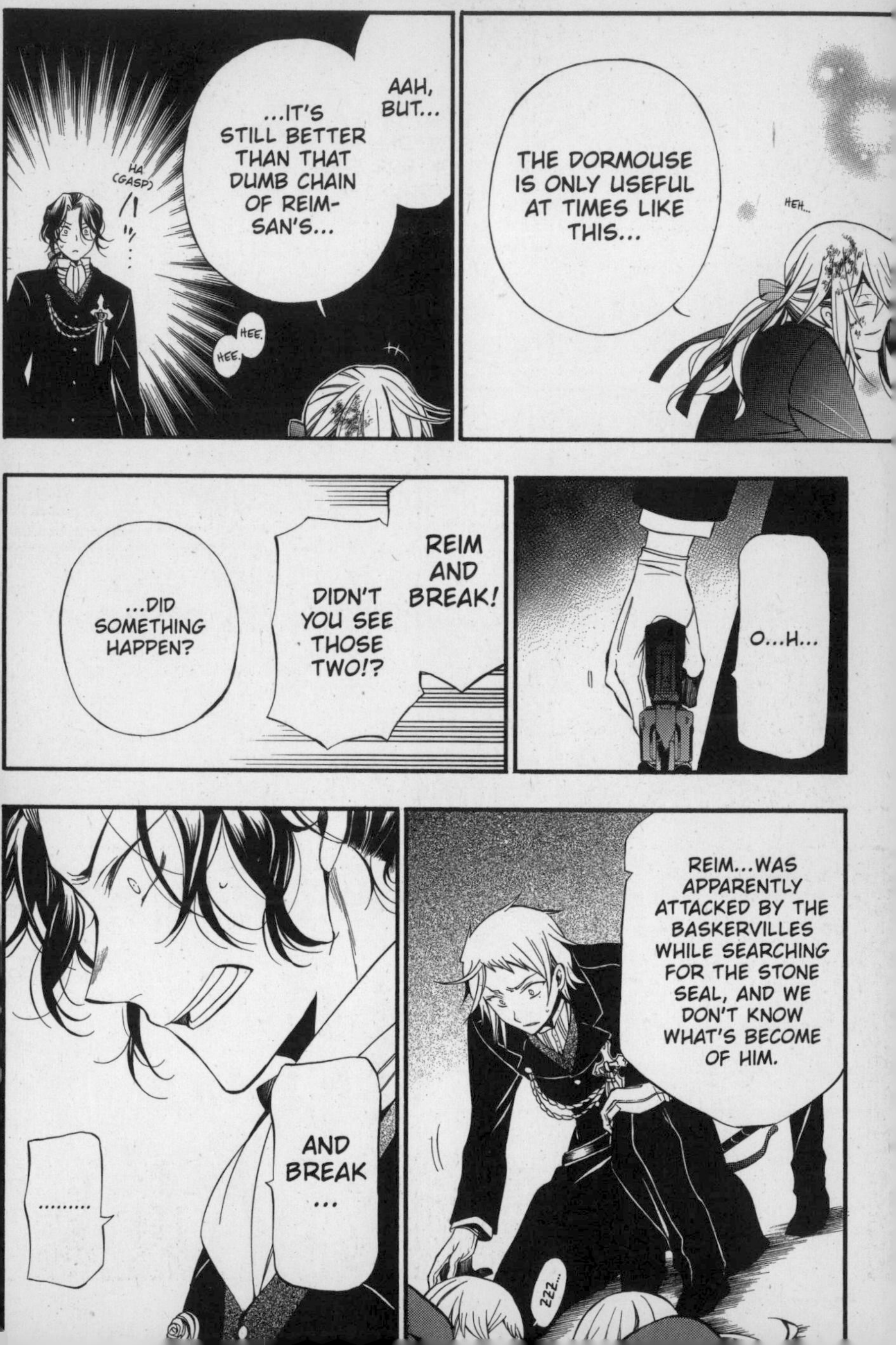
THE DORMOUSE IS ONLY USEFUL AT TIMES LIKE THIS...
HEH...
AAH, BUT...
...IT'S STILL BETTER THAN THAT DUMB CHAIN OF REIM-SAN'S...
HA (GASP)
HEE. HEE.
O...H...
REIM AND BREAK!
DIDN'T YOU SEE THOSE TWO!?
...DID SOMETHING HAPPEN?
REIM...WAS APPARENTLY ATTACKED BY THE BASKERVILLES WHILE SEARCHING FOR THE STONE SEAL, AND WE DON'T KNOW WHAT'S BECOME OF HIM.
ZZZ...
AND BREAK...
....

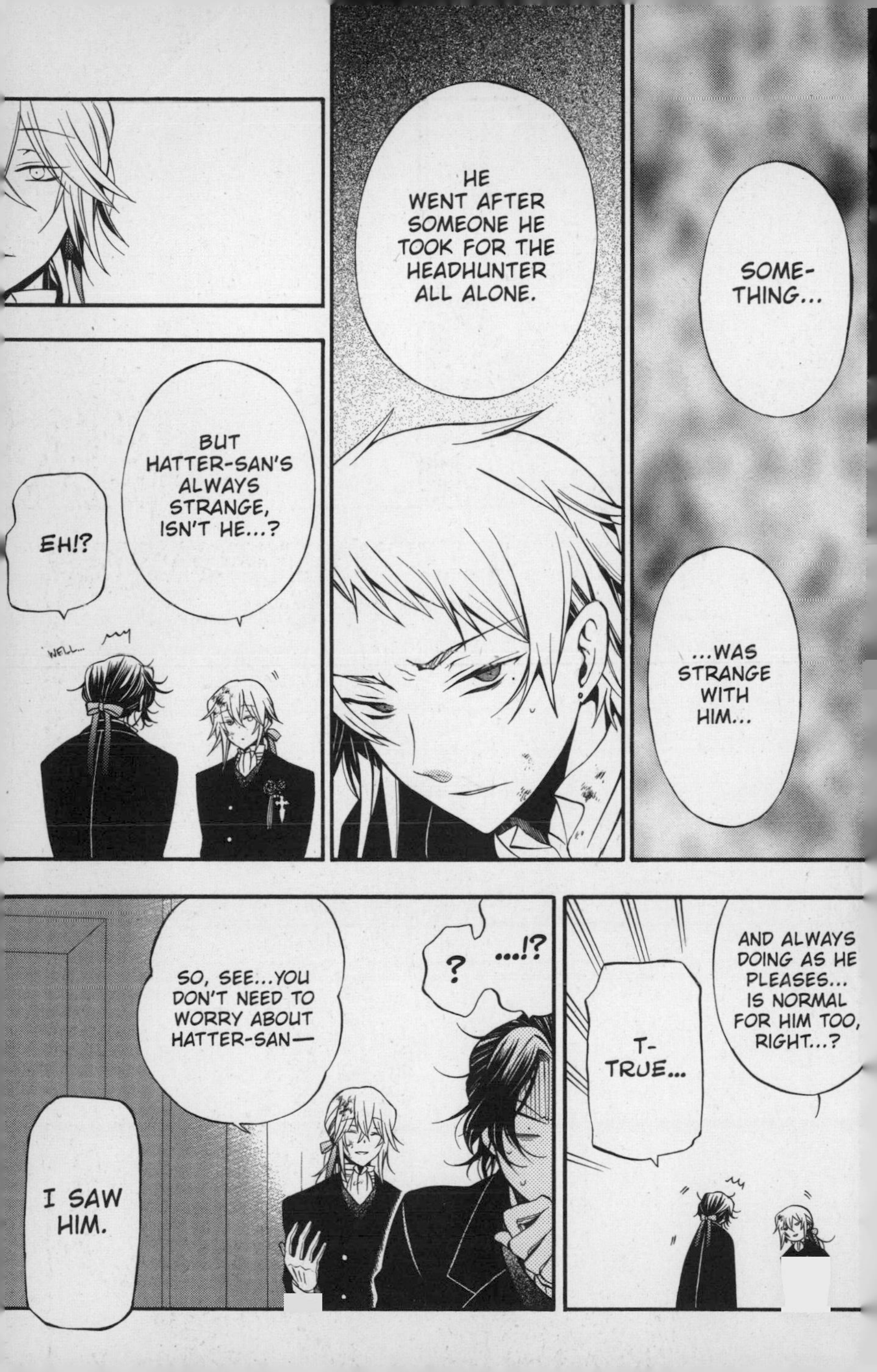
SOMETHING...
...WAS STRANGE WITH HIM...
HE WENT AFTER SOMEONE HE TOOK FOR THE HEADHUNTER ALL ALONE.
BUT HATTER-SAN'S ALWAYS STRANGE, ISN'T HE...?
EH!?
WELL...
AND ALWAYS DOING AS HE PLEASES... IS NORMAL FOR HIM TOO, RIGHT...?
T-TRUE...
...!?
?
SO, SEE...YOU DON'T NEED TO WORRY ABOUT HATTER-SAN—
I SAW HIM.

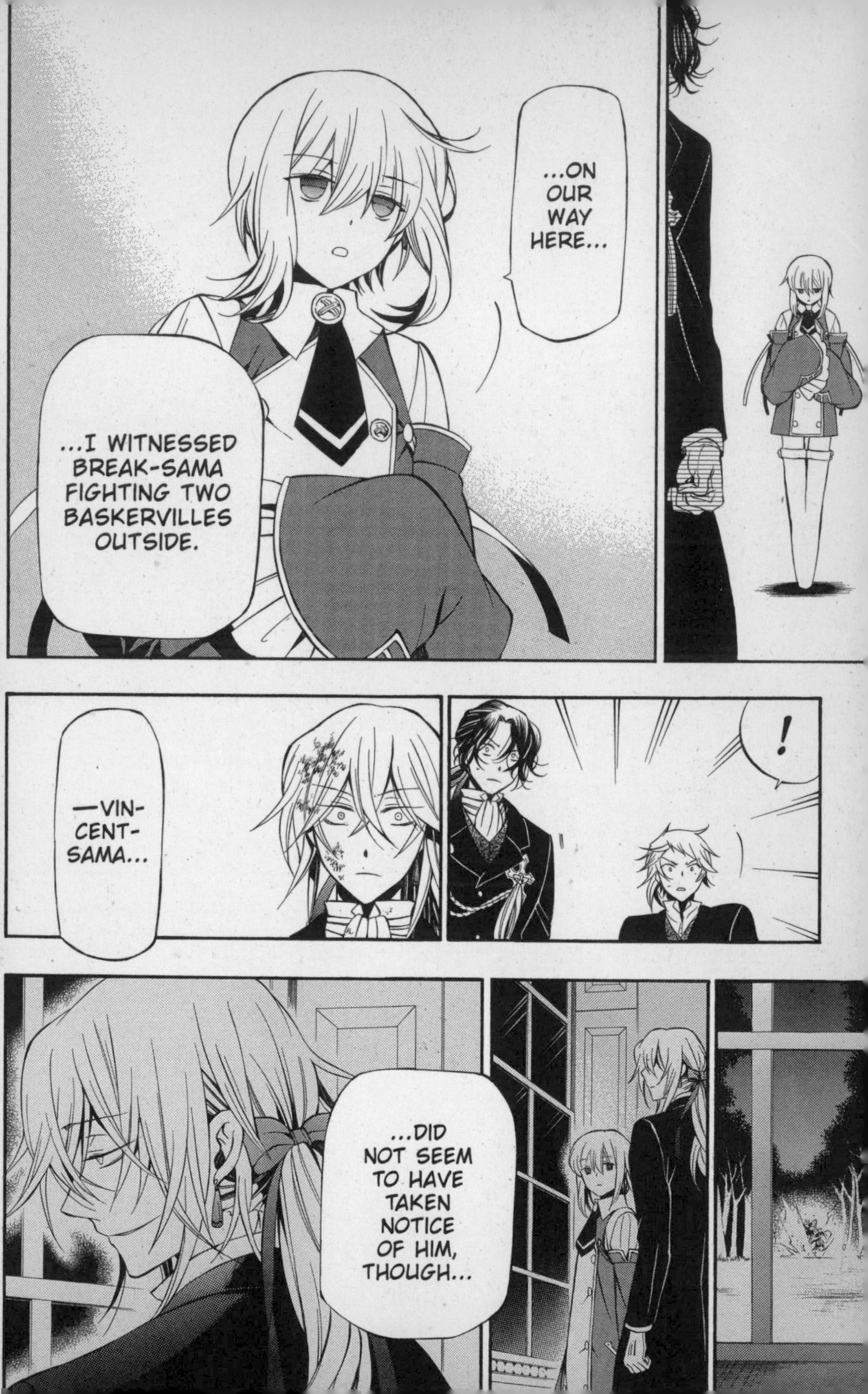
...ON OUR WAY HERE...
...I WITNESSED BREAK-SAMA FIGHTING TWO BASKERVILLES OUTSIDE.
!
—VIN-CENT-SAMA...
...DID NOT SEEM TO HAVE TAKEN NOTICE OF HIM, THOUGH...

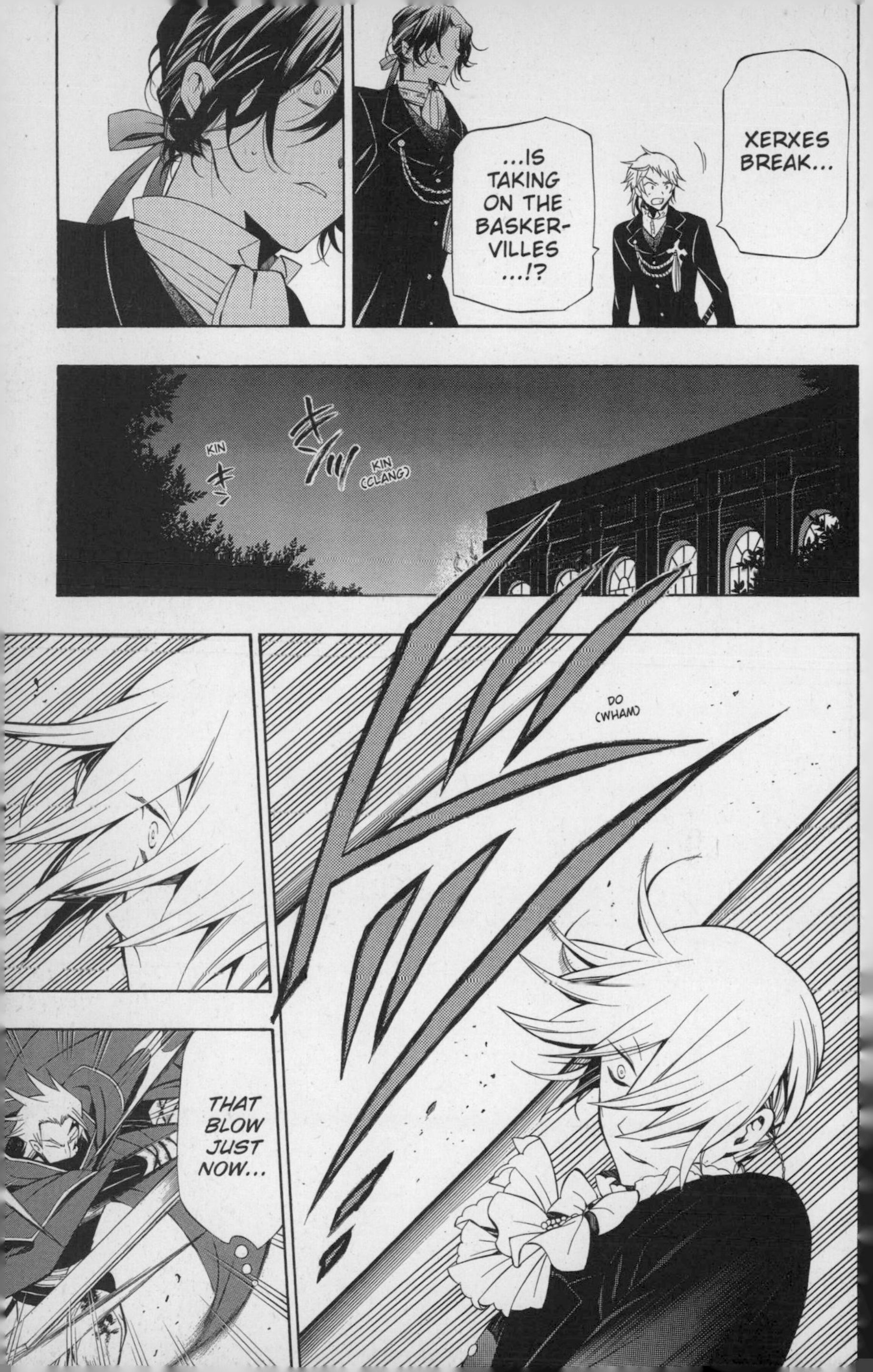
XERXES BREAK...
...IS TAKING ON THE BASKER-VILLES ...!?
KIN (CLANG)
KIN
DO (WHAM)
THAT BLOW JUST NOW...

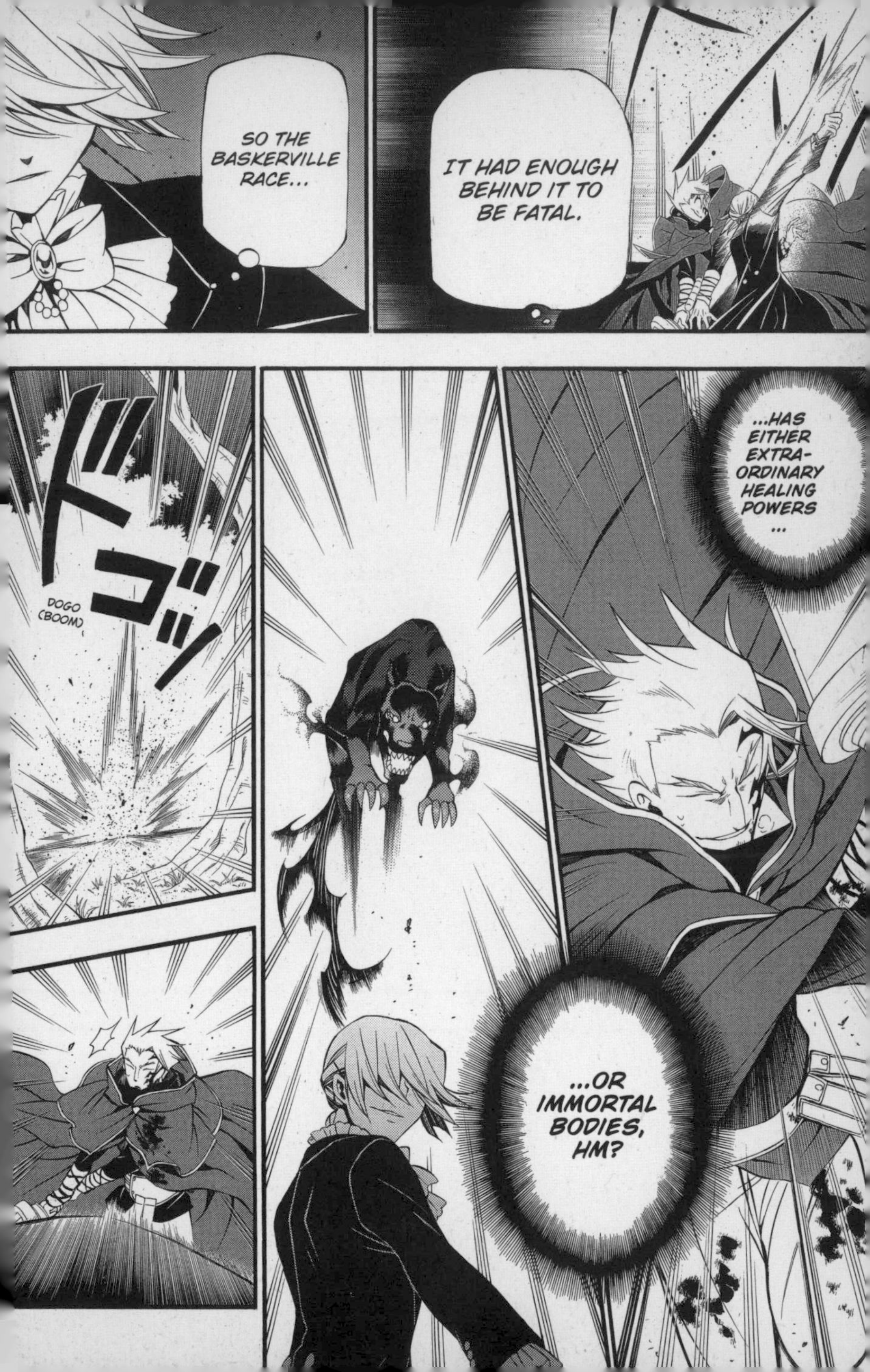
IT HAD ENOUGH BEHIND IT TO BE FATAL.
SO THE BASKERVILLE RACE...
...HAS EITHER EXTRA-ORDINARY HEALING POWERS...
DOGO (BOOM)
...OR IMMORTAL BODIES, HM?

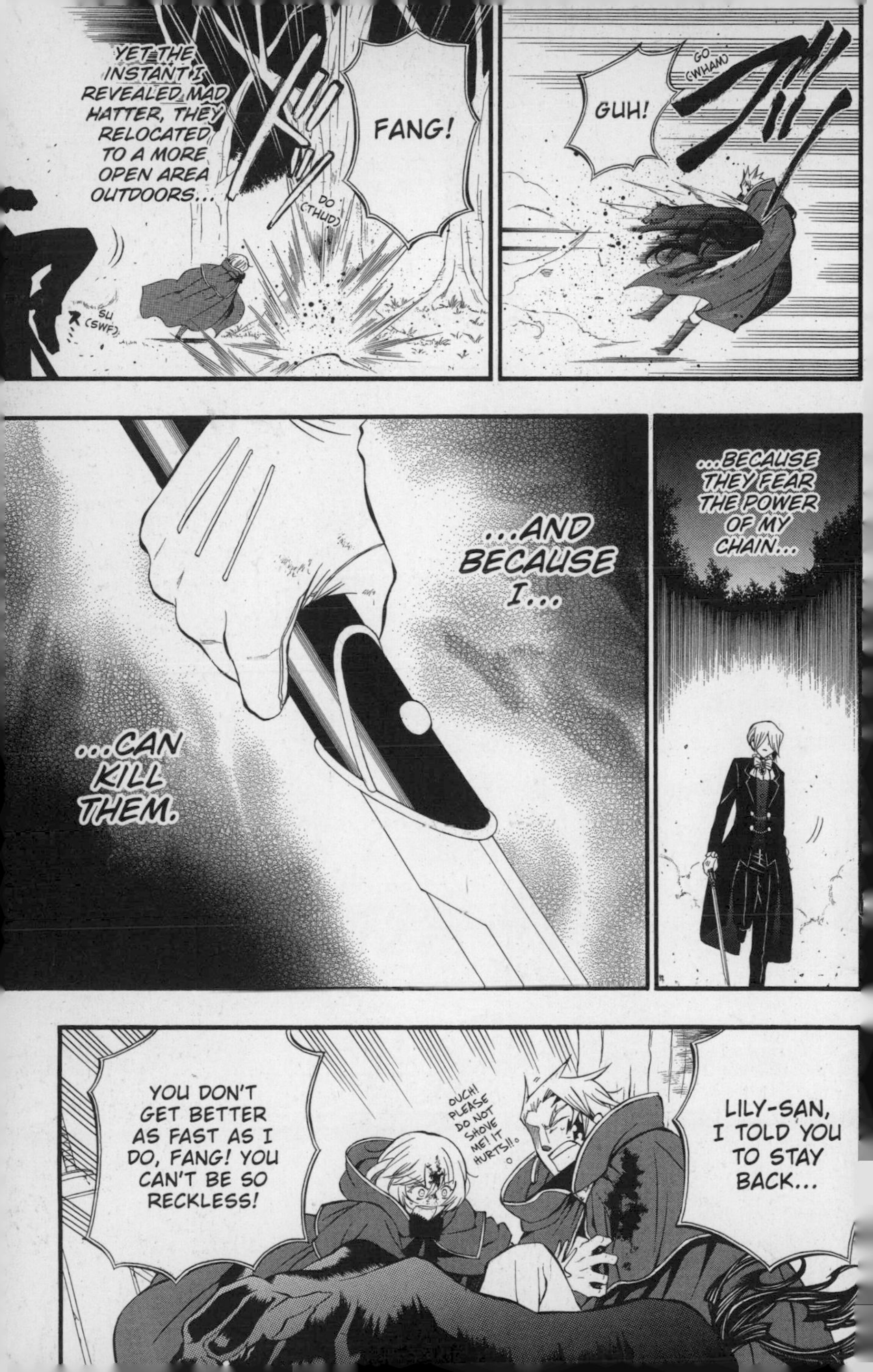
GO (WHAM)
GUH!
FANG!
DO (THUD)
YET THE INSTANT I REVEALED MAD HATTER, THEY RELOCATED TO A MORE OPEN AREA OUTDOORS...
SU (SWF)
...BECAUSE THEY FEAR THE POWER OF MY CHAIN...
...AND BECAUSE I...
...CAN KILL THEM.
LILY-SAN, I TOLD YOU TO STAY BACK...
OUCH! PLEASE DO NOT SHOVE ME! IT HURTS!!
YOU DON'T GET BETTER AS FAST AS I DO, FANG! YOU CAN'T BE SO RECKLESS!

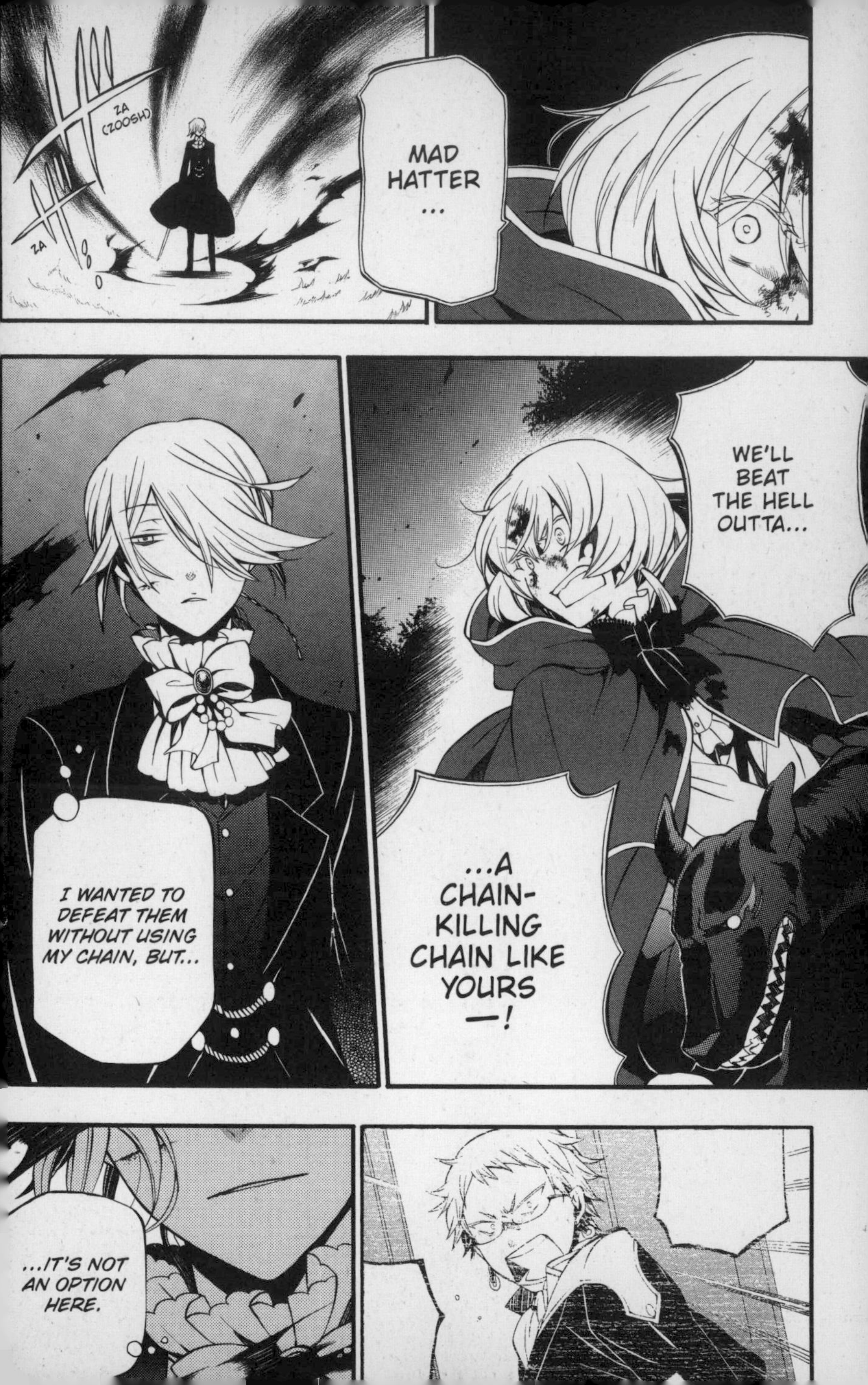
MAD HATTER ...
ZA (ZOOSH)
ZA
WE'LL BEAT THE HELL OUTTA...
...A CHAIN-KILLING CHAIN LIKE YOURS —!
I WANTED TO DEFEAT THEM WITHOUT USING MY CHAIN, BUT...
...IT'S NOT AN OPTION HERE.

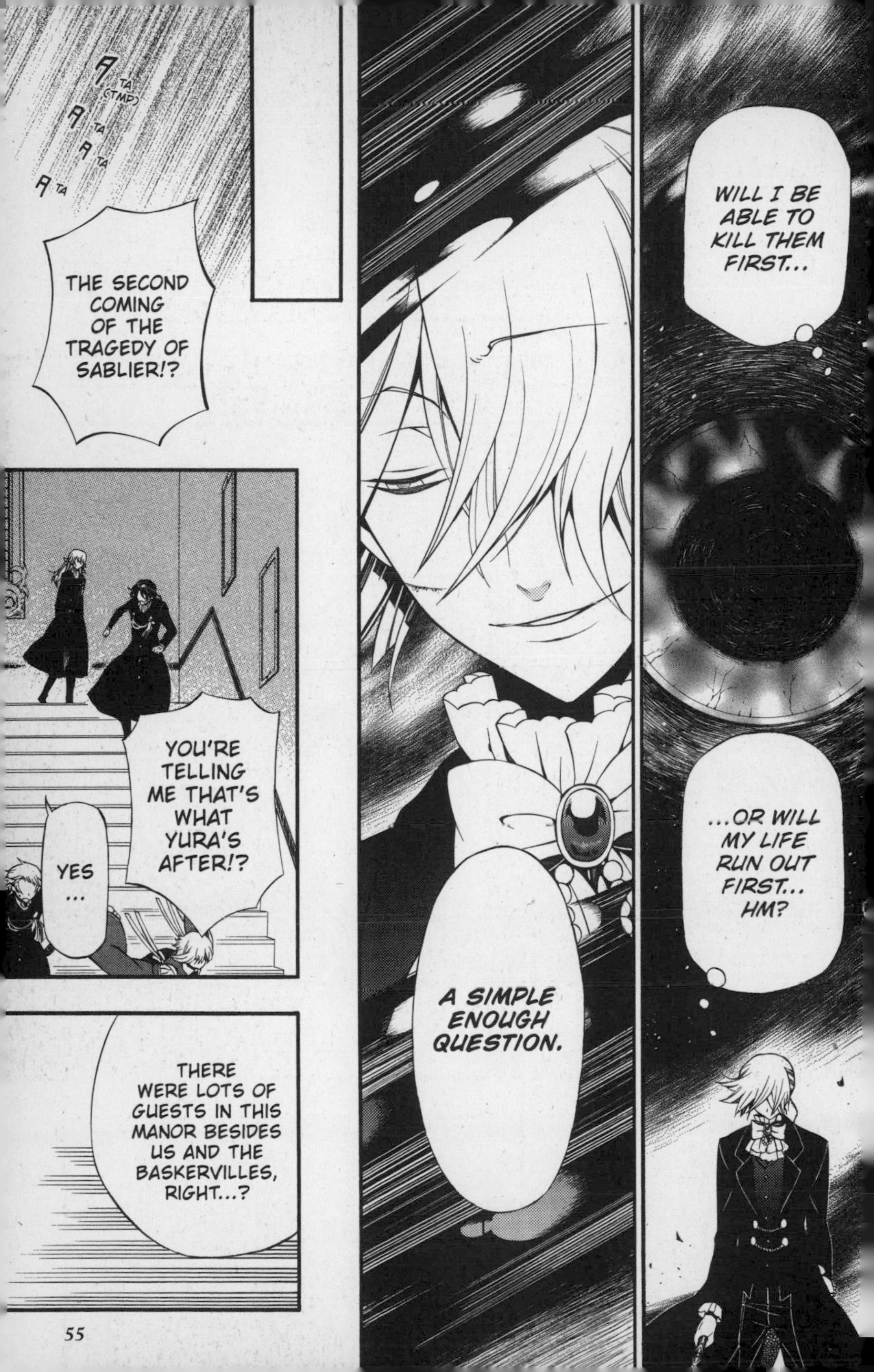
WILL I BE ABLE TO KILL THEM FIRST...
...OR WILL MY LIFE RUN OUT FIRST... HM?
A SIMPLE ENOUGH QUESTION.
TA (TMP)
TA
TA
TA
THE SECOND COMING OF THE TRAGEDY OF SABLIER!?
YOU'RE TELLING ME THAT'S WHAT YURA'S AFTER!?
YES...
THERE WERE LOTS OF GUESTS IN THIS MANOR BESIDES US AND THE BASKERVILLES, RIGHT...?

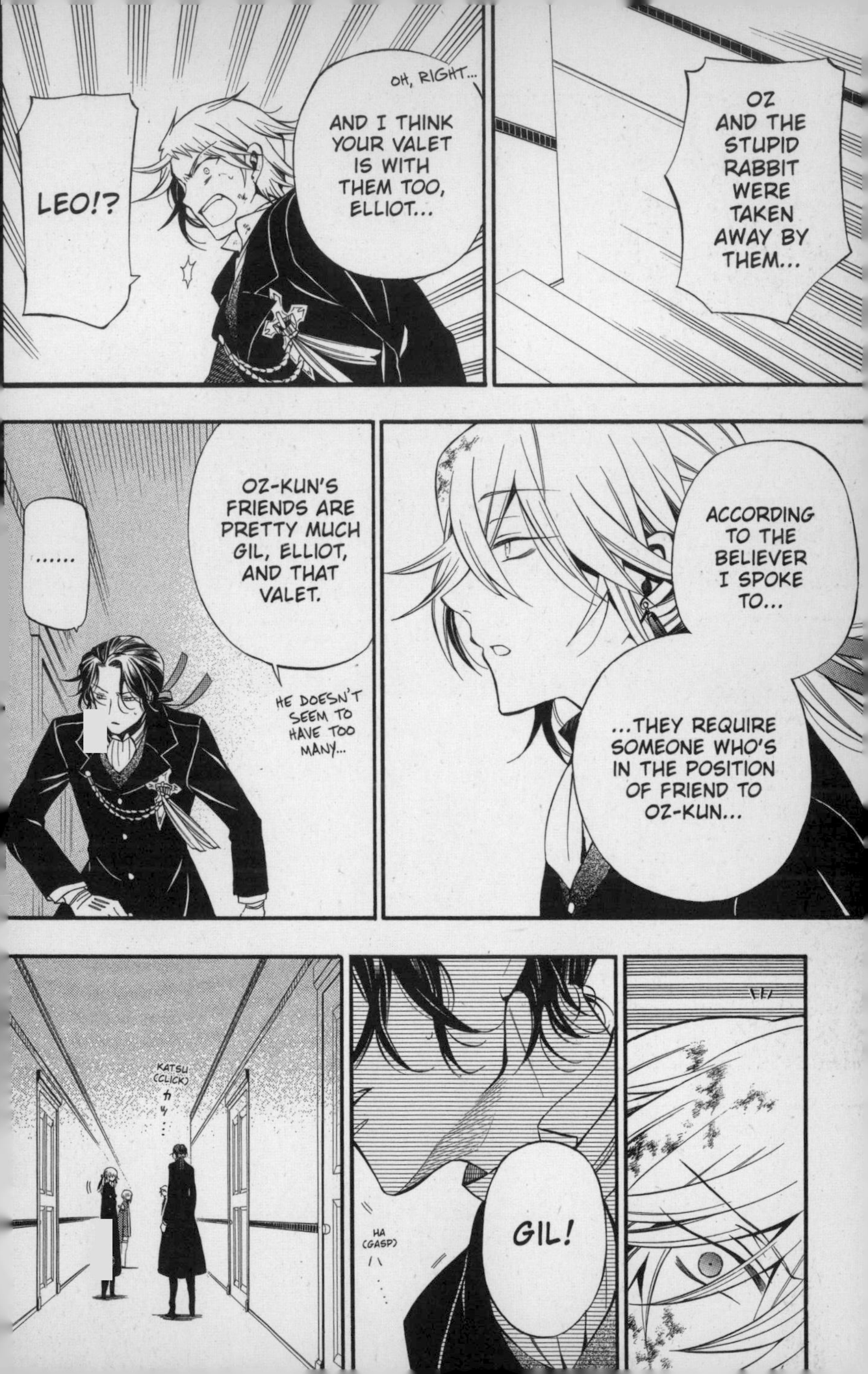
OZ AND THE STUPID RABBIT WERE TAKEN AWAY BY THEM...
OH, RIGHT...
AND I THINK YOUR VALET IS WITH THEM TOO, ELLIOT...
LEO!?
ACCORDING TO THE BELIEVER I SPOKE TO...
...THEY REQUIRE SOMEONE WHO'S IN THE POSITION OF FRIEND TO OZ-KUN...
OZ-KUN'S FRIENDS ARE PRETTY MUCH GIL, ELLIOT, AND THAT VALET.
HE DOESN'T SEEM TO HAVE TOO MANY...
......
GIL!
HA (GASP)
KATSU (CLICK)
カッ…

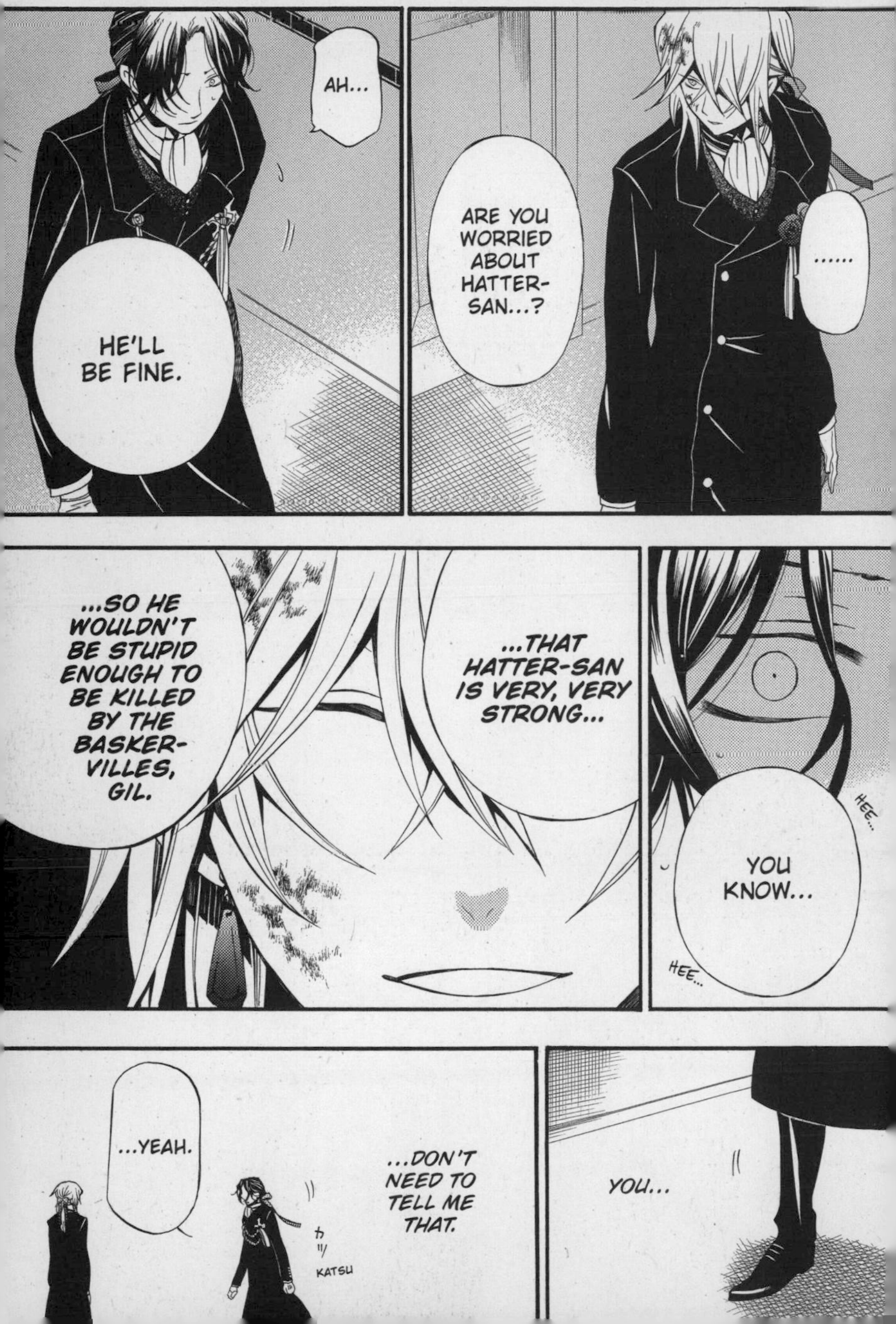
......
ARE YOU WORRIED ABOUT HATTER-SAN...?
AH...
HE'LL BE FINE.
HEE...
YOU KNOW...
HEE...
...THAT HATTER-SAN IS VERY, VERY STRONG...
...SO HE WOULDN'T BE STUPID ENOUGH TO BE KILLED BY THE BASKER-VILLES, GIL.
YOU...
...DON'T NEED TO TELL ME THAT.
カッ
KATSU
...YEAH.

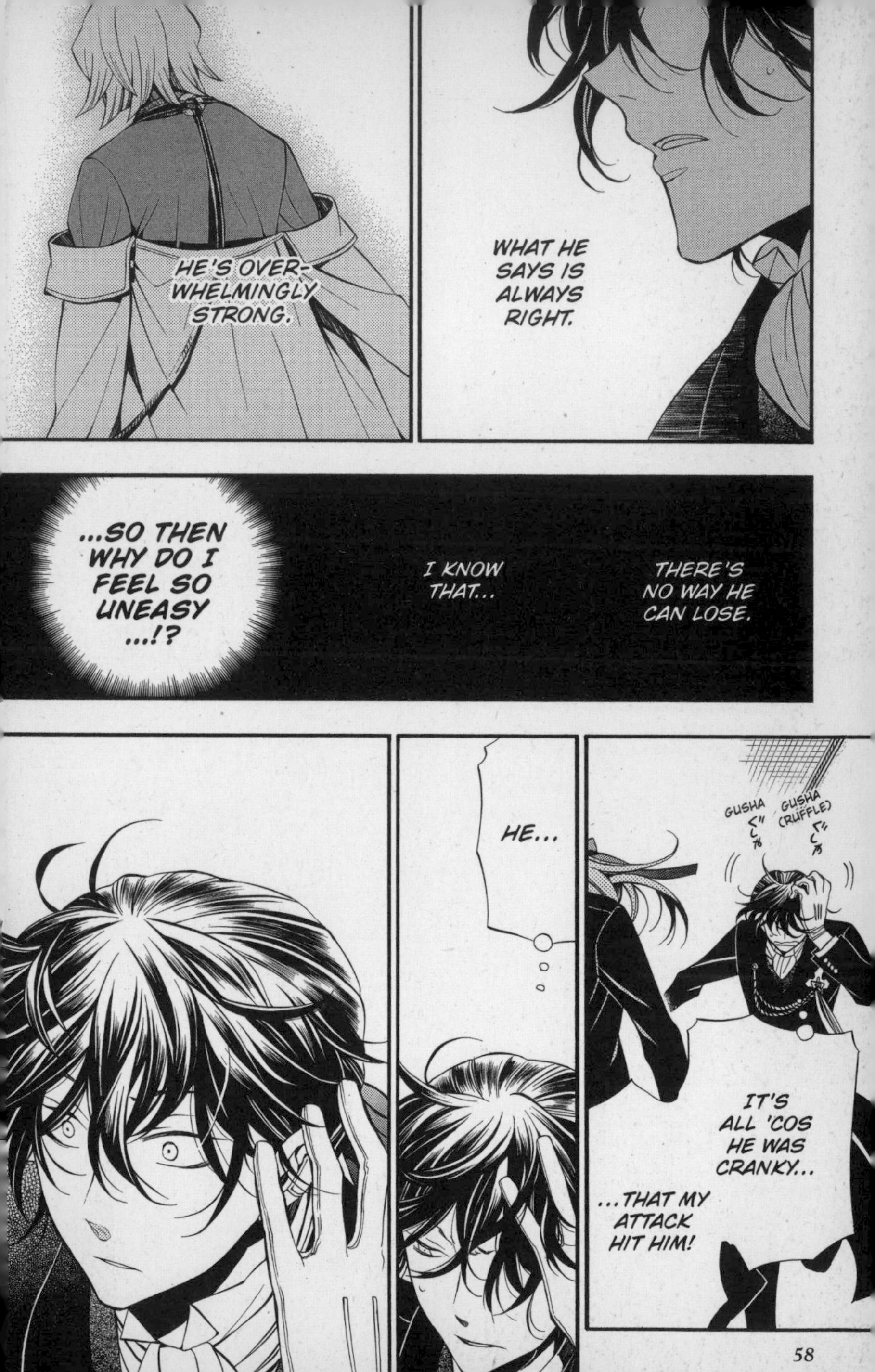
WHAT HE SAYS IS ALWAYS RIGHT.
HE'S OVER-WHELMINGLY STRONG.
THERE'S NO WAY HE CAN LOSE.
I KNOW THAT...
...SO THEN WHY DO I FEEL SO UNEASY ...!?
GUSHA
GUSHA (RUFFLE)
IT'S ALL 'COS HE WAS CRANKY...
...THAT MY ATTACK HIT HIM!
HE...

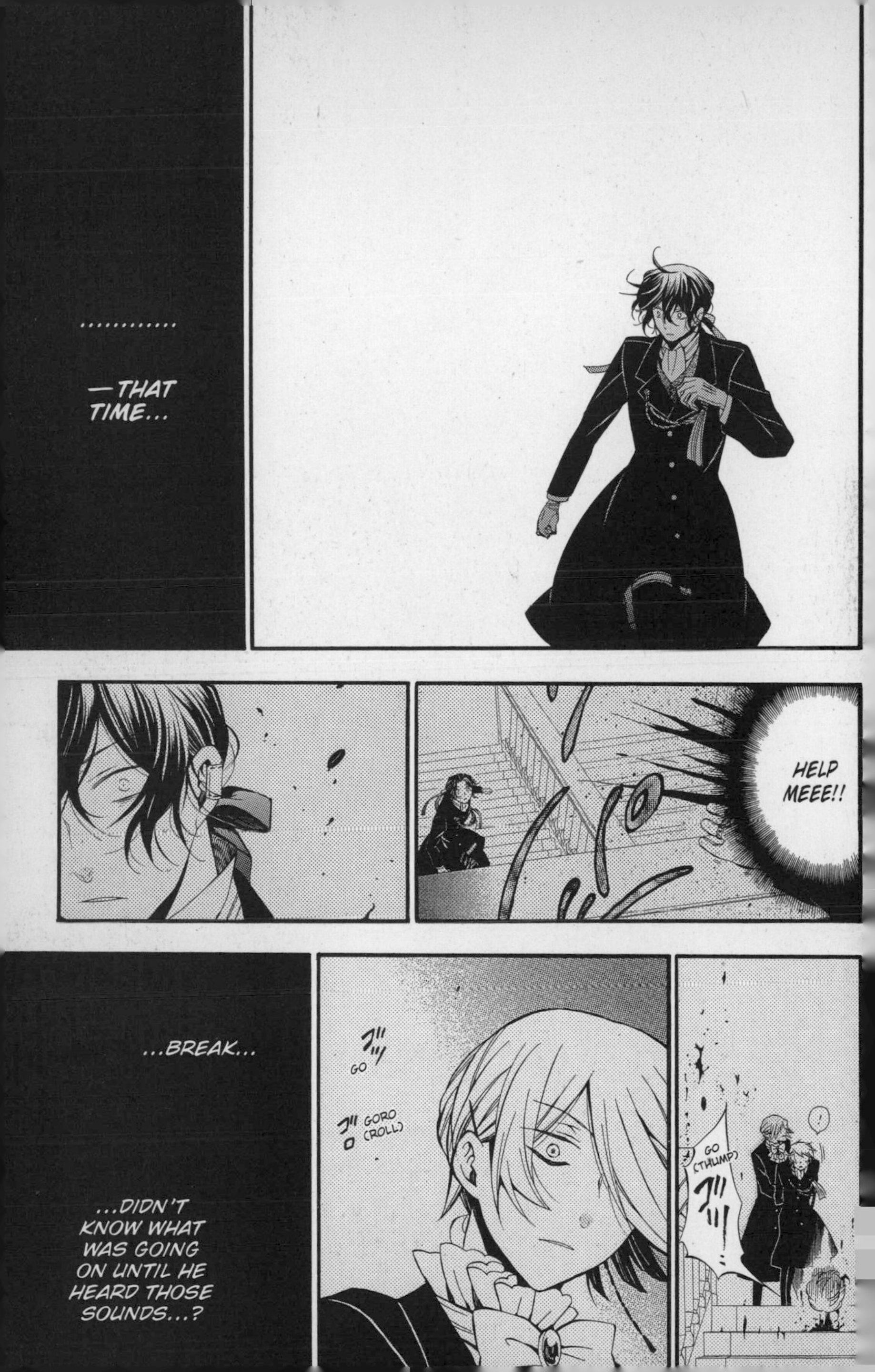
....
—THAT TIME...
HELP MEEE!!
!
GO (THUMP)
GO
GORO (ROLL)
...BREAK...
...DIDN'T KNOW WHAT WAS GOING ON UNTIL HE HEARD THOSE SOUNDS...?

WHY ARE YOU SO KEEN ON GETTING ME TO DO THAT!?

WHY, YOU!!

NO.

IT CAN'T BE...!

DOKUN

DOKUN (BADUM)

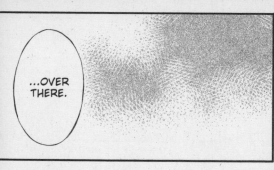

...OVER THERE.

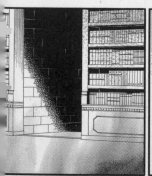

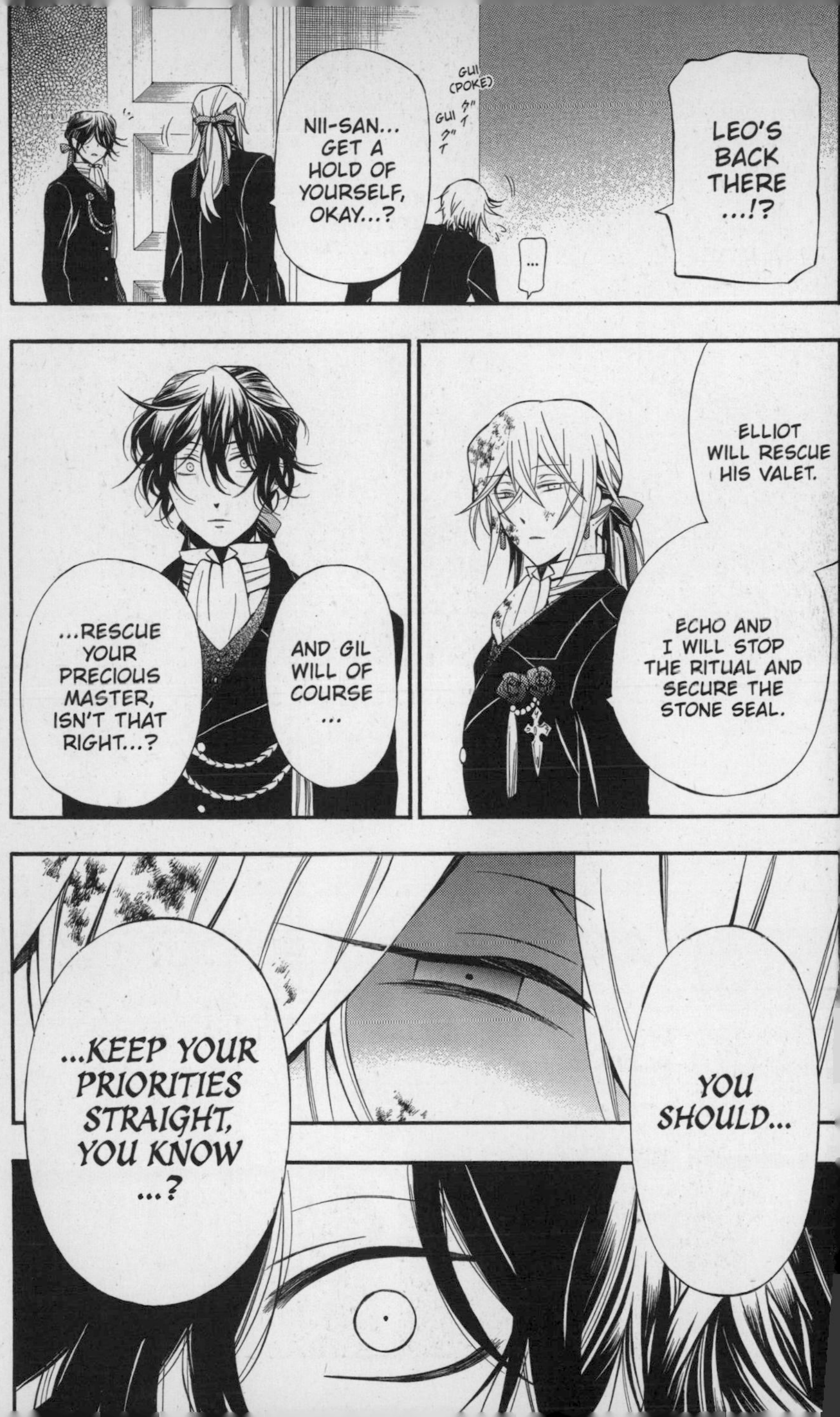
LEO'S BACK THERE ...!?
GUI (POKE)
GUI
NII-SAN... GET A HOLD OF YOURSELF, OKAY...?
...
ELLIOT WILL RESCUE HIS VALET.
ECHO AND I WILL STOP THE RITUAL AND SECURE THE STONE SEAL.
AND GIL WILL OF COURSE ...
...RESCUE YOUR PRECIOUS MASTER, ISN'T THAT RIGHT...?
YOU SHOULD...
...KEEP YOUR PRIORITIES STRAIGHT, YOU KNOW ...?

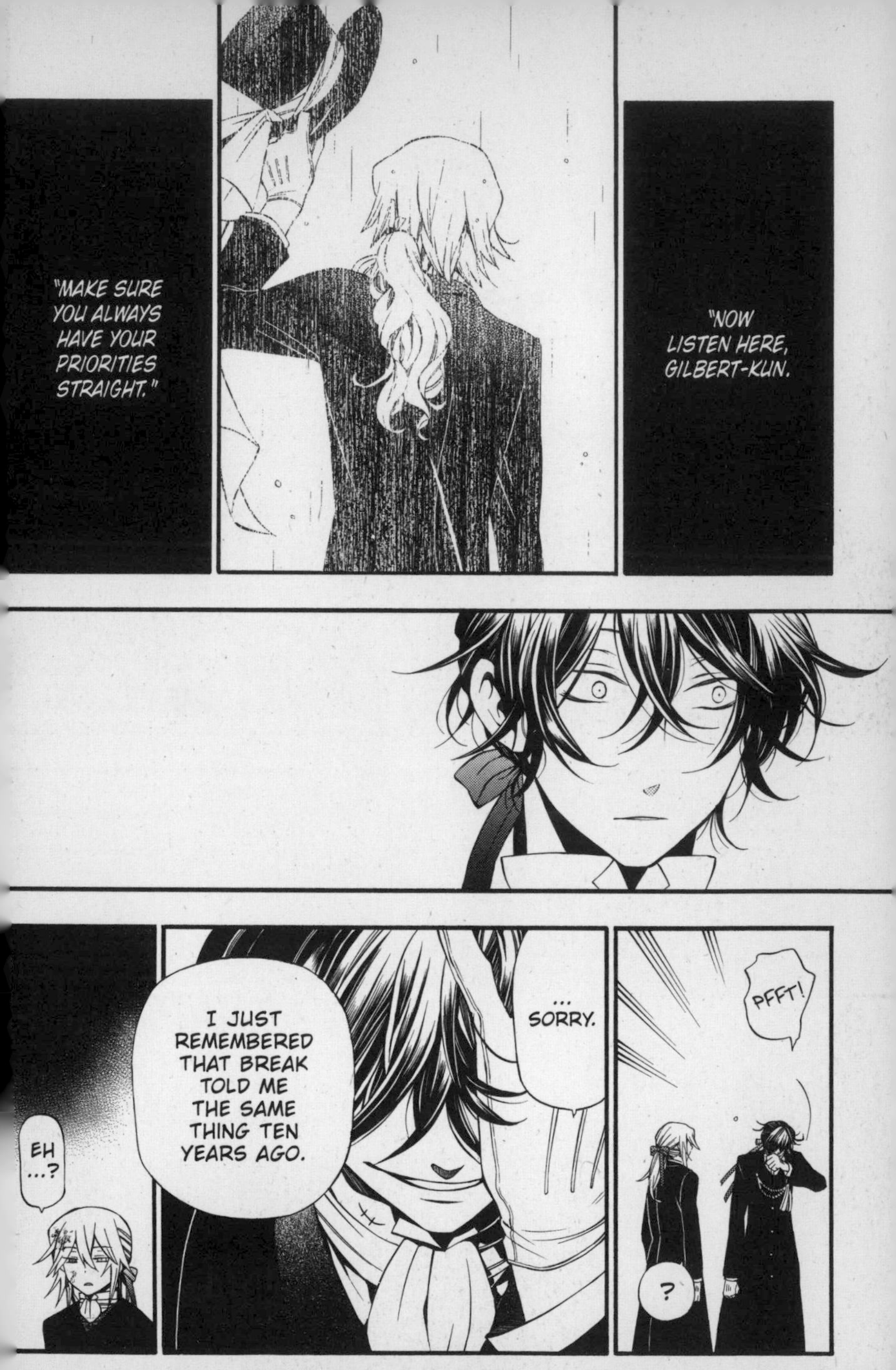
"NOW LISTEN HERE, GILBERT-KUN.
"MAKE SURE YOU ALWAYS HAVE YOUR PRIORITIES STRAIGHT."
PFFT!
?
... SORRY.
I JUST REMEMBERED THAT BREAK TOLD ME THE SAME THING TEN YEARS AGO.
EH ...?

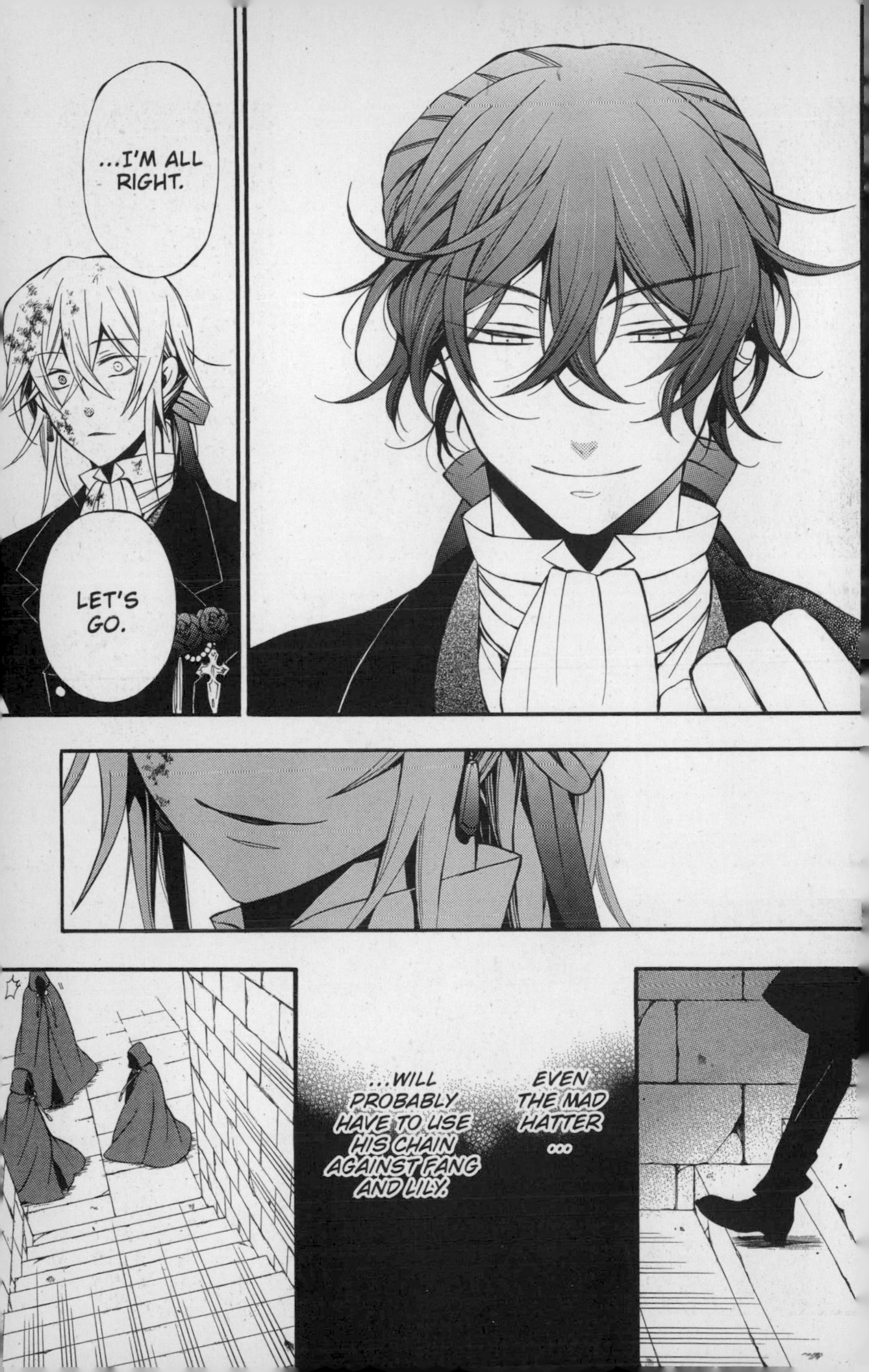
...I'M ALL RIGHT.
LET'S GO.
EVEN THE MAD HATTER...
...WILL PROBABLY HAVE TO USE HIS CHAIN AGAINST FANG AND LILY.

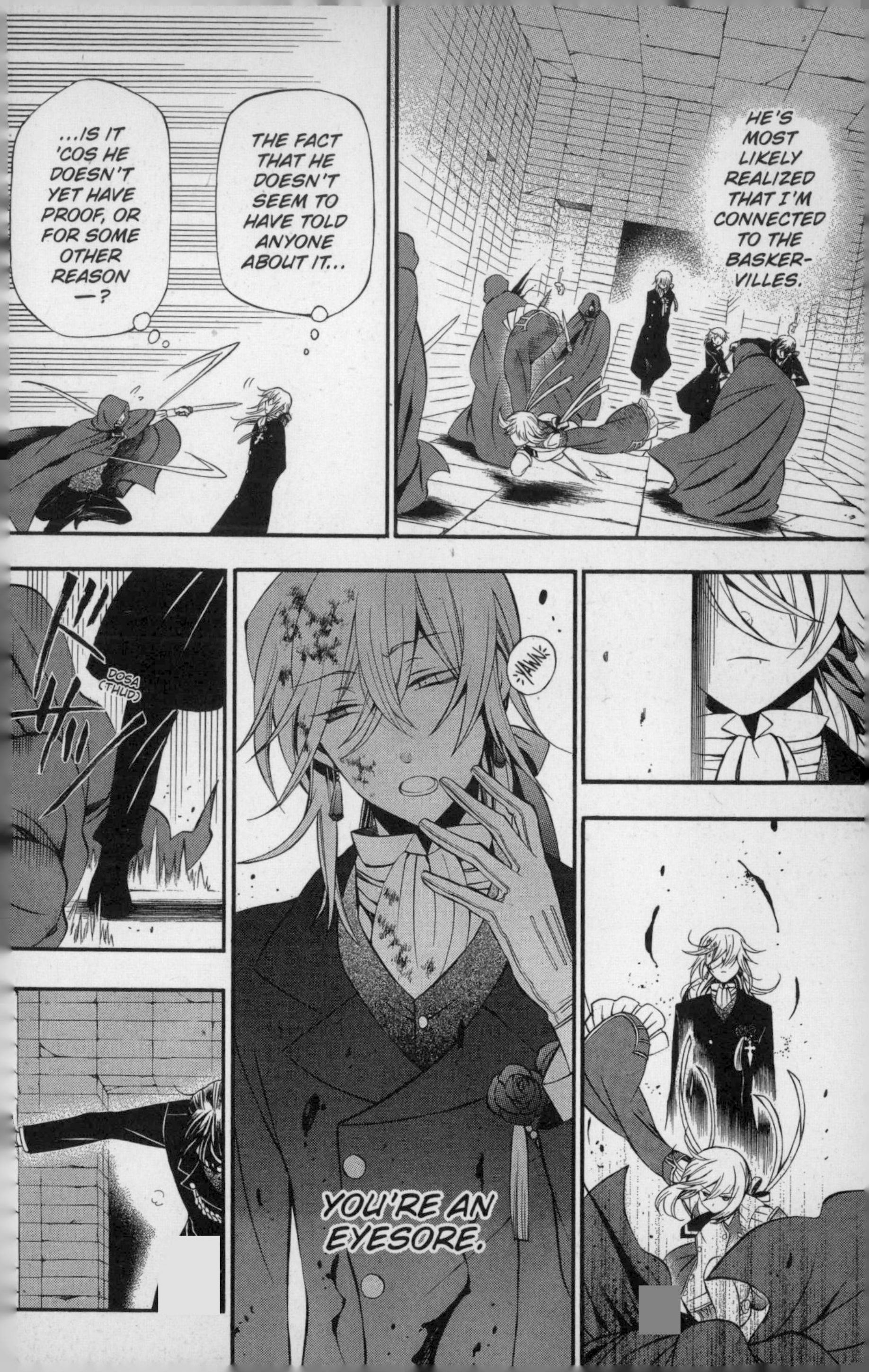
HE'S MOST LIKELY REALIZED THAT I'M CONNECTED TO THE BASKER-VILLES.
THE FACT THAT HE DOESN'T SEEM TO HAVE TOLD ANYONE ABOUT IT...
...IS IT 'COS HE DOESN'T YET HAVE PROOF, OR FOR SOME OTHER REASON —?
YAWN
YOU'RE AN EYESORE.
DOSA (THUD)

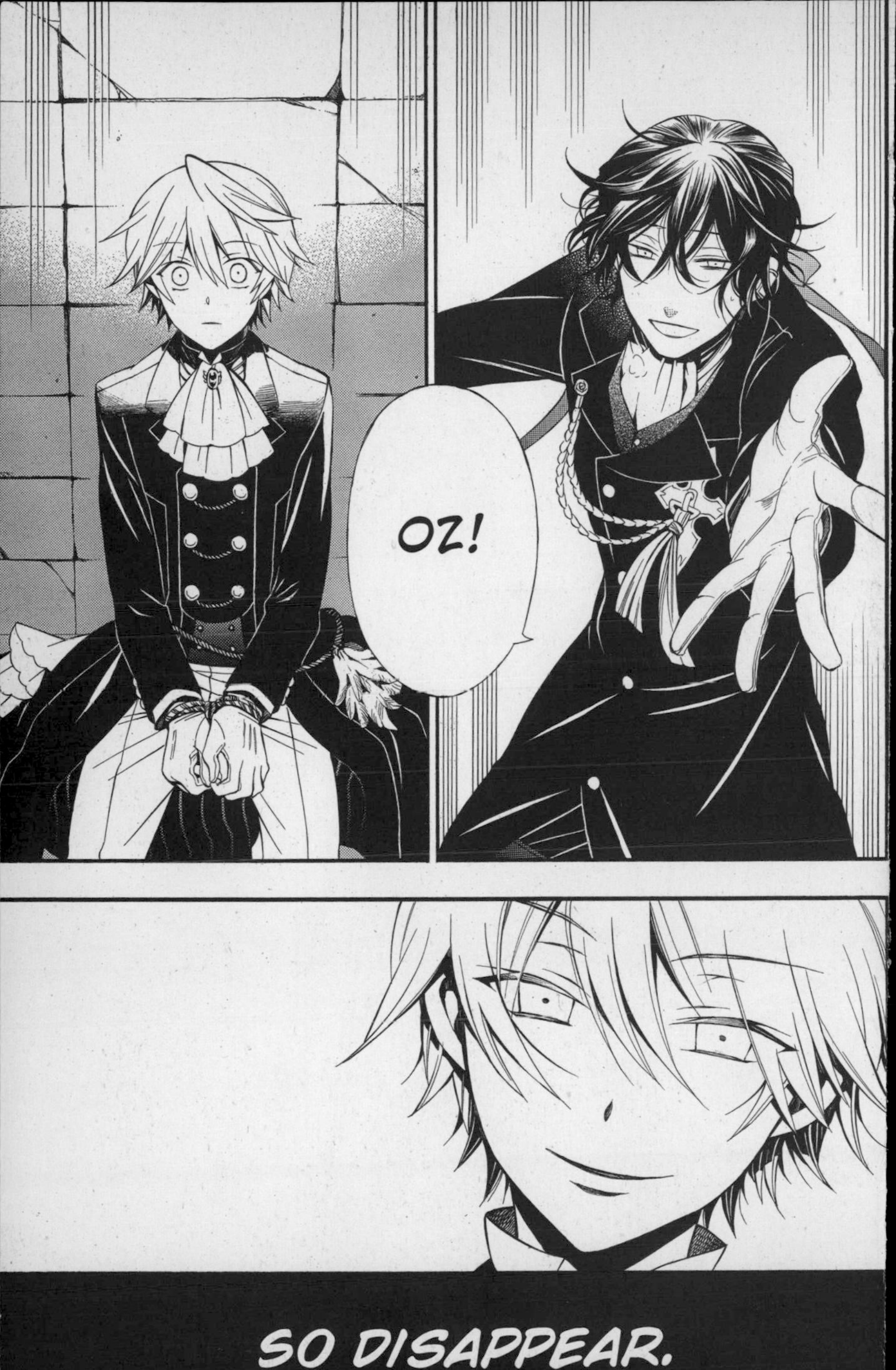
OZ!
SO DISAPPEAR.

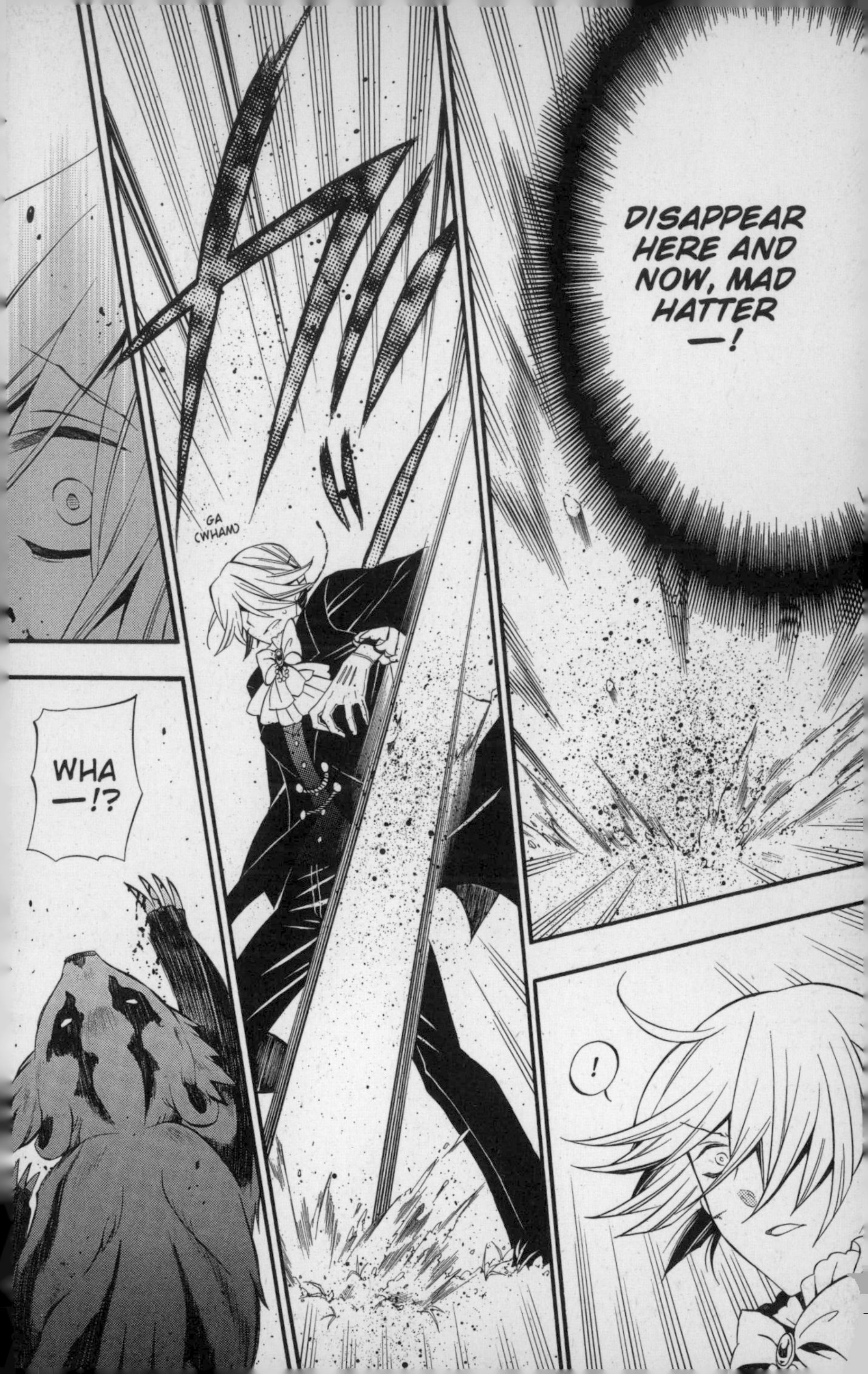
DISAPPEAR HERE AND NOW, MAD HATTER —!
GA (WHAM)
WHA —!?
!

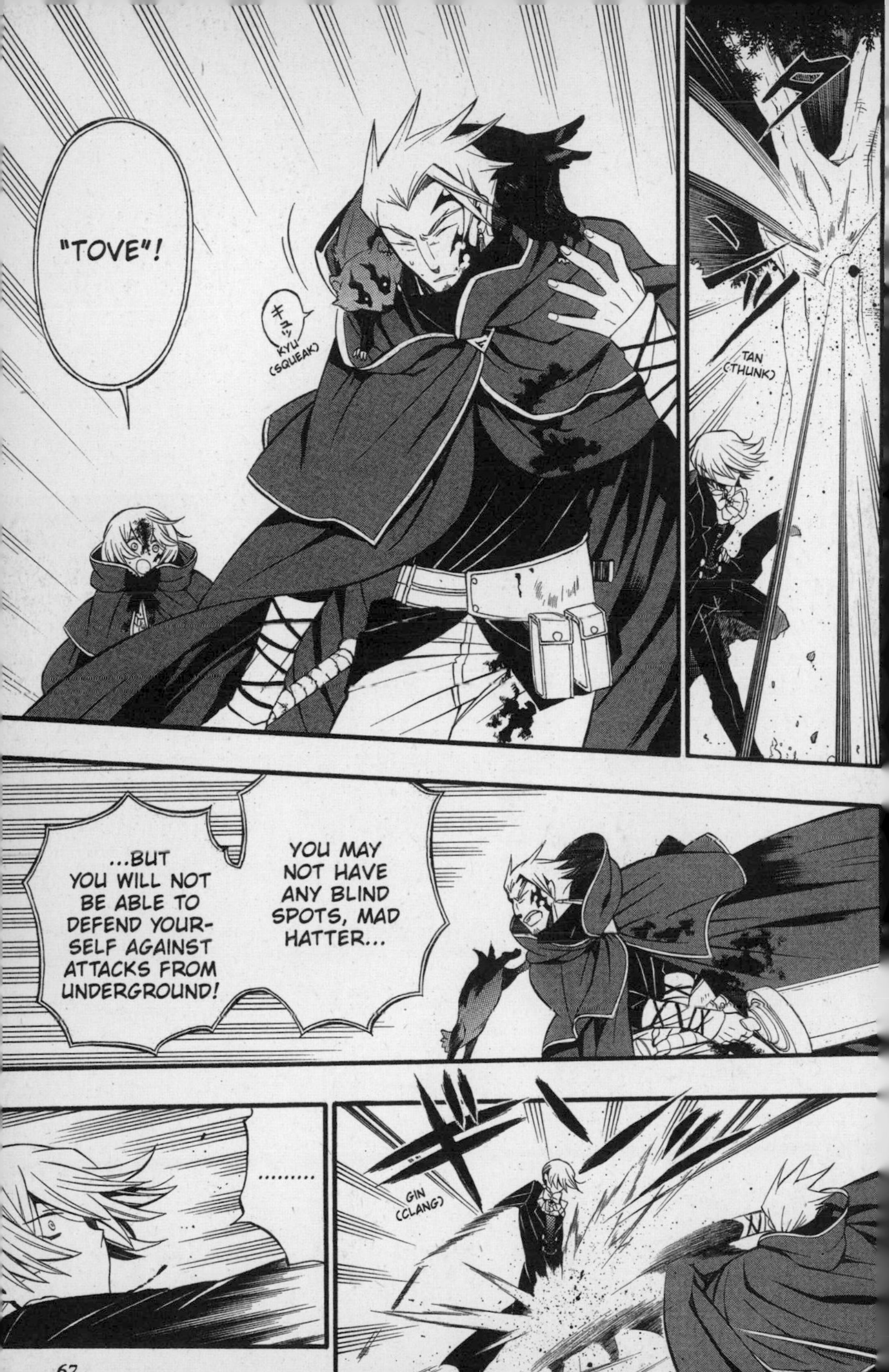
TAN
(THUNK)
"TOVE"!
キュッ
KYU
(SQUEAK)
YOU MAY NOT HAVE ANY BLIND SPOTS, MAD HATTER...
...BUT YOU WILL NOT BE ABLE TO DEFEND YOUR-SELF AGAINST ATTACKS FROM UNDERGROUND!
GIN
(CLANG)
....
...

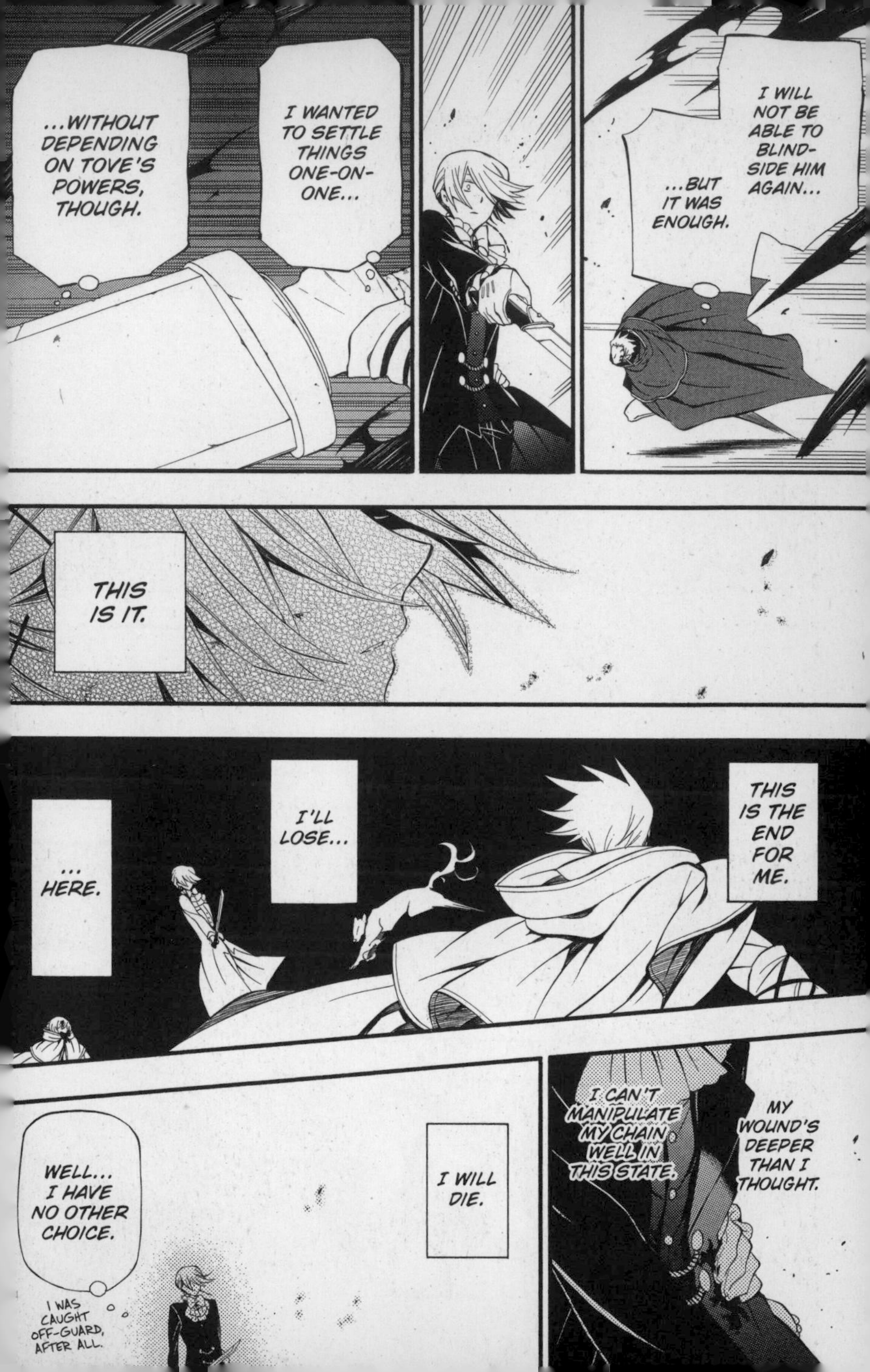
I WILL NOT BE ABLE TO BLIND-SIDE HIM AGAIN...
...BUT IT WAS ENOUGH.
I WANTED TO SETTLE THINGS ONE-ON-ONE...
...WITHOUT DEPENDING ON TOVE'S POWERS, THOUGH.
THIS IS IT.
THIS IS THE END FOR ME.
I'LL LOSE...
...HERE.
MY WOUND'S DEEPER THAN I THOUGHT.
I CAN'T MANIPULATE MY CHAIN WELL IN THIS STATE.
I WILL DIE.
WELL... I HAVE NO OTHER CHOICE.
I WAS CAUGHT OFF-GUARD, AFTER ALL.

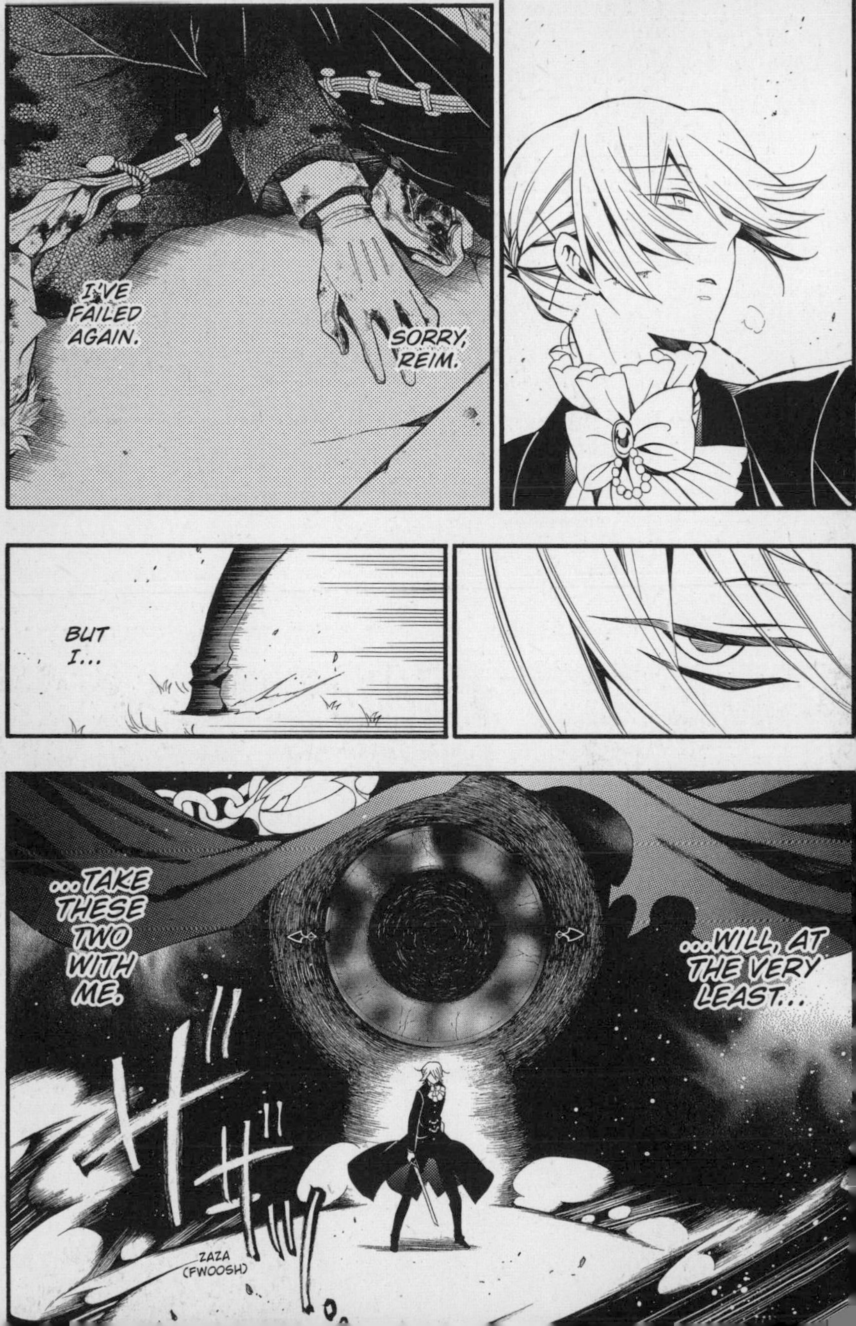
SORRY, REIM.
I'VE FAILED AGAIN.
BUT I...
...WILL, AT THE VERY LEAST...
...TAKE THESE TWO WITH ME.
ZAZA (FWOOSH)

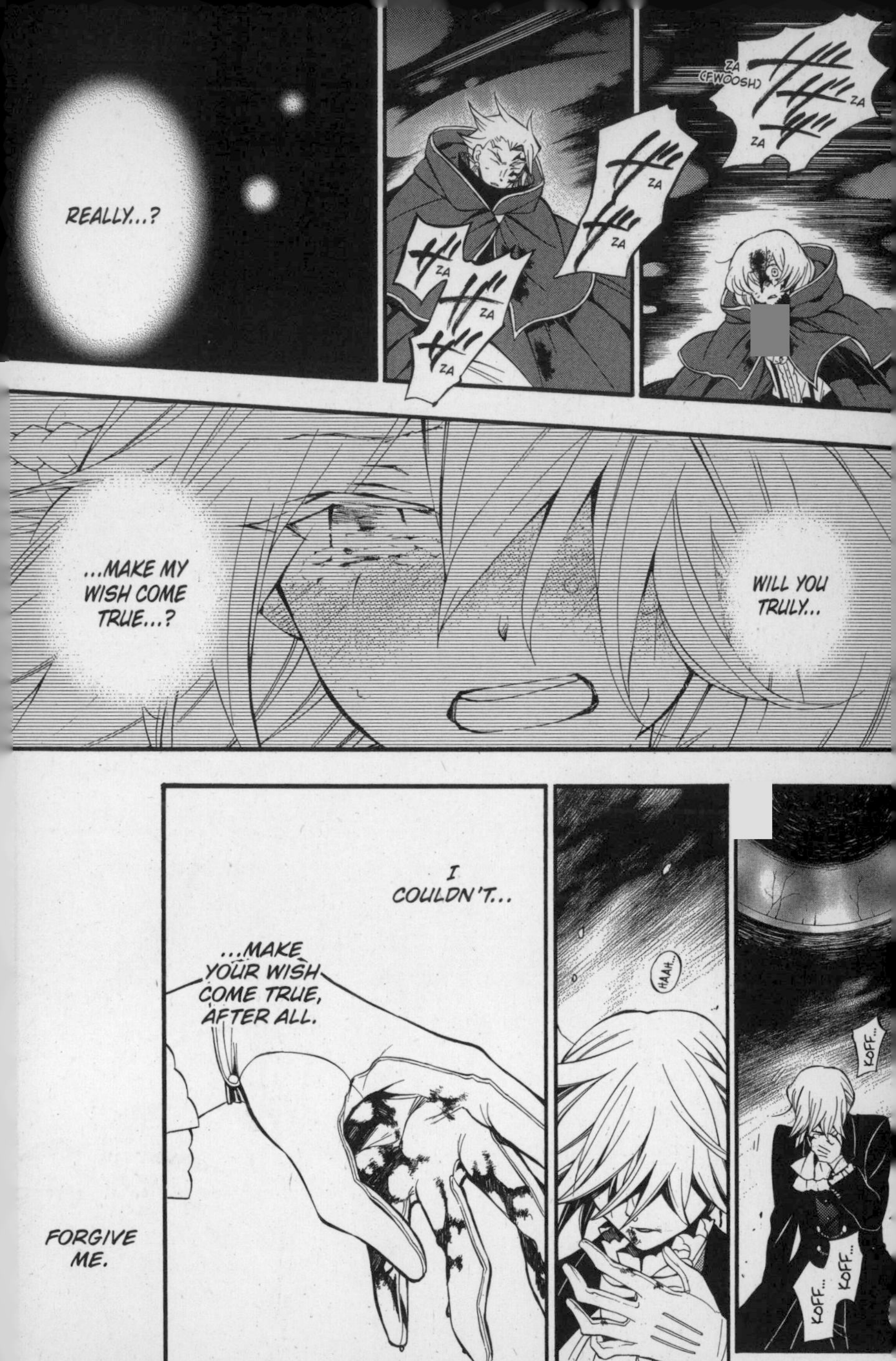
ZA (FWOOSH)
ZA
ZA
ZA
ZA
ZA
ZA
ZA
REALLY...?
WILL YOU TRULY...
...MAKE MY WISH COME TRUE...?
KOFF...
KOFF... KOFF...
HAAH...
I COULDN'T...
...MAKE YOUR WISH COME TRUE, AFTER ALL.
FORGIVE ME.

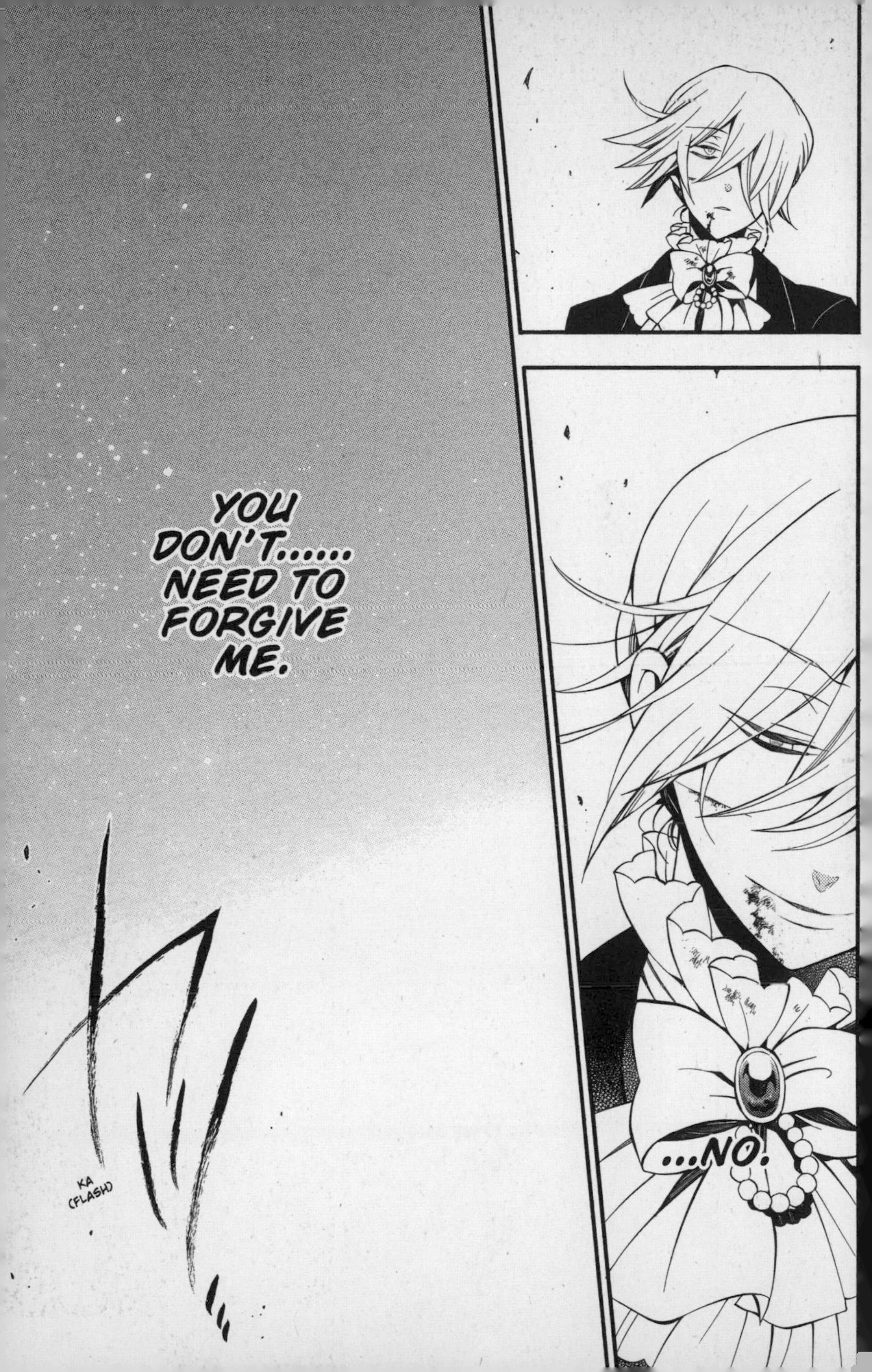
...NO.
YOU DON'T...... NEED TO FORGIVE ME.
KA (FLASH)

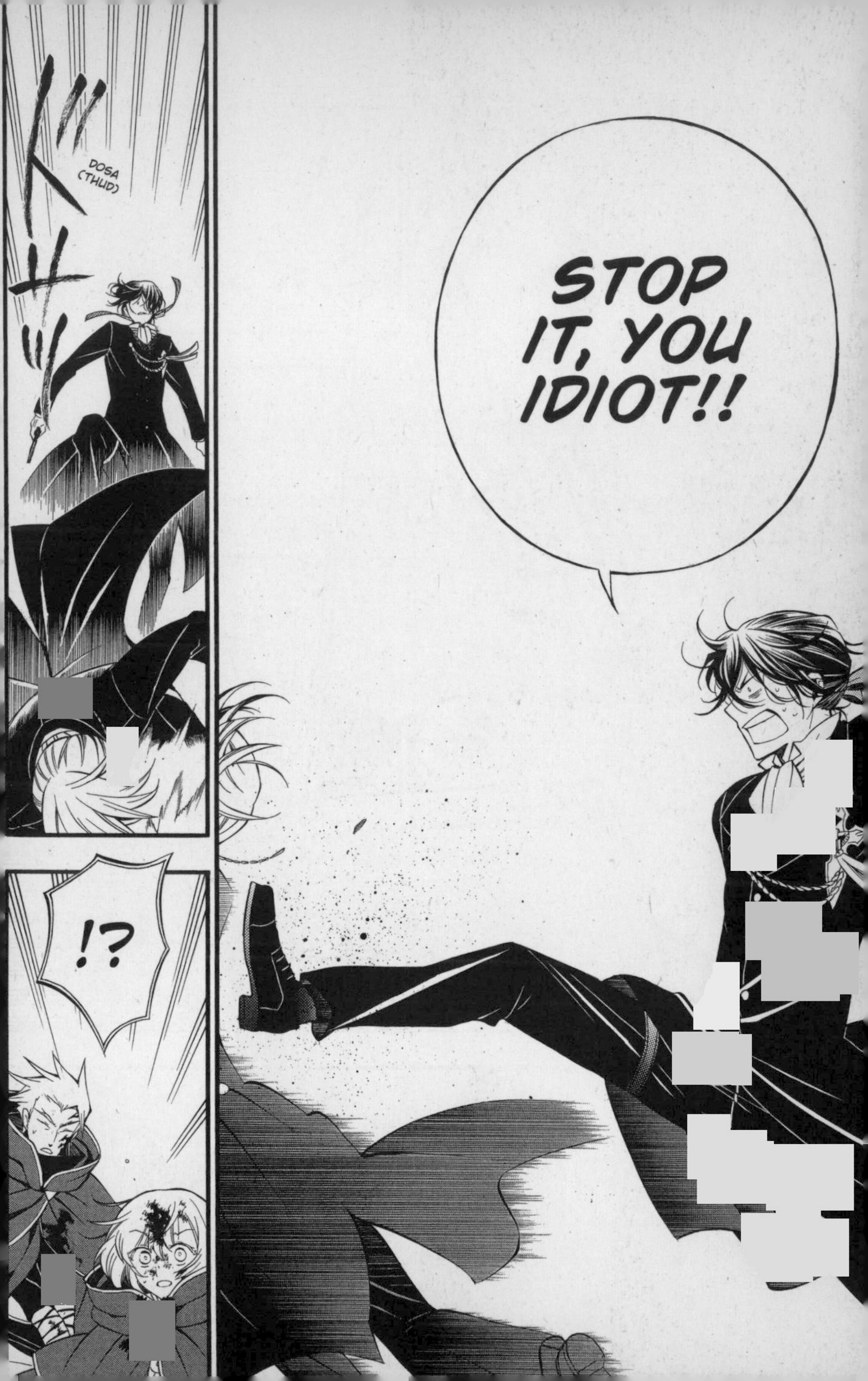
STOP IT, YOU IDIOT!!
DOSA (THUD)
!?

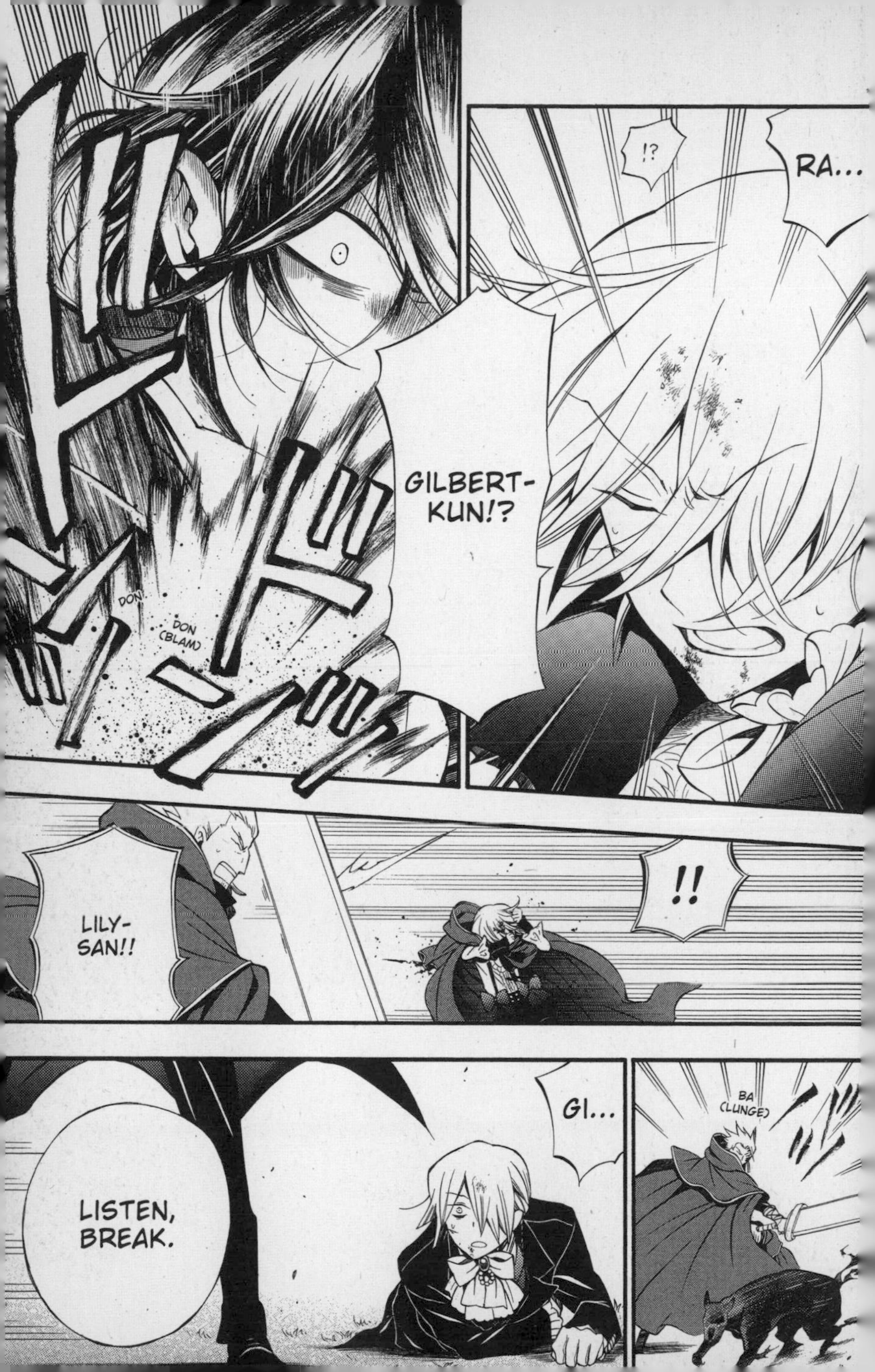
RA...
!?
GILBERT-KUN!?
DON
DON (BLAM)
!!
LILY-SAN!!
BA (LUNGE)
GI...
LISTEN, BREAK.

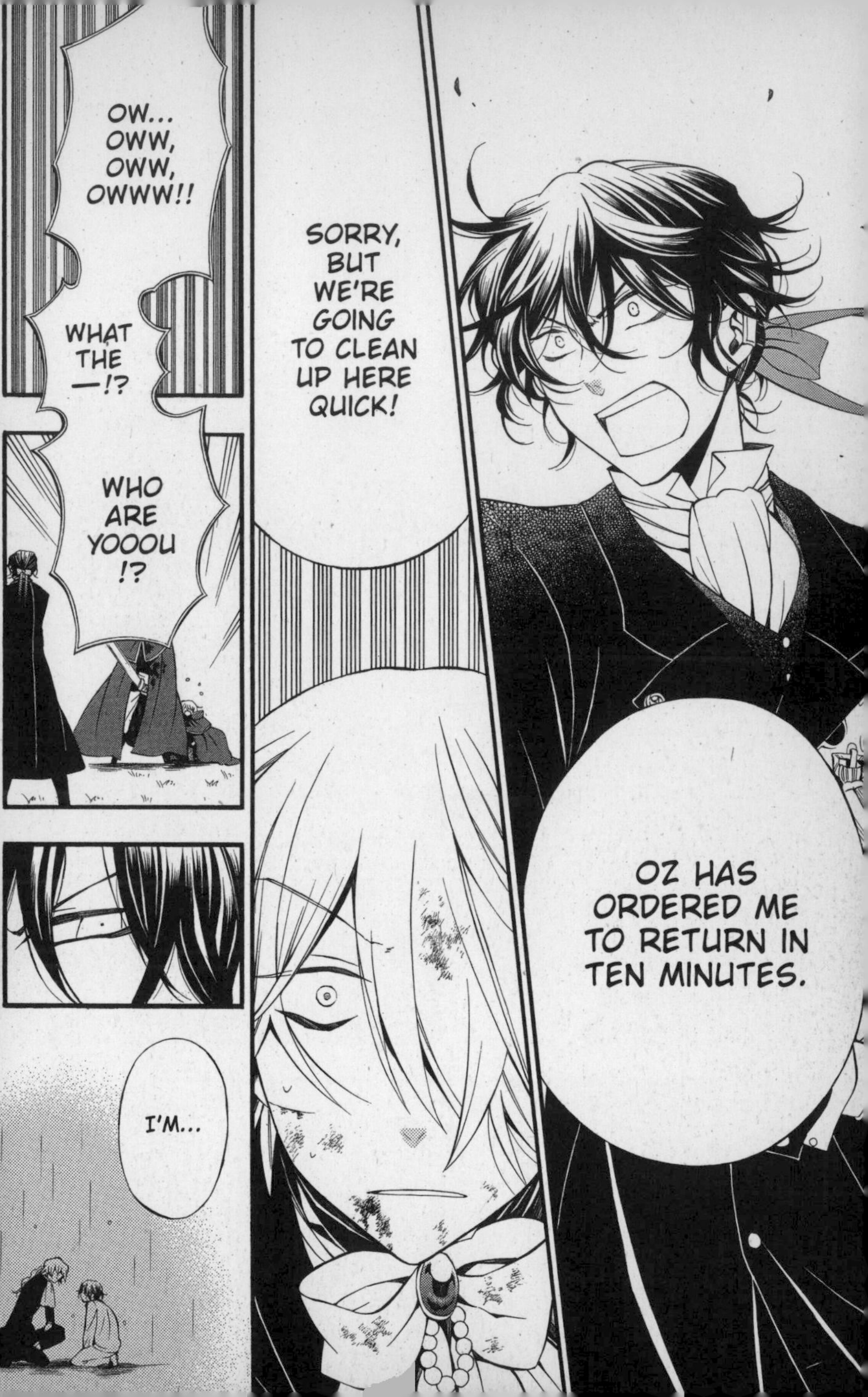
SORRY, BUT WE'RE GOING TO CLEAN UP HERE QUICK!
OZ HAS ORDERED ME TO RETURN IN TEN MINUTES.
OW... OWW, OWW, OWWW!!
WHAT THE —!?
WHO ARE YOOOU !?
I'M...

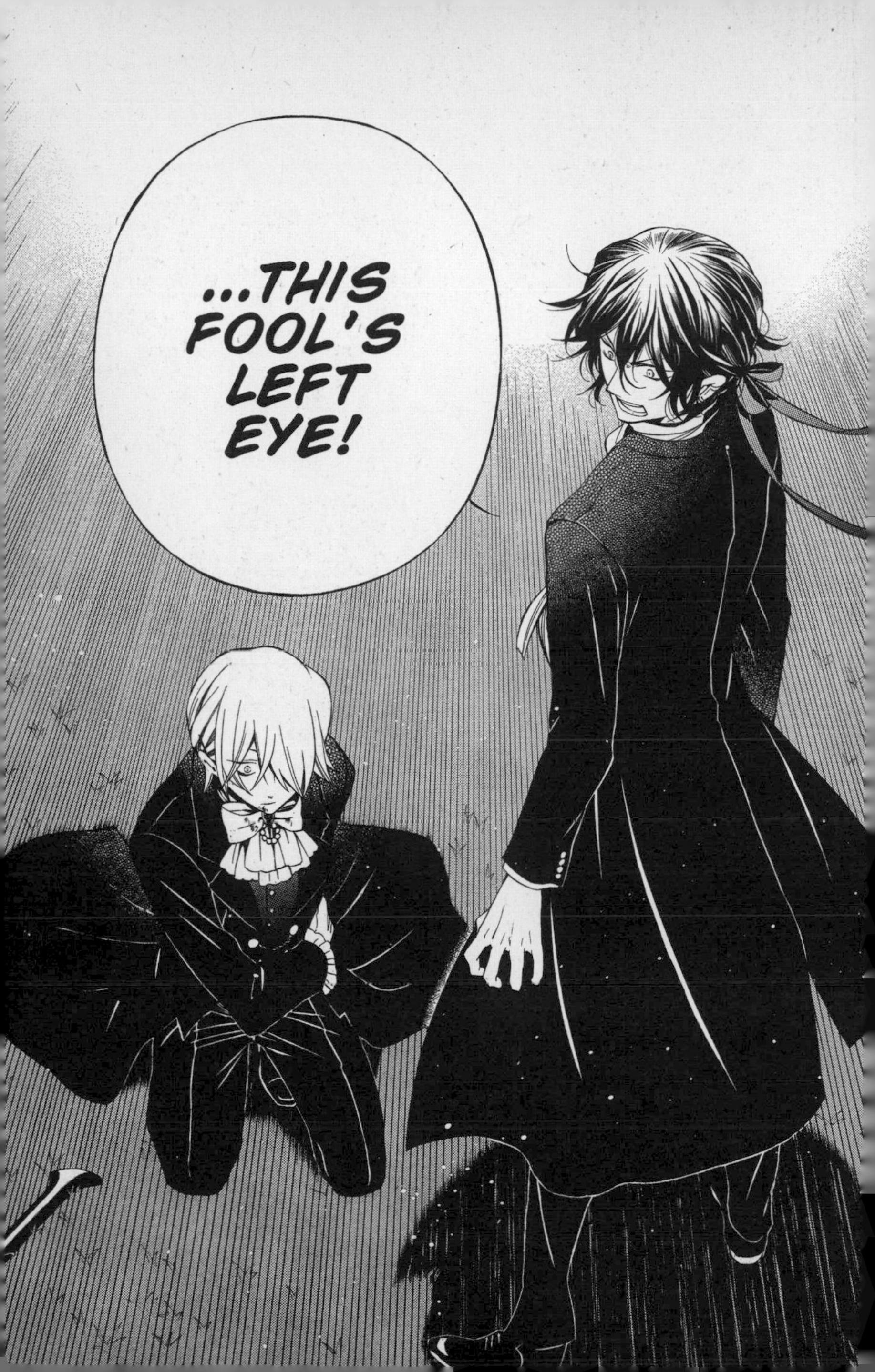
...THIS FOOL'S LEFT EYE!

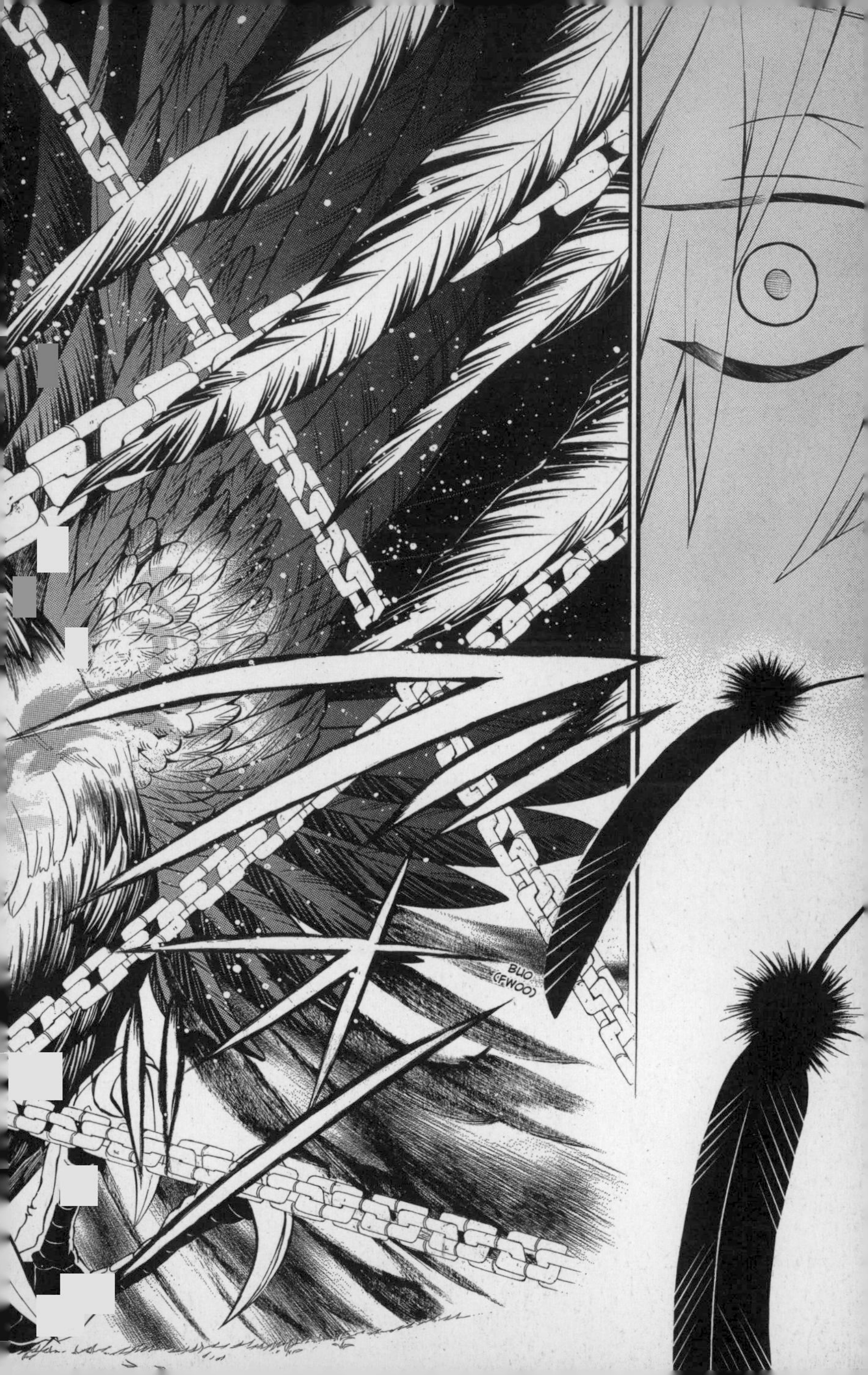
BUO
(FWOO)

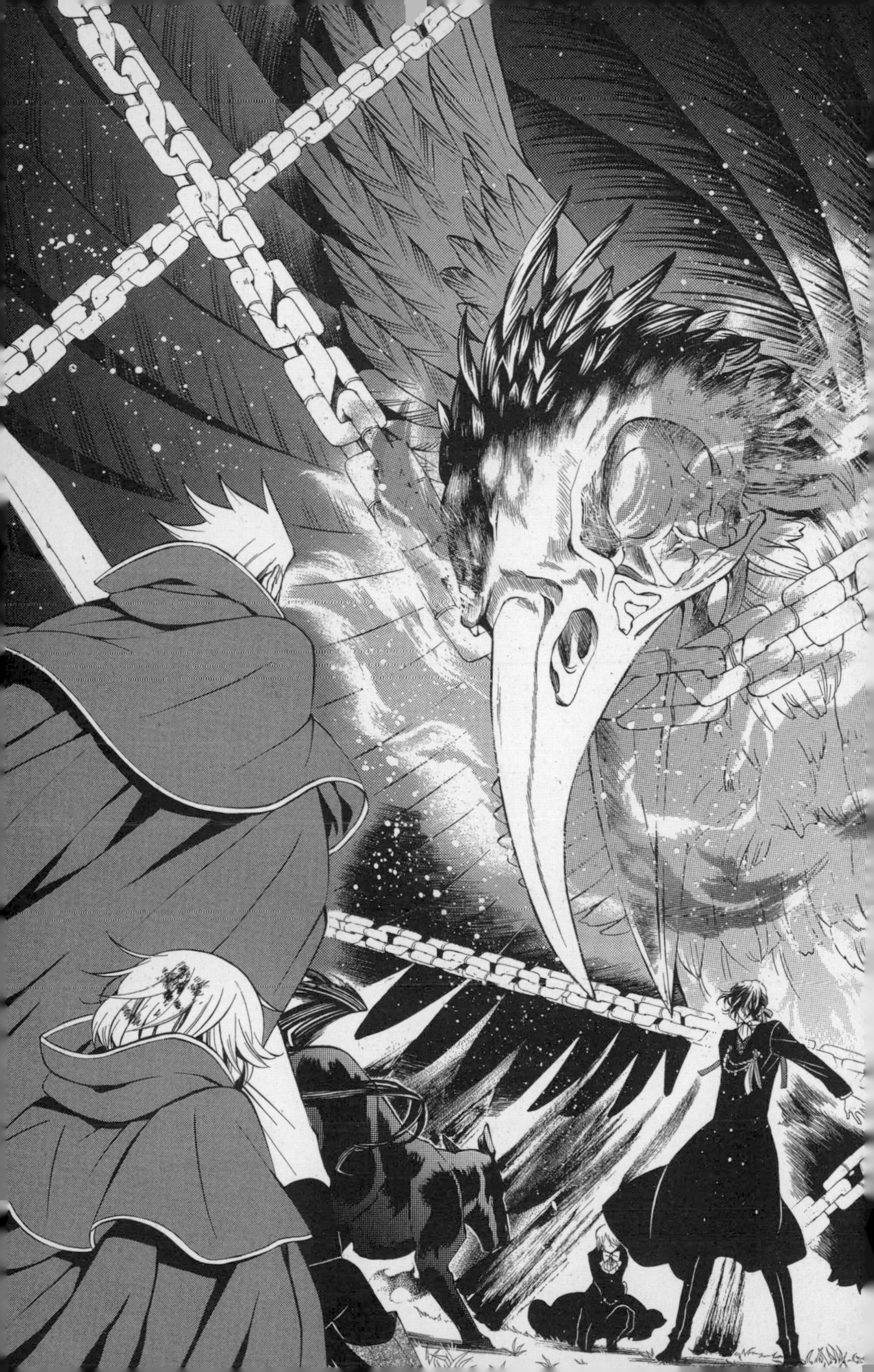

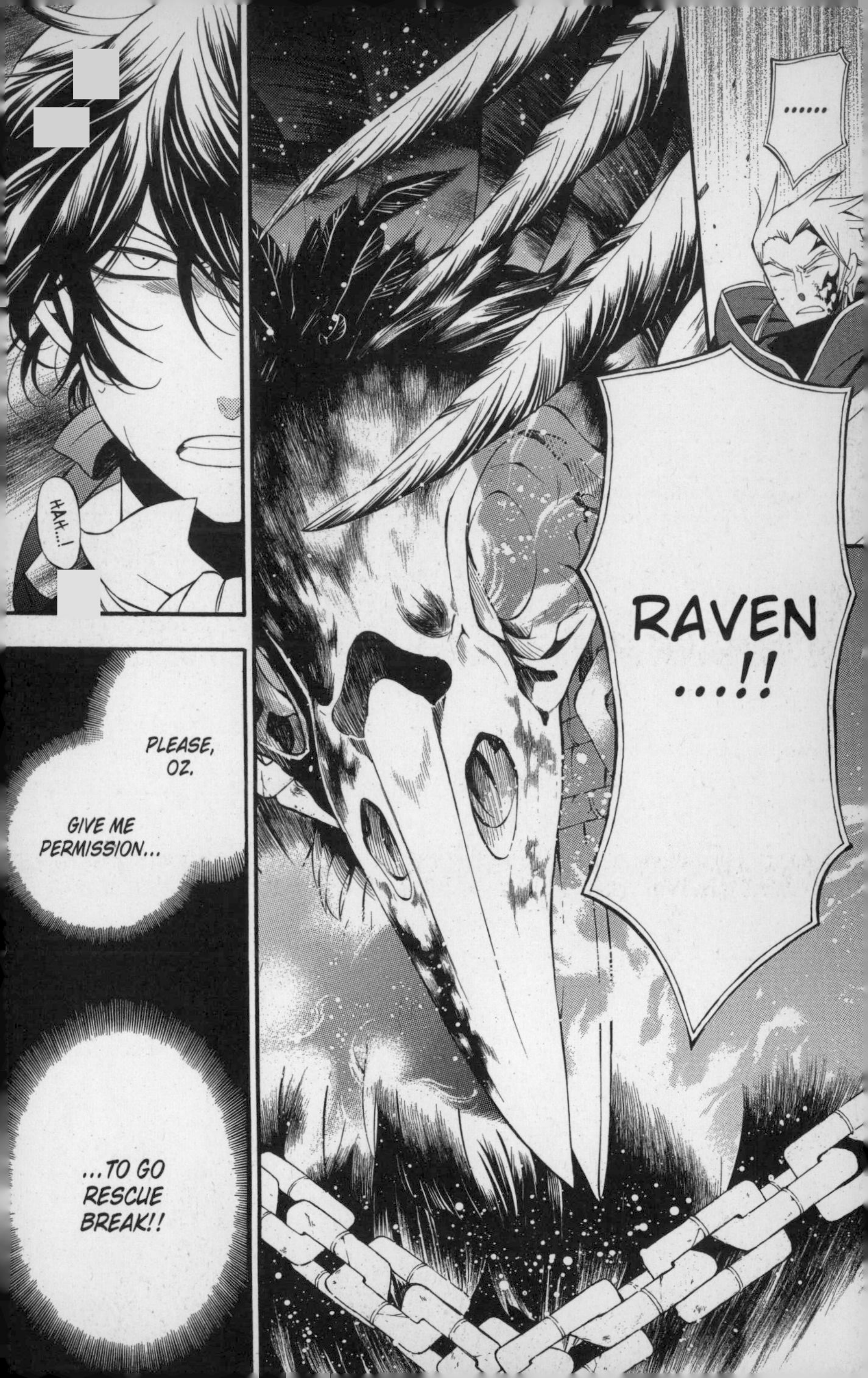
......
RAVEN ...!!
HAH...!
PLEASE, OZ.
GIVE ME PERMISSION...
...TO GO RESCUE BREAK!!

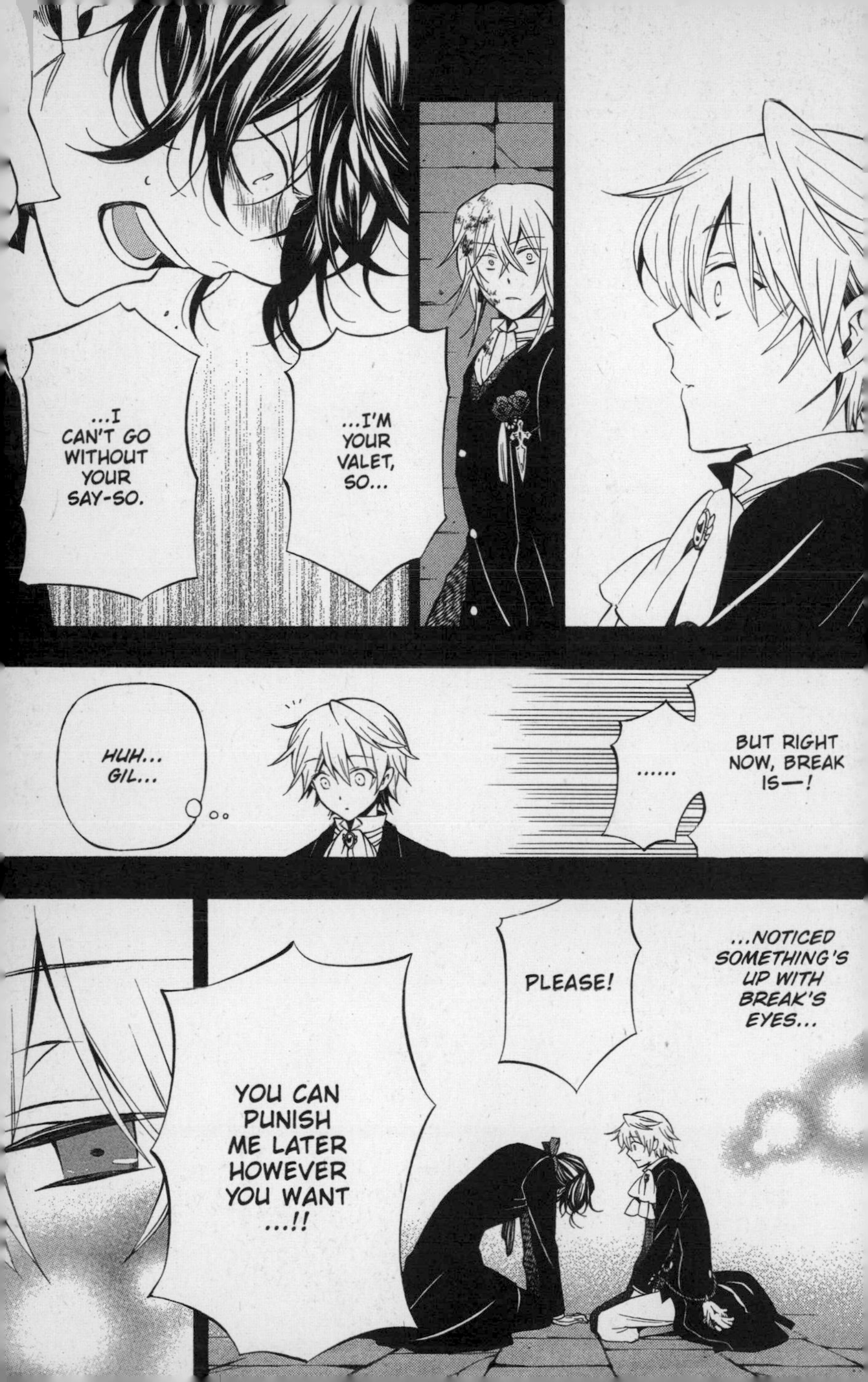
...I'M YOUR VALET, SO...
...I CAN'T GO WITHOUT YOUR SAY-SO.
BUT RIGHT NOW, BREAK IS—!
......
HUH... GIL...
...NOTICED SOMETHING'S UP WITH BREAK'S EYES...
PLEASE!
YOU CAN PUNISH ME LATER HOWEVER YOU WANT ...!!

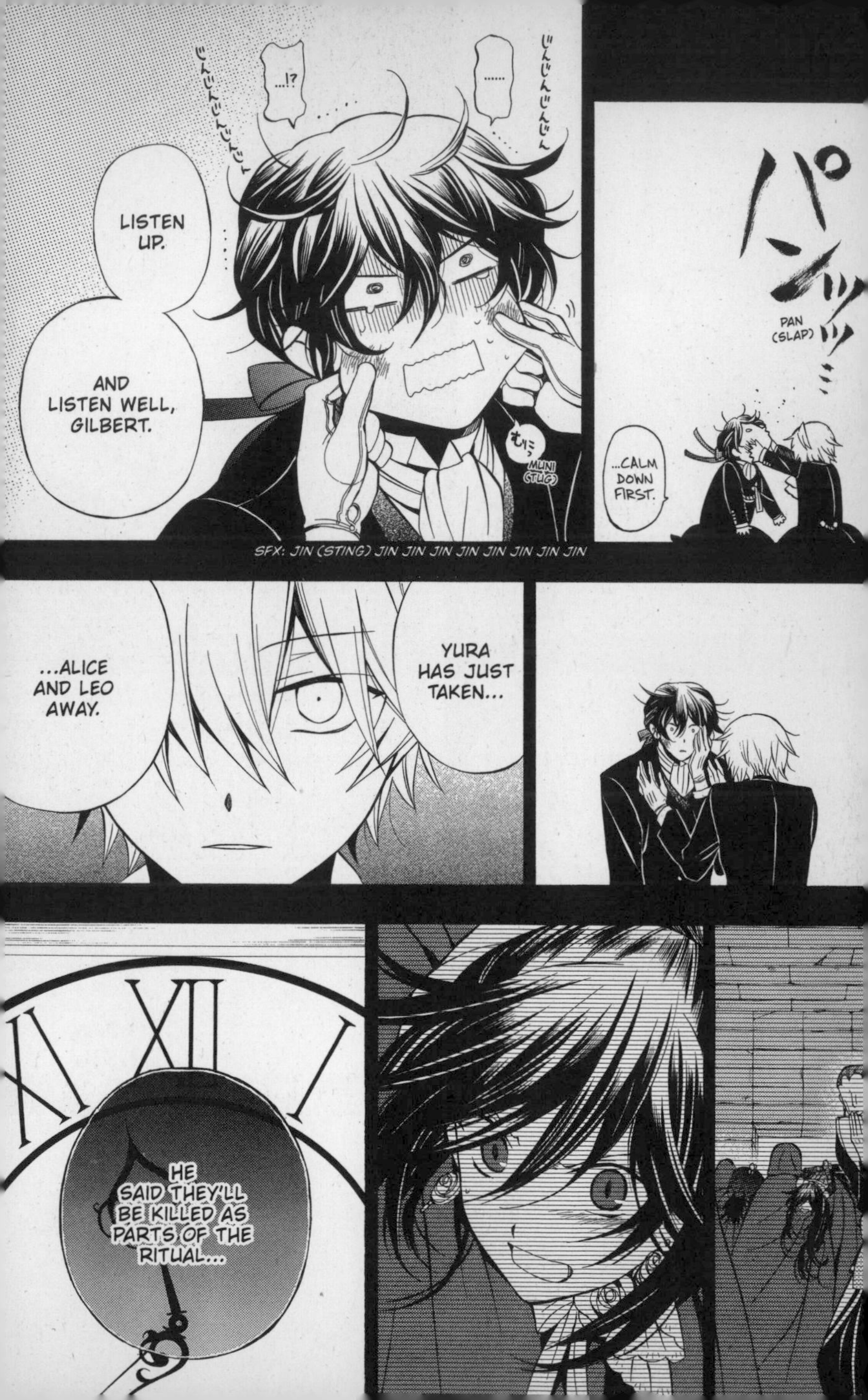
パンッ
PAN (SLAP)
...CALM DOWN FIRST.
じんじんじん
......
...!?
じんじんじんじんじん
LISTEN UP.
AND LISTEN WELL, GILBERT.
むにっ
MUNI (TUG)
SFX: JIN (STING) JIN JIN JIN JIN JIN JIN JIN JIN
YURA HAS JUST TAKEN...
...ALICE AND LEO AWAY.
XII
HE SAID THEY'LL BE KILLED AS PARTS OF THE RITUAL...

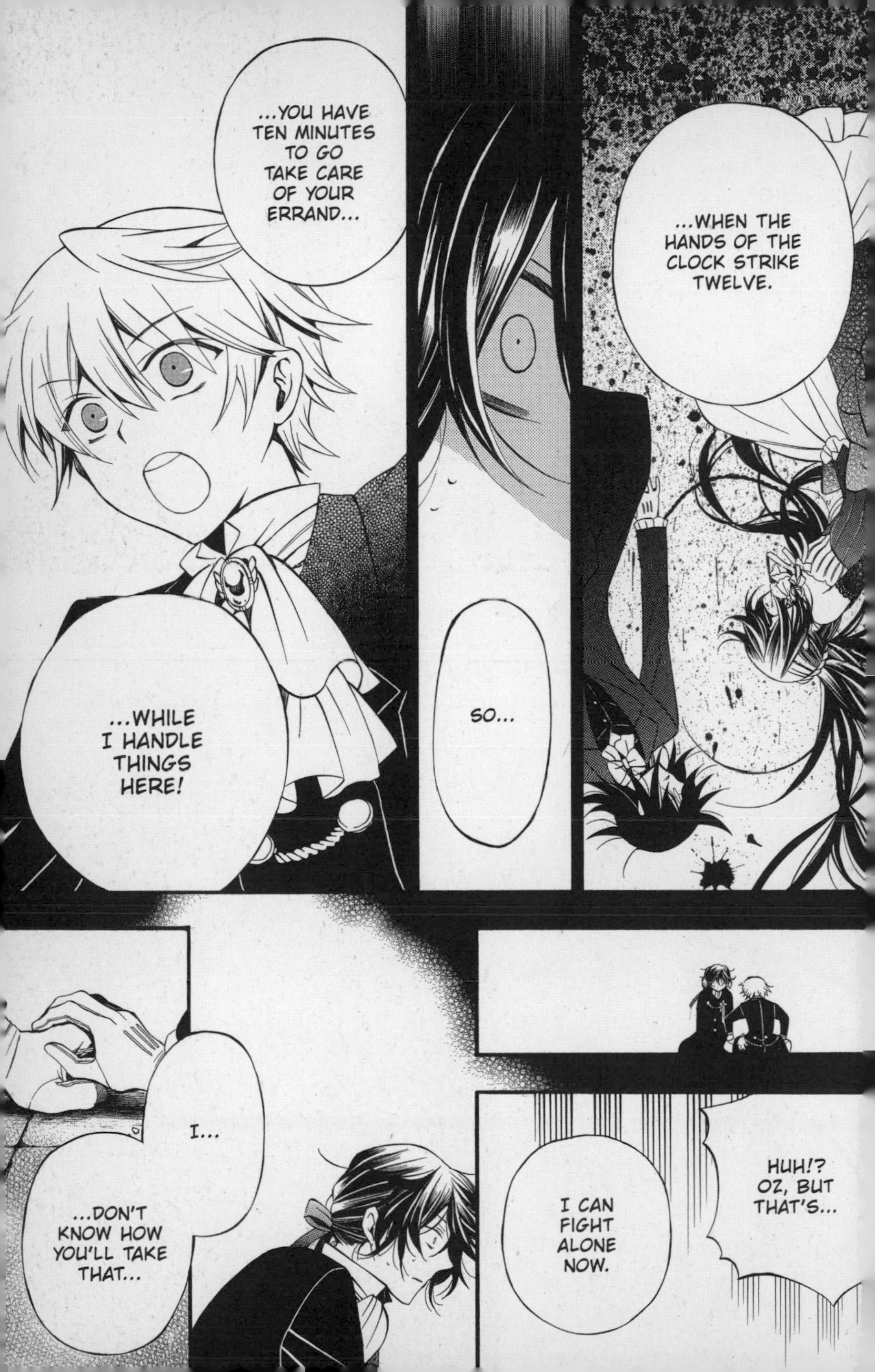
...WHEN THE HANDS OF THE CLOCK STRIKE TWELVE.
SO...
...YOU HAVE TEN MINUTES TO GO TAKE CARE OF YOUR ERRAND...
...WHILE I HANDLE THINGS HERE!
HUH!? OZ, BUT THAT'S...
I CAN FIGHT ALONE NOW.
I...
...DON'T KNOW HOW YOU'LL TAKE THAT...

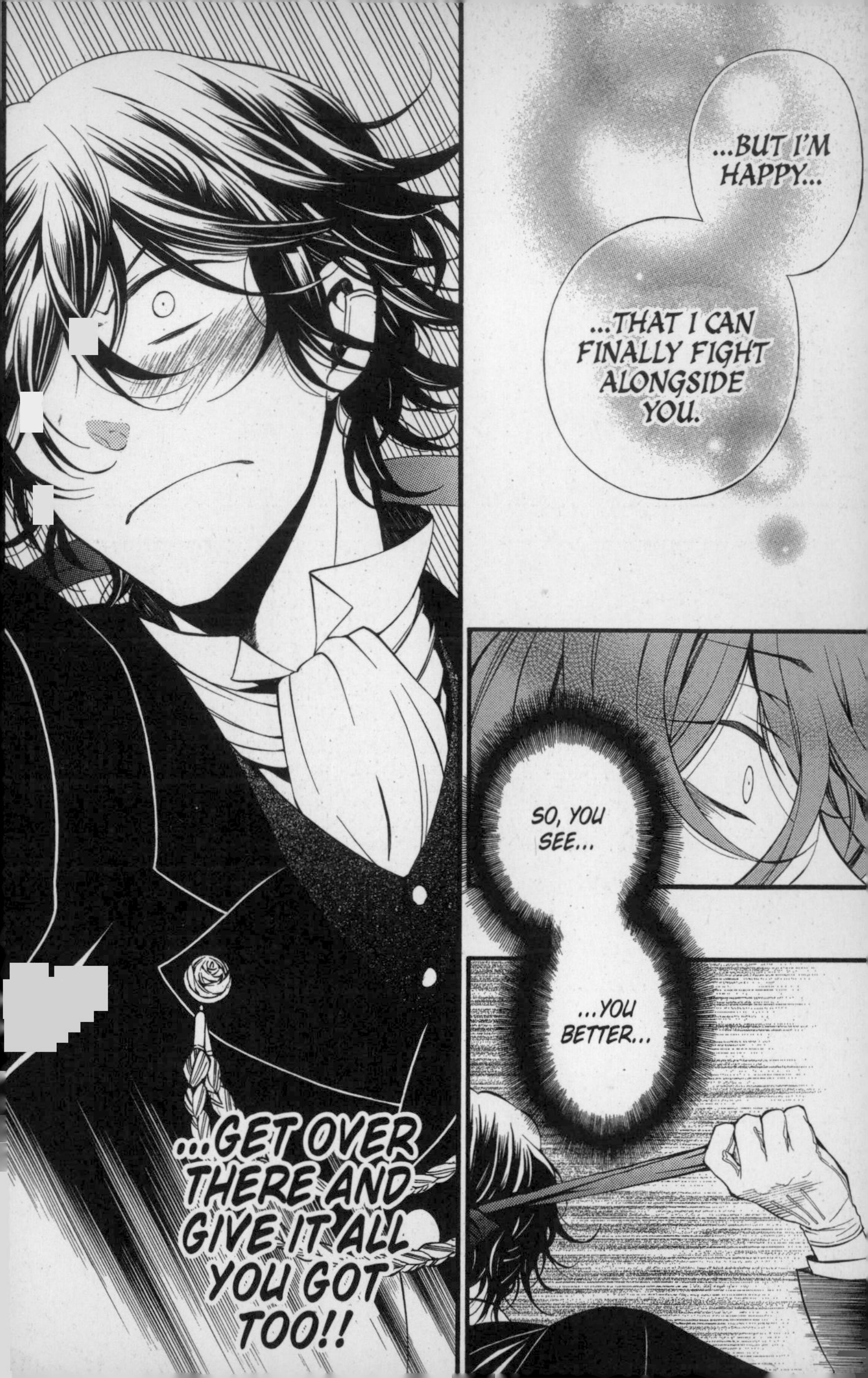
...BUT I'M HAPPY...
...THAT I CAN FINALLY FIGHT ALONGSIDE YOU.
SO, YOU SEE...
...YOU BETTER...
...GET OVER THERE AND GIVE IT ALL YOU GOT TOO!!

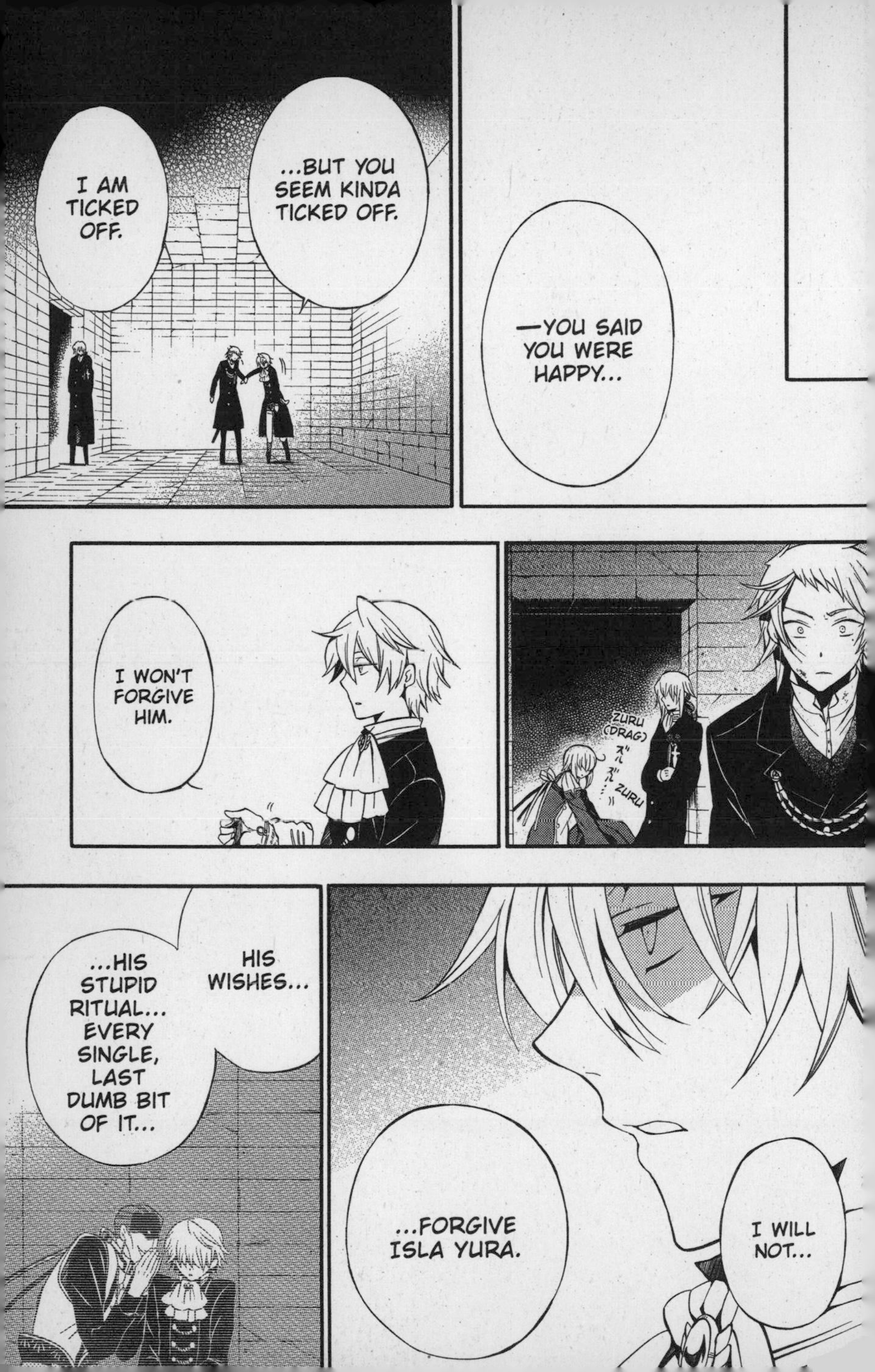
—YOU SAID YOU WERE HAPPY...
...BUT YOU SEEM KINDA TICKED OFF.
I AM TICKED OFF.
ZURU (DRAG)
ズルズル…
ZURU
I WON'T FORGIVE HIM.
I WILL NOT...
...FORGIVE ISLA YURA.
HIS WISHES...
...HIS STUPID RITUAL... EVERY SINGLE, LAST DUMB BIT OF IT...

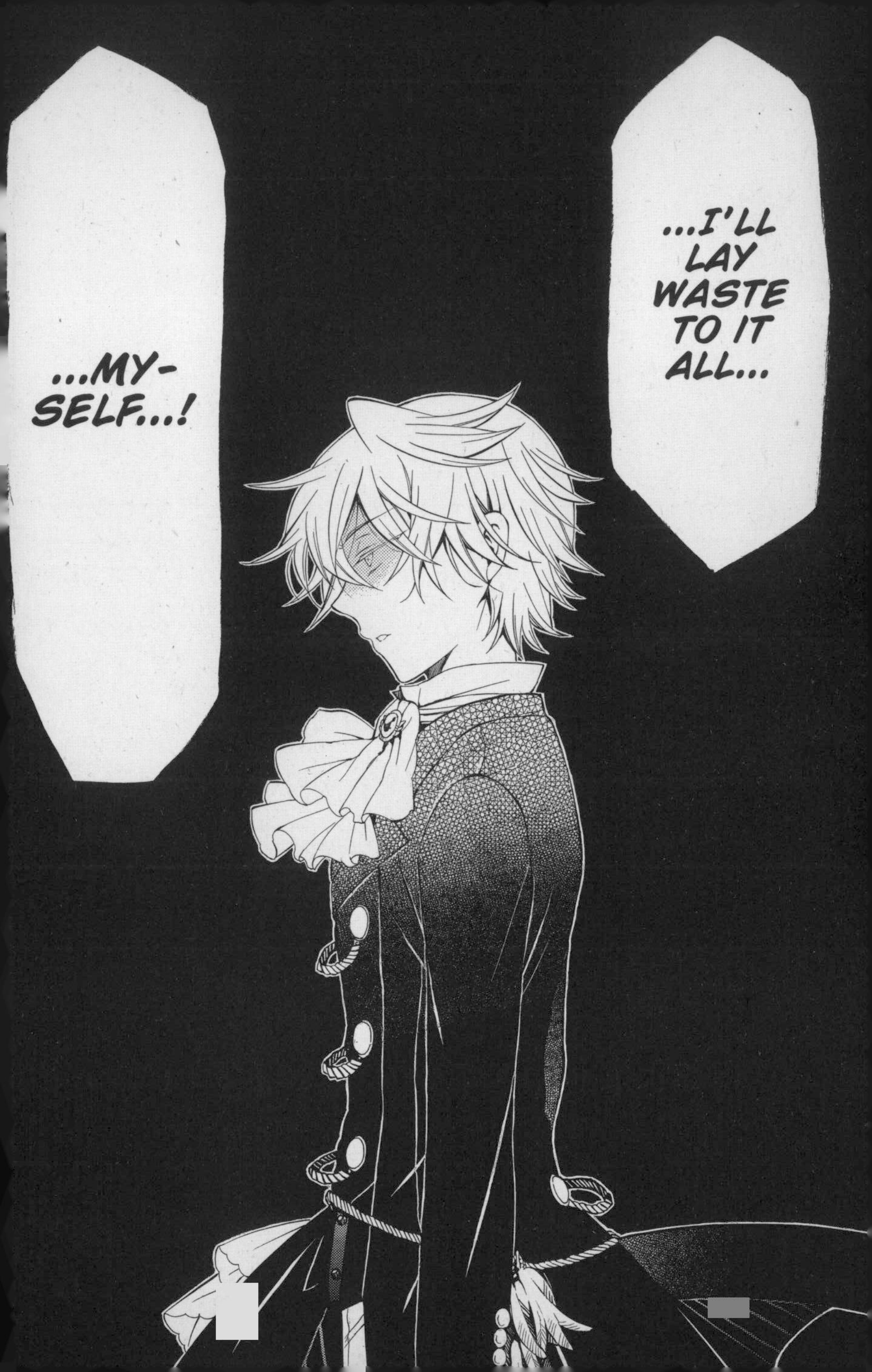
...I'LL LAY WASTE TO IT ALL...
...MY-SELF...!

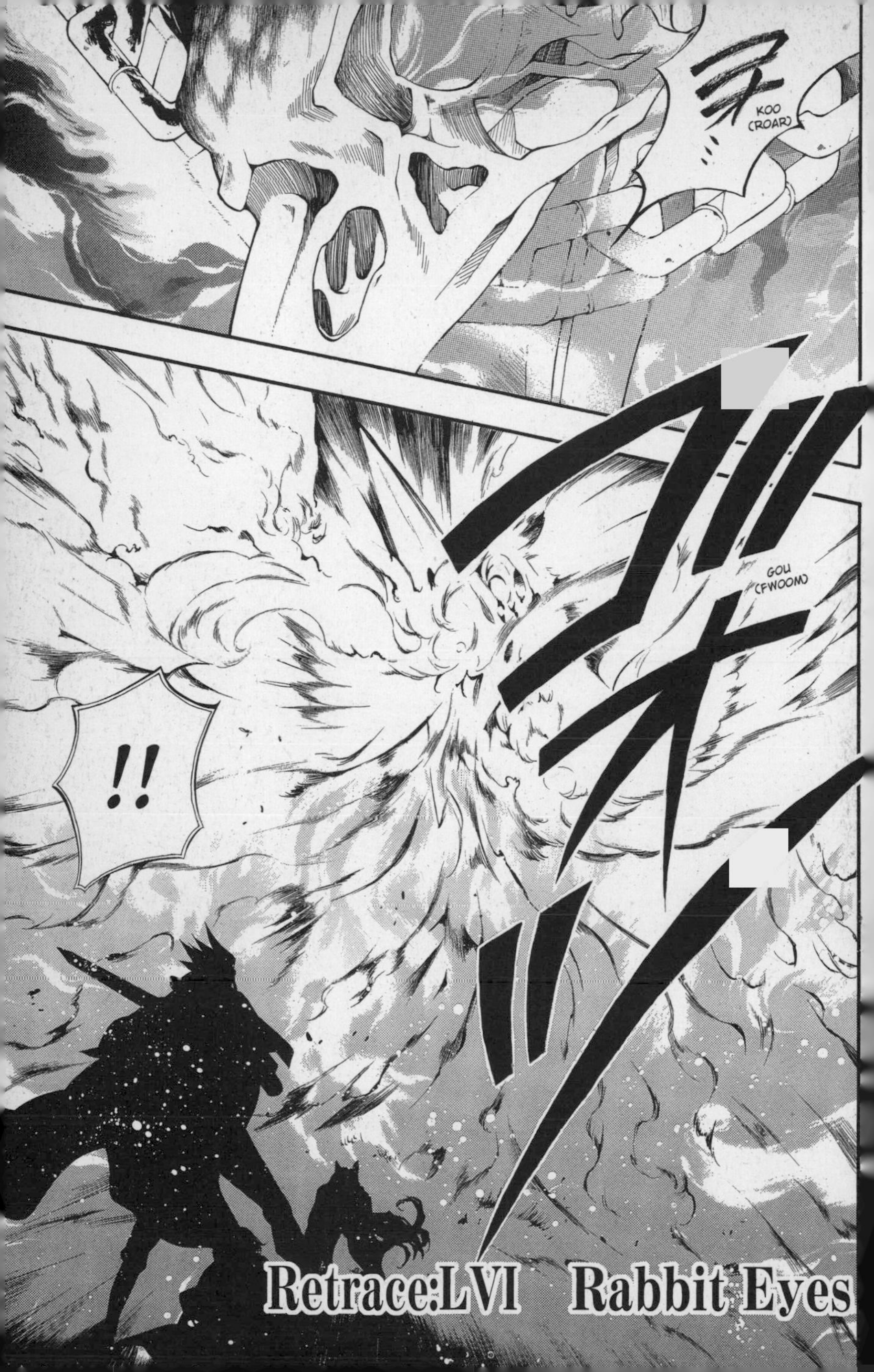
KOO
(ROAR)
GOU
(FWOOM)
!!

Retrace:LVI Rabbit Eyes

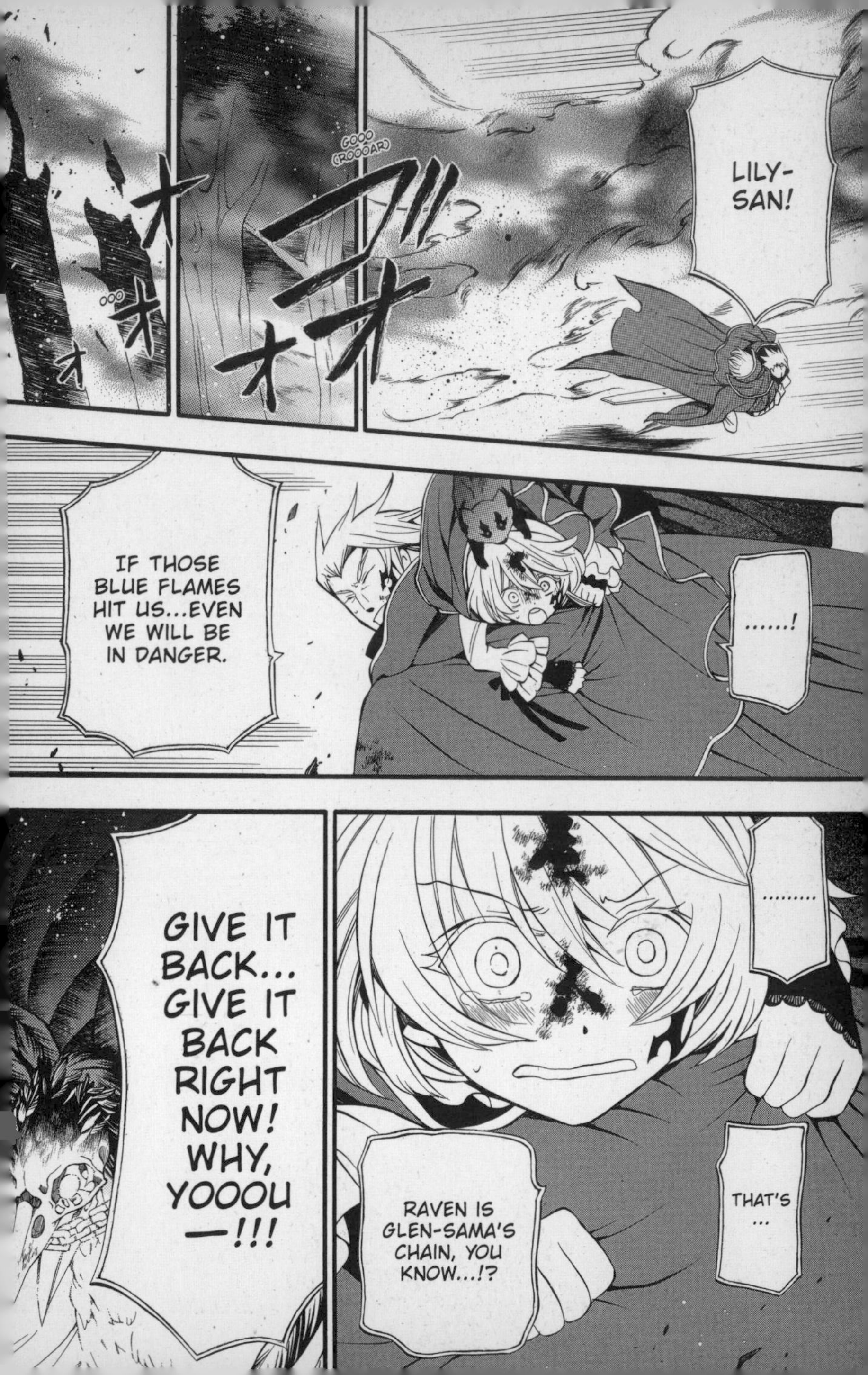
LILY-SAN!
GOOO (ROOOAR)
OOO
......!
IF THOSE BLUE FLAMES HIT US...EVEN WE WILL BE IN DANGER.
....
THAT'S ...
RAVEN IS GLEN-SAMA'S CHAIN, YOU KNOW...!?
GIVE IT BACK... GIVE IT BACK RIGHT NOW! WHY, YOOOU—!!!

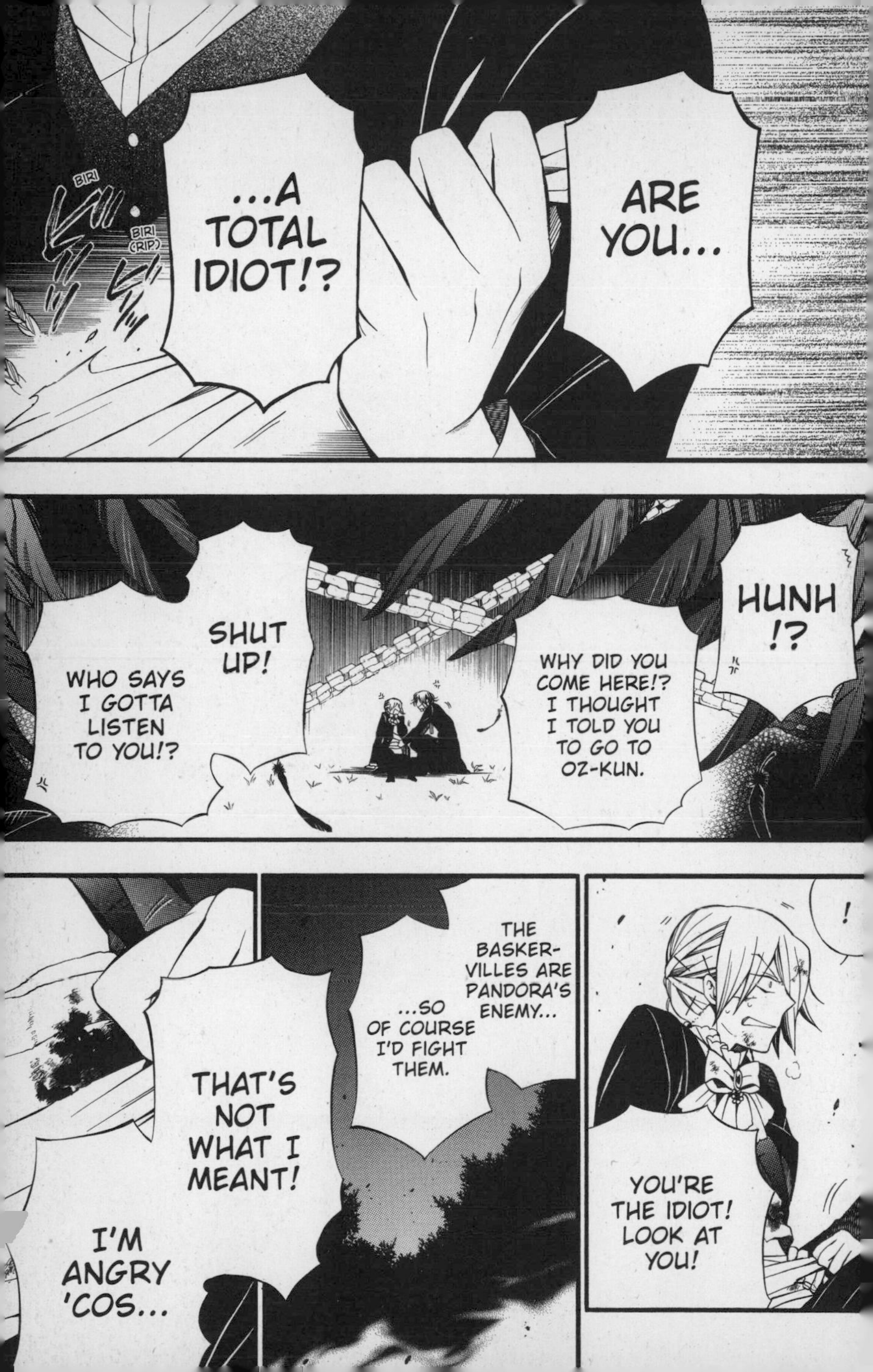
ARE YOU...
...A TOTAL IDIOT!?
BIRI
BIRI (RIP)
HUNH !?
WHY DID YOU COME HERE!? I THOUGHT I TOLD YOU TO GO TO OZ-KUN.
SHUT UP!
WHO SAYS I GOTTA LISTEN TO YOU!?
!
YOU'RE THE IDIOT! LOOK AT YOU!
THE BASKER-VILLES ARE PANDORA'S ENEMY...
...SO OF COURSE I'D FIGHT THEM.
THAT'S NOT WHAT I MEANT!
I'M ANGRY 'COS...

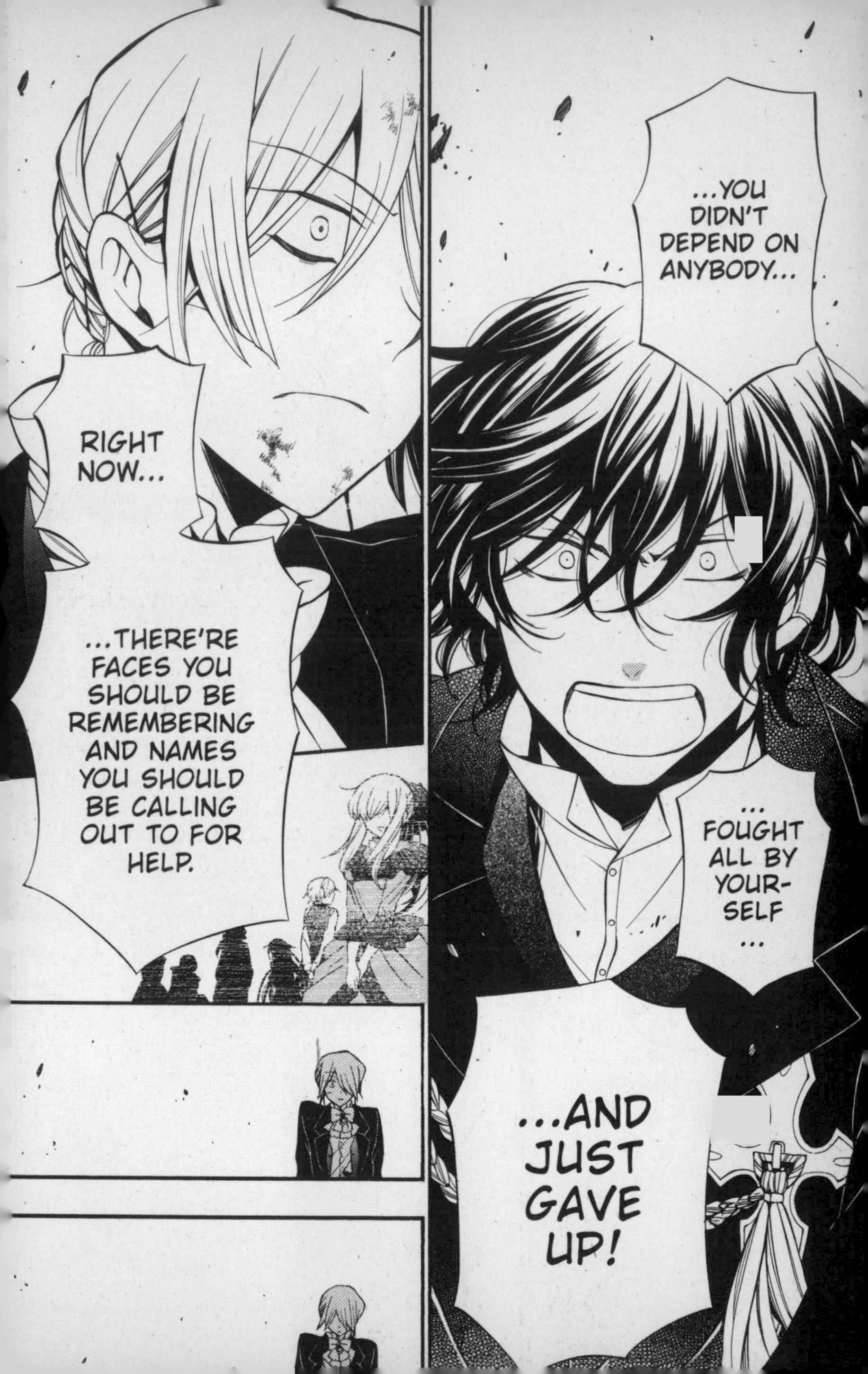
...YOU DIDN'T DEPEND ON ANYBODY...
...FOUGHT ALL BY YOUR-SELF...
...AND JUST GAVE UP!
RIGHT NOW...
...THERE'RE FACES YOU SHOULD BE REMEMBERING AND NAMES YOU SHOULD BE CALLING OUT TO FOR HELP.

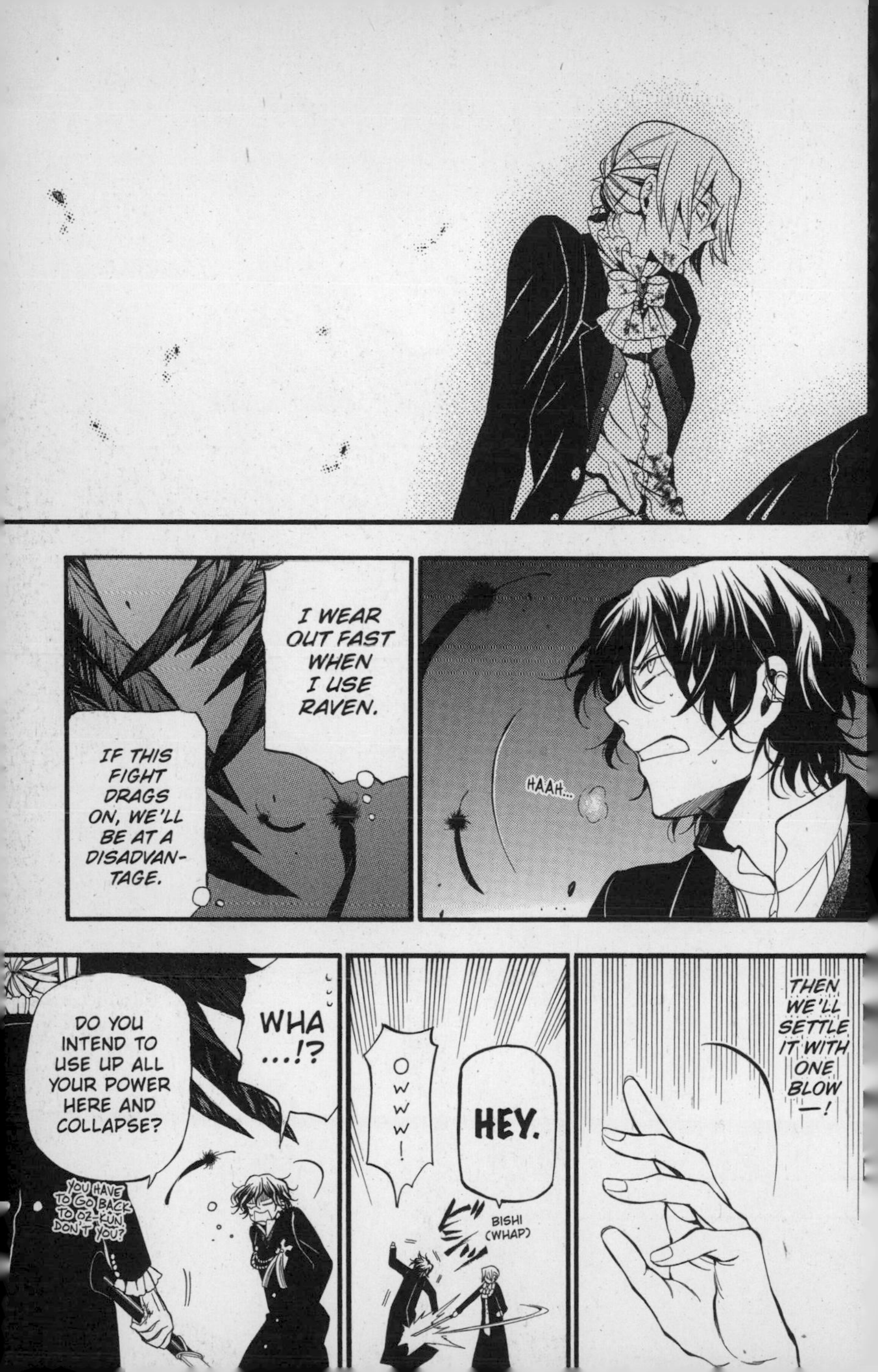
HAAH...
I WEAR OUT FAST WHEN I USE RAVEN.
IF THIS FIGHT DRAGS ON, WE'LL BE AT A DISADVANTAGE.
THEN WE'LL SETTLE IT WITH ONE BLOW—!
HEY.
OWWW!
BISHI (WHAP)
WHA...!?
DO YOU INTEND TO USE UP ALL YOUR POWER HERE AND COLLAPSE?
YOU HAVE TO GO BACK TO OZ-KUN, DON'T YOU?

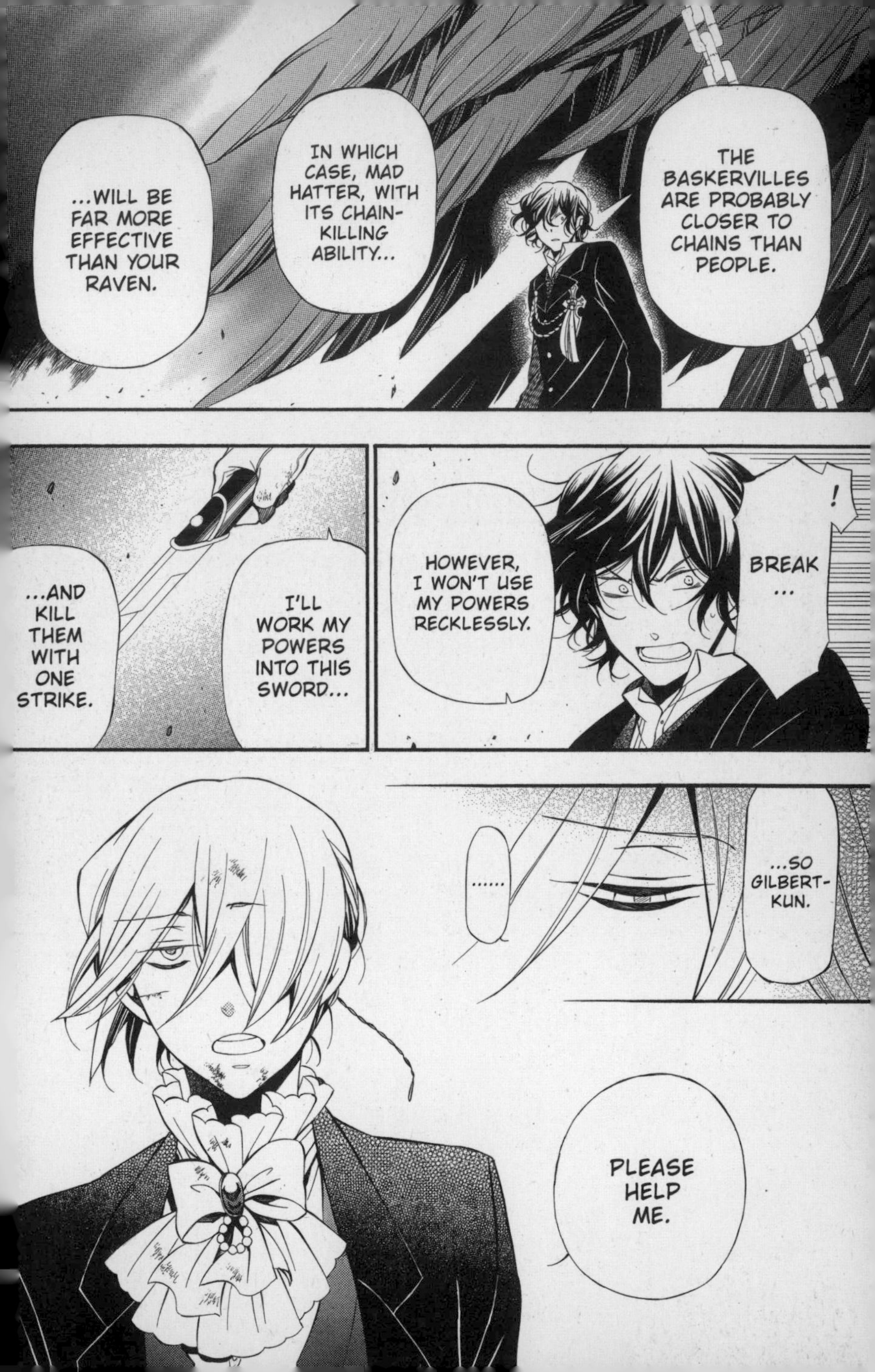
THE BASKERVILLES ARE PROBABLY CLOSER TO CHAINS THAN PEOPLE.
IN WHICH CASE, MAD HATTER, WITH ITS CHAIN-KILLING ABILITY...
...WILL BE FAR MORE EFFECTIVE THAN YOUR RAVEN.
!
BREAK...
HOWEVER, I WON'T USE MY POWERS RECKLESSLY.
I'LL WORK MY POWERS INTO THIS SWORD...
...AND KILL THEM WITH ONE STRIKE.
...SO GILBERT-KUN.
......
PLEASE HELP ME.

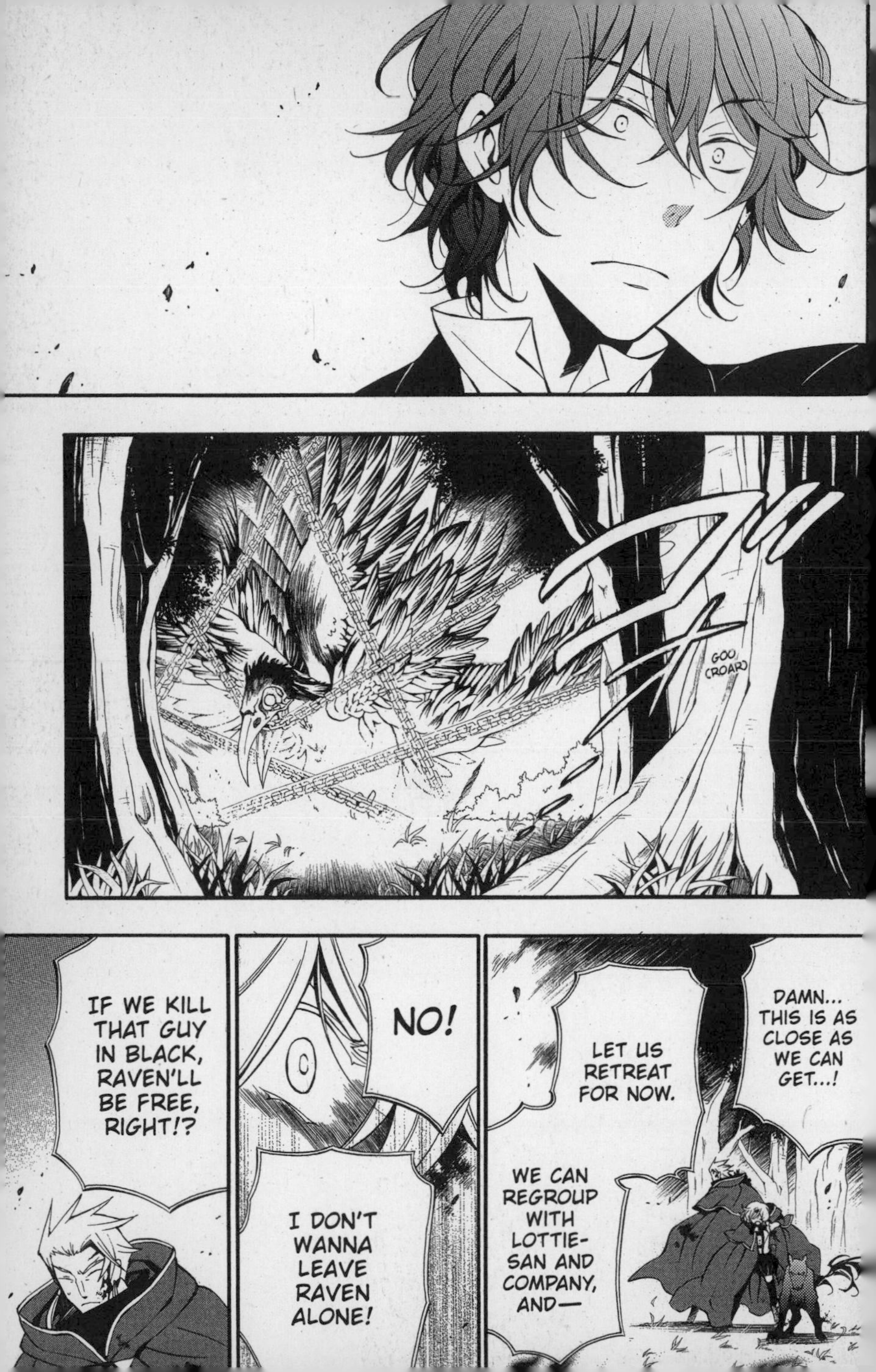

GOO (ROAR)
DAMN... THIS IS AS CLOSE AS WE CAN GET...!
LET US RETREAT FOR NOW.
WE CAN REGROUP WITH LOTTIE-SAN AND COMPANY, AND—
NO!
I DON'T WANNA LEAVE RAVEN ALONE!
IF WE KILL THAT GUY IN BLACK, RAVEN'LL BE FREE, RIGHT!?

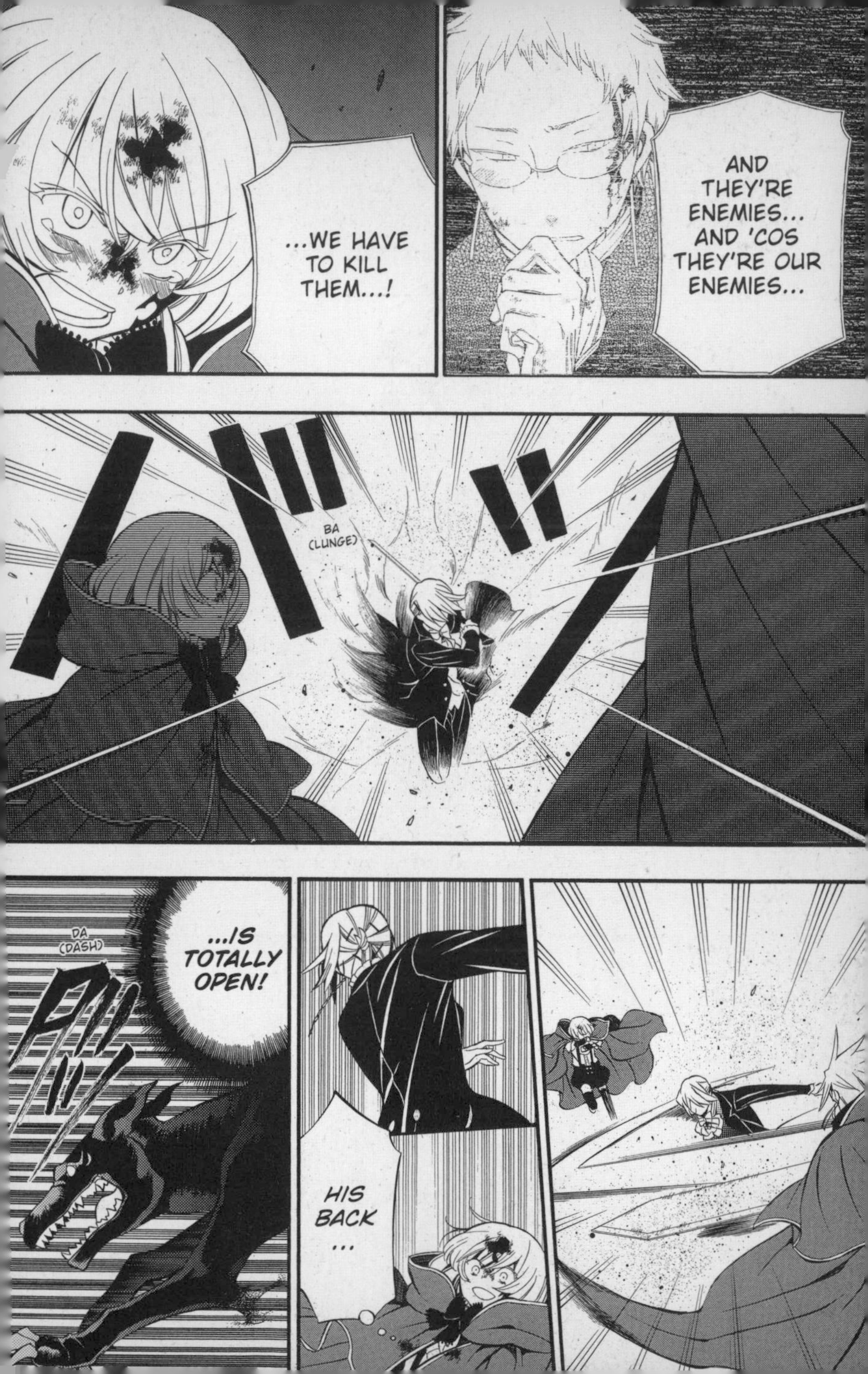
AND THEY'RE ENEMIES... AND 'COS THEY'RE OUR ENEMIES...
...WE HAVE TO KILL THEM...!
BA (LUNGE)
HIS BACK ...
...IS TOTALLY OPEN!
DA (DASH)

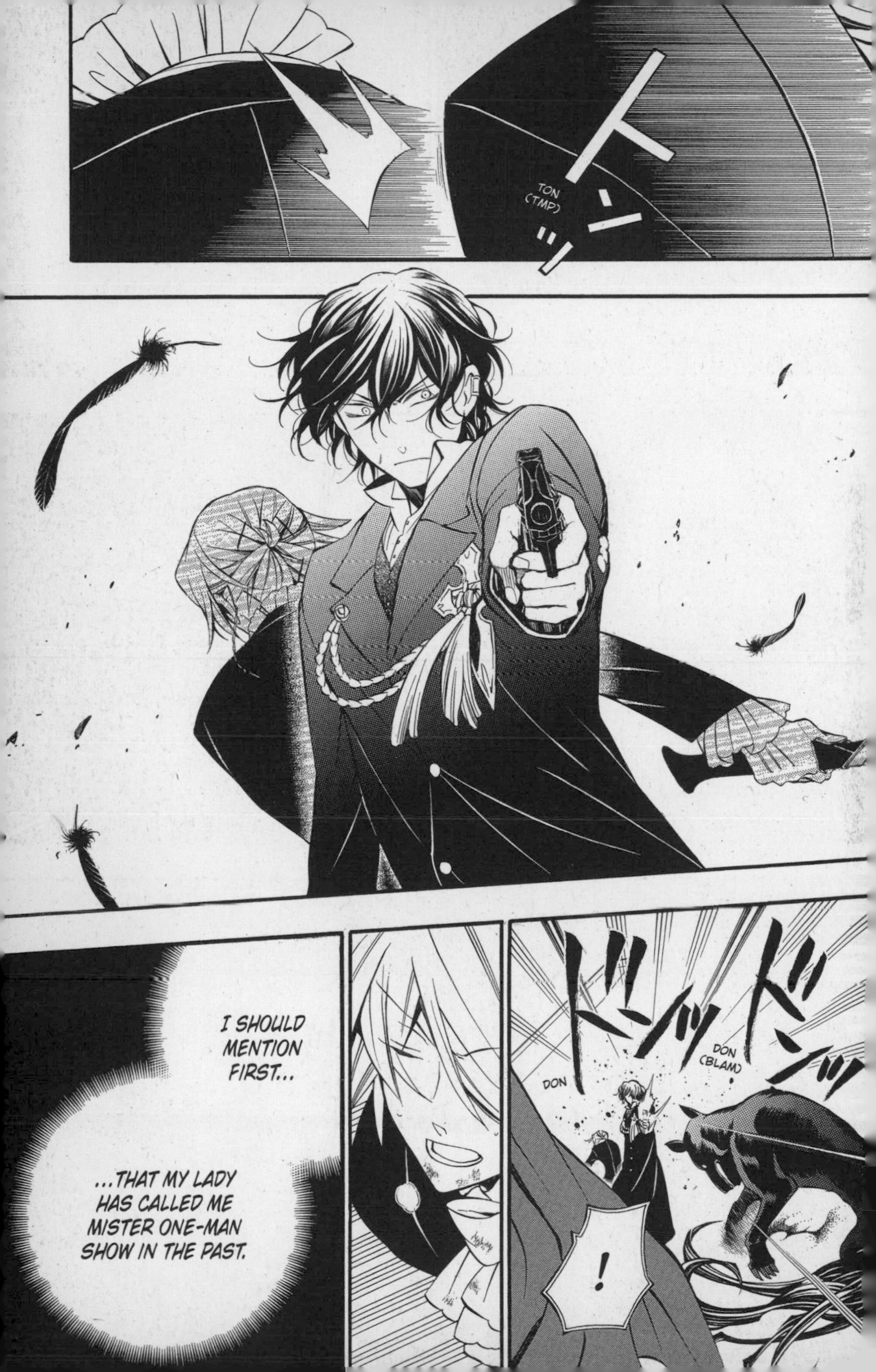
TON
(TMP)
DON
(BLAM)
DON
!
I SHOULD MENTION FIRST...
...THAT MY LADY HAS CALLED ME MISTER ONE-MAN SHOW IN THE PAST.

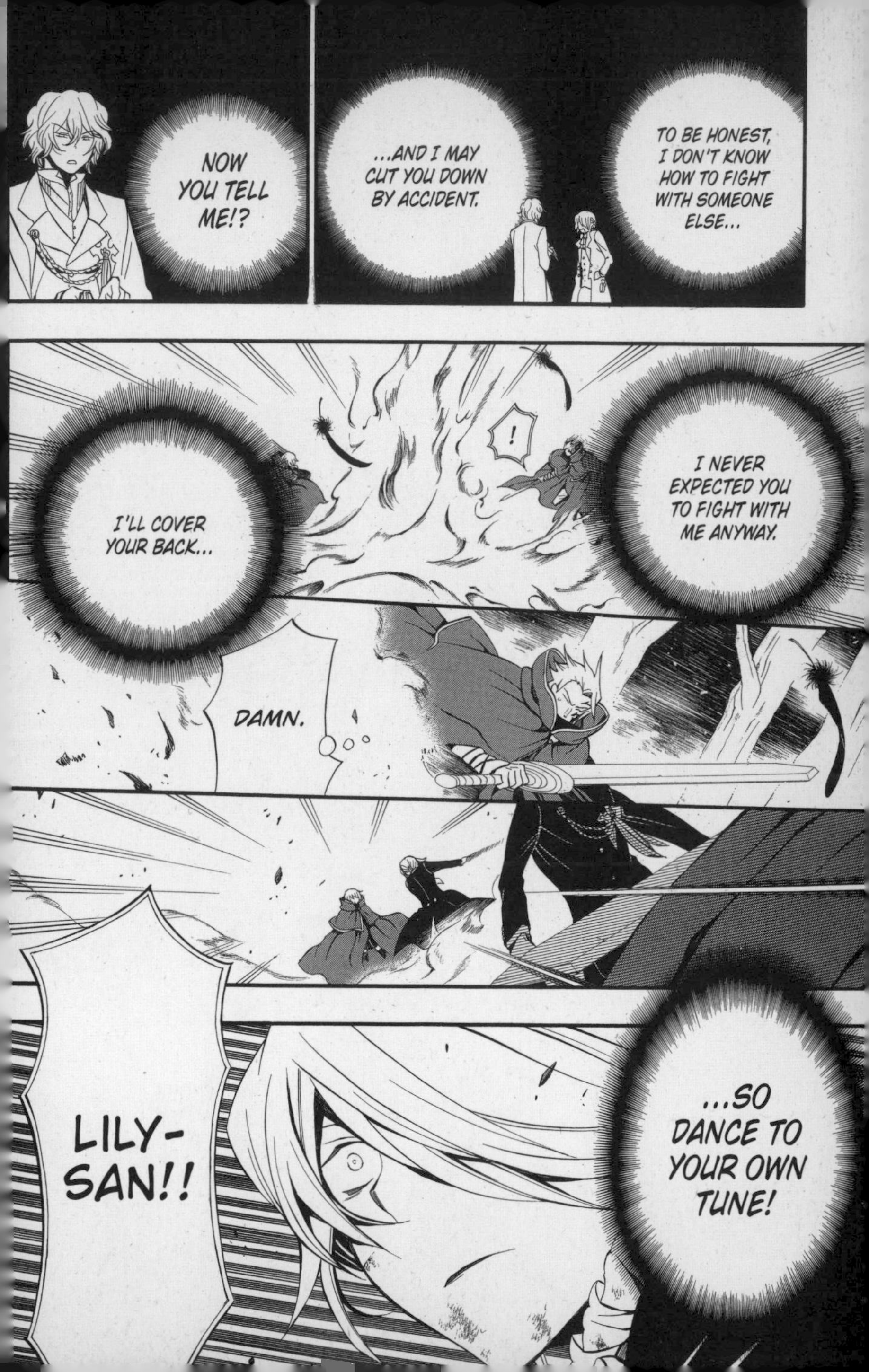
TO BE HONEST, I DON'T KNOW HOW TO FIGHT WITH SOMEONE ELSE...
...AND I MAY CUT YOU DOWN BY ACCIDENT.
NOW YOU TELL ME!?
I NEVER EXPECTED YOU TO FIGHT WITH ME ANYWAY.
!
I'LL COVER YOUR BACK...
DAMN.
...SO DANCE TO YOUR OWN TUNE!
LILY-SAN!!

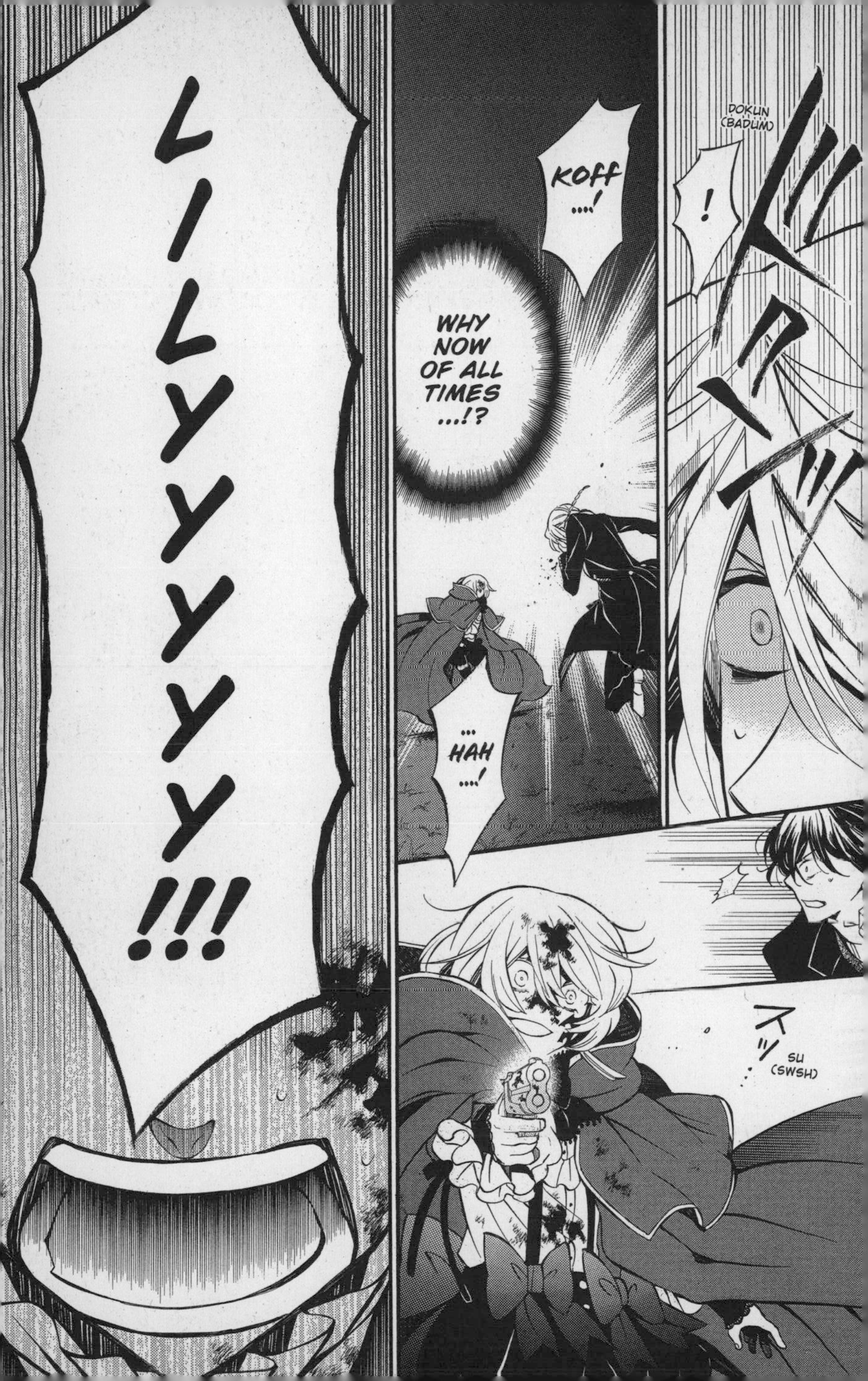
DOKUN (BADUMP)
!
KOFF ...!
WHY NOW OF ALL TIMES ...!?
...HAH ...!
SU (SWSH)
LILYYYYYY!!!

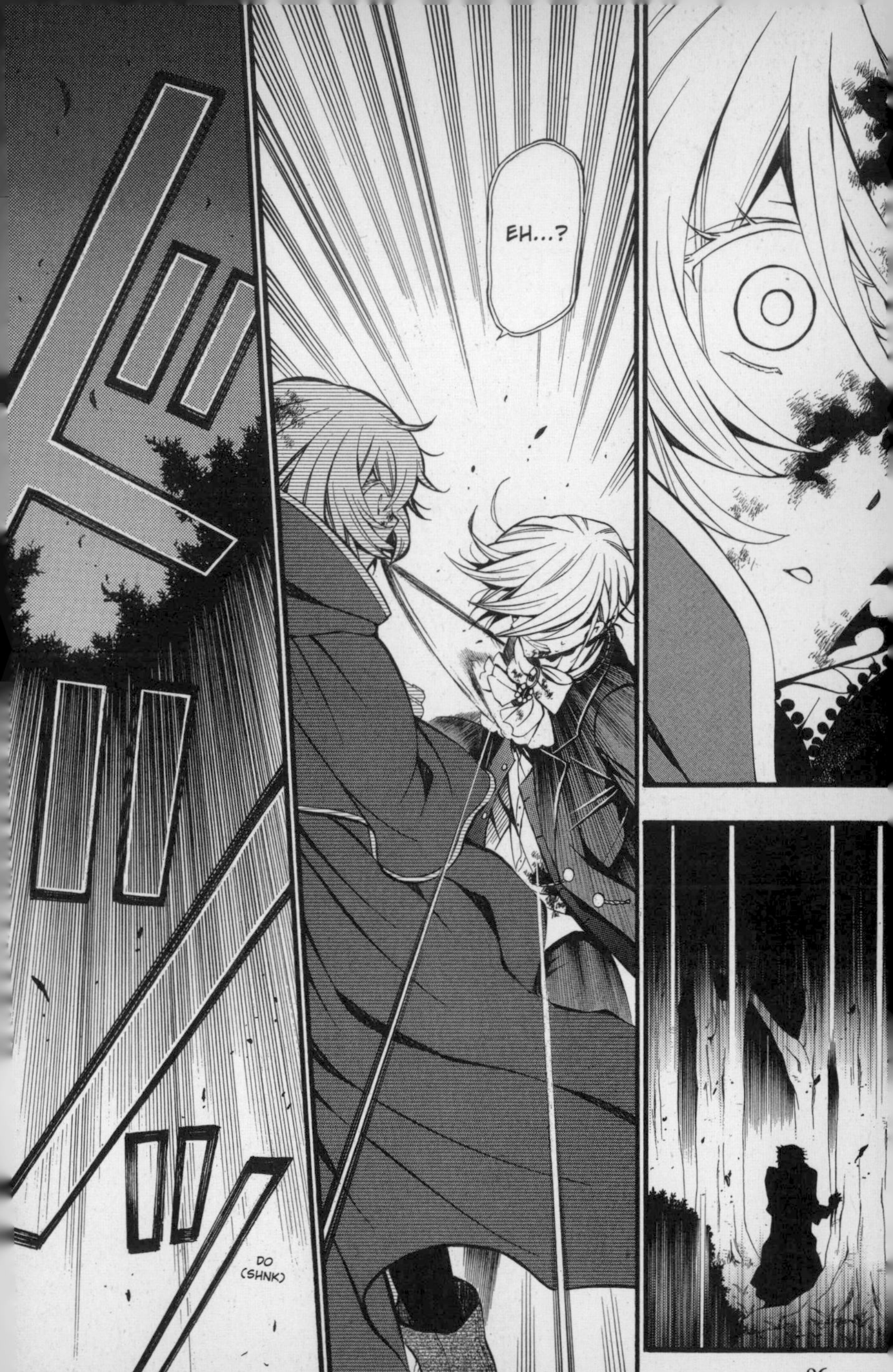
EH...?
DO
(SHNK)

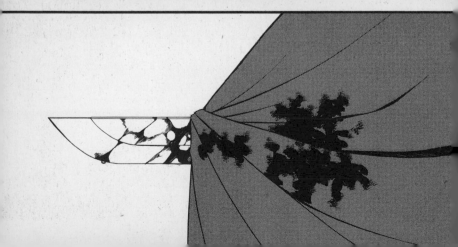

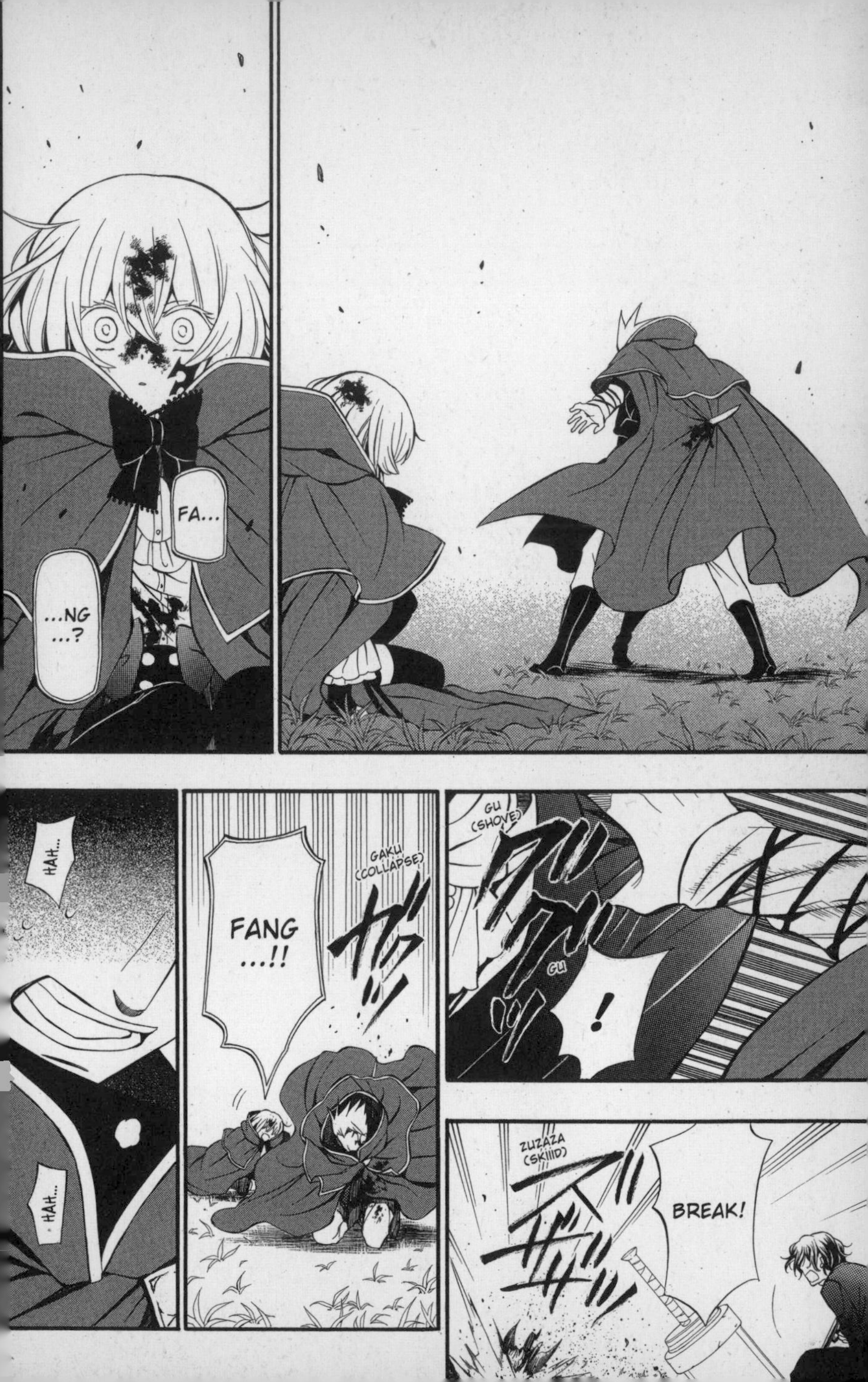
FA...
...NG ...?
GU (SHOVE)
GU
!
ZUZAZA (SKIIID)
BREAK!
GAKU (COLLAPSE)
FANG ...!!
HAH...
HAH...

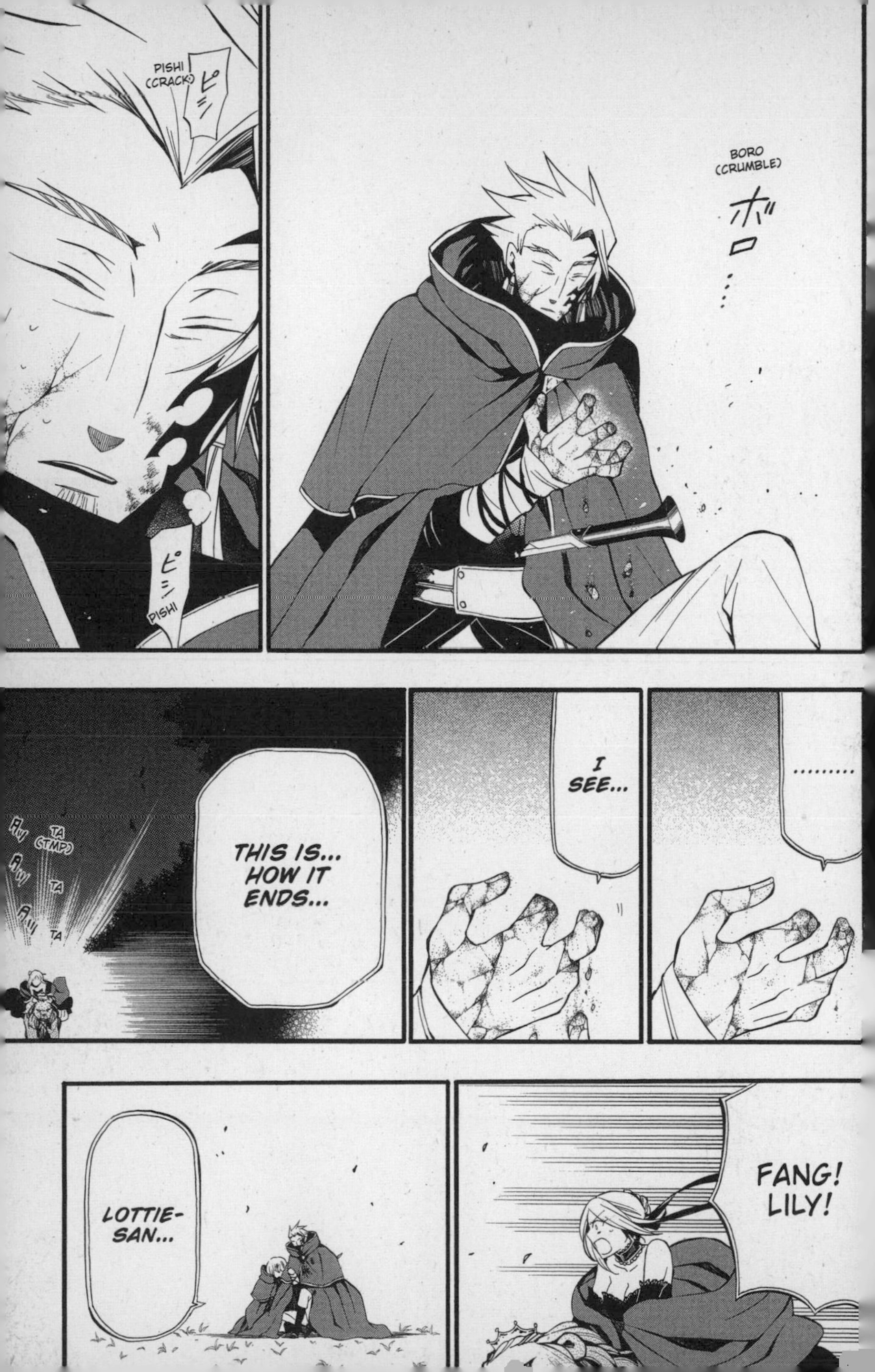
ボロ…
BORO (CRUMBLE)
ピシ
PISHI (CRACK)
ピシ
PISHI
....
I SEE...
THIS IS... HOW IT ENDS...
TA (TMP)
TA
TA
FANG! LILY!
LOTTIE-SAN...

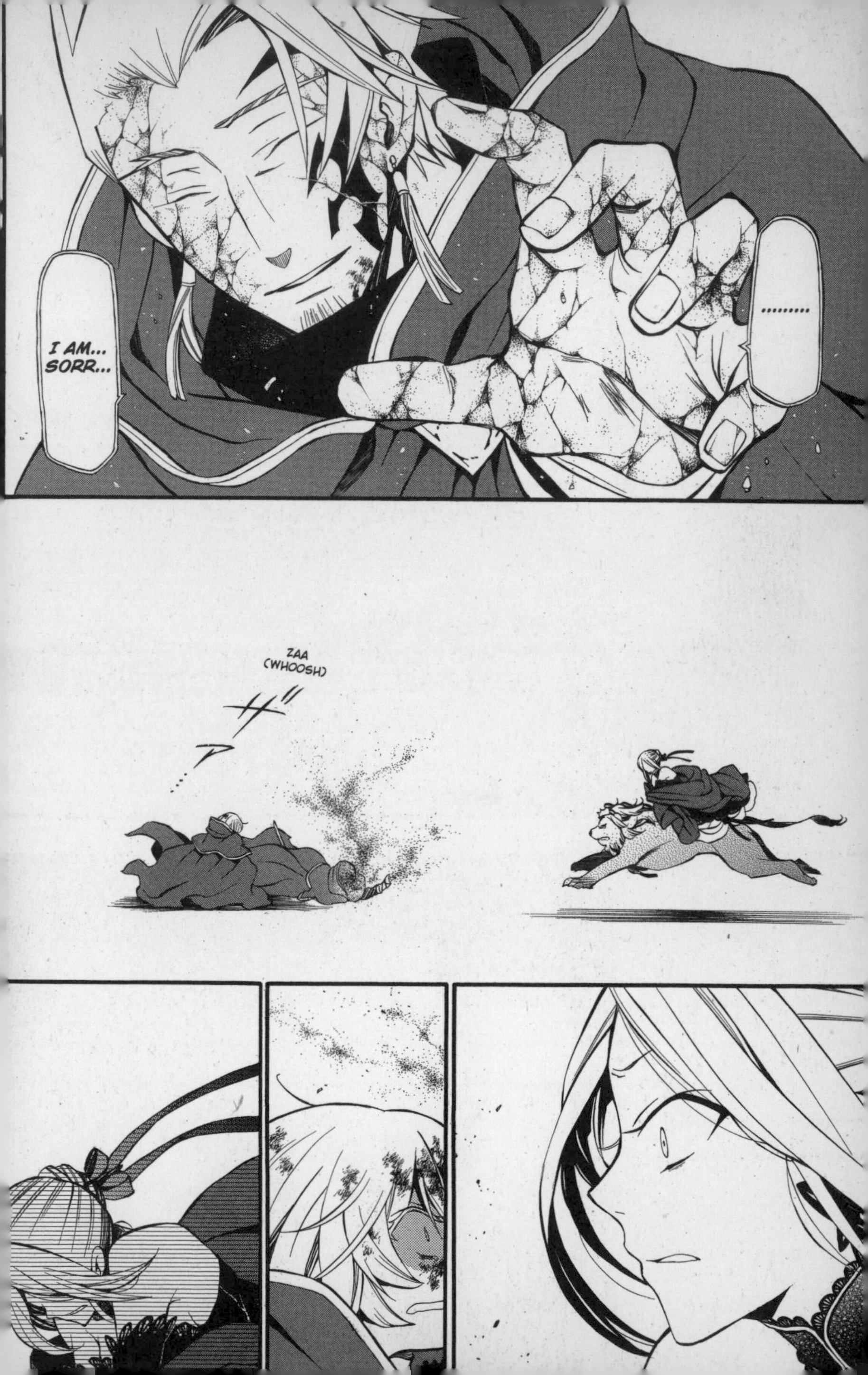
....
I AM... SORR...
ZAA (WHOOSH)

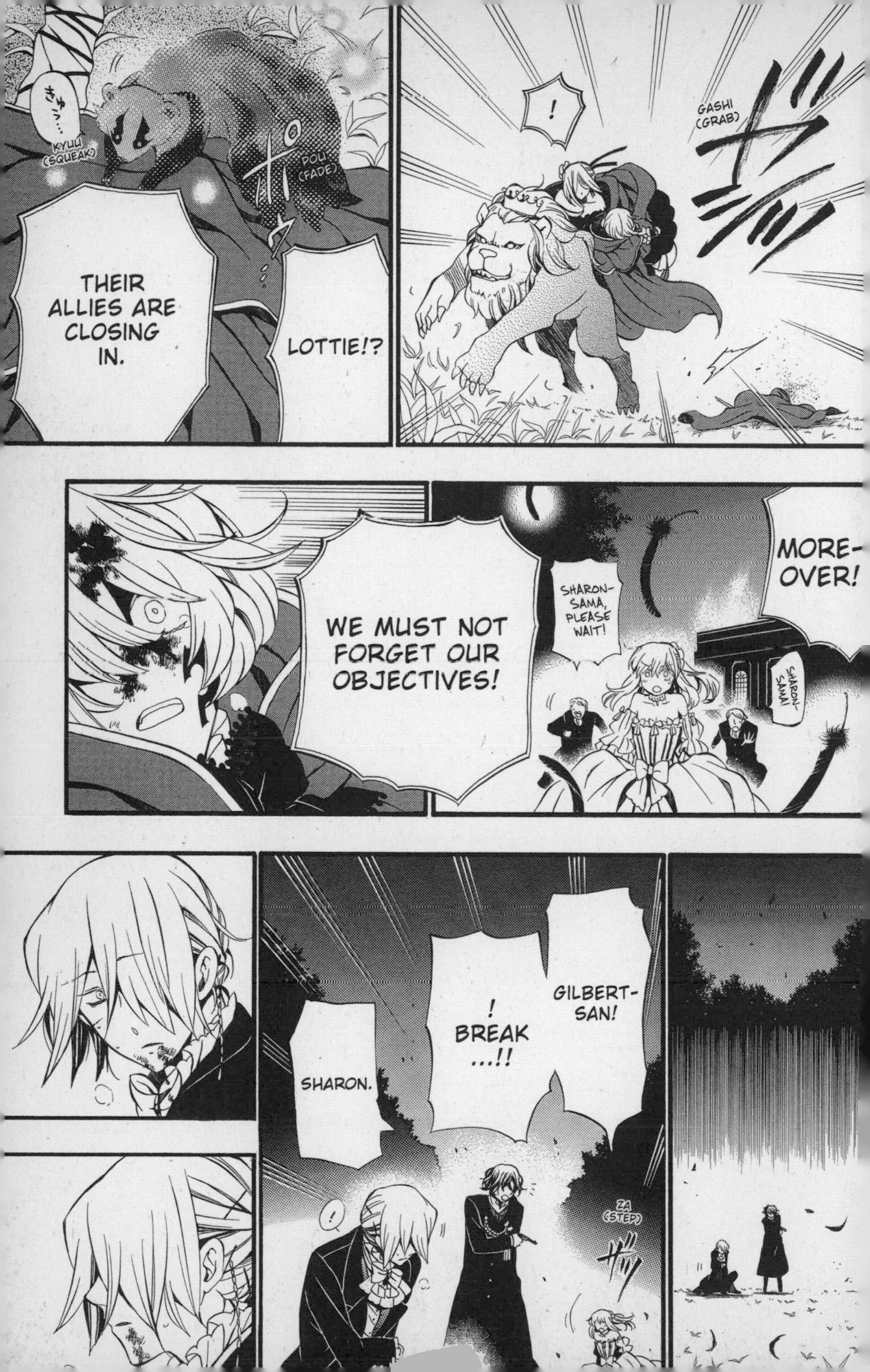

!
GASHI (GRAB)
きゅぅ…
KYUU (SQUEAK)
POU (FADE)
LOTTIE!?
THEIR ALLIES ARE CLOSING IN.
MORE-OVER!
SHARON-SAMA!
SHARON-SAMA, PLEASE WAIT!
WE MUST NOT FORGET OUR OBJECTIVES!
ZA (STEP)
GILBERT-SAN!
! BREAK ...!!
SHARON.
!

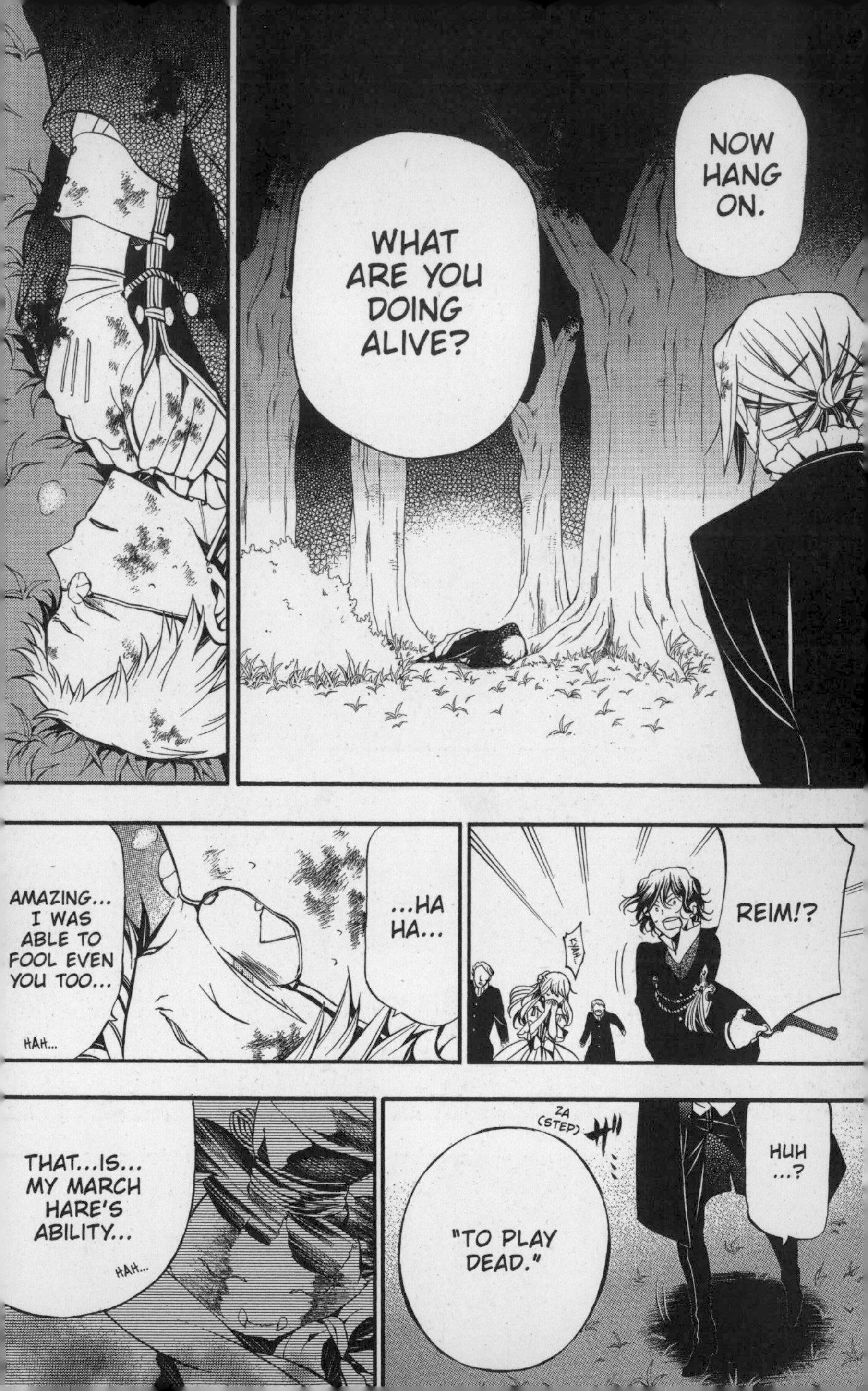
NOW HANG ON.
WHAT ARE YOU DOING ALIVE?
REIM!?
KYAH...
...HA HA...
AMAZING... I WAS ABLE TO FOOL EVEN YOU TOO...
HAH...
ZA (STEP)
HUH ...?
"TO PLAY DEAD."
THAT...IS... MY MARCH HARE'S ABILITY...
HAH...

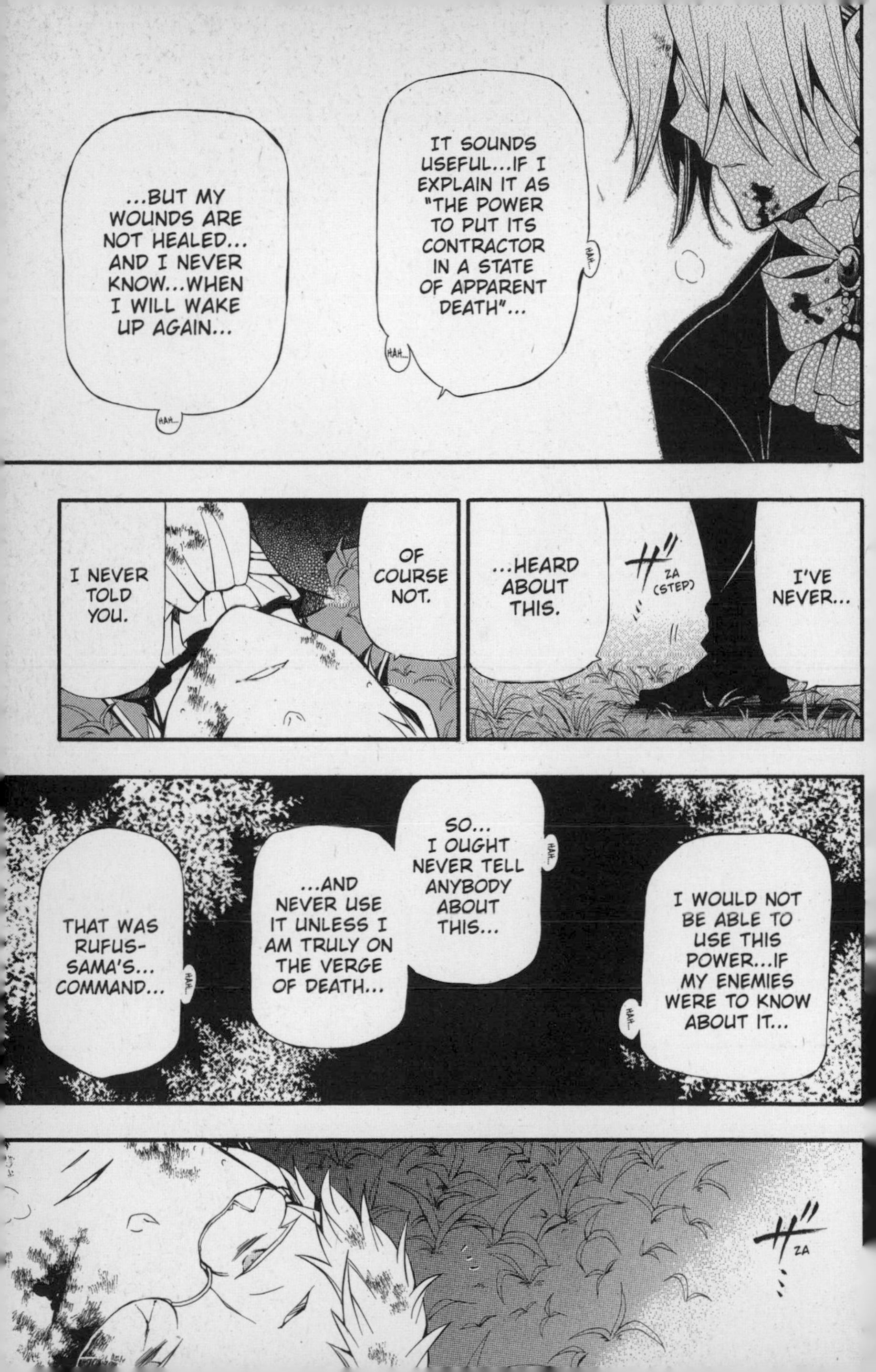
HAH...
IT SOUNDS USEFUL...IF I EXPLAIN IT AS "THE POWER TO PUT ITS CONTRACTOR IN A STATE OF APPARENT DEATH"...
HAH...
...BUT MY WOUNDS ARE NOT HEALED... AND I NEVER KNOW...WHEN I WILL WAKE UP AGAIN...
HAH...
I'VE NEVER...
ZA (STEP)
...HEARD ABOUT THIS.
OF COURSE NOT.
I NEVER TOLD YOU.
HAH...
I WOULD NOT BE ABLE TO USE THIS POWER...IF MY ENEMIES WERE TO KNOW ABOUT IT...
HAH...
SO... I OUGHT NEVER TELL ANYBODY ABOUT THIS...
...AND NEVER USE IT UNLESS I AM TRULY ON THE VERGE OF DEATH...
HAH...
THAT WAS RUFUS-SAMA'S... COMMAND...
ZA

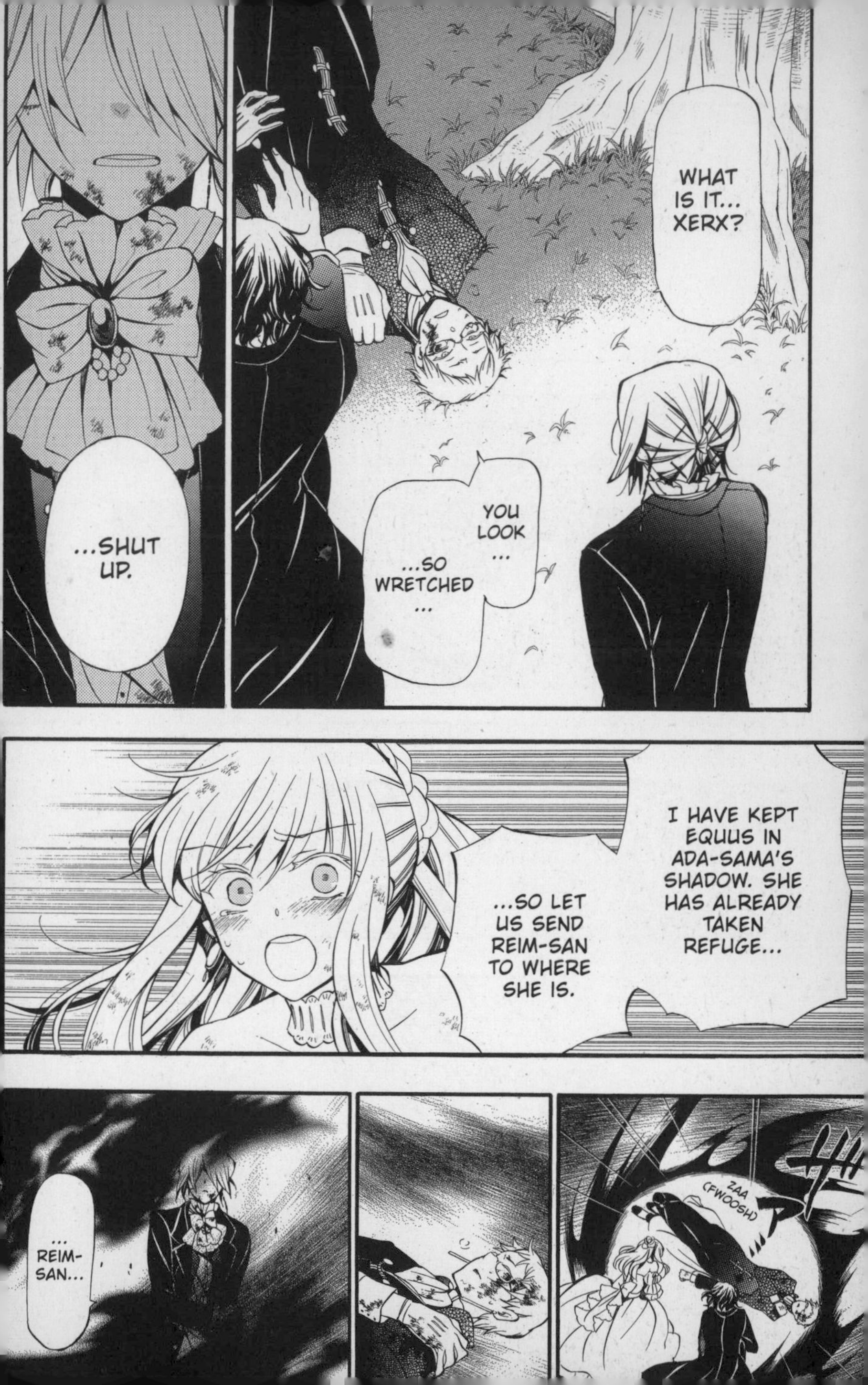
WHAT IS IT... XERX?
YOU LOOK ... ...SO WRETCHED ...
...SHUT UP.
I HAVE KEPT EQUUS IN ADA-SAMA'S SHADOW. SHE HAS ALREADY TAKEN REFUGE...
...SO LET US SEND REIM-SAN TO WHERE SHE IS.
ZAA (FWOOSH)
... REIM-SAN...

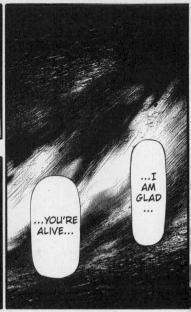

...YOU'RE ALIVE...

...I AM GLAD...

LILYYYYY!!!

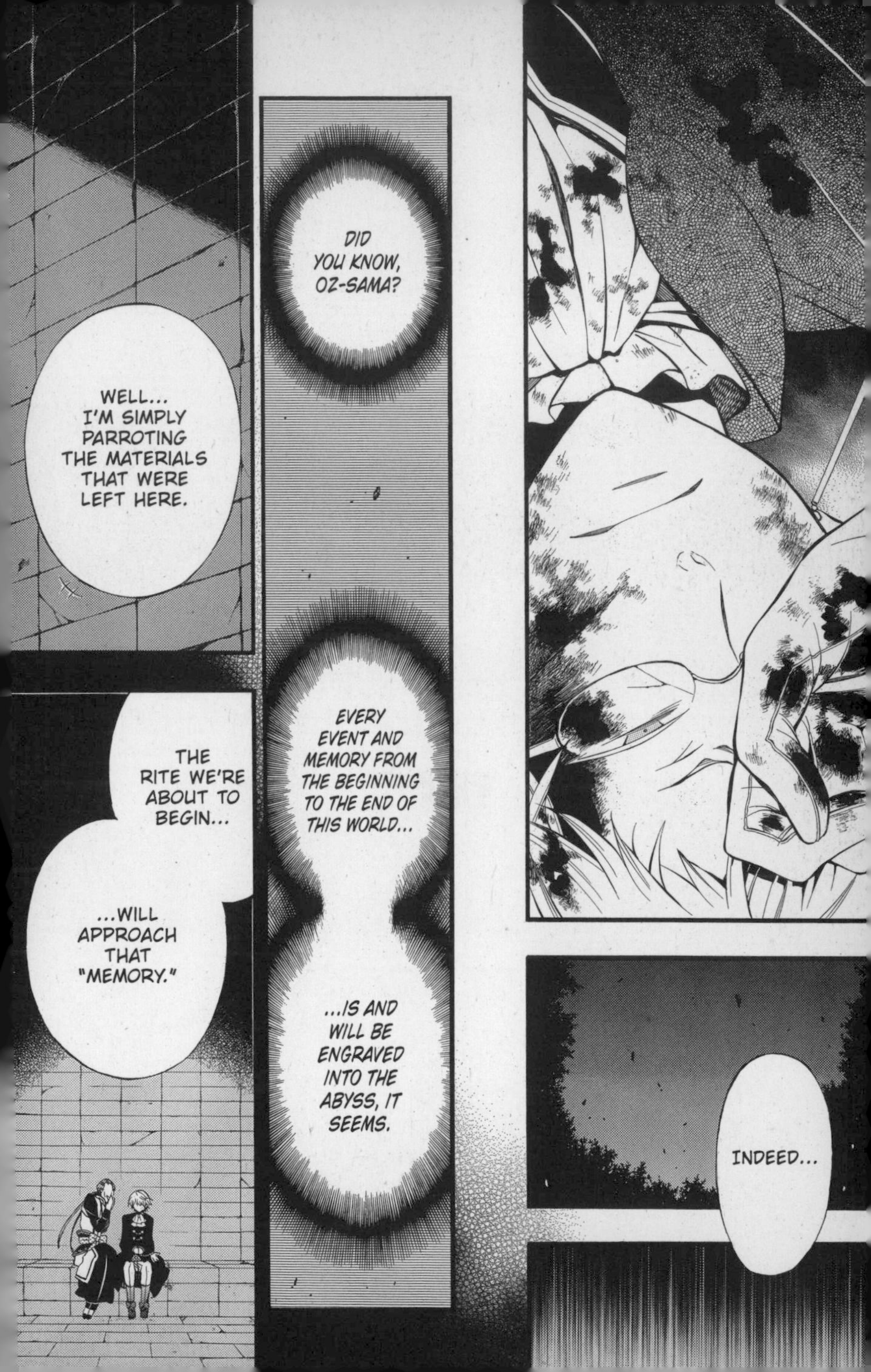
INDEED...
DID YOU KNOW, OZ-SAMA?
EVERY EVENT AND MEMORY FROM THE BEGINNING TO THE END OF THIS WORLD...
...IS AND WILL BE ENGRAVED INTO THE ABYSS, IT SEEMS.
WELL... I'M SIMPLY PARROTING THE MATERIALS THAT WERE LEFT HERE.
THE RITE WE'RE ABOUT TO BEGIN...
...WILL APPROACH THAT "MEMORY."

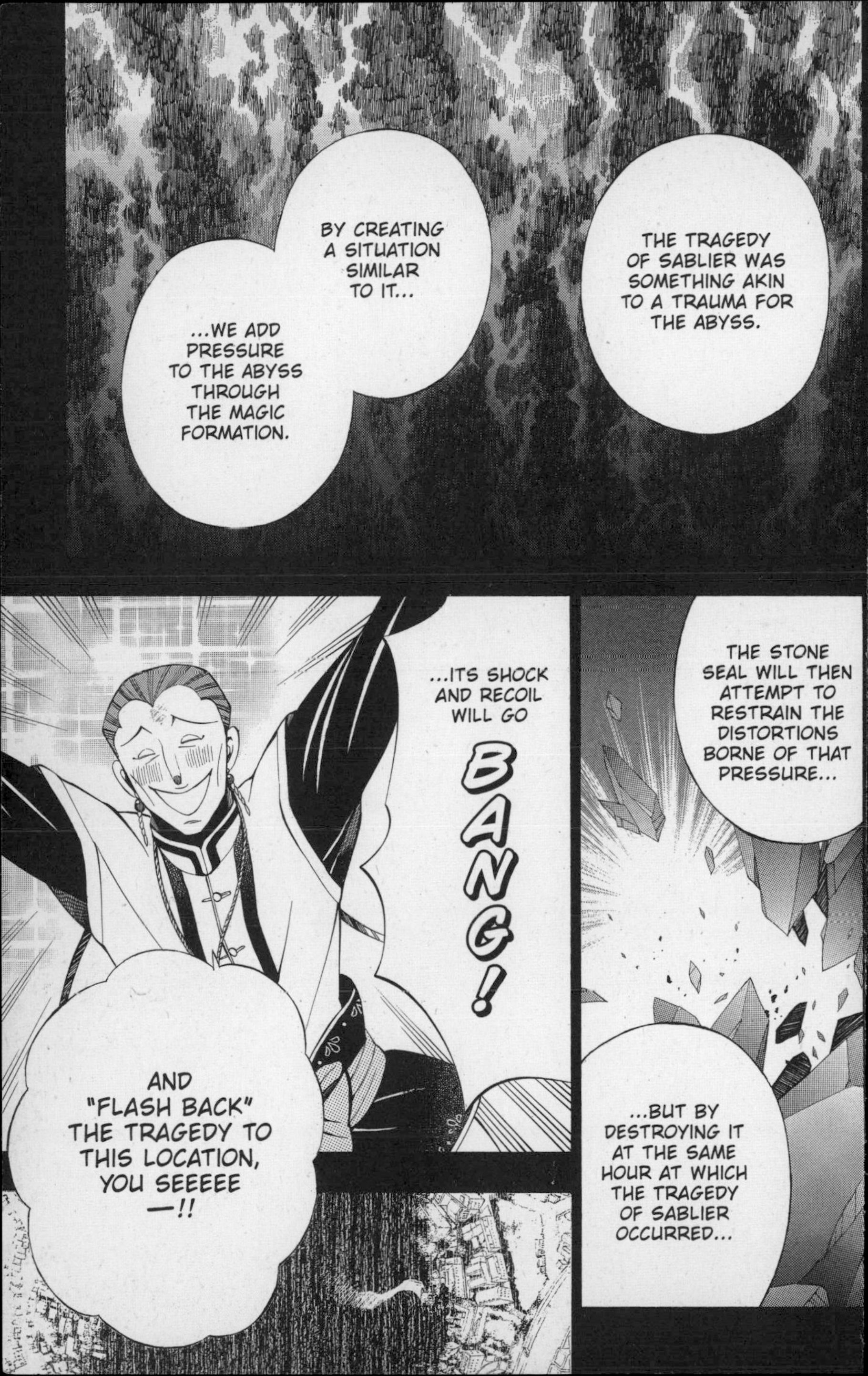
THE TRAGEDY OF SABLIER WAS SOMETHING AKIN TO A TRAUMA FOR THE ABYSS.
BY CREATING A SITUATION SIMILAR TO IT...
...WE ADD PRESSURE TO THE ABYSS THROUGH THE MAGIC FORMATION.
THE STONE SEAL WILL THEN ATTEMPT TO RESTRAIN THE DISTORTIONS BORNE OF THAT PRESSURE...
...BUT BY DESTROYING IT AT THE SAME HOUR AT WHICH THE TRAGEDY OF SABLIER OCCURRED...
...ITS SHOCK AND RECOIL WILL GO
BANG!
AND "FLASH BACK" THE TRAGEDY TO THIS LOCATION, YOU SEEEEE—!!

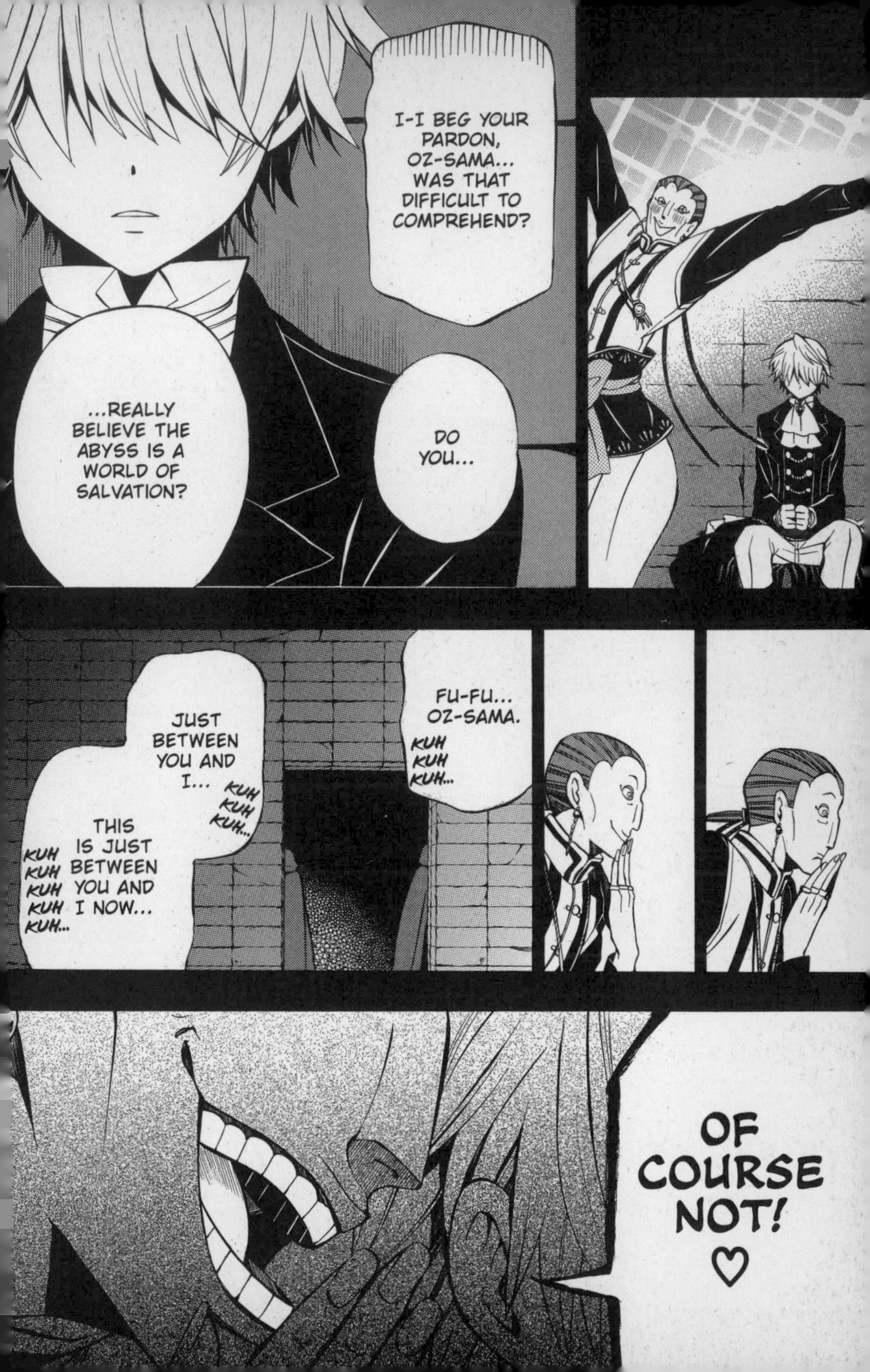
I-I BEG YOUR PARDON, OZ-SAMA... WAS THAT DIFFICULT TO COMPREHEND?
DO YOU...
...REALLY BELIEVE THE ABYSS IS A WORLD OF SALVATION?
FU-FU... OZ-SAMA.
KUH KUH KUH...
JUST BETWEEN YOU AND I...
KUH KUH KUH...
THIS IS JUST BETWEEN YOU AND I NOW...
KUH KUH KUH KUH KUH...
OF COURSE NOT! ♡

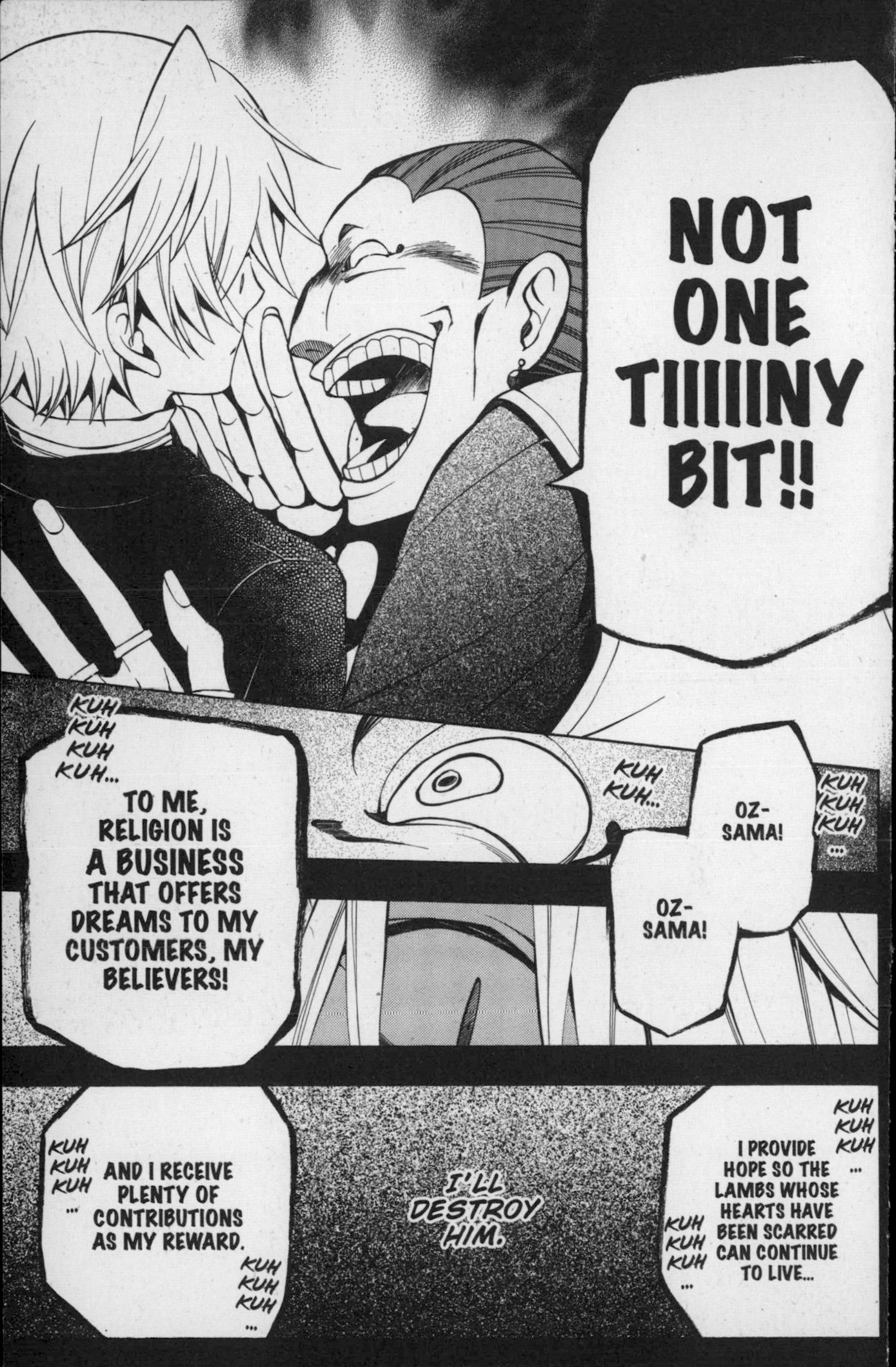
NOT ONE TIIIIINY BIT!!
KUH KUH KUH ...
OZ-SAMA!
OZ-SAMA!
KUH KUH...
KUH KUH KUH KUH...
TO ME, RELIGION IS A BUSINESS THAT OFFERS DREAMS TO MY CUSTOMERS, MY BELIEVERS!
KUH KUH KUH ...
I PROVIDE HOPE SO THE LAMBS WHOSE HEARTS HAVE BEEN SCARRED CAN CONTINUE TO LIVE...
KUH KUH KUH ...
I'LL DESTROY HIM.
KUH KUH KUH ...
AND I RECEIVE PLENTY OF CONTRIBUTIONS AS MY REWARD.
KUH KUH KUH ...

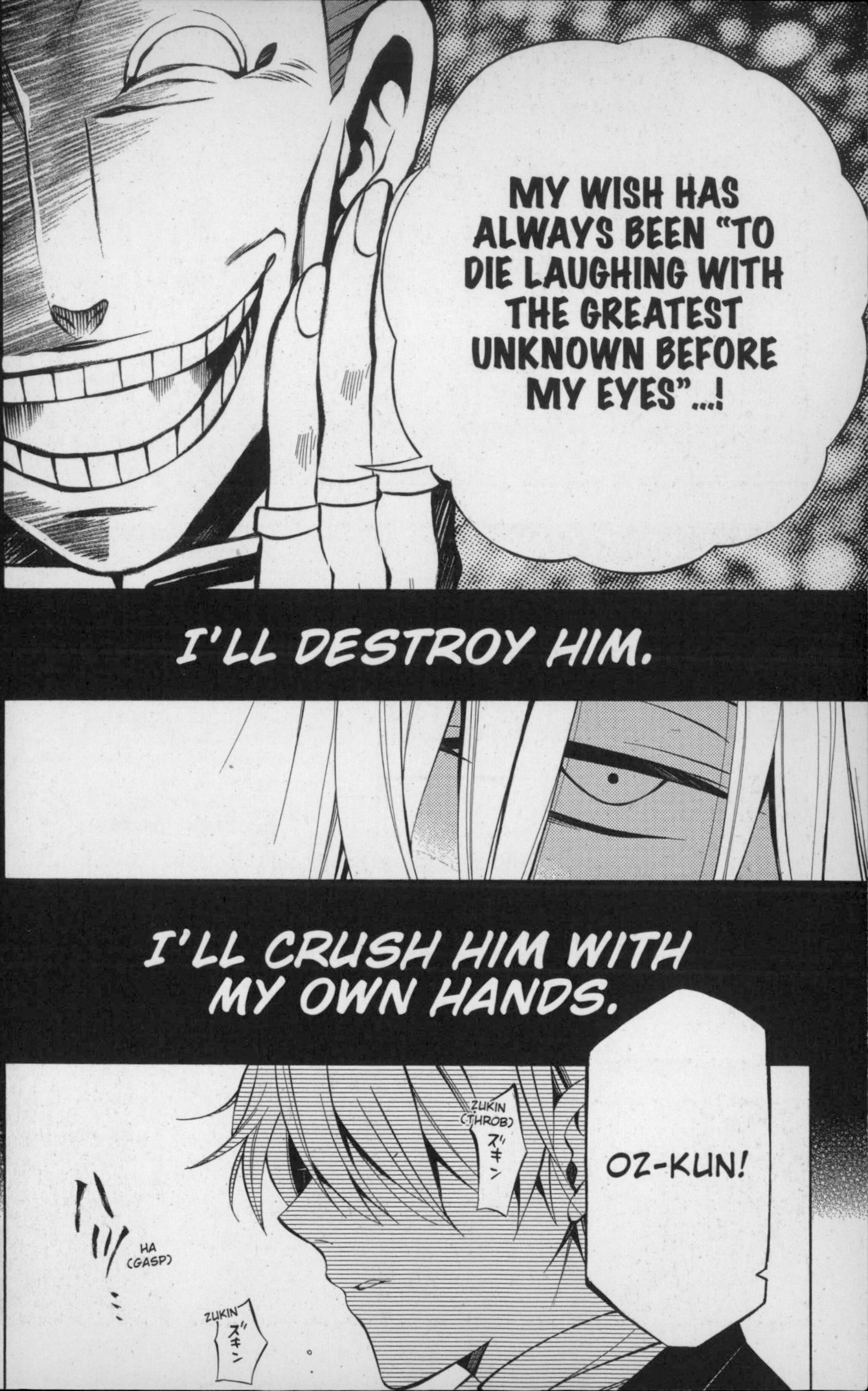
MY WISH HAS ALWAYS BEEN "TO DIE LAUGHING WITH THE GREATEST UNKNOWN BEFORE MY EYES"...!
I'LL DESTROY HIM.
I'LL CRUSH HIM WITH MY OWN HANDS.
OZ-KUN!
ZUKIN (THROB)
ズキン
ハッ
HA (GASP)
ZUKIN
ズキン

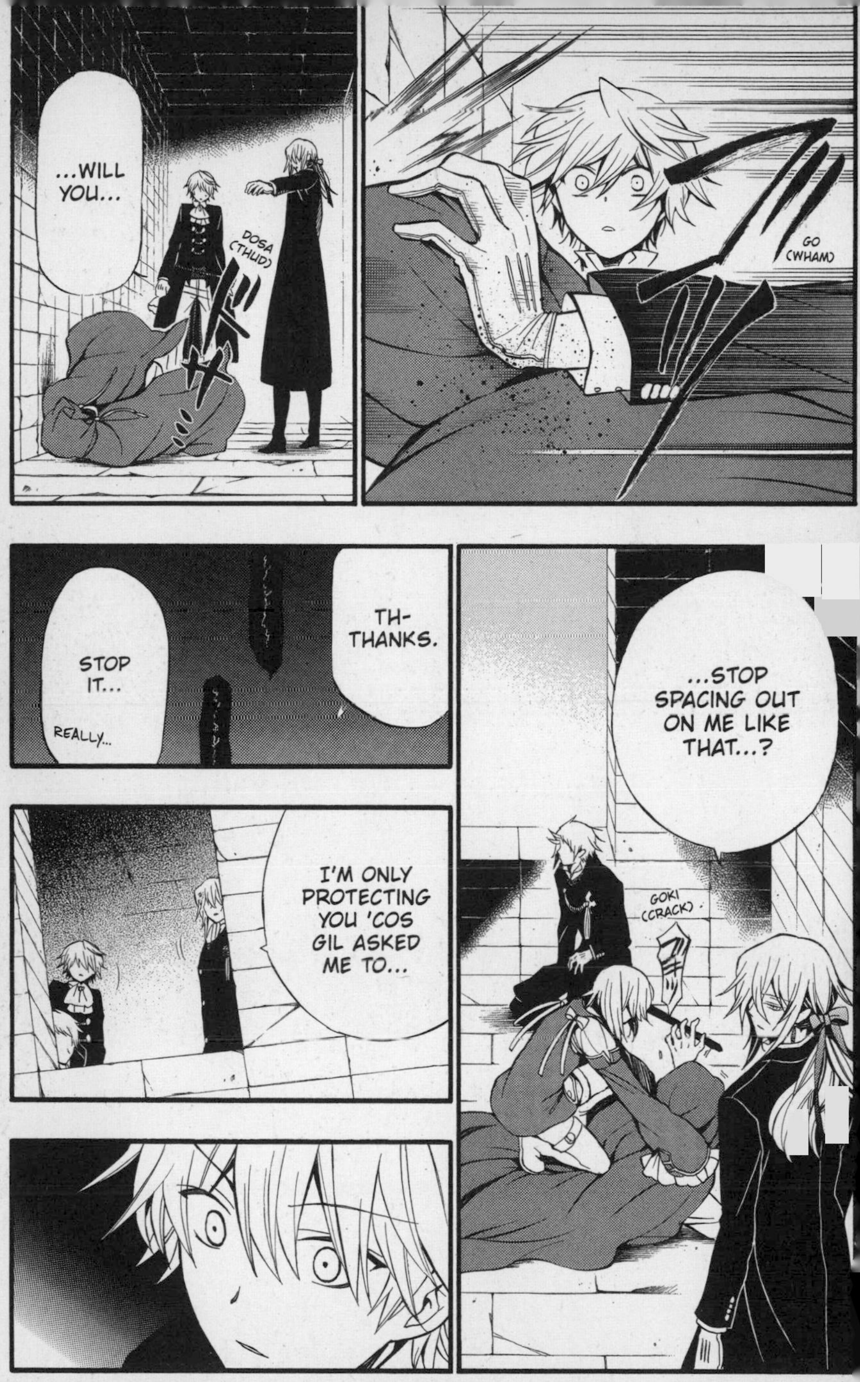
GO (WHAM)
...WILL YOU...
DOSA (THUD)
...STOP SPACING OUT ON ME LIKE THAT...?
GOKI (CRACK)
TH-THANKS.
STOP IT...
REALLY...
I'M ONLY PROTECTING YOU 'COS GIL ASKED ME TO...

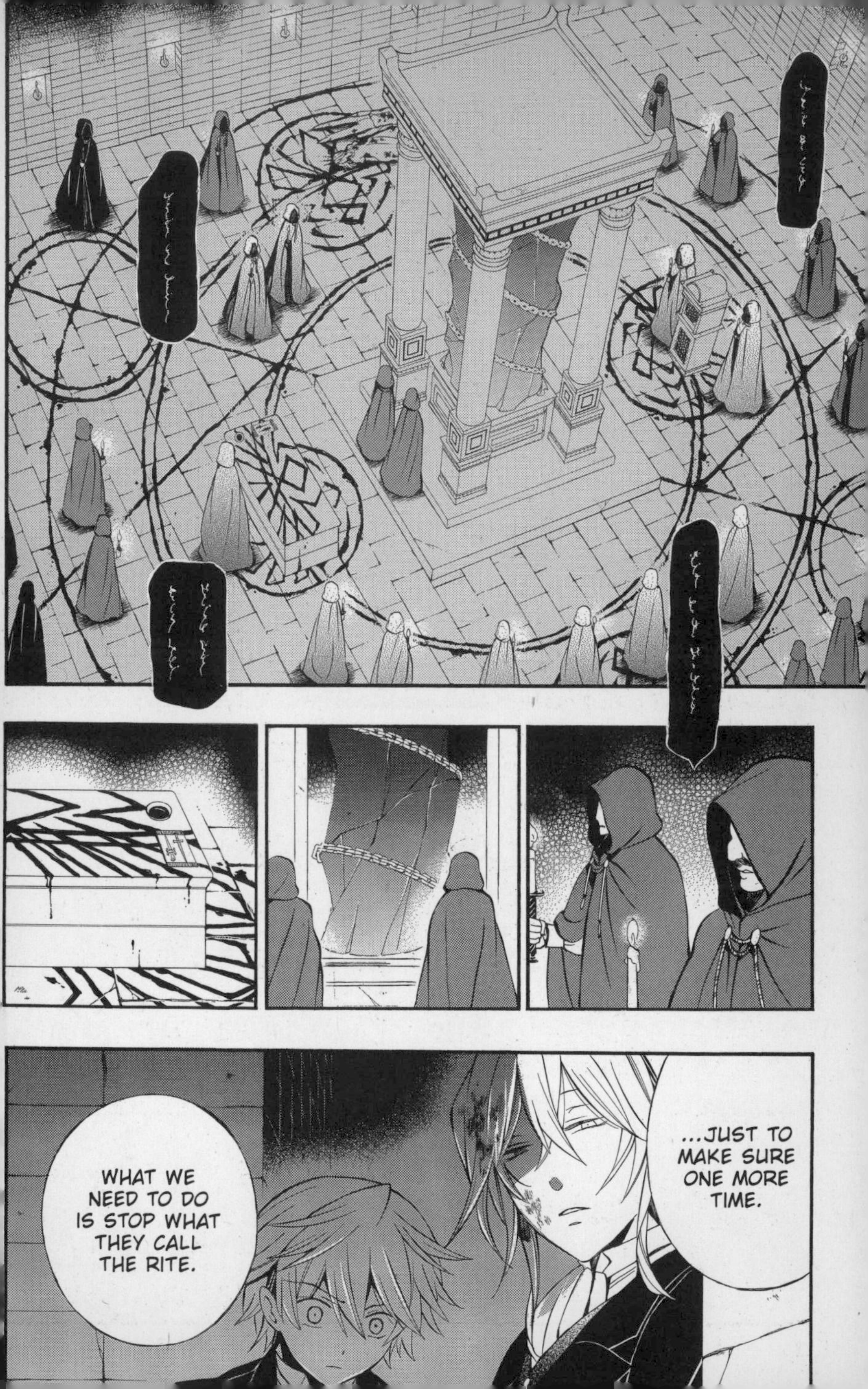
...JUST TO MAKE SURE ONE MORE TIME.
WHAT WE NEED TO DO IS STOP WHAT THEY CALL THE RITE.

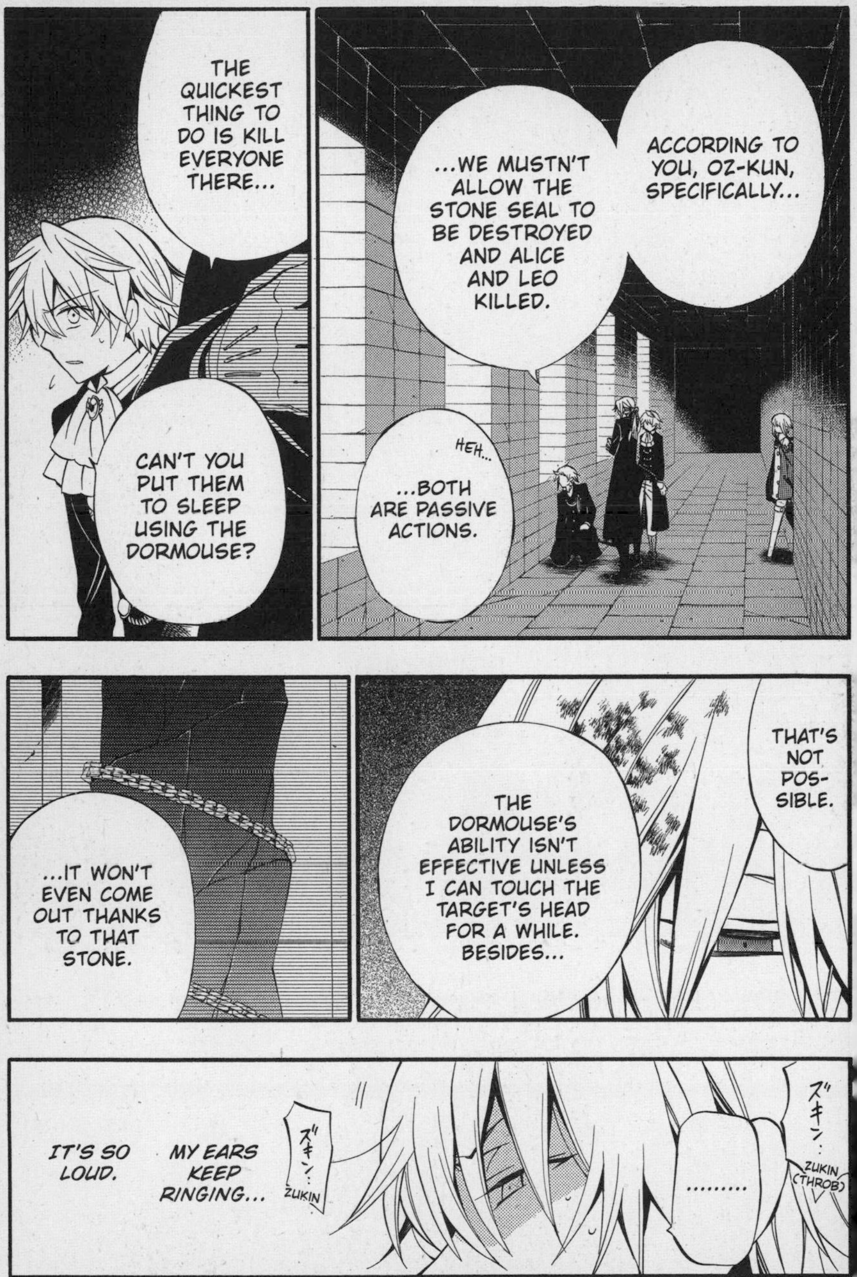
ACCORDING TO YOU, OZ-KUN, SPECIFICALLY...
...WE MUSTN'T ALLOW THE STONE SEAL TO BE DESTROYED AND ALICE AND LEO KILLED.
HEH...
...BOTH ARE PASSIVE ACTIONS.
THE QUICKEST THING TO DO IS KILL EVERYONE THERE...
CAN'T YOU PUT THEM TO SLEEP USING THE DORMOUSE?
THAT'S NOT POS-SIBLE.
THE DORMOUSE'S ABILITY ISN'T EFFECTIVE UNLESS I CAN TOUCH THE TARGET'S HEAD FOR A WHILE. BESIDES...
...IT WON'T EVEN COME OUT THANKS TO THAT STONE.
ズキン…
ZUKIN (THROB)
....
ズキン…
ZUKIN
MY EARS KEEP RINGING...
IT'S SO LOUD.

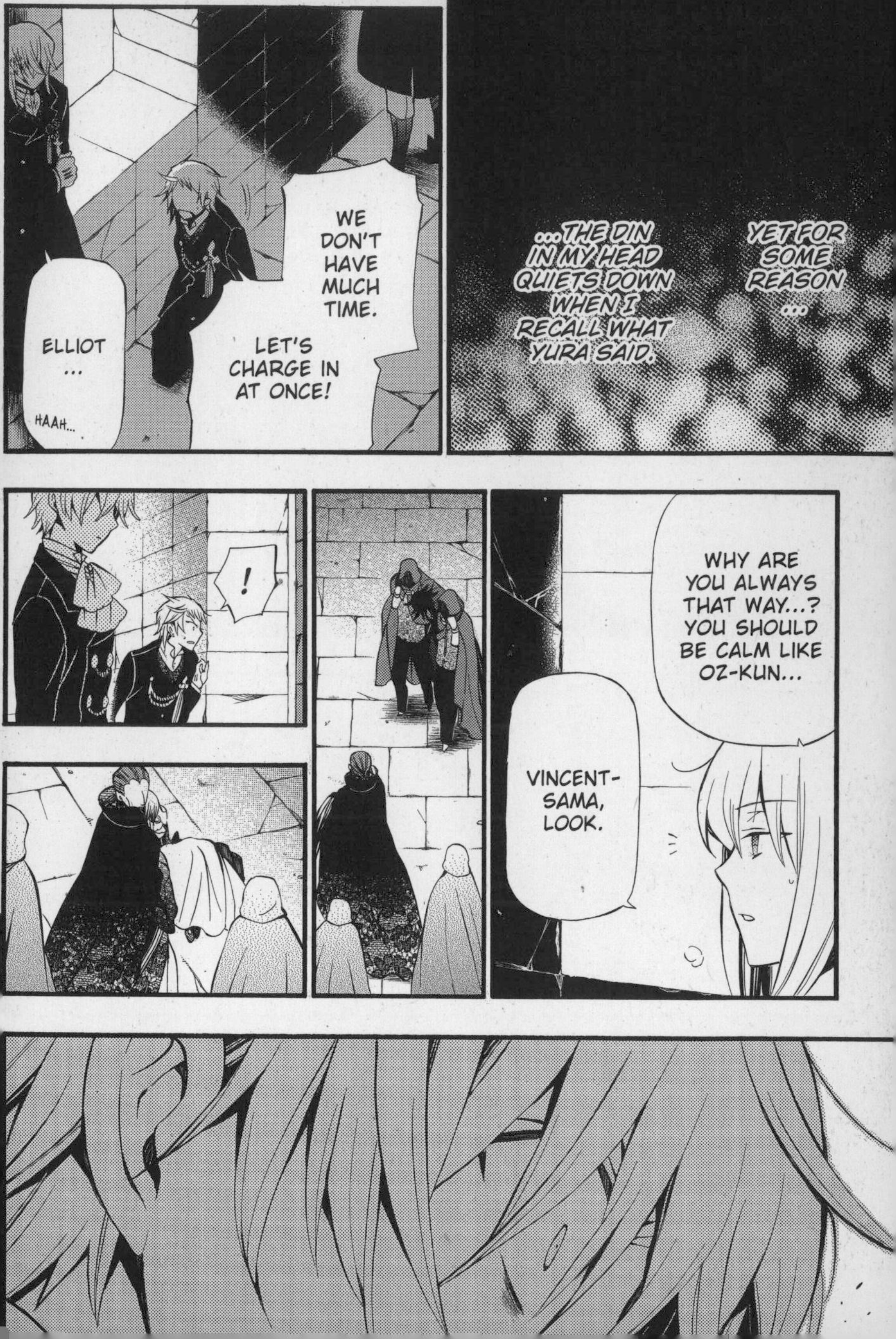
YET FOR SOME REASON ...
...THE DIN IN MY HEAD QUIETS DOWN WHEN I RECALL WHAT YURA SAID.
WE DON'T HAVE MUCH TIME.
LET'S CHARGE IN AT ONCE!
ELLIOT ...
HAAH...
WHY ARE YOU ALWAYS THAT WAY...? YOU SHOULD BE CALM LIKE OZ-KUN...
VINCENT-SAMA, LOOK.
!

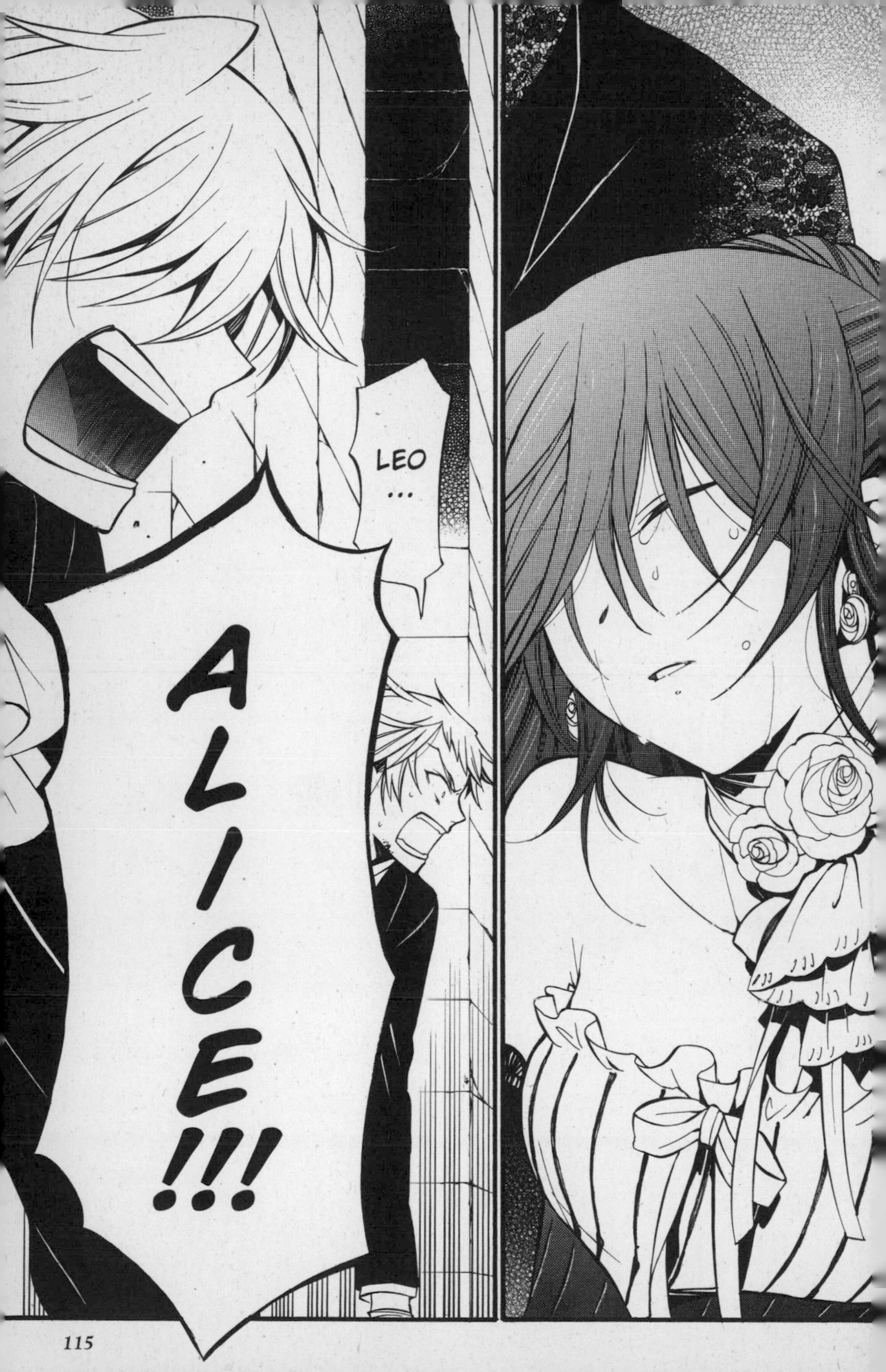
LEO ...
ALICE!!!

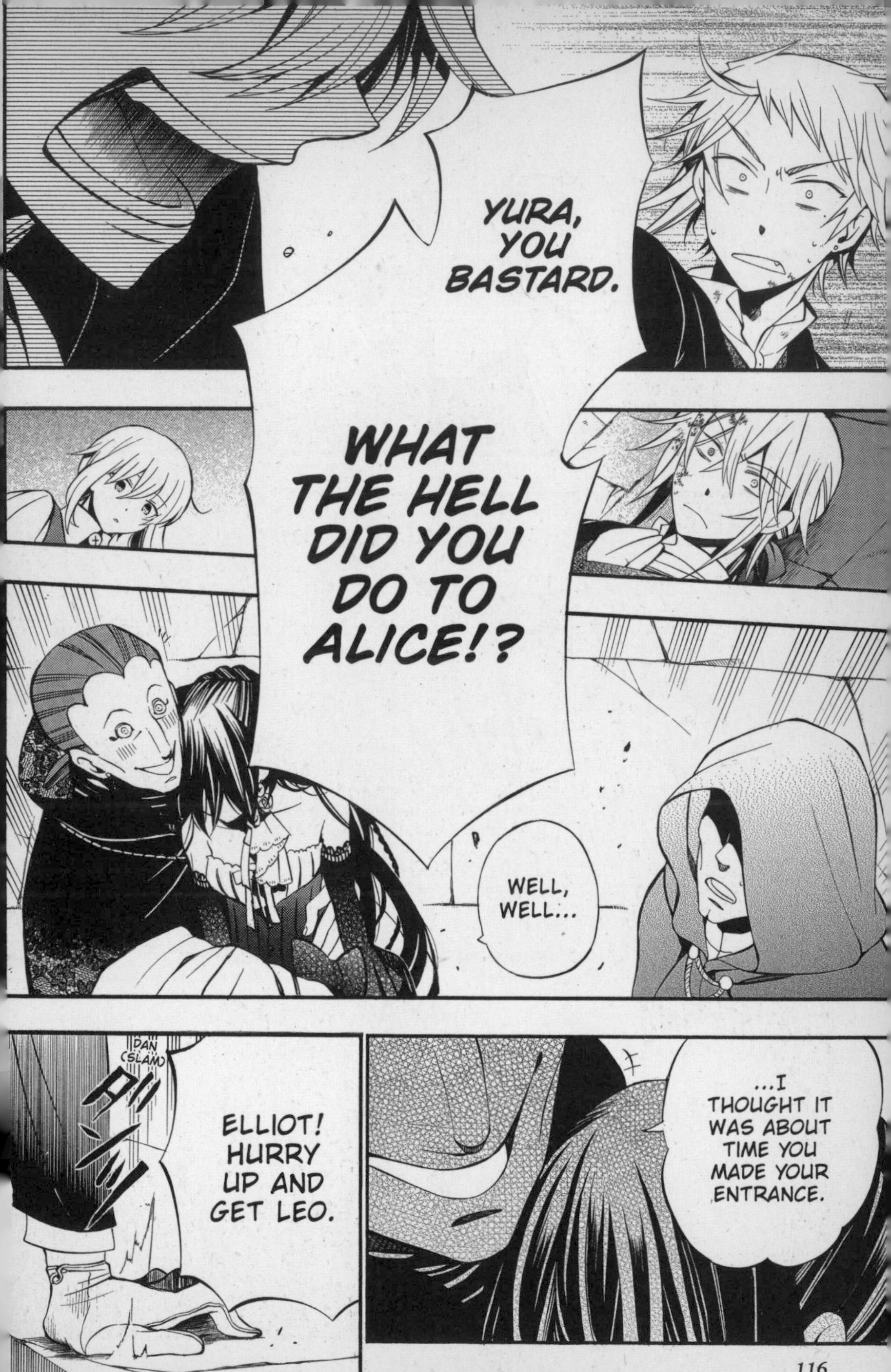
YURA, YOU BASTARD.
WHAT THE HELL DID YOU DO TO ALICE!?
WELL, WELL...
...I THOUGHT IT WAS ABOUT TIME YOU MADE YOUR ENTRANCE.
DAN (SLAM)
ELLIOT! HURRY UP AND GET LEO.

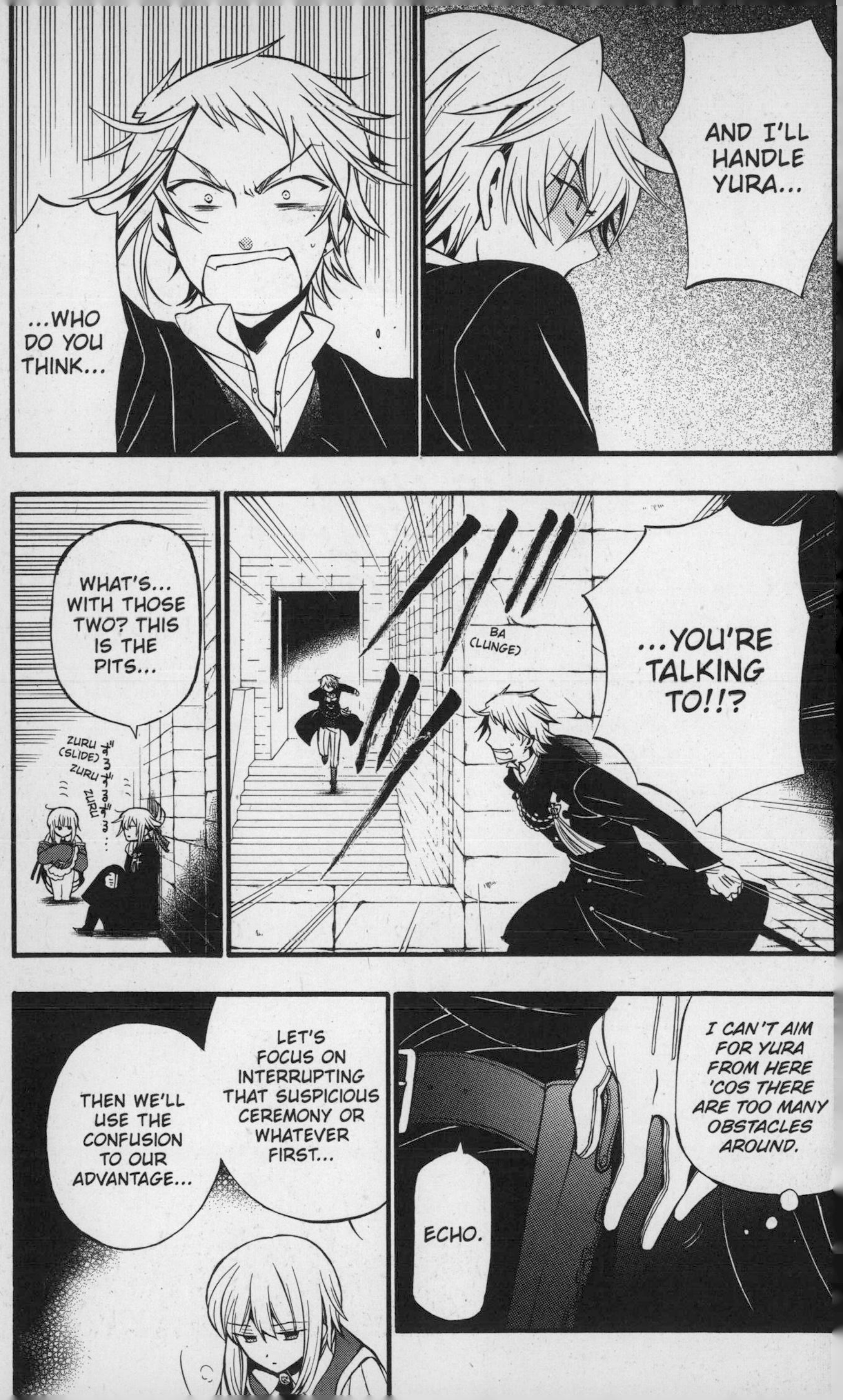
AND I'LL HANDLE YURA...
...WHO DO YOU THINK...
...YOU'RE TALKING TO!!?
BA (LUNGE)
WHAT'S... WITH THOSE TWO? THIS IS THE PITS...
ZURU (SLIDE) ZURU ZURU
I CAN'T AIM FOR YURA FROM HERE 'COS THERE ARE TOO MANY OBSTACLES AROUND.
ECHO.
LET'S FOCUS ON INTERRUPTING THAT SUSPICIOUS CEREMONY OR WHATEVER FIRST...
THEN WE'LL USE THE CONFUSION TO OUR ADVANTAGE...

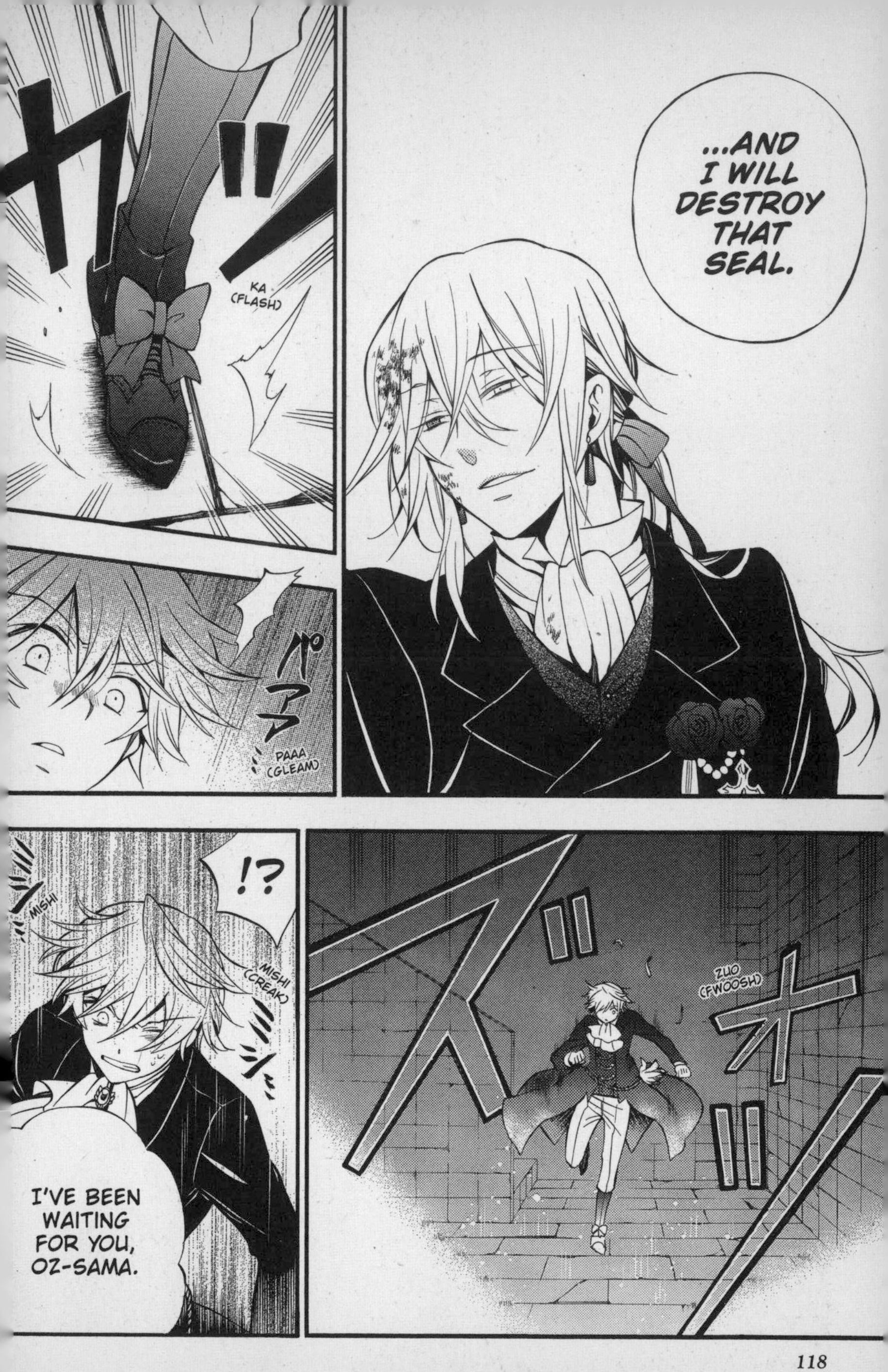
...AND I WILL DESTROY THAT SEAL.
KA (FLASH)
PAAA (GLEAM)
ZUO (FWOOSH)
!?
MISHI
MISHI (CREAK)
I'VE BEEN WAITING FOR YOU, OZ-SAMA.

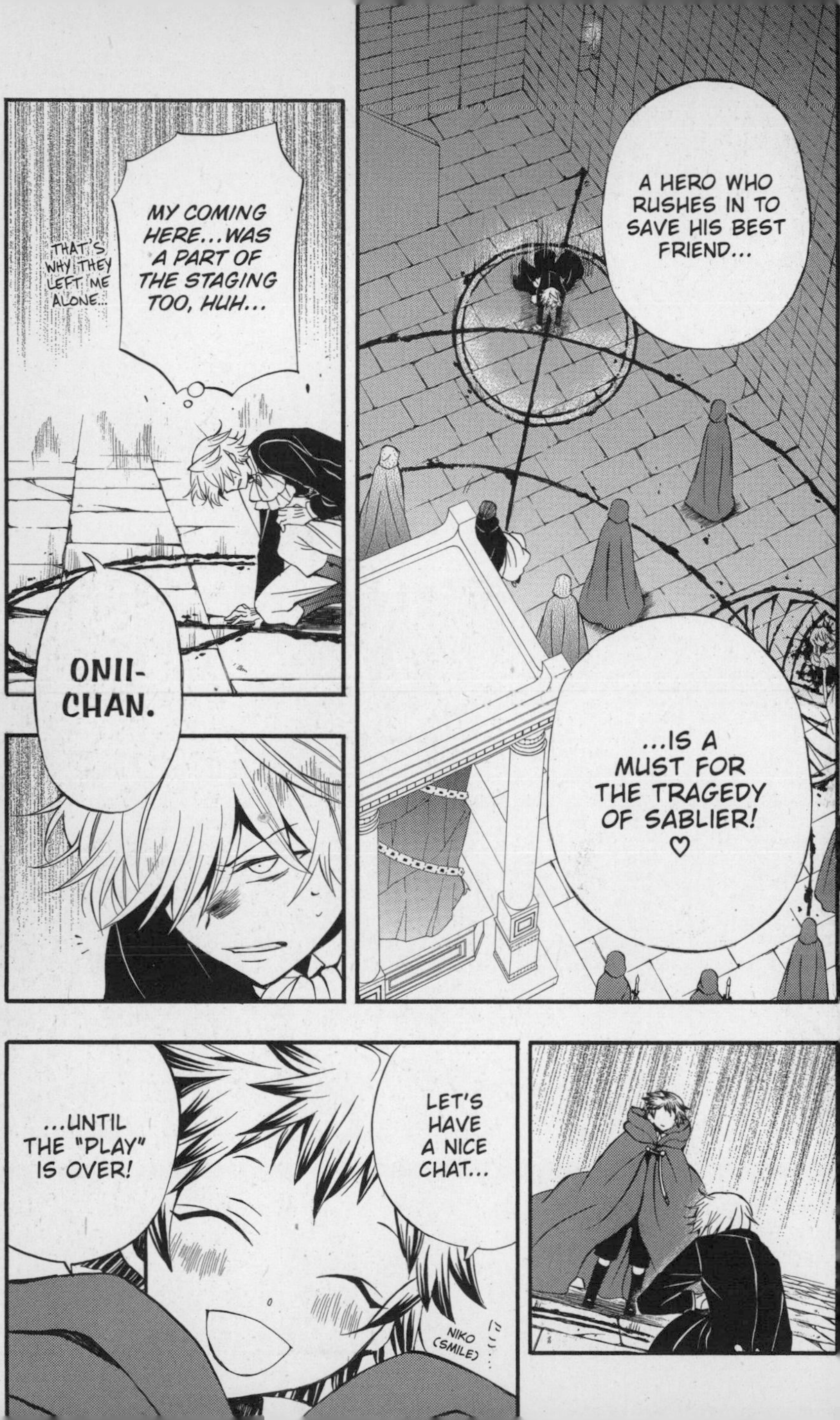
A HERO WHO RUSHES IN TO SAVE HIS BEST FRIEND...
...IS A MUST FOR THE TRAGEDY OF SABLIER! ♡
MY COMING HERE...WAS A PART OF THE STAGING TOO, HUH...
THAT'S WHY THEY LEFT ME ALONE...
ONII-CHAN.
LET'S HAVE A NICE CHAT...
...UNTIL THE "PLAY" IS OVER!
NIKO (SMILE)

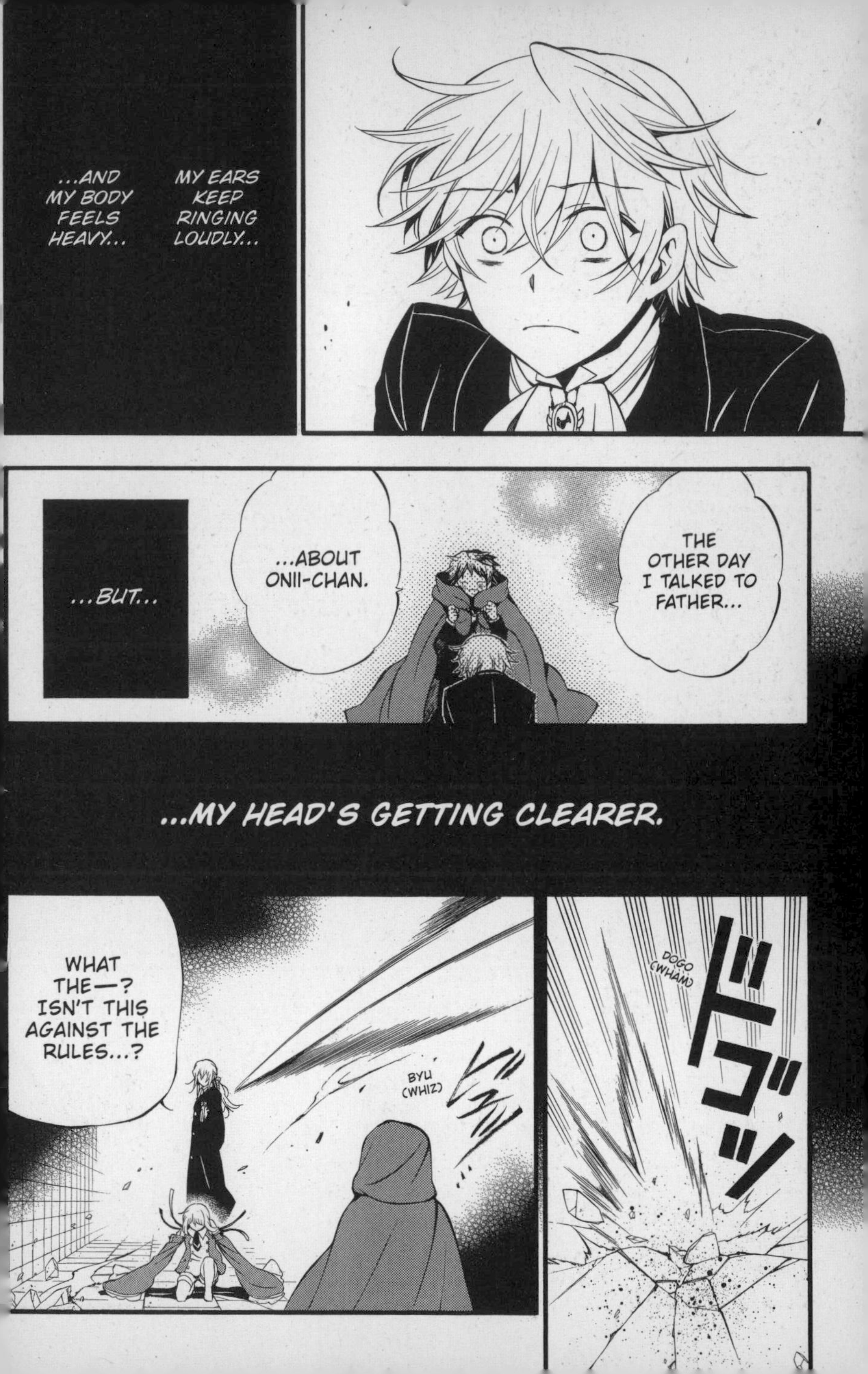
MY EARS KEEP RINGING LOUDLY...
...AND MY BODY FEELS HEAVY...
THE OTHER DAY I TALKED TO FATHER...
...ABOUT ONII-CHAN.
...BUT...
...MY HEAD'S GETTING CLEARER.
ドゴッ
DOGO (WHAM)
BYU (WHIZ)
WHAT THE—? ISN'T THIS AGAINST THE RULES...?

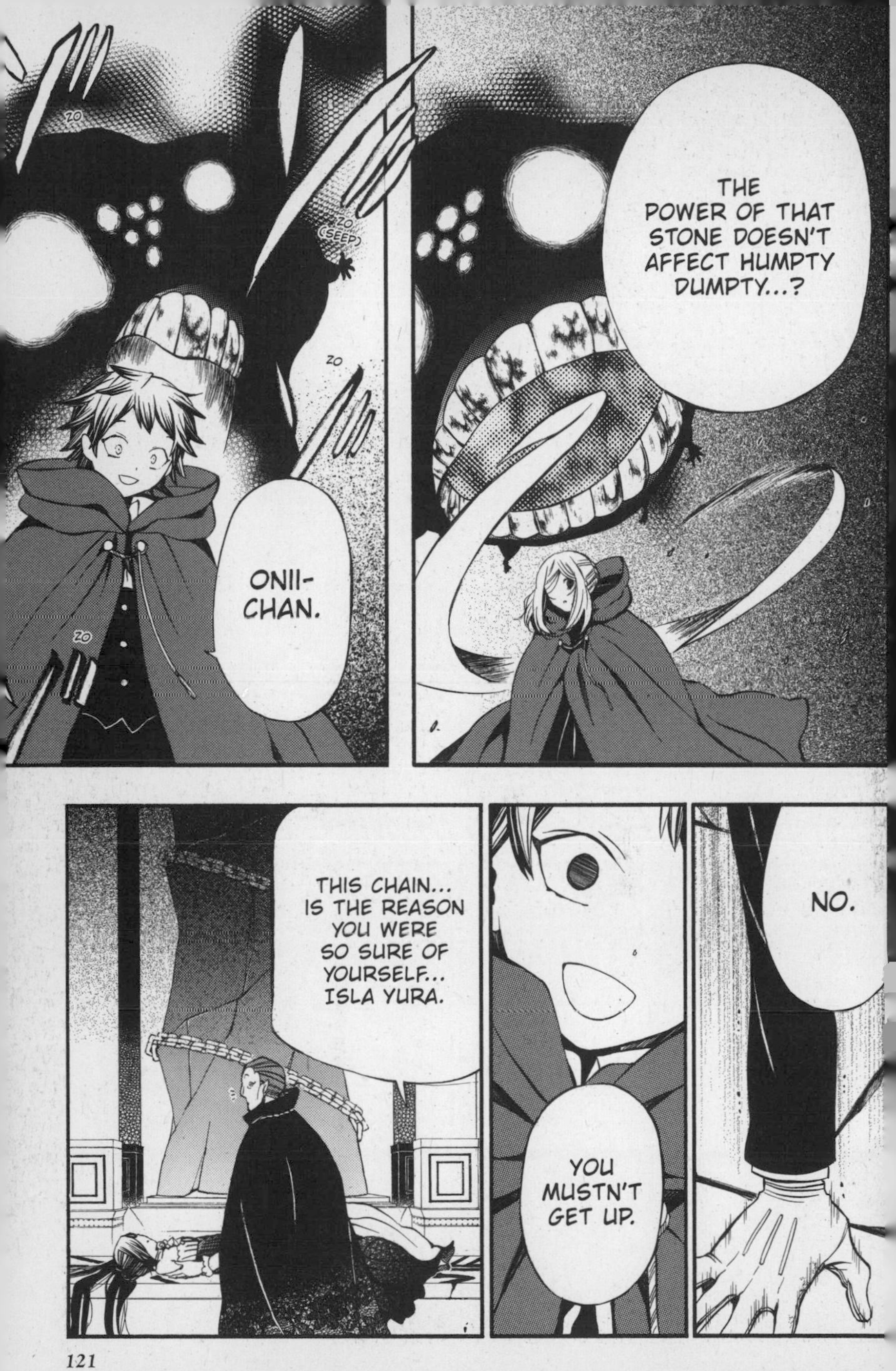
THE POWER OF THAT STONE DOESN'T AFFECT HUMPTY DUMPTY...?
ZO
ZO (SEEP)
ZO
ONII-CHAN.
ZO
NO.
YOU MUSTN'T GET UP.
THIS CHAIN... IS THE REASON YOU WERE SO SURE OF YOURSELF... ISLA YURA.

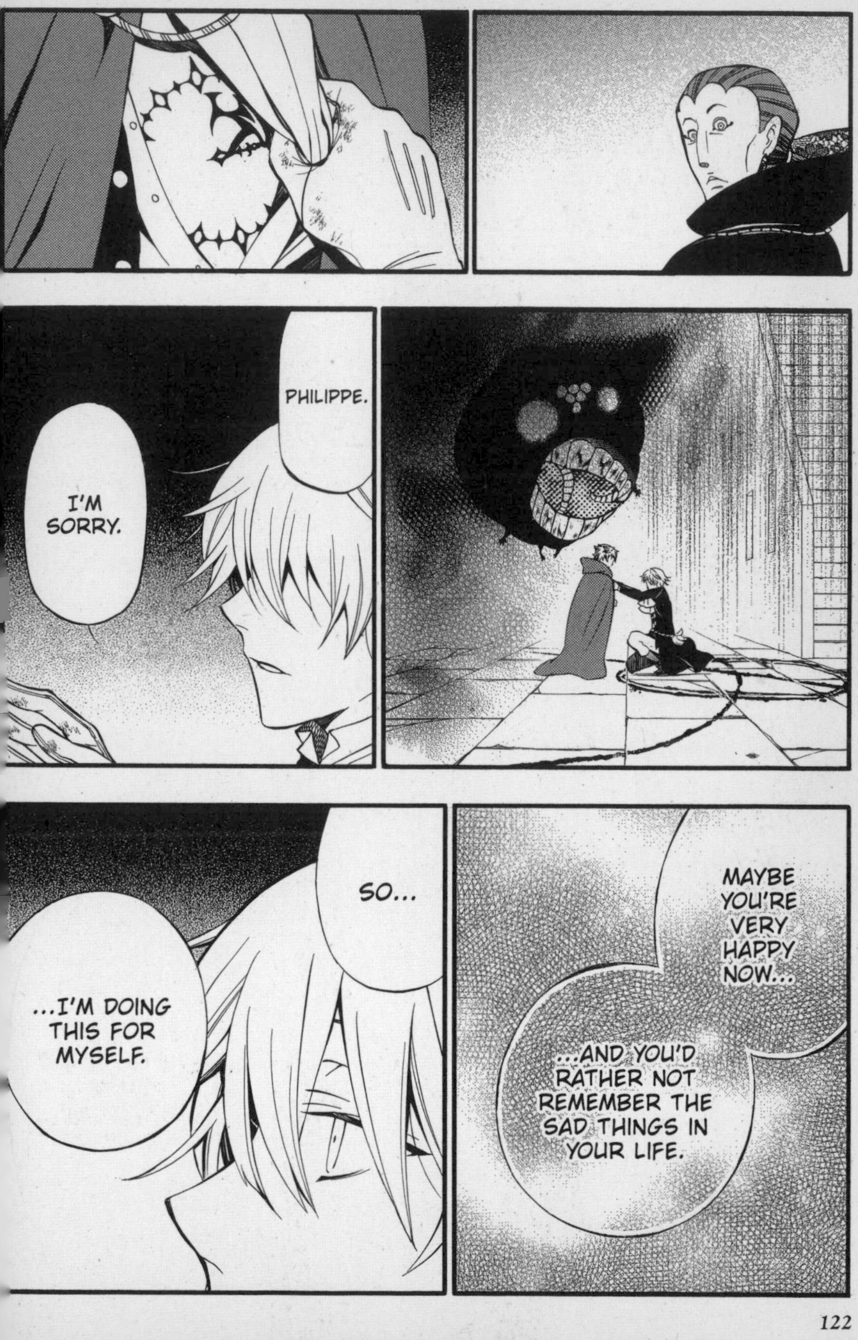
PHILIPPE.
I'M SORRY.
MAYBE YOU'RE VERY HAPPY NOW...
...AND YOU'D RATHER NOT REMEMBER THE SAD THINGS IN YOUR LIFE.
SO...
...I'M DOING THIS FOR MYSELF.

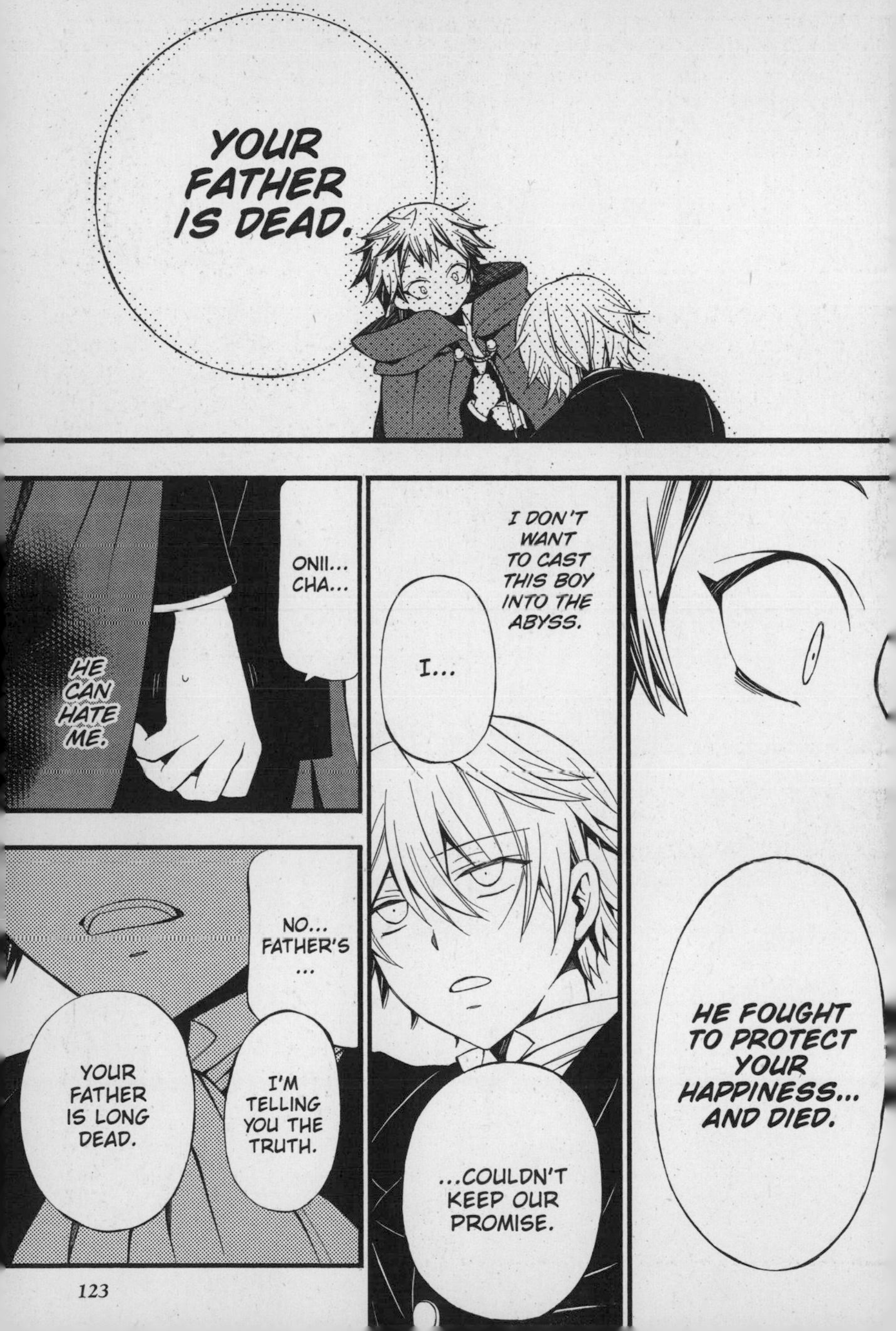
YOUR FATHER IS DEAD.
HE FOUGHT TO PROTECT YOUR HAPPINESS... AND DIED.
I DON'T WANT TO CAST THIS BOY INTO THE ABYSS.
I...
...COULDN'T KEEP OUR PROMISE.
ONII... CHA...
HE CAN HATE ME.
NO... FATHER'S ...
I'M TELLING YOU THE TRUTH.
YOUR FATHER IS LONG DEAD.

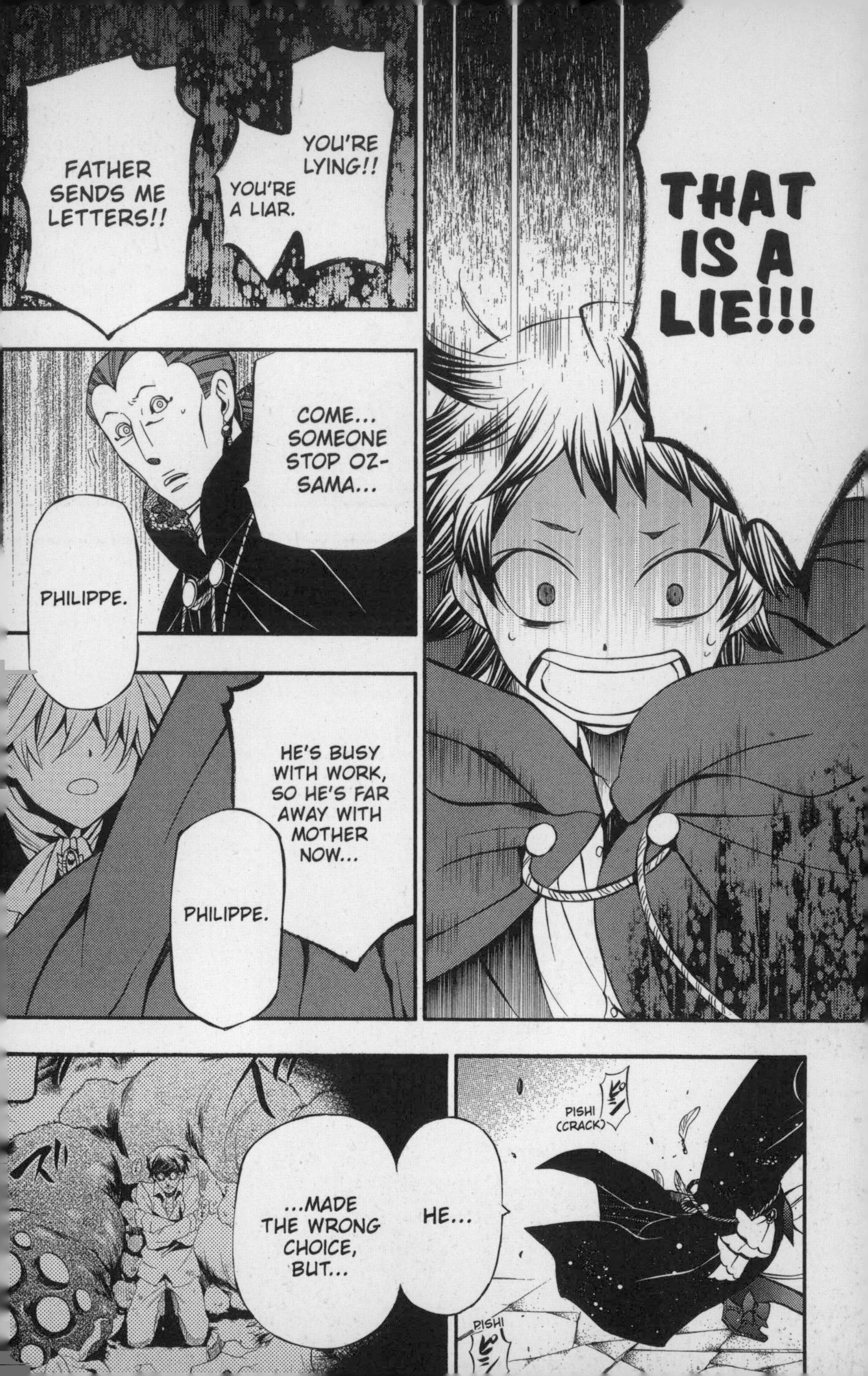
THAT IS A LIE!!!
YOU'RE LYING!!
YOU'RE A LIAR.
FATHER SENDS ME LETTERS!!
COME... SOMEONE STOP OZ-SAMA...
PHILIPPE.
HE'S BUSY WITH WORK, SO HE'S FAR AWAY WITH MOTHER NOW...
PHILIPPE.
PISHI (CRACK)
PISHI
HE...
...MADE THE WRONG CHOICE, BUT...

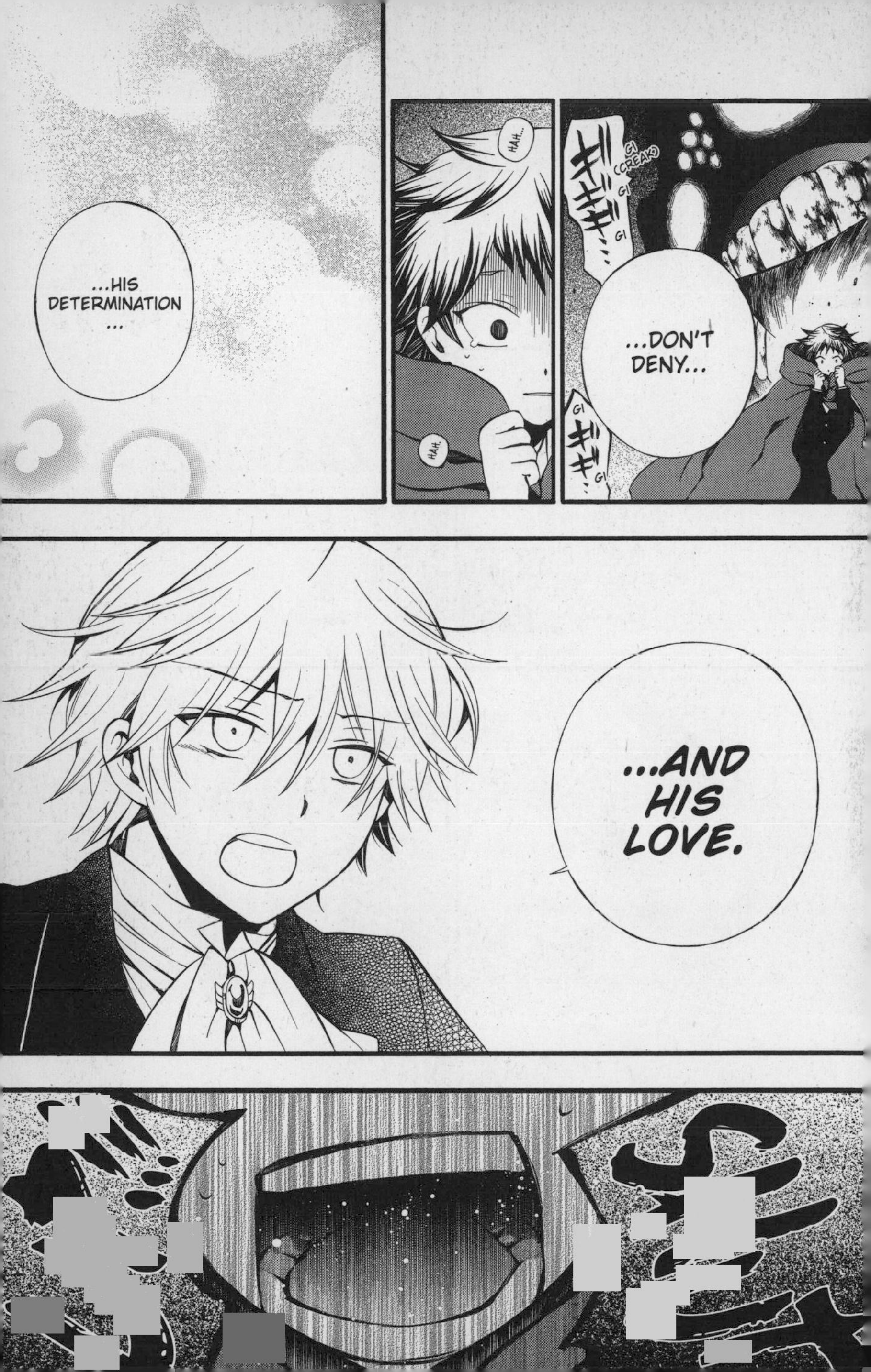
GI (CREAK) GI GI
...DON'T DENY...
GI GI
HAH...
HAH.
...HIS DETERMINATION ...
...AND HIS LOVE.

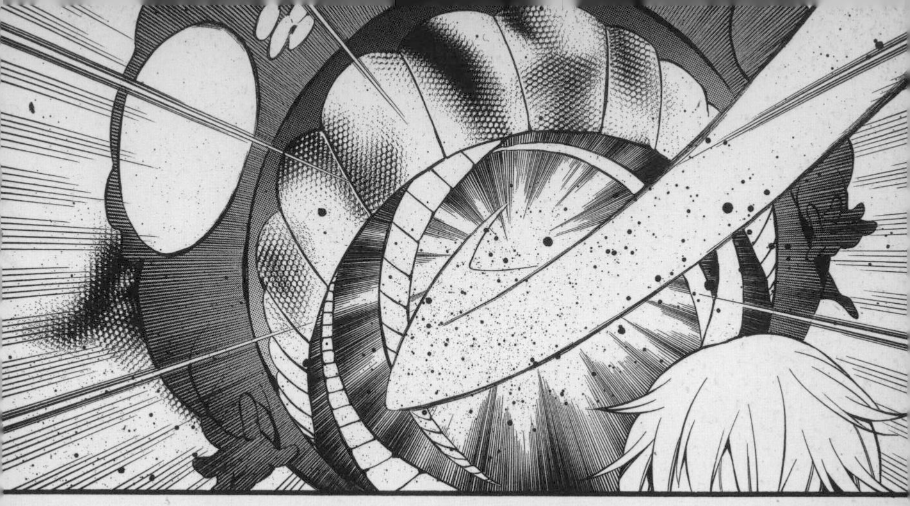

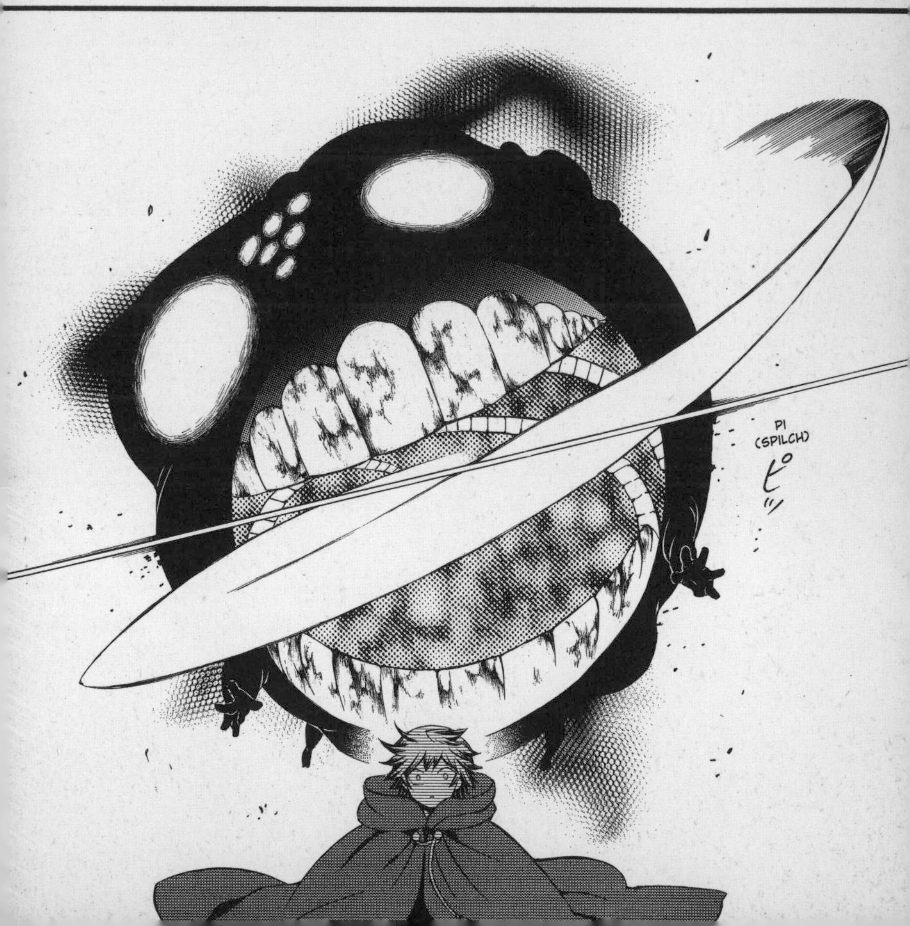
PI
(SPILCH)
ピッ

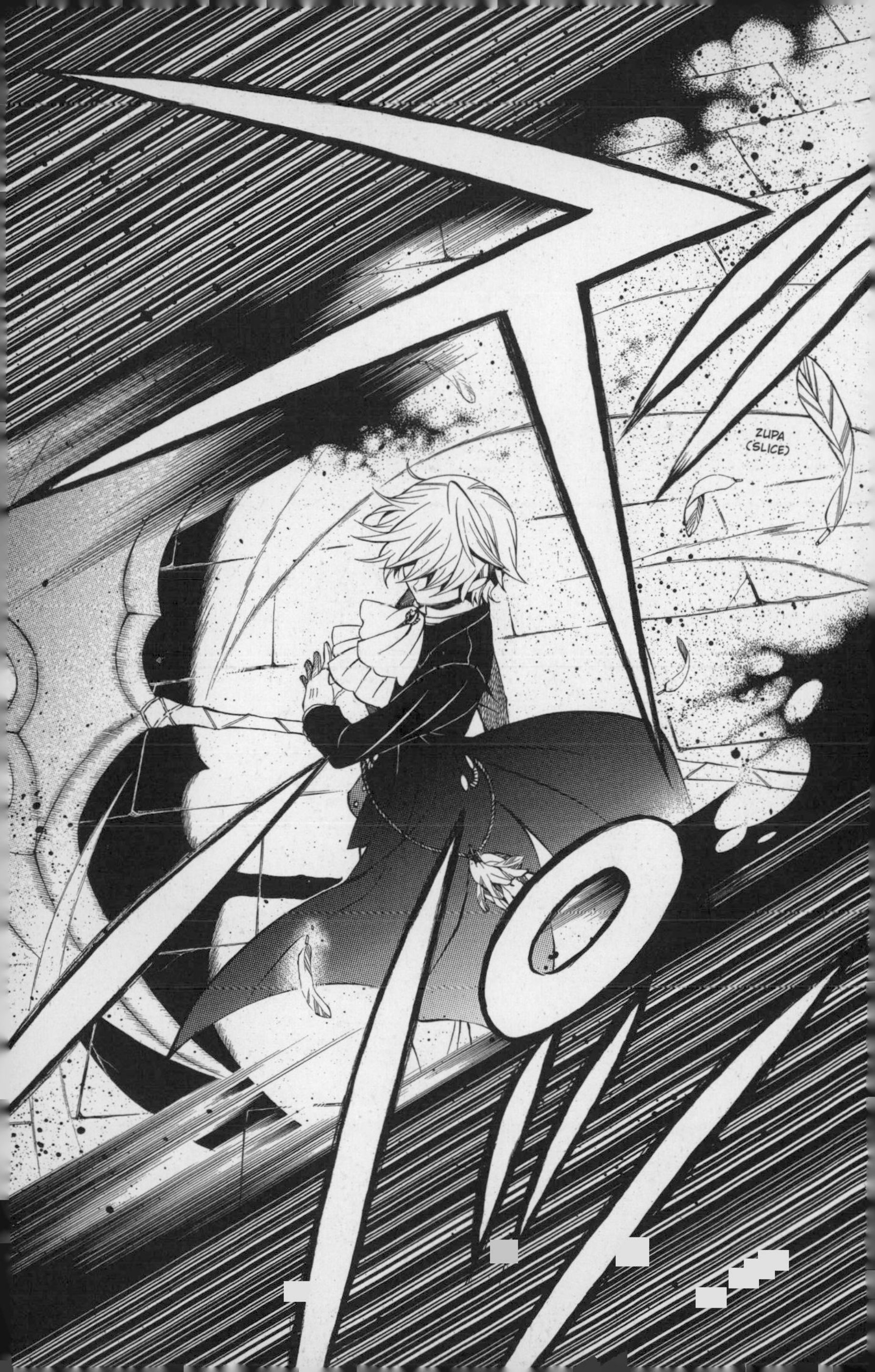
ZUPA
(SLICE)

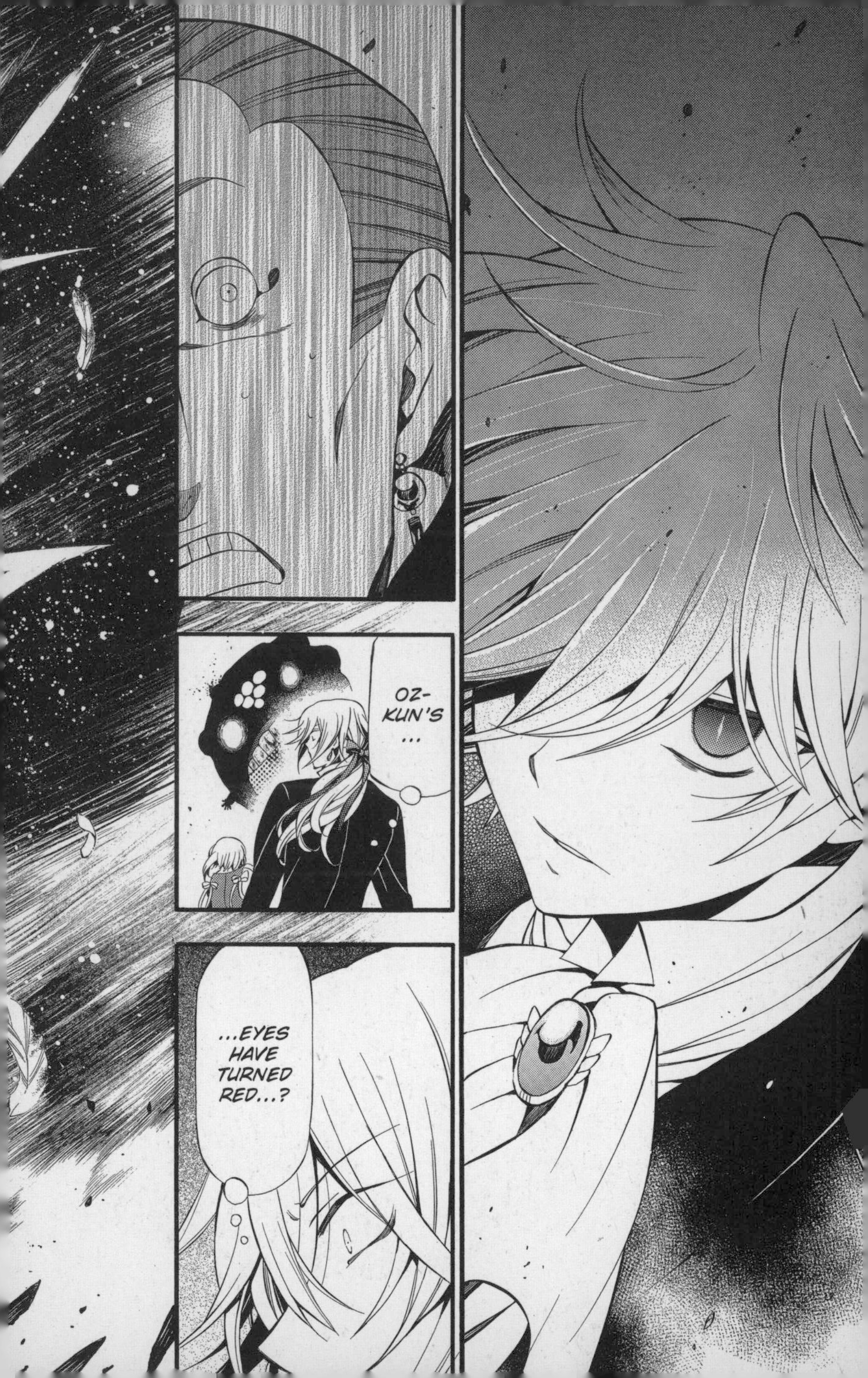
OZ-KUN'S ...
...EYES HAVE TURNED RED...?

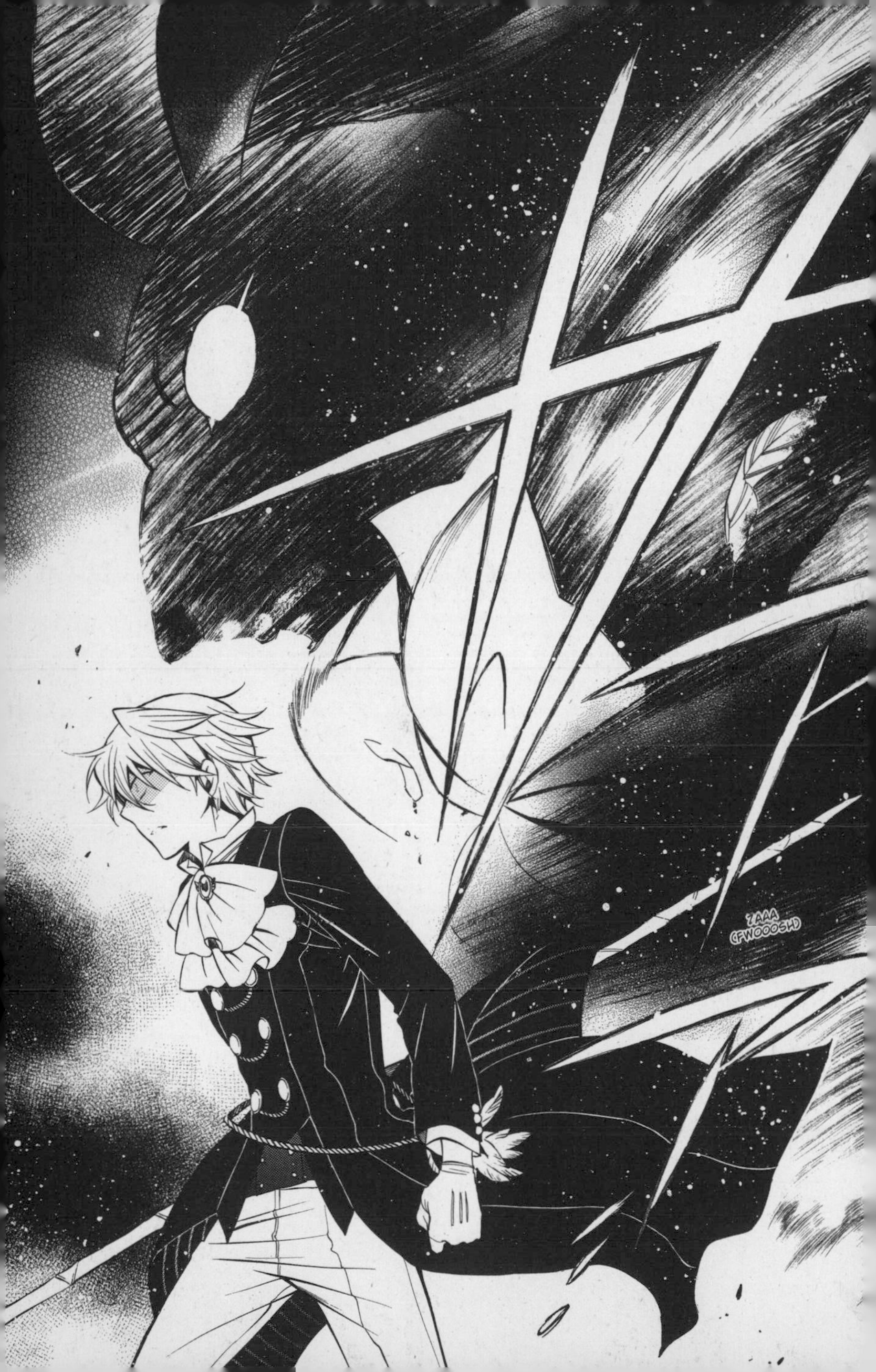
ZAAA
(FWOOOSH)

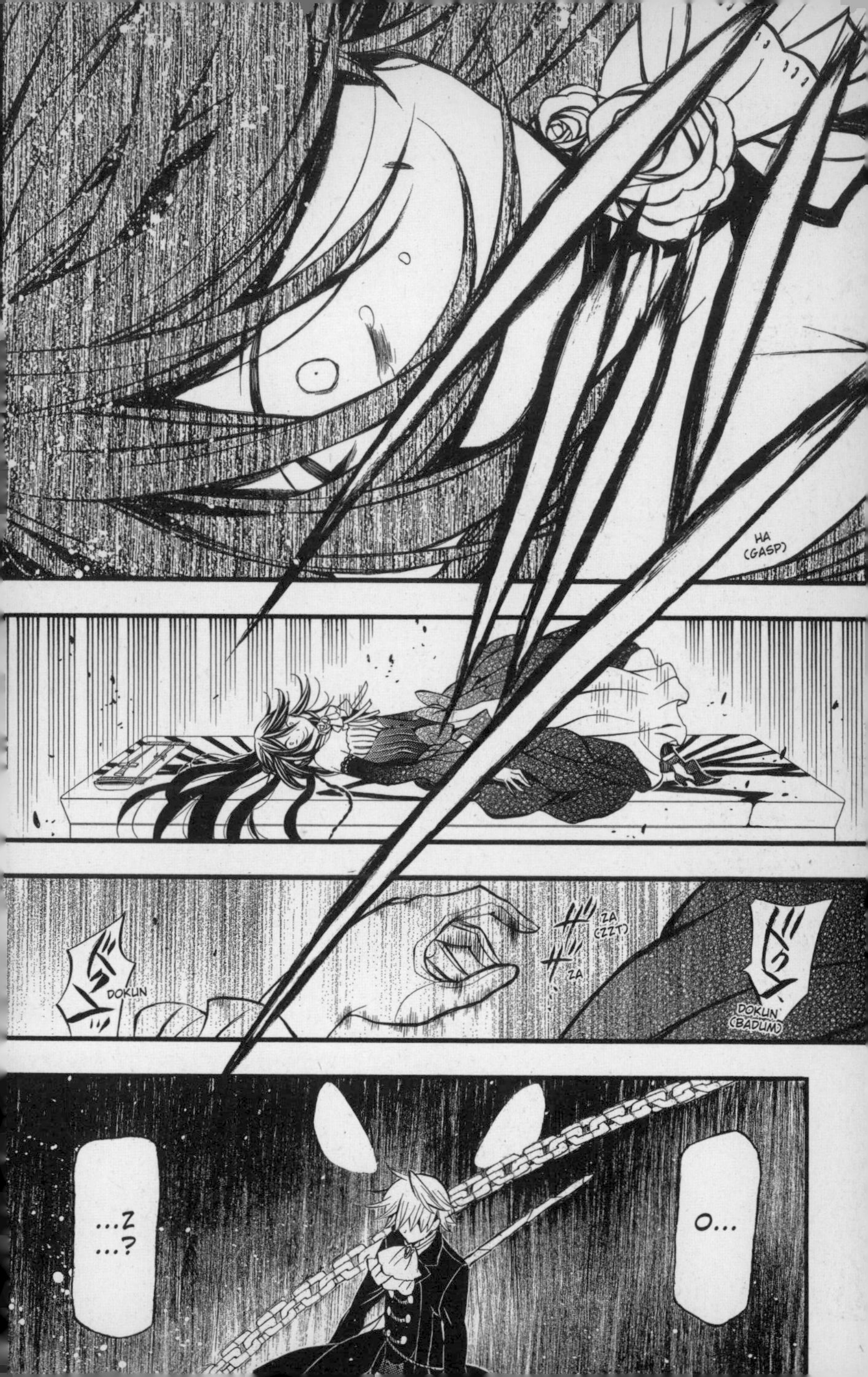
HA
(GASP)
DOKUN
(BADUM)
ZA
(ZZT)
ZA
DOKUN
O...
...Z
...?

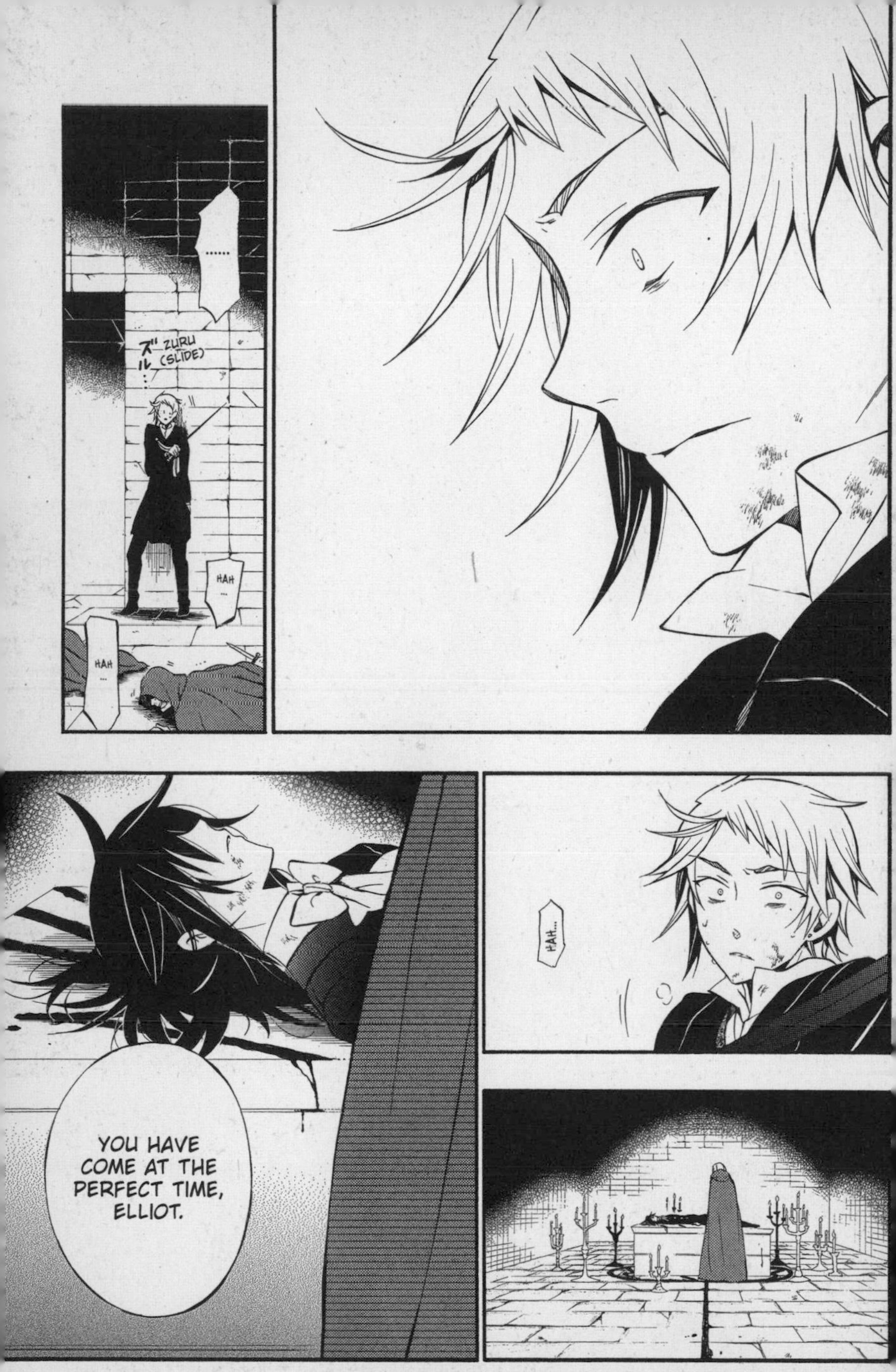
......
ズル ZURU (SLIDE)
HAH...
HAH...
HAH...
YOU HAVE COME AT THE PERFECT TIME, ELLIOT.

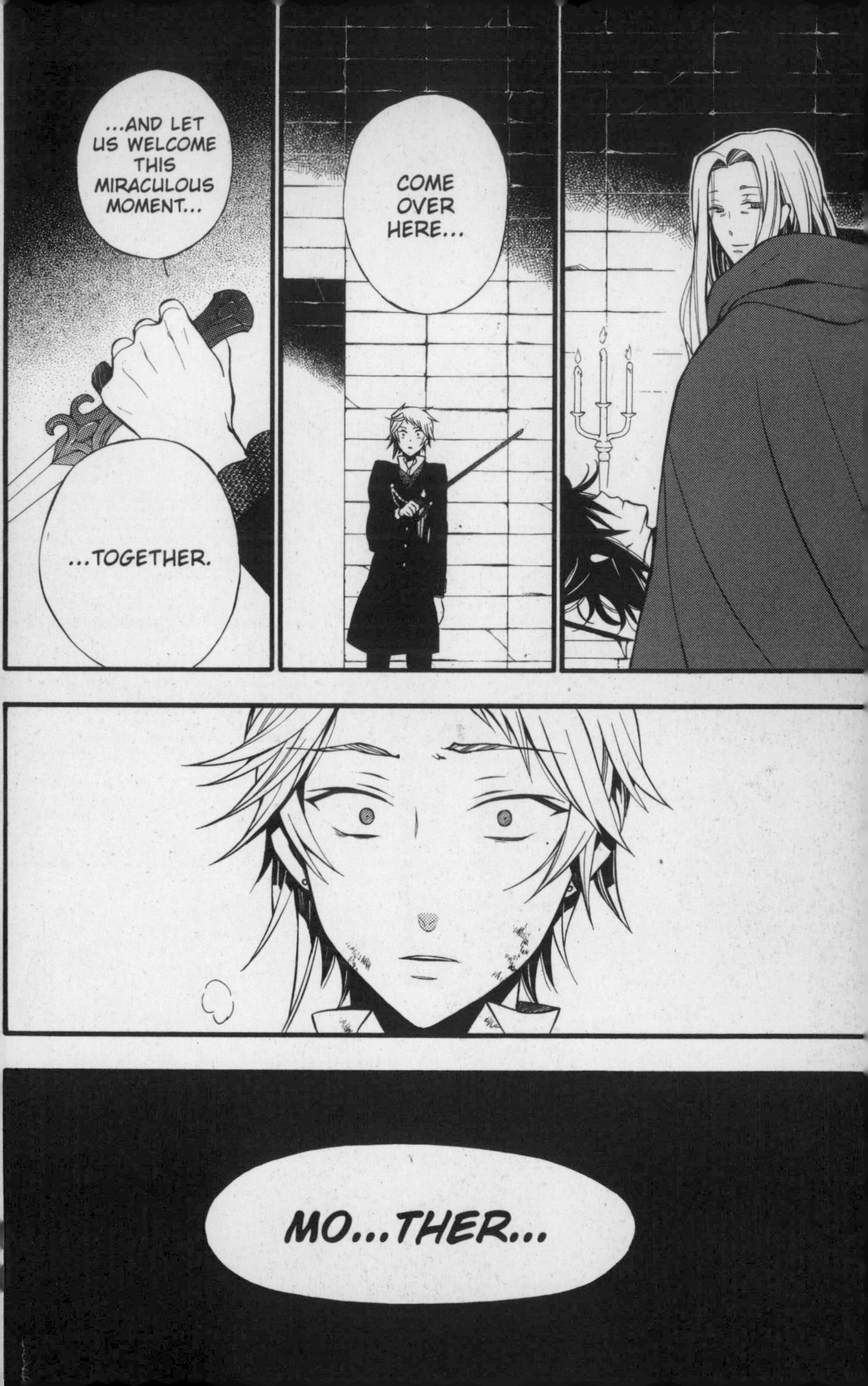
COME OVER HERE...
...AND LET US WELCOME THIS MIRACULOUS MOMENT...
...TOGETHER.
MO...THER...

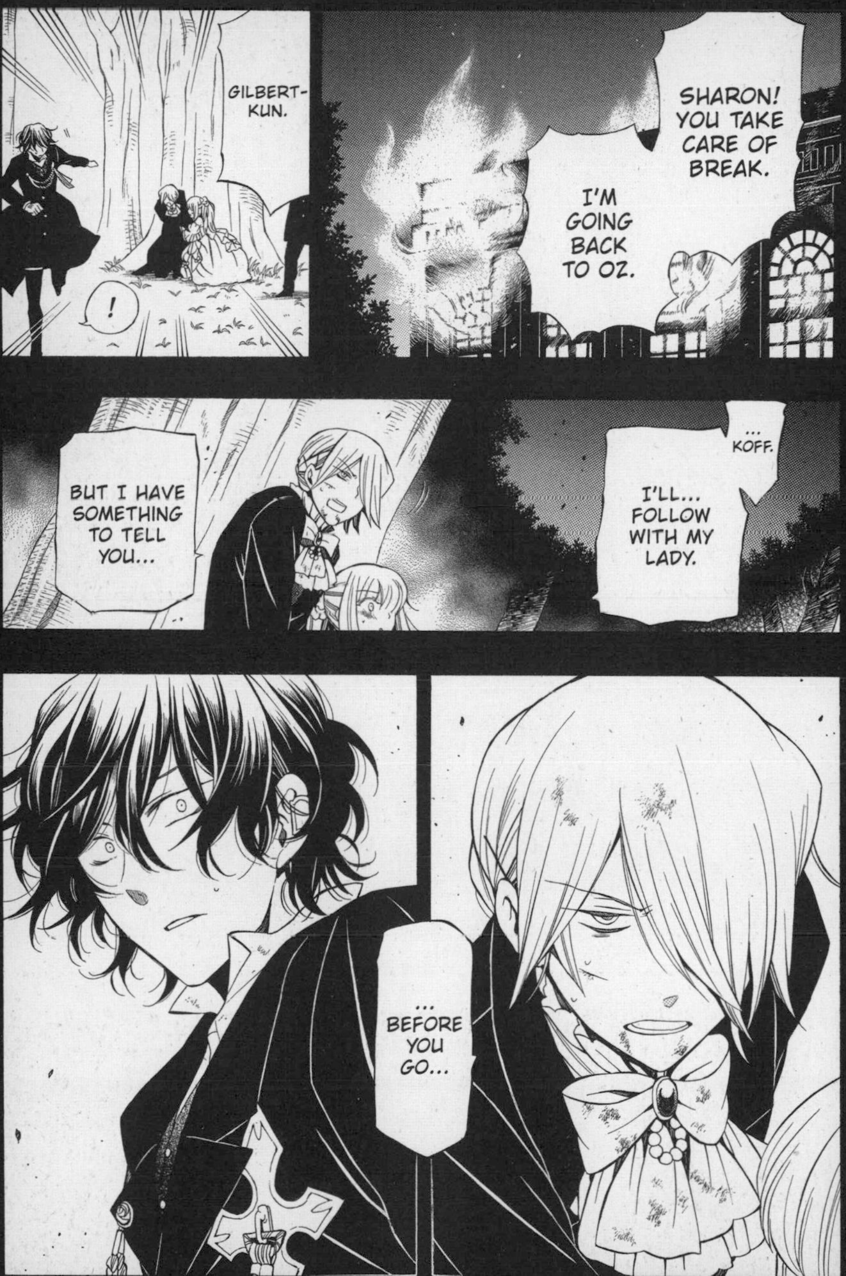
SHARON! YOU TAKE CARE OF BREAK.
I'M GOING BACK TO OZ.
GILBERT-KUN.
!
...KOFF.
I'LL... FOLLOW WITH MY LADY.
BUT I HAVE SOMETHING TO TELL YOU...
...BEFORE YOU GO...

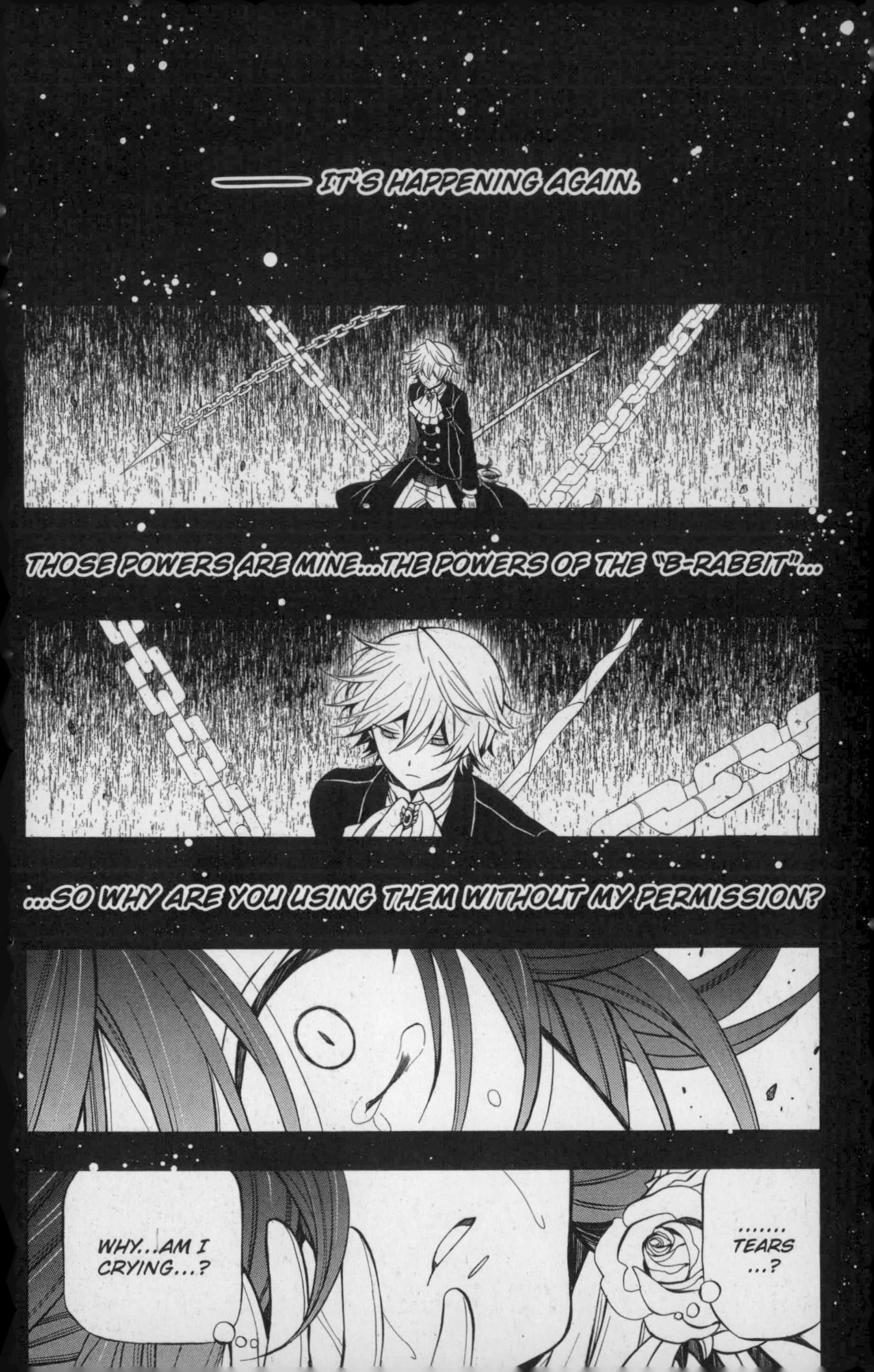
——IT'S HAPPENING AGAIN.
THOSE POWERS ARE MINE...THE POWERS OF THE "B-RABBIT"...
...SO WHY ARE YOU USING THEM WITHOUT MY PERMISSION?
.......TEARS...?
WHY...AM I CRYING...?

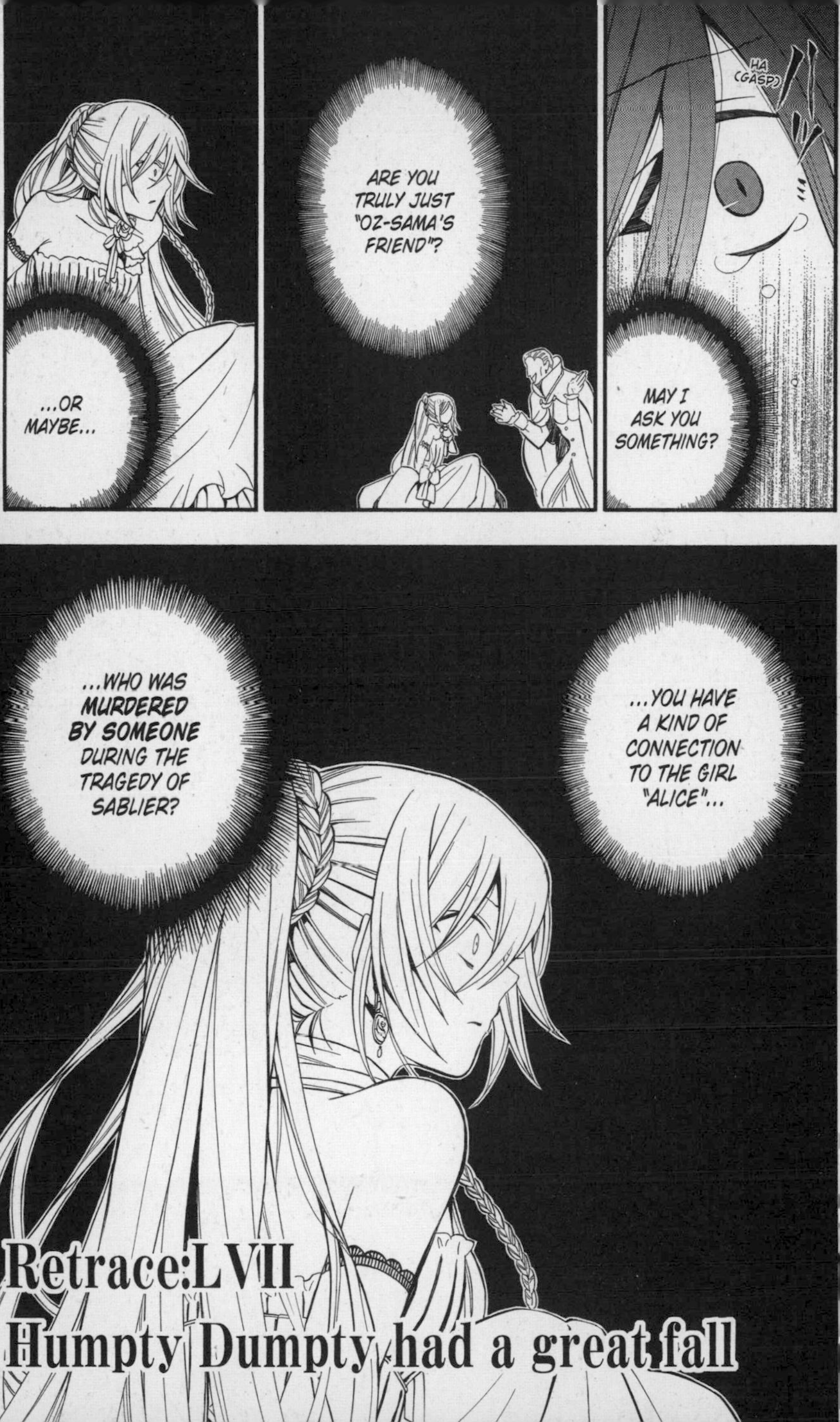
HA (GASP)
MAY I ASK YOU SOMETHING?
ARE YOU TRULY JUST "OZ-SAMA'S FRIEND"?
...OR MAYBE...
...YOU HAVE A KIND OF CONNECTION TO THE GIRL "ALICE"...
...WHO WAS MURDERED BY SOMEONE DURING THE TRAGEDY OF SABLIER?
Retrace:LVII
Humpty Dumpty had a great fall

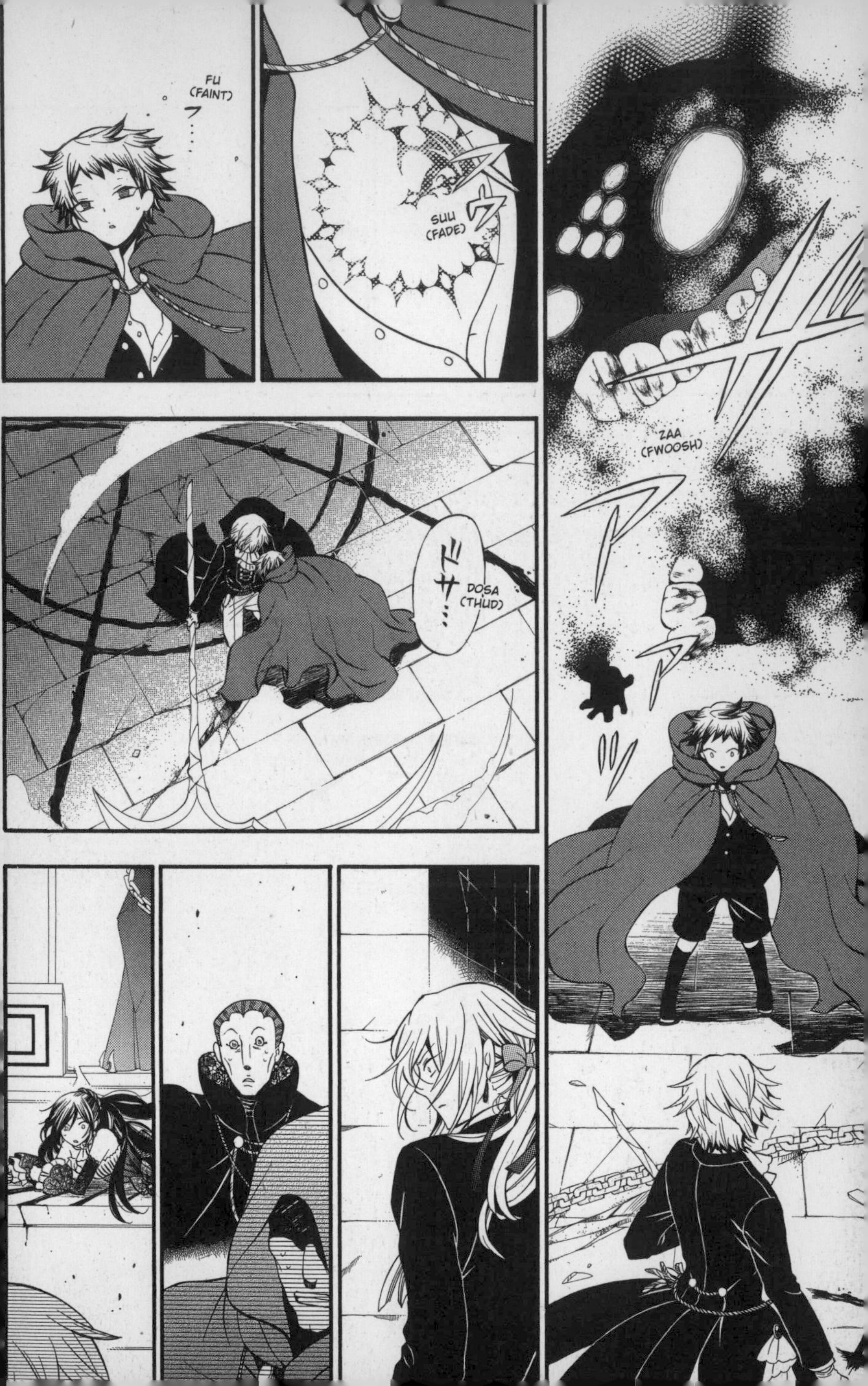
ZAA
(FWOOSH)
SUU
(FADE)
FU
(FAINT)
ドサ…
DOSA
(THUD)

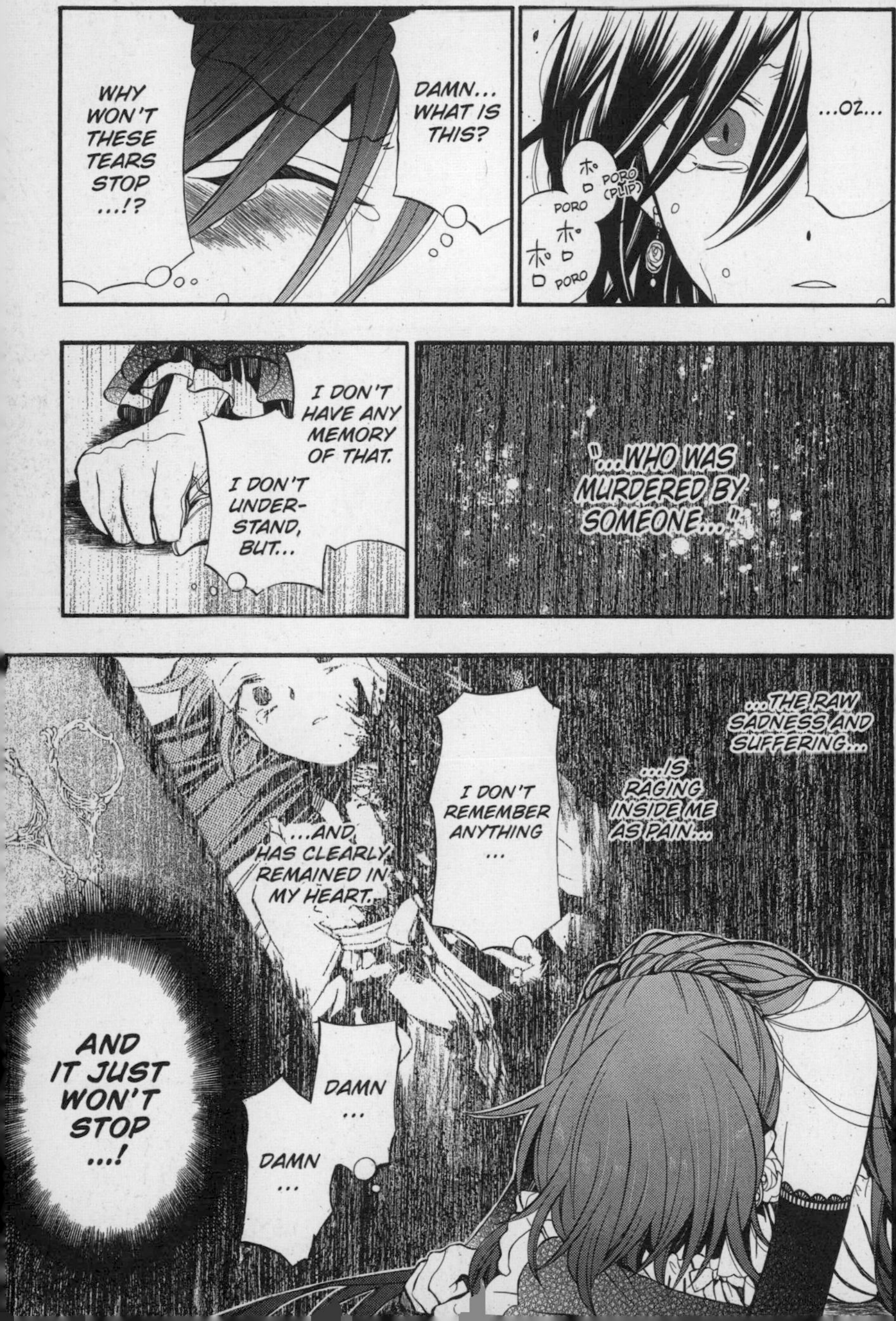
...OZ...
ポロ
PORO (PLIP)
PORO
ポロ
ポロ
PORO
DAMN... WHAT IS THIS?
WHY WON'T THESE TEARS STOP ...!?
"...WHO WAS MURDERED BY SOMEONE..."
I DON'T HAVE ANY MEMORY OF THAT.
I DON'T UNDERSTAND, BUT...
...THE RAW SADNESS AND SUFFERING...
...IS RAGING INSIDE ME AS PAIN...
I DON'T REMEMBER ANYTHING ...
...AND HAS CLEARLY REMAINED IN MY HEART.
DAMN ...
DAMN ...
AND IT JUST WON'T STOP ...!

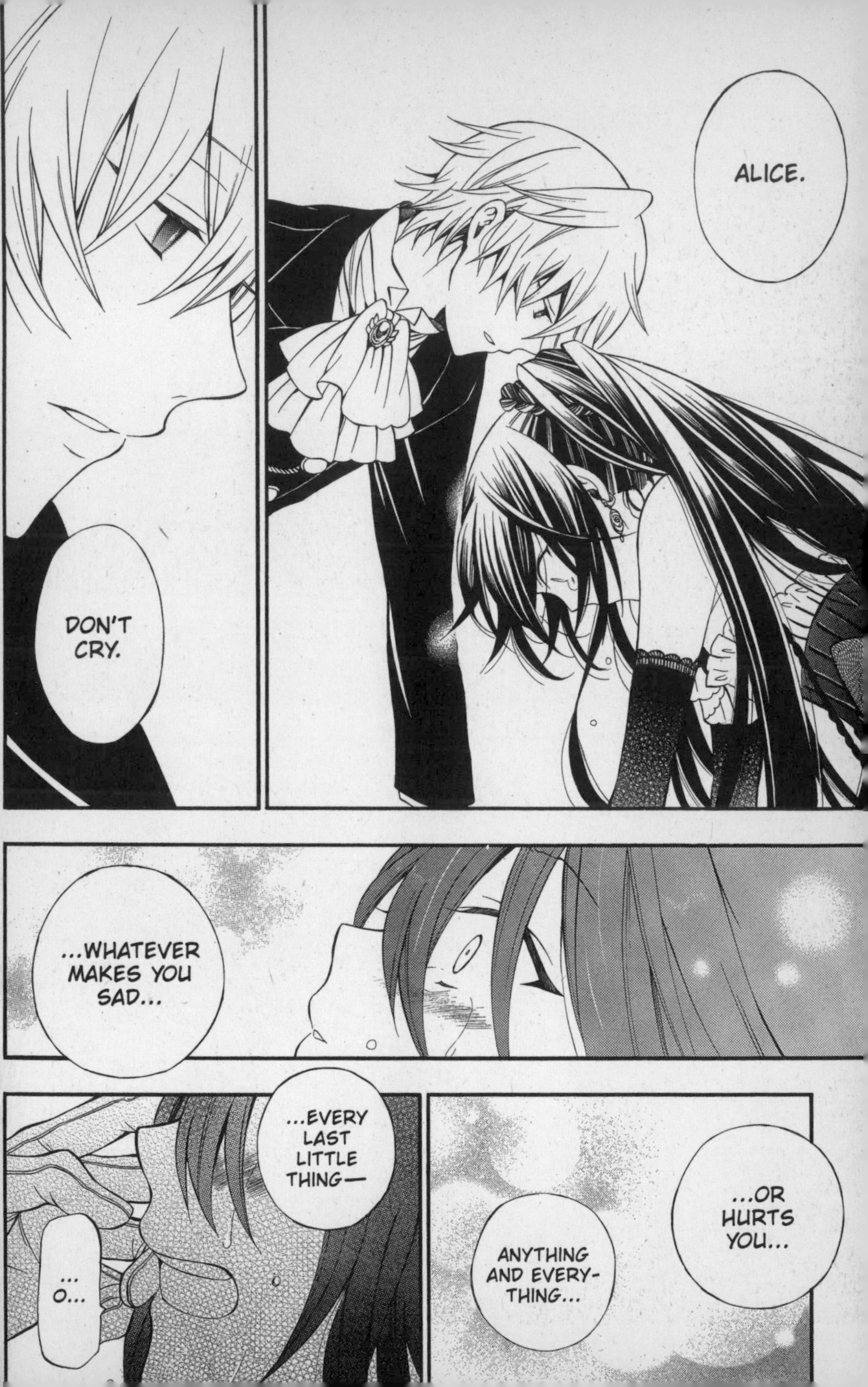
ALICE.
DON'T CRY.
...WHATEVER MAKES YOU SAD...
...OR HURTS YOU...
ANYTHING AND EVERY-THING...
...EVERY LAST LITTLE THING—
... O...

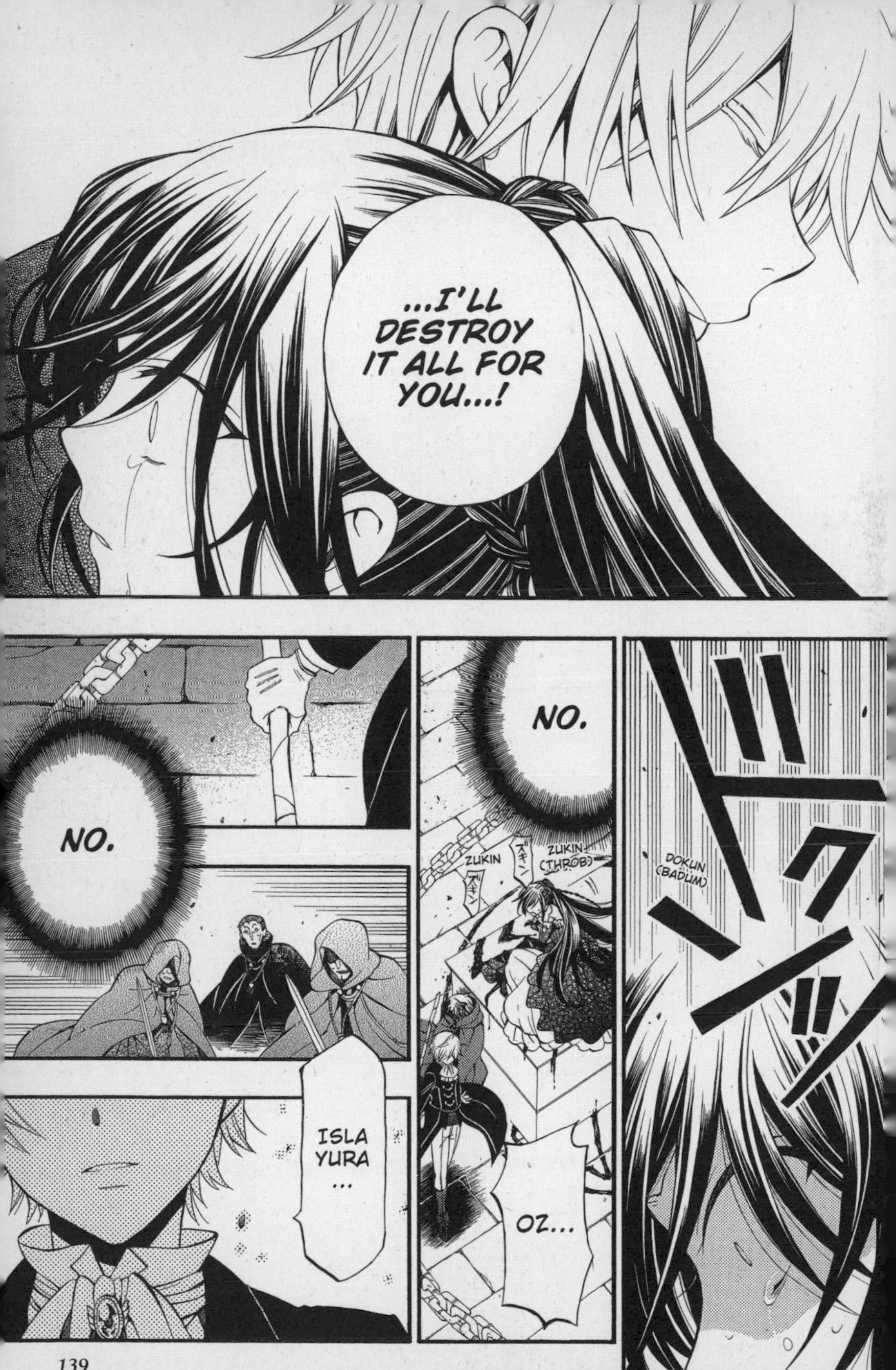
...I'LL DESTROY IT ALL FOR YOU...!
DOKUN (BADUM)
NO.
ZUKIN (THROB)
ズキン
ZUKIN
ズキン
OZ...
NO.
ISLA YURA ...

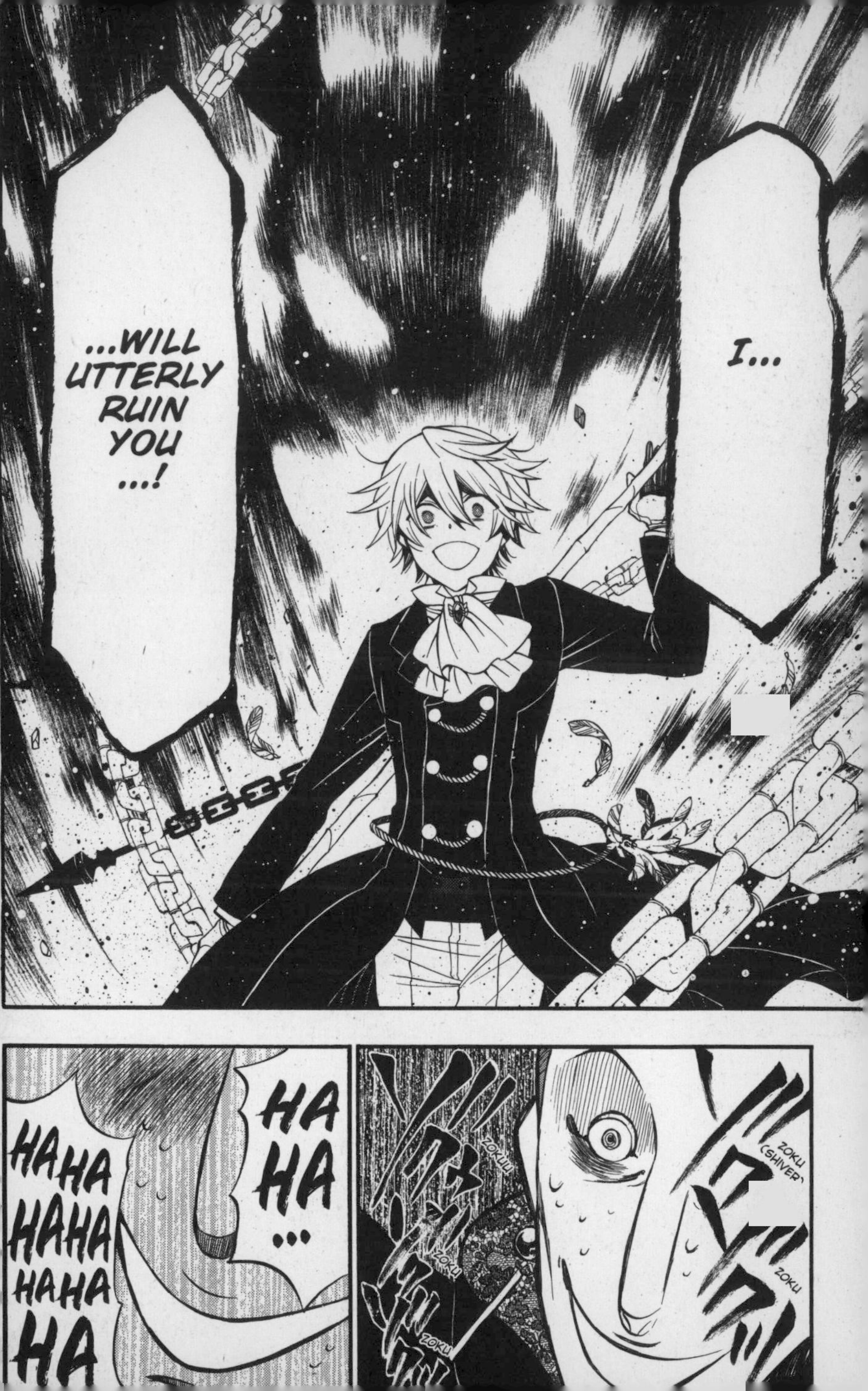
I...
...WILL UTTERLY RUIN YOU ...!
ZOKU (SHIVER)
ZOKU
ZOKU
ZOKU
ZOKU
HA HA ...
HAHA HAHA HAHA HA

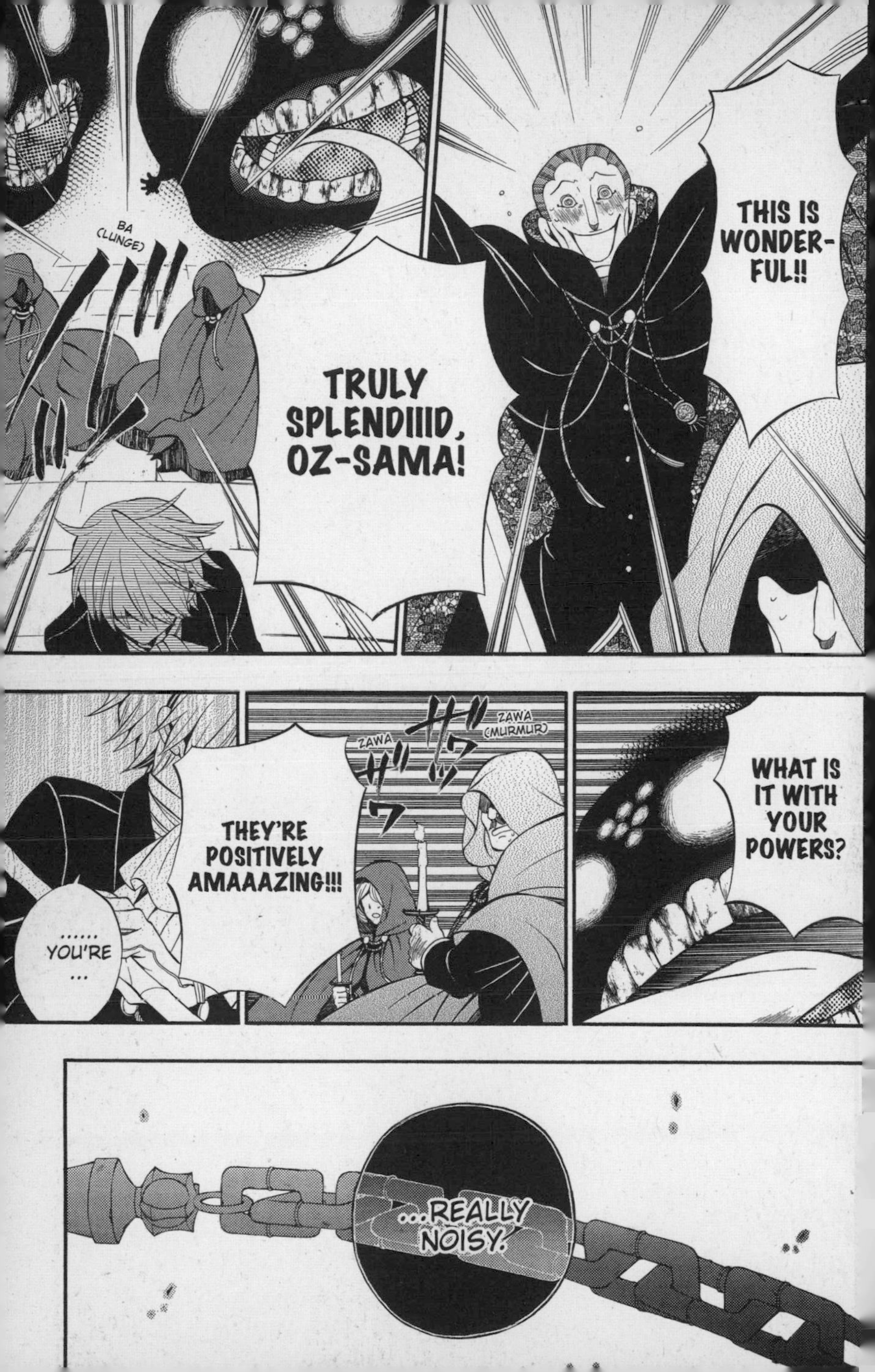
THIS IS WONDERFUL!!
TRULY SPLENDIIIID, OZ-SAMA!
BA (LUNGE)
WHAT IS IT WITH YOUR POWERS?
ZAWA (MURMUR)
ZAWA
THEY'RE POSITIVELY AMAAAZING!!!
...... YOU'RE ...
...REALLY NOISY.

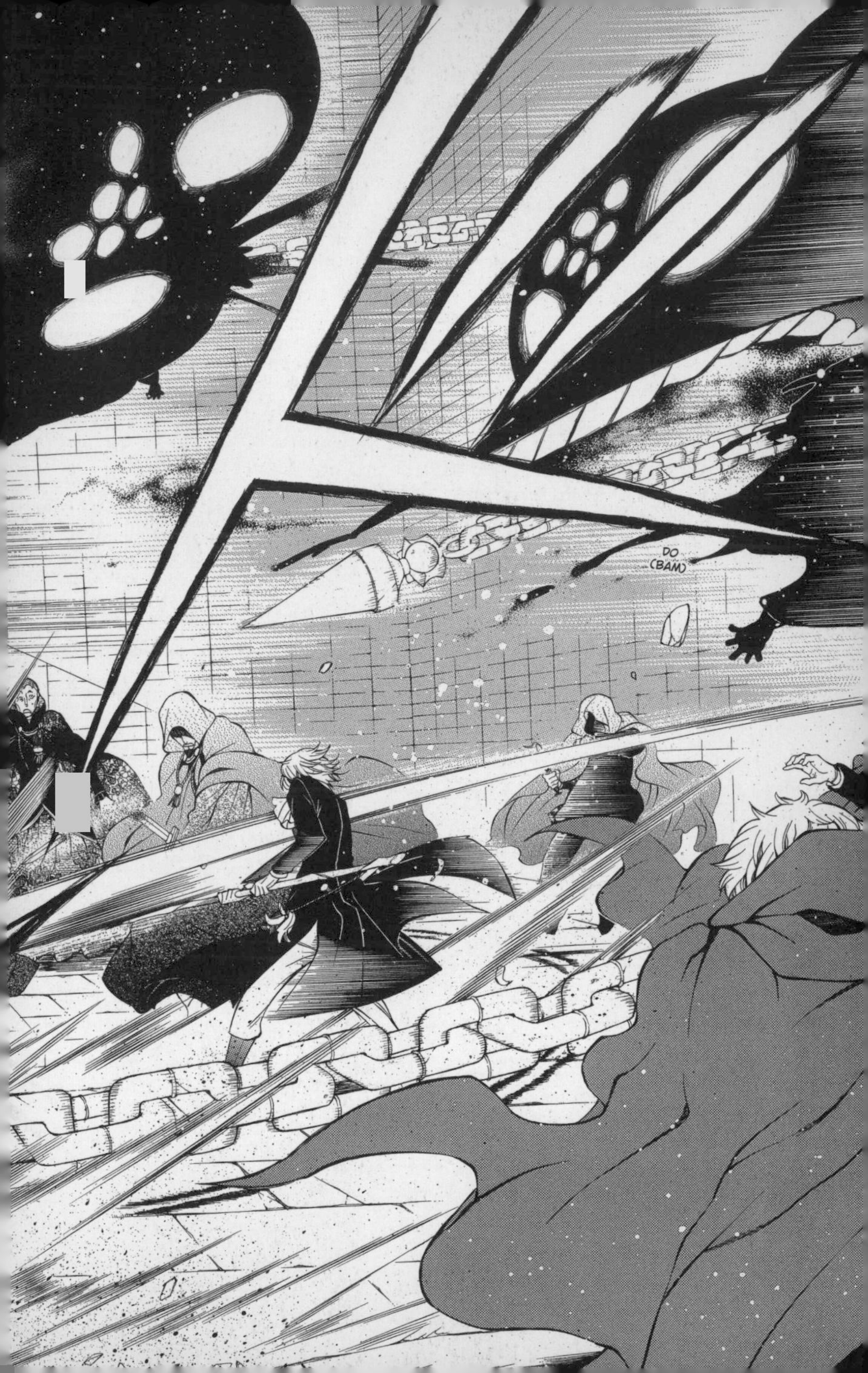
DO
(BAM)

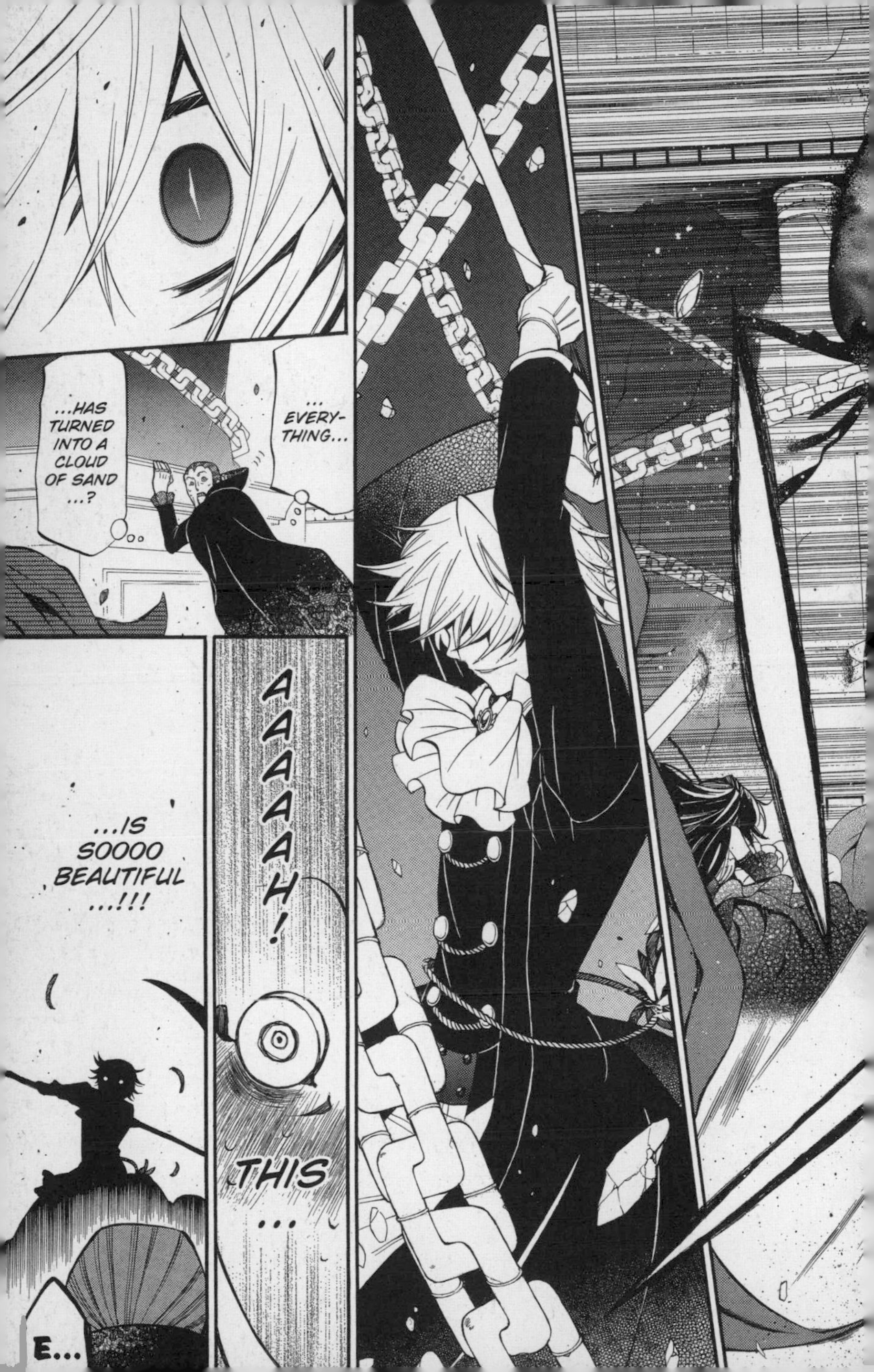

...EVERY-THING...
...HAS TURNED INTO A CLOUD OF SAND ...?
AAAAAAH!
THIS ...
...IS SOOOO BEAUTIFUL ...!!!
E...

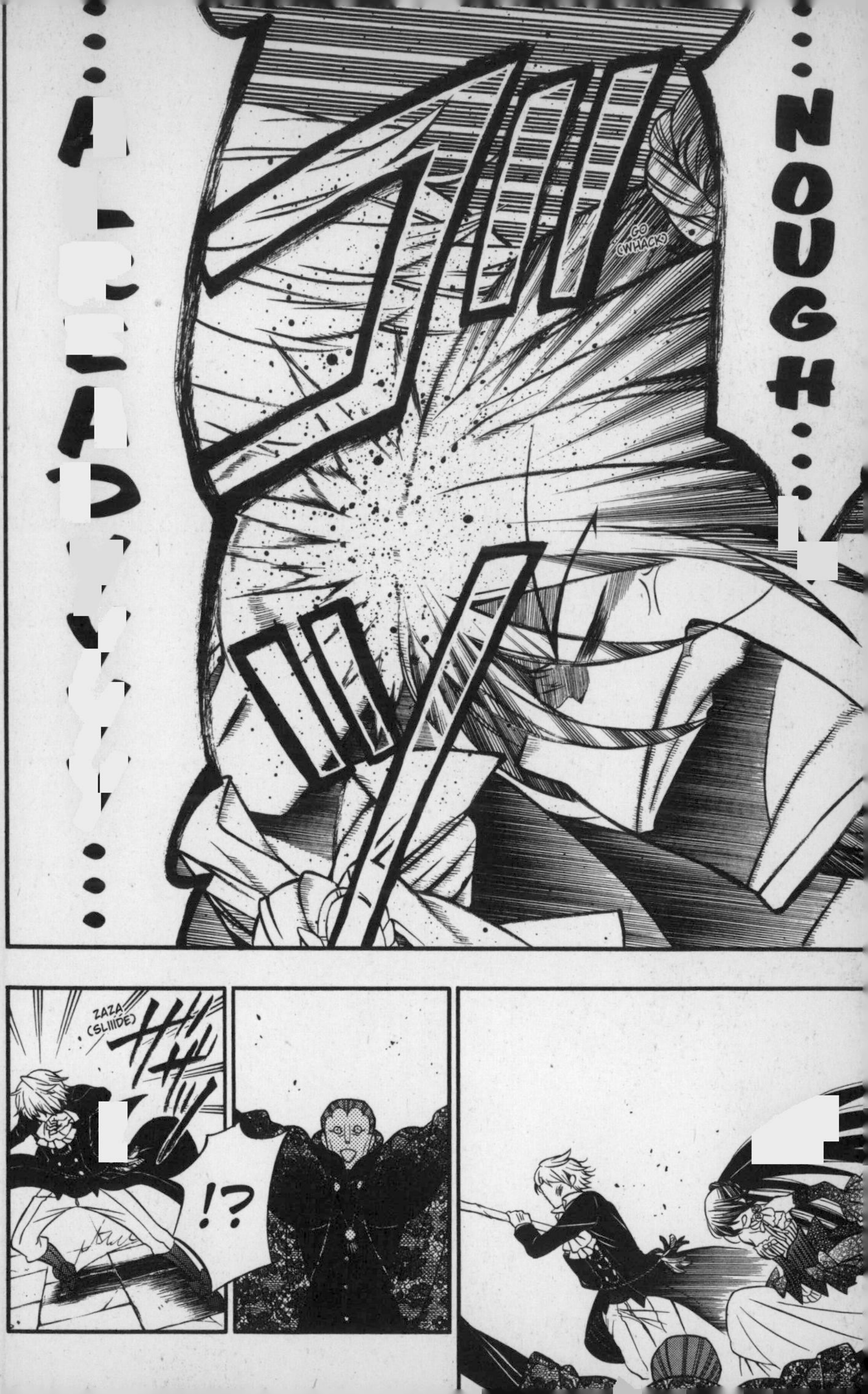
...NOUGH...
GO (WHACK)
!?
ZAZA (SLIIIDE)

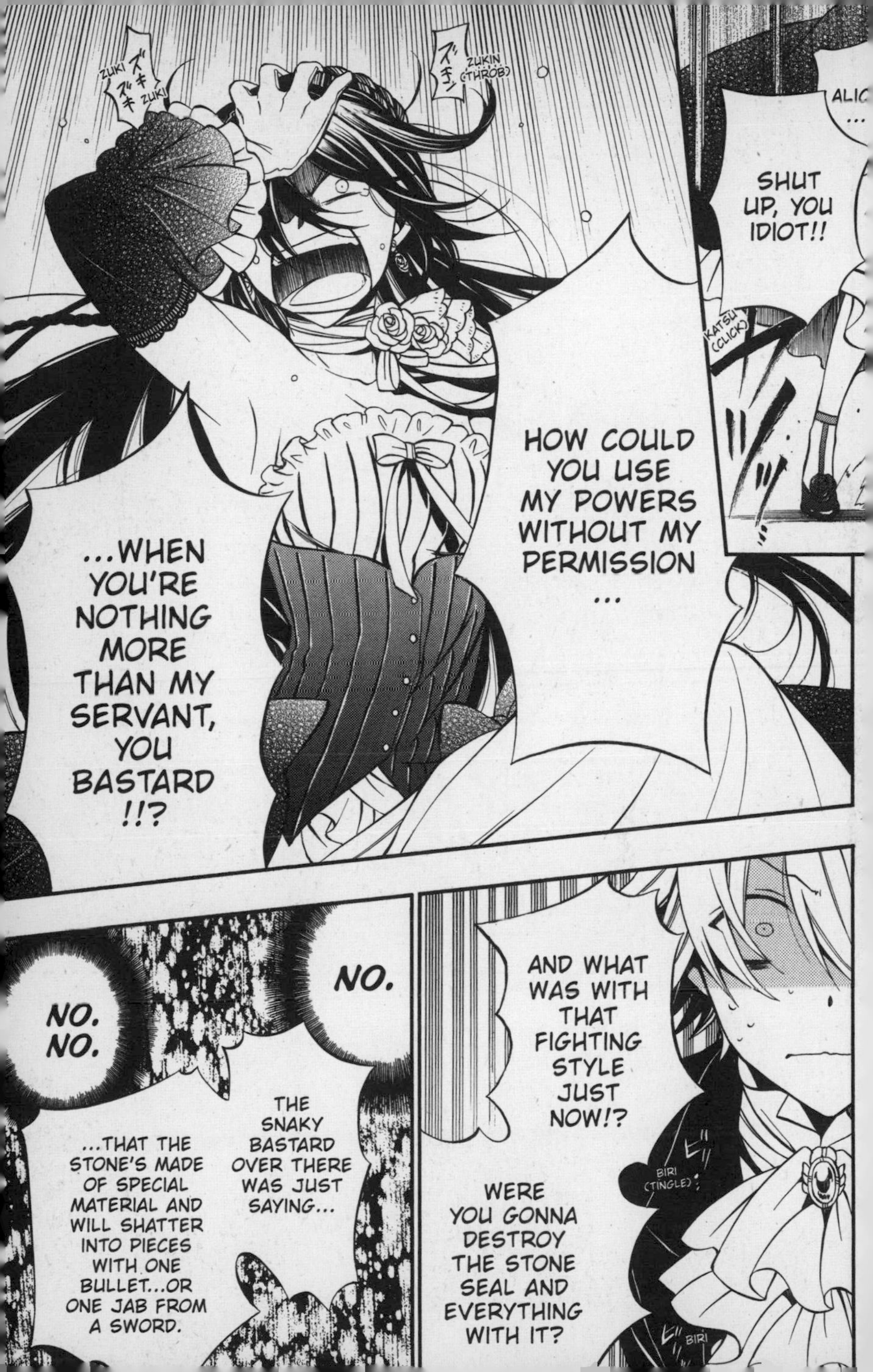
ALIC...
SHUT UP, YOU IDIOT!!
KATSU (CLICK)
ZUKI ZUKI
ZUKIN (THROB)
HOW COULD YOU USE MY POWERS WITHOUT MY PERMISSION...
...WHEN YOU'RE NOTHING MORE THAN MY SERVANT, YOU BASTARD!!?
AND WHAT WAS WITH THAT FIGHTING STYLE JUST NOW!?
BIRI (TINGLE)
WERE YOU GONNA DESTROY THE STONE SEAL AND EVERYTHING WITH IT?
BIRI
NO.
NO. NO.
THE SNAKY BASTARD OVER THERE WAS JUST SAYING...
...THAT THE STONE'S MADE OF SPECIAL MATERIAL AND WILL SHATTER INTO PIECES WITH ONE BULLET...OR ONE JAB FROM A SWORD.

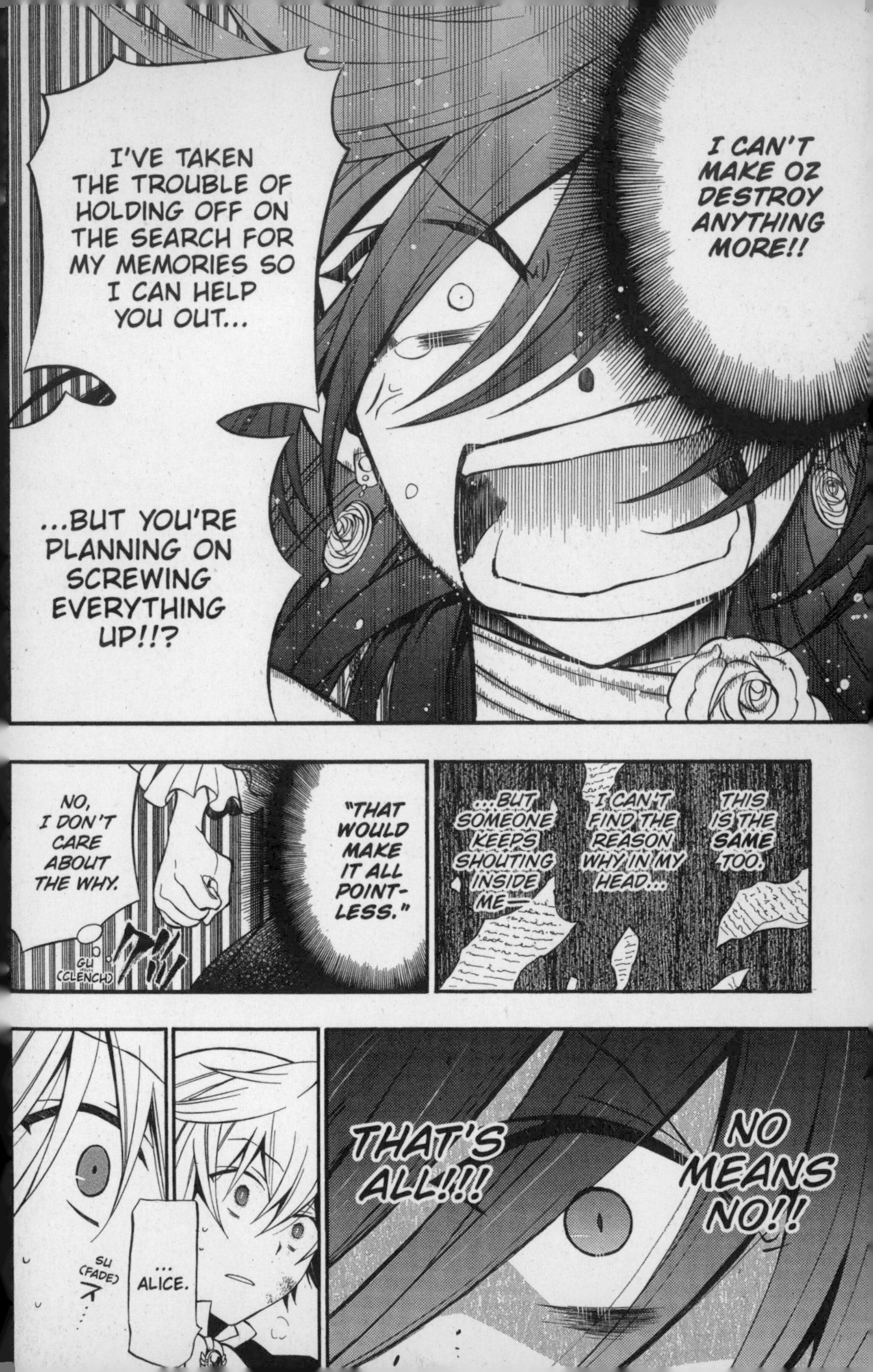
I CAN'T MAKE OZ DESTROY ANYTHING MORE!!
I'VE TAKEN THE TROUBLE OF HOLDING OFF ON THE SEARCH FOR MY MEMORIES SO I CAN HELP YOU OUT...
...BUT YOU'RE PLANNING ON SCREWING EVERYTHING UP!!?
THIS IS THE SAME TOO.
I CAN'T FIND THE REASON WHY IN MY HEAD...
...BUT SOMEONE KEEPS SHOUTING INSIDE ME—
"THAT WOULD MAKE IT ALL POINT-LESS."
NO, I DON'T CARE ABOUT THE WHY.
GU (CLENCH)
NO MEANS NO!!
THAT'S ALL!!!
... ALICE.
SU (FADE)

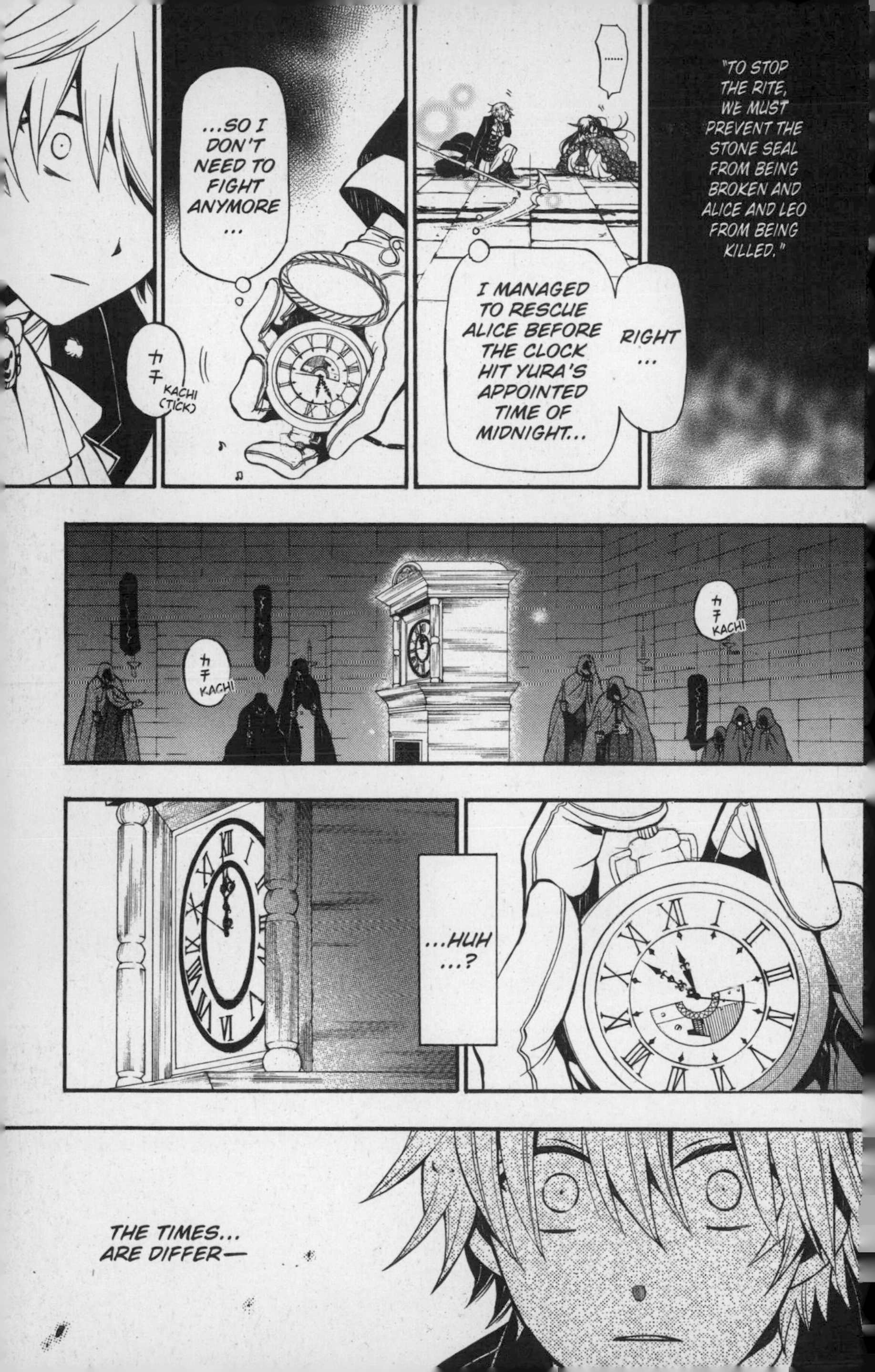
"TO STOP THE RITE, WE MUST PREVENT THE STONE SEAL FROM BEING BROKEN AND ALICE AND LEO FROM BEING KILLED."
......
RIGHT...
I MANAGED TO RESCUE ALICE BEFORE THE CLOCK HIT YURA'S APPOINTED TIME OF MIDNIGHT...
...SO I DON'T NEED TO FIGHT ANYMORE...
カチ KACHI (TICK)
カチ KACHI
カチ KACHI
...HUH...?
THE TIMES... ARE DIFFER—

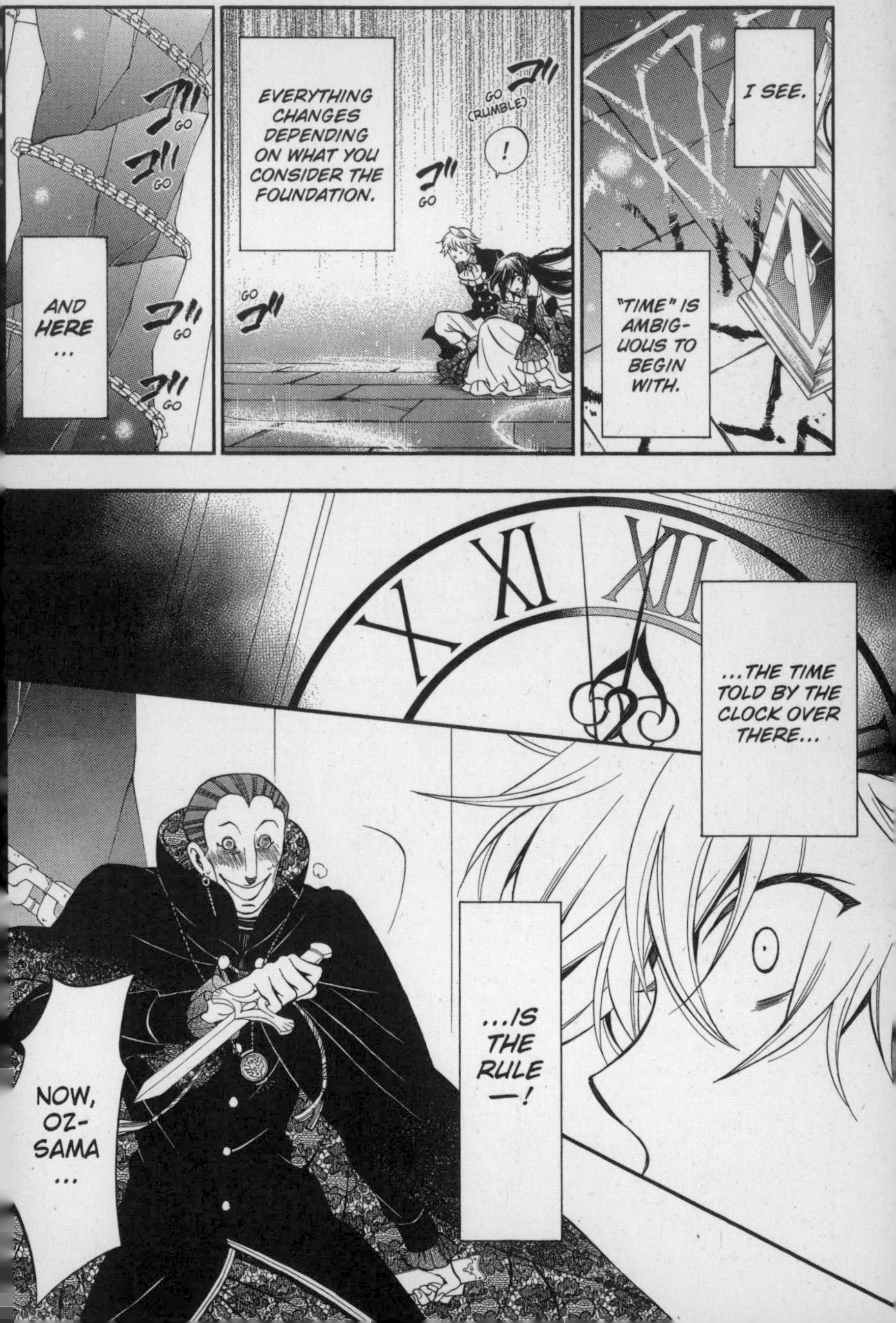
I SEE.
"TIME" IS AMBIGUOUS TO BEGIN WITH.
EVERYTHING CHANGES DEPENDING ON WHAT YOU CONSIDER THE FOUNDATION.
ゴゴ GO (RUMBLE)
!
ゴ GO
ゴ GO
AND HERE ...
ゴ GO
ゴ GO
ゴ GO
ゴ GO
XII
XI
X
...THE TIME TOLD BY THE CLOCK OVER THERE...
...IS THE RULE—!
NOW, OZ-SAMA ...

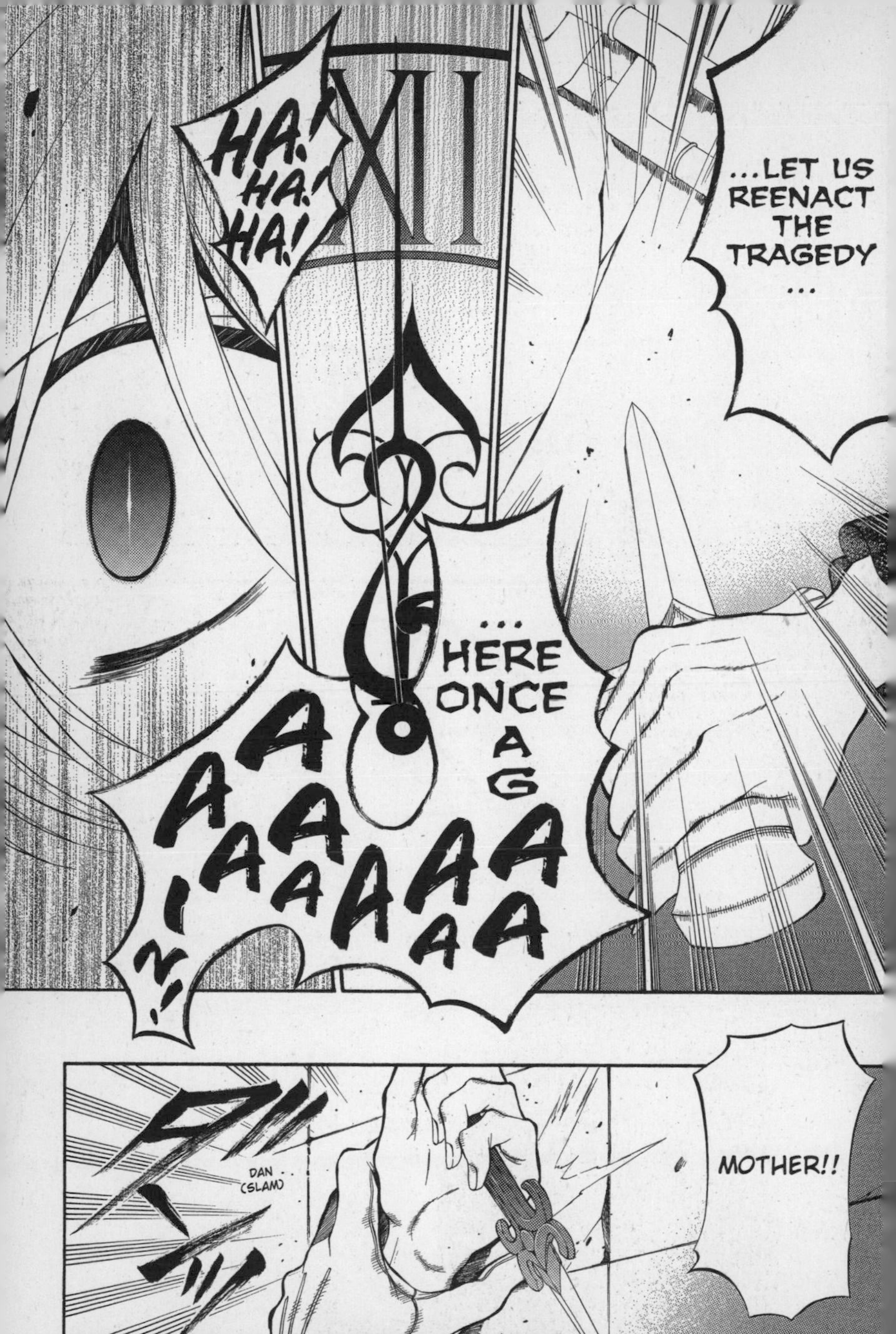
...LET US REENACT THE TRAGEDY ...
HA! HA! HA!
...HERE ONCE AG
AAAAAAAAAAAAAAA!?
MOTHER!!
DAN (SLAM)

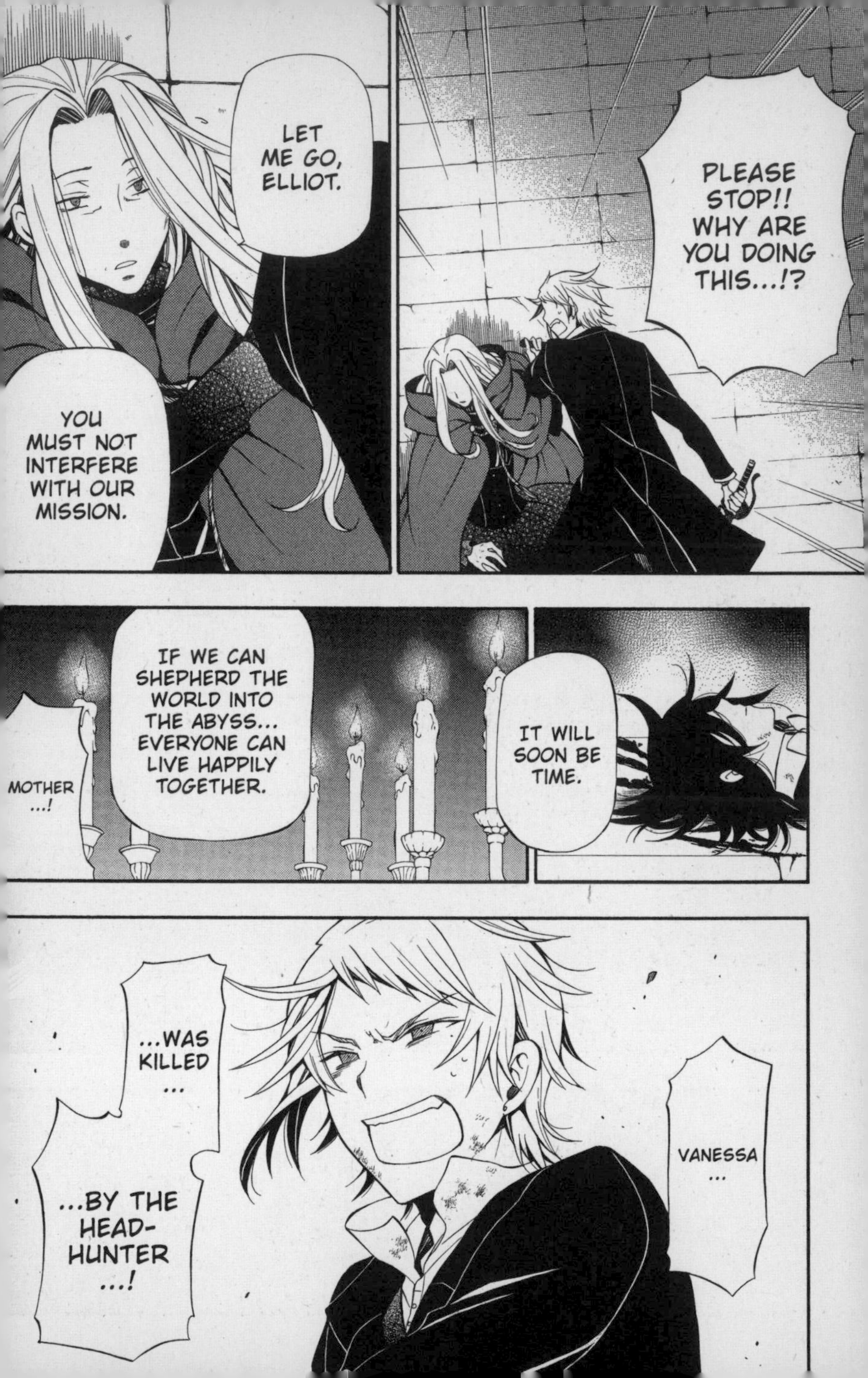
PLEASE STOP!! WHY ARE YOU DOING THIS...!?
LET ME GO, ELLIOT.
YOU MUST NOT INTERFERE WITH OUR MISSION.
IT WILL SOON BE TIME.
IF WE CAN SHEPHERD THE WORLD INTO THE ABYSS... EVERYONE CAN LIVE HAPPILY TOGETHER.
MOTHER ...!
VANESSA ...
...WAS KILLED ...
...BY THE HEAD-HUNTER ...!

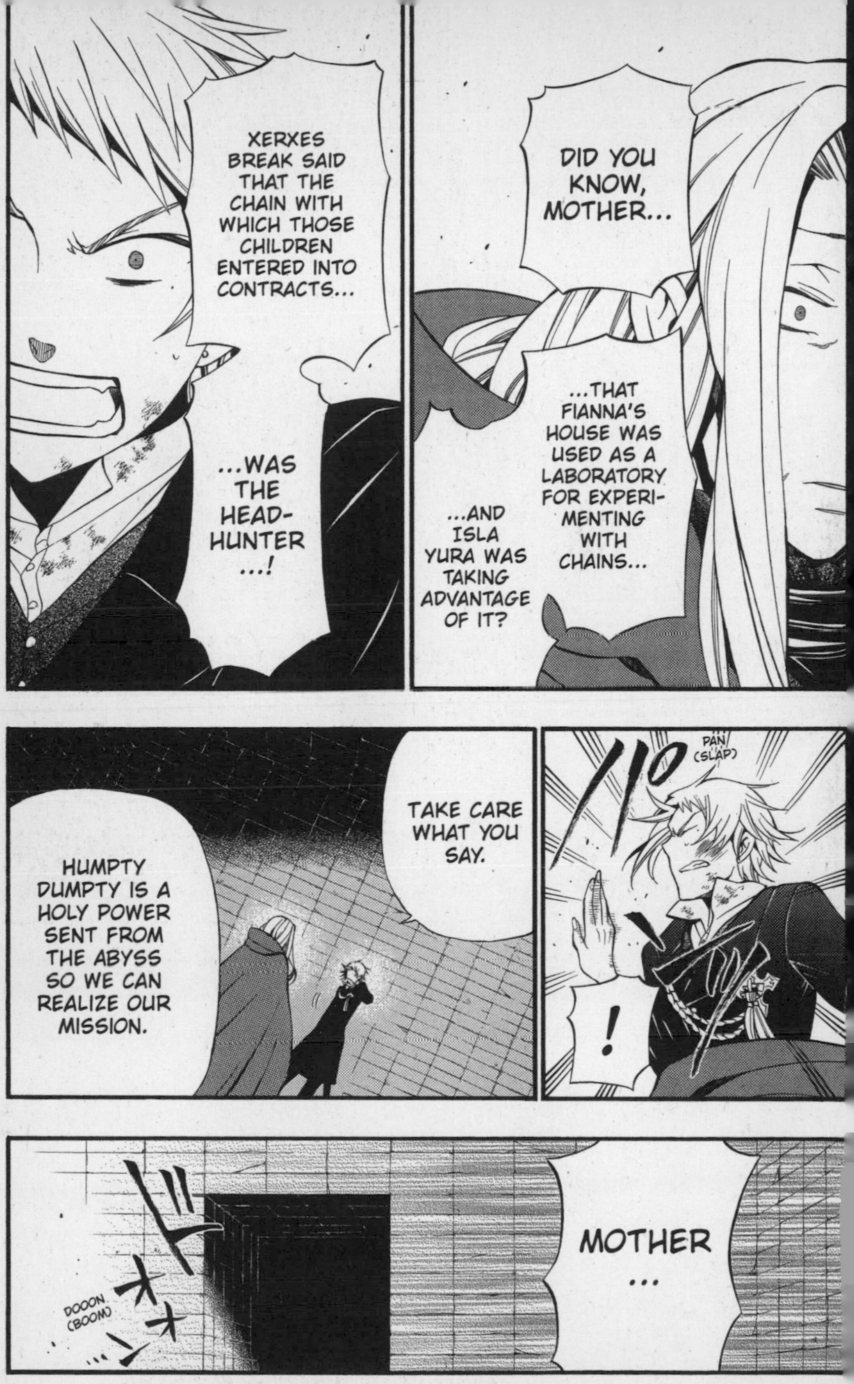
DID YOU KNOW, MOTHER...
...THAT FIANNA'S HOUSE WAS USED AS A LABORATORY FOR EXPERI-MENTING WITH CHAINS...
...AND ISLA YURA WAS TAKING ADVANTAGE OF IT?
XERXES BREAK SAID THAT THE CHAIN WITH WHICH THOSE CHILDREN ENTERED INTO CONTRACTS...
...WAS THE HEAD-HUNTER ...!
PAN (SLAP)
!
TAKE CARE WHAT YOU SAY.
HUMPTY DUMPTY IS A HOLY POWER SENT FROM THE ABYSS SO WE CAN REALIZE OUR MISSION.
MOTHER ...
DOOON (BOOM)

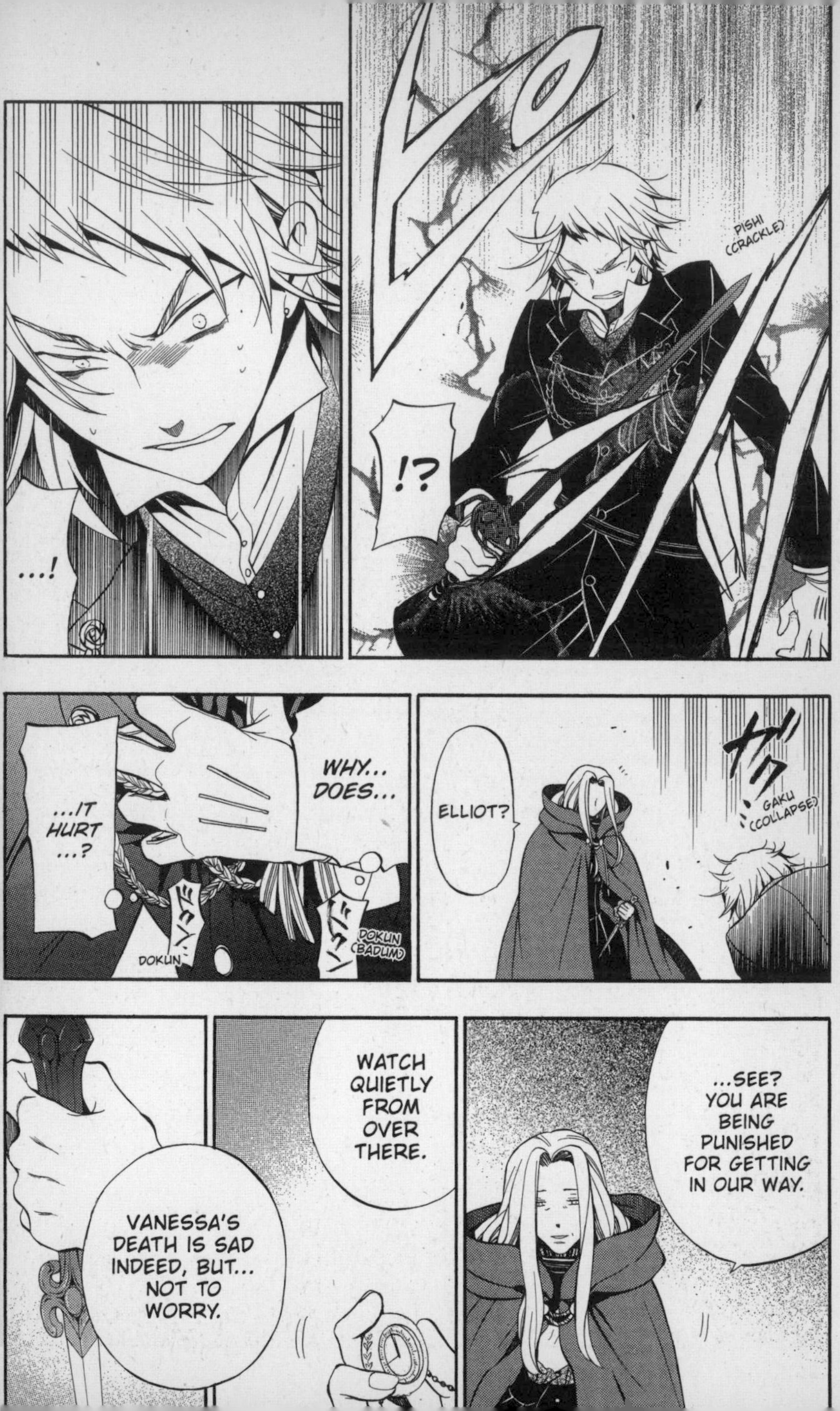
PISHI (CRACKLE)
!?
...!
GAKU (COLLAPSE)
ELLIOT?
WHY... DOES...
...IT HURT ...?
DOKUN (BADUMP)
DOKUN
...SEE? YOU ARE BEING PUNISHED FOR GETTING IN OUR WAY.
WATCH QUIETLY FROM OVER THERE.
VANESSA'S DEATH IS SAD INDEED, BUT... NOT TO WORRY.

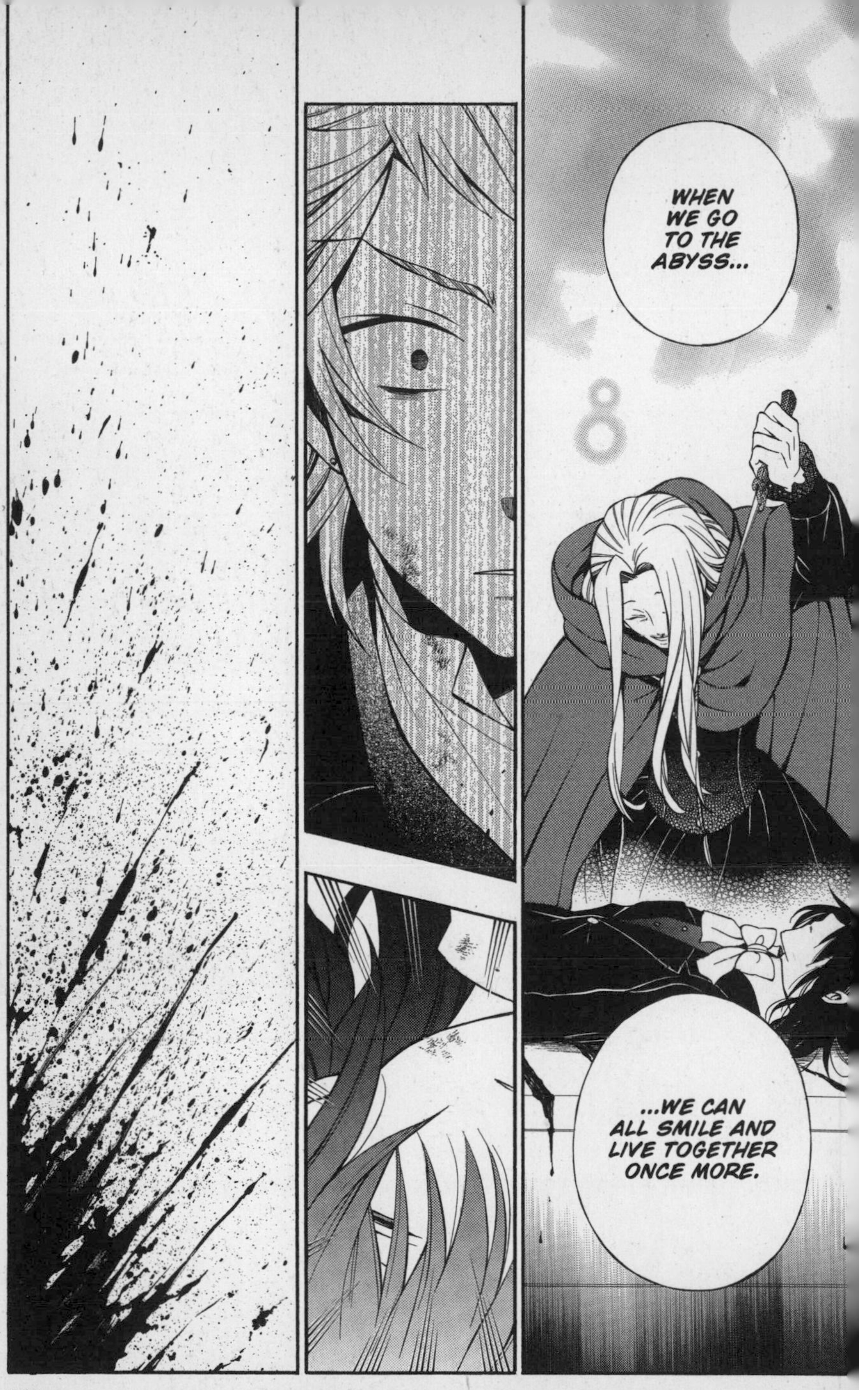
WHEN WE GO TO THE ABYSS...
...WE CAN ALL SMILE AND LIVE TOGETHER ONCE MORE.

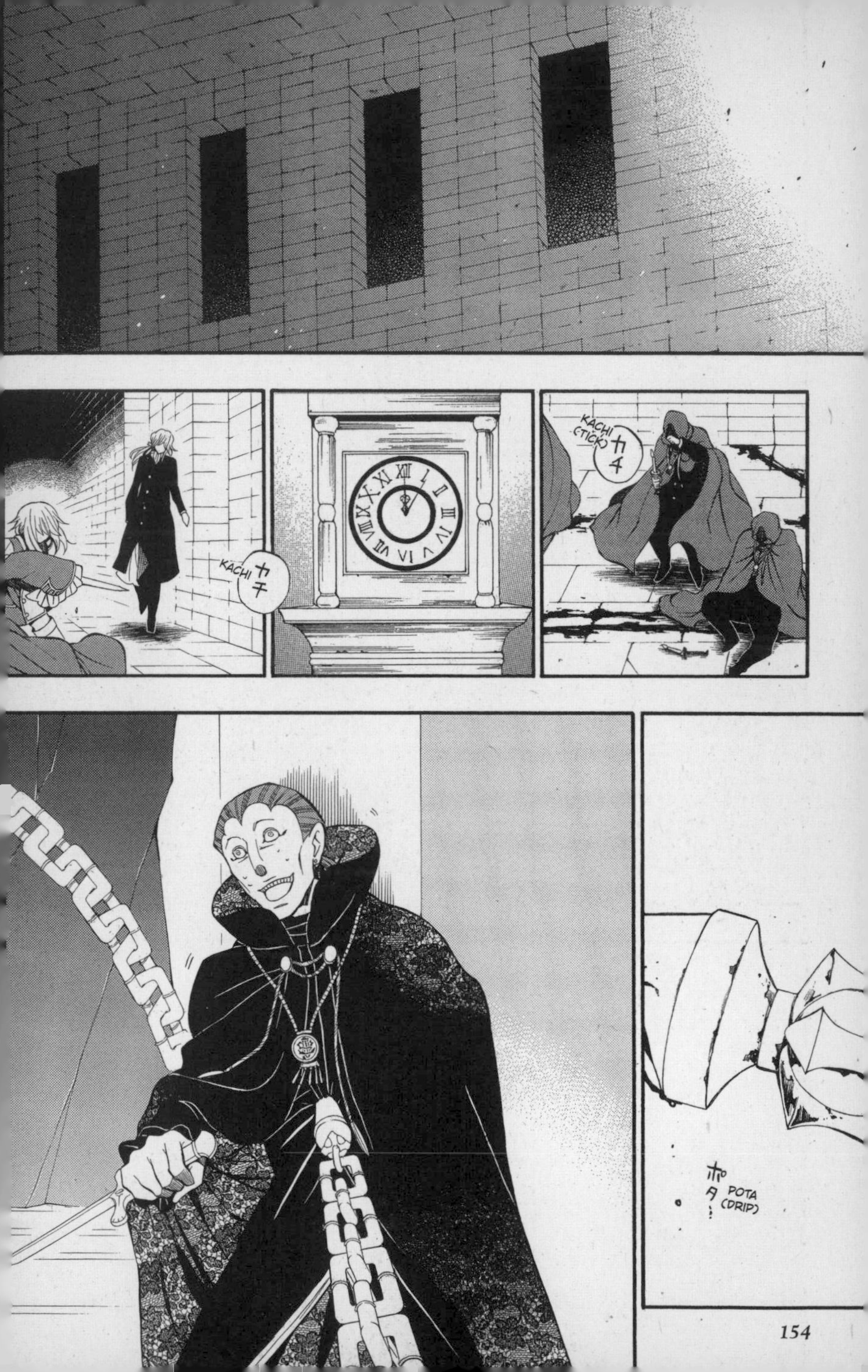
カチ
KACHI (TICK)
カチ
KACHI
ポタ
POTA (DRIP)

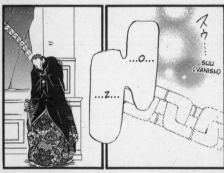

...O...

...Z...

スウ......
SUU
(VANISH)

DON'T WORRY, ALICE.

...IT'S OKAY.

KARAN
(CLANK)

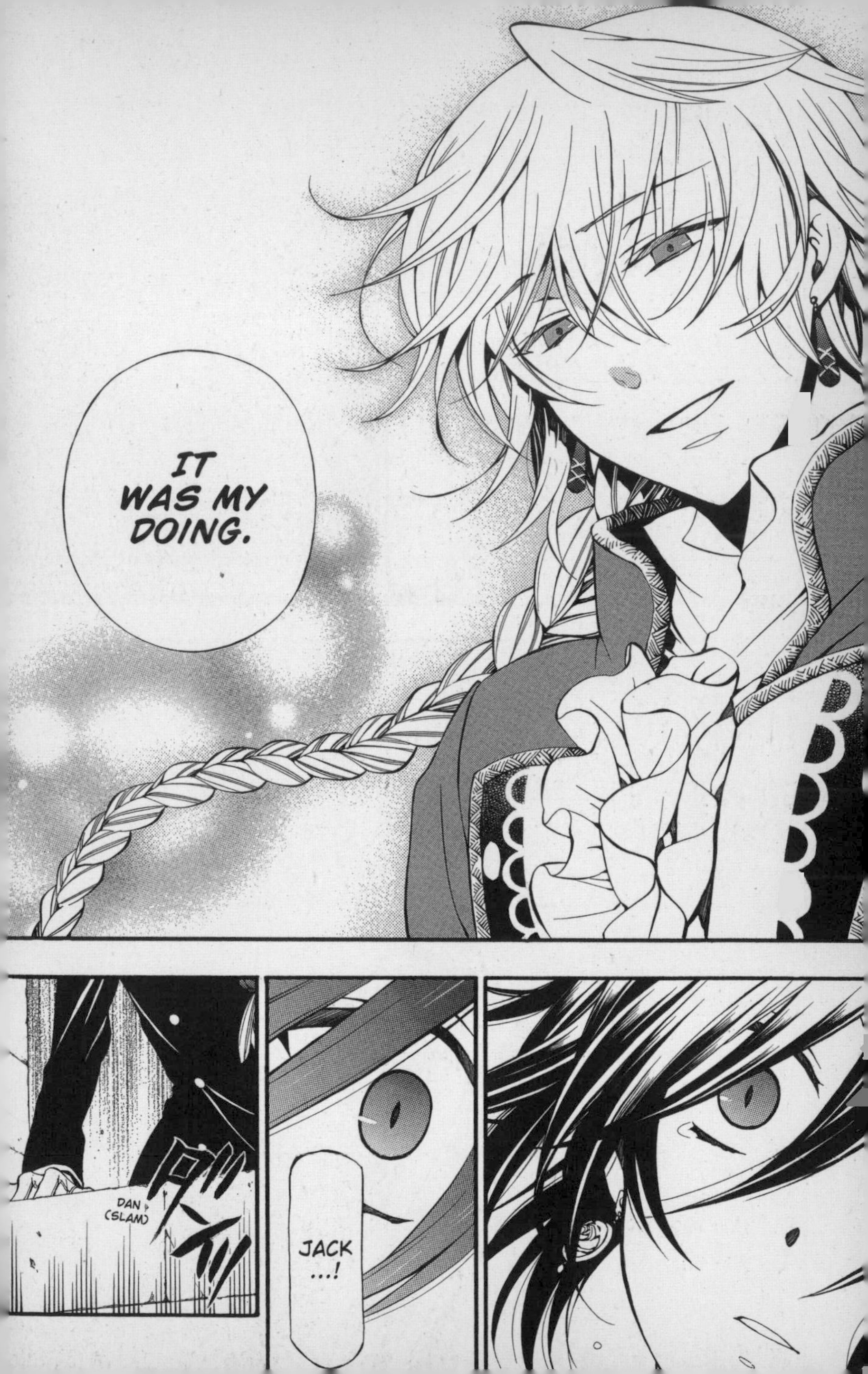
IT WAS MY DOING.
JACK ...!
DAN
(SLAM)

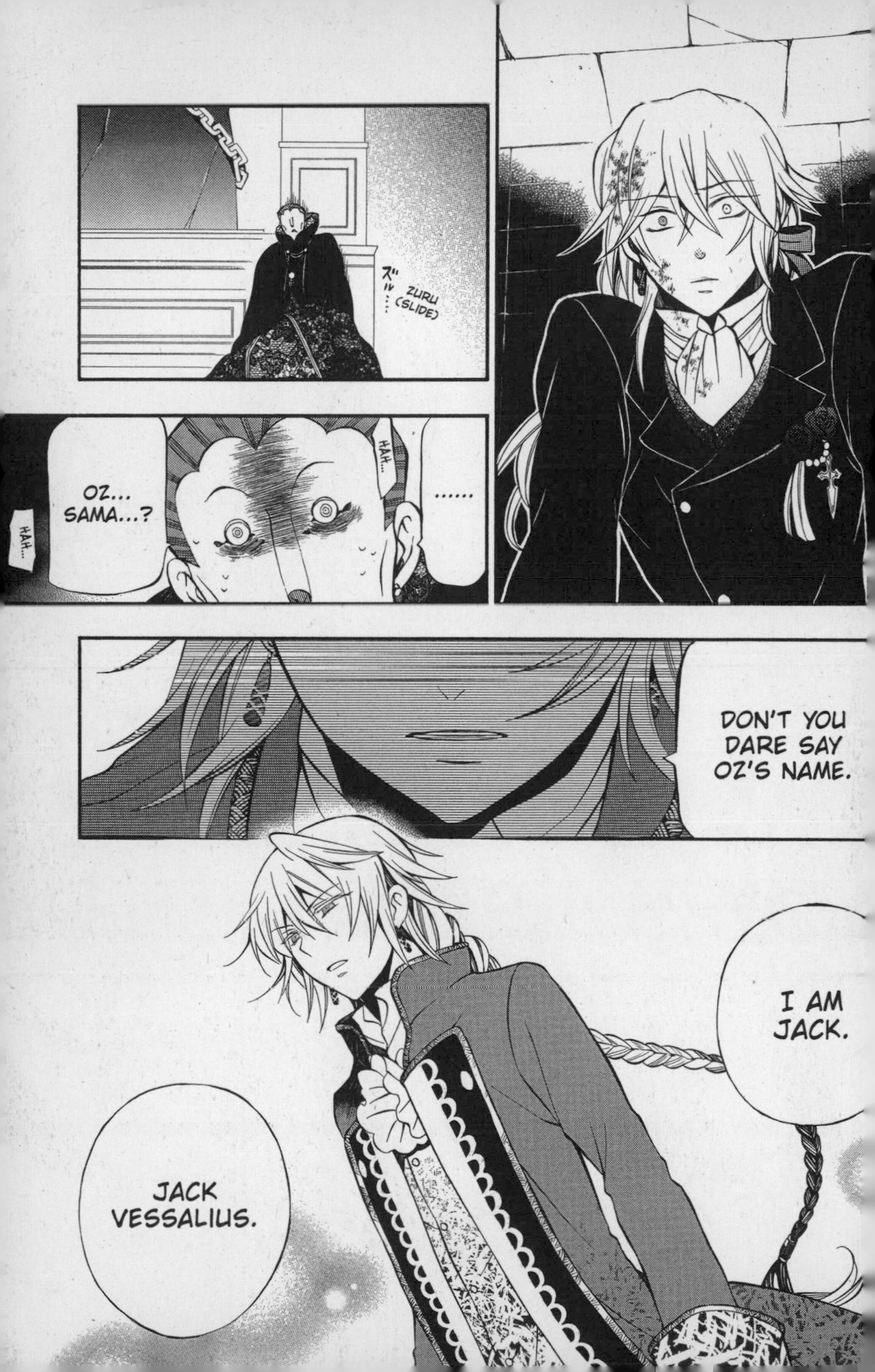
ズル…
ZURU (SLIDE)
HAH...
......
OZ... SAMA...?
HAH...
DON'T YOU DARE SAY OZ'S NAME.
I AM JACK.
JACK VESSALIUS.

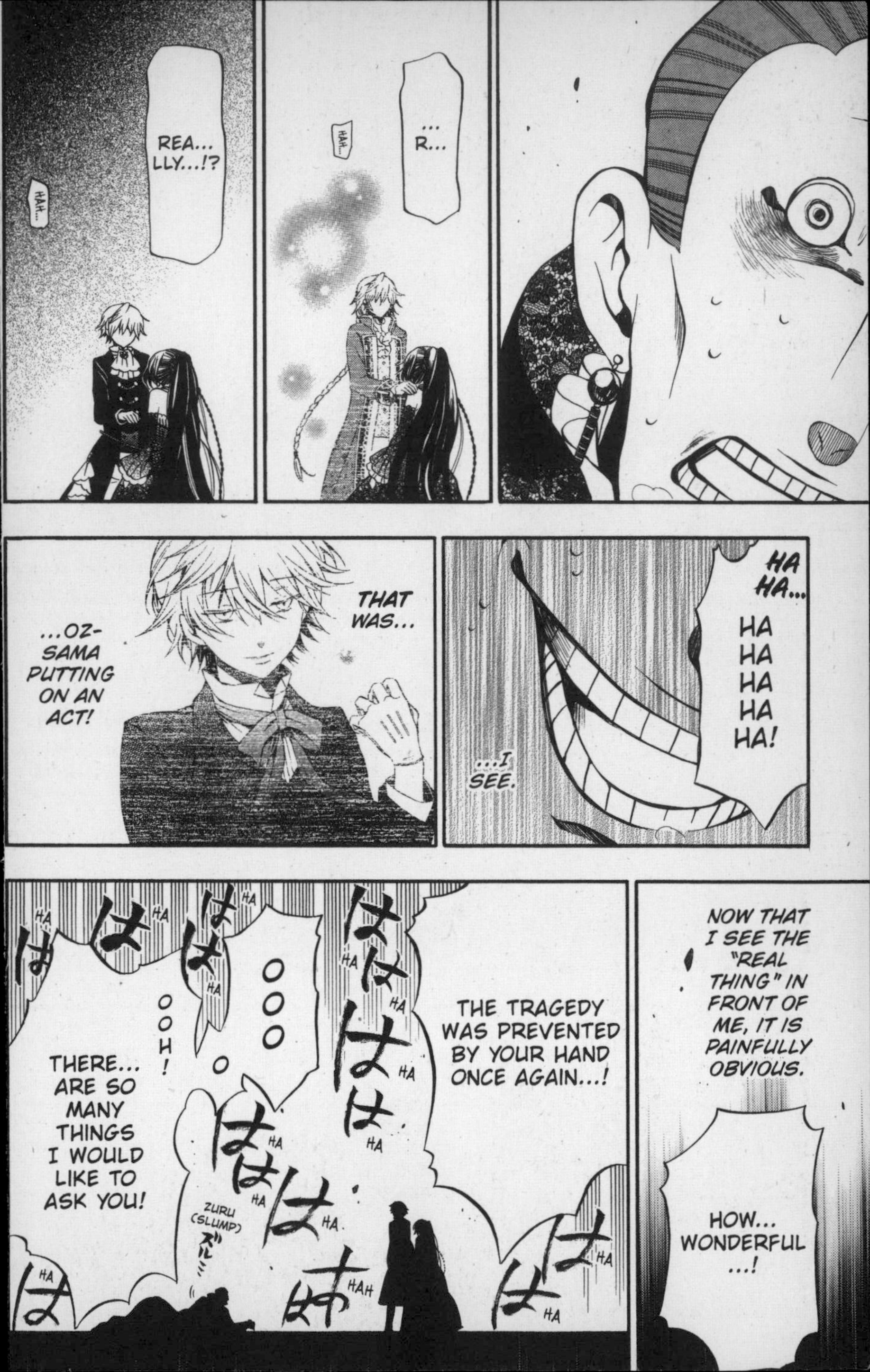
... R...
HAH...
REA... LLY...!?
HAH...
HA HA...
HA HA HA HA HA!
...I SEE.
THAT WAS...
...OZ-SAMA PUTTING ON AN ACT!
NOW THAT I SEE THE "REAL THING" IN FRONT OF ME, IT IS PAINFULLY OBVIOUS.
HOW... WONDERFUL ...!
THE TRAGEDY WAS PREVENTED BY YOUR HAND ONCE AGAIN...!
OOOO
OOH!
THERE... ARE SO MANY THINGS I WOULD LIKE TO ASK YOU!
ZURU (SLUMP)
HAH

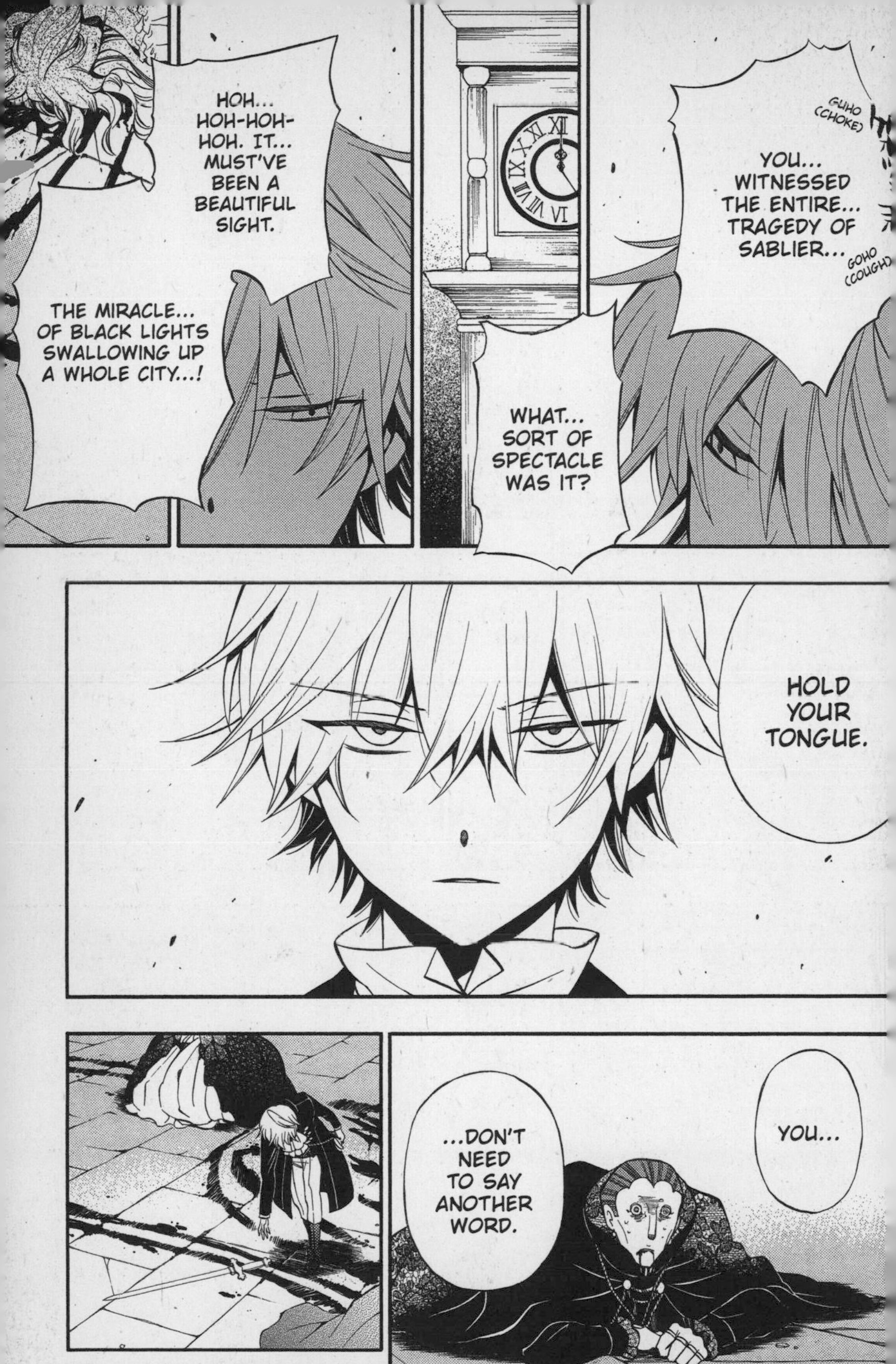
GUHO (CHOKE)
YOU... WITNESSED THE ENTIRE... TRAGEDY OF SABLIER...
GOHO (COUGH)
WHAT... SORT OF SPECTACLE WAS IT?
HOH... HOH-HOH-HOH. IT... MUST'VE BEEN A BEAUTIFUL SIGHT.
THE MIRACLE... OF BLACK LIGHTS SWALLOWING UP A WHOLE CITY...!
HOLD YOUR TONGUE.
YOU...
...DON'T NEED TO SAY ANOTHER WORD.

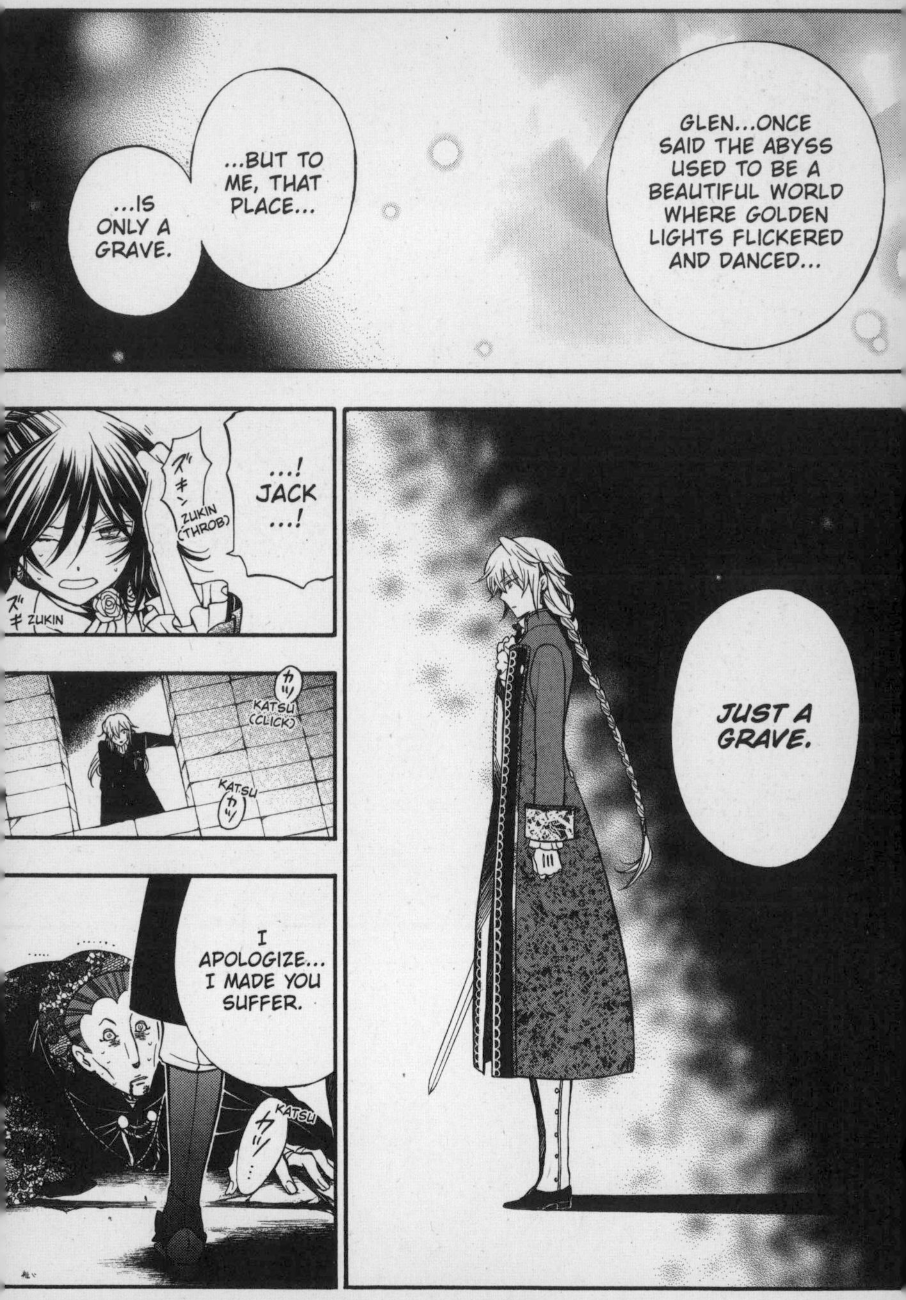
GLEN...ONCE SAID THE ABYSS USED TO BE A BEAUTIFUL WORLD WHERE GOLDEN LIGHTS FLICKERED AND DANCED...
...BUT TO ME, THAT PLACE...
...IS ONLY A GRAVE.
JUST A GRAVE.
...! JACK ...!
ズキン ZUKIN (THROB)
ズキ ZUKIN
カッ KATSU (CLICK)
KATSU カッ
I APOLOGIZE... I MADE YOU SUFFER.
KATSU カッ

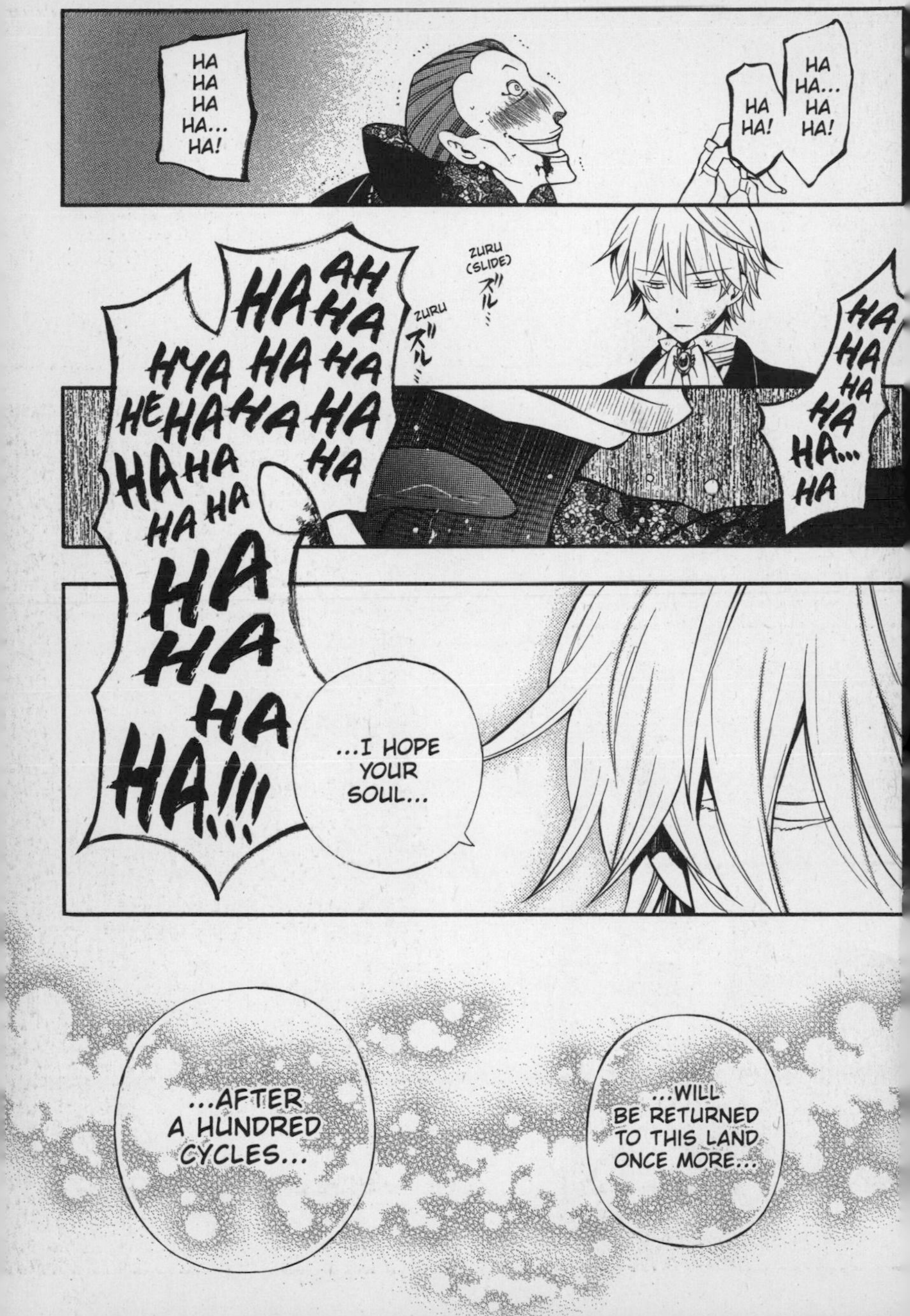
HA HA... HA HA!
HA HA!
HA HA HA HA... HA!
HA HA HA HA HA... HA
ZURU (SLIDE) ズル
ZURU ズル
AH HA HA HA HA HA HA HA HYA HEHA HA HA HA HA HA HA HA HA HA HA HA HA HA!!!
...I HOPE YOUR SOUL...
...WILL BE RETURNED TO THIS LAND ONCE MORE...
...AFTER A HUNDRED CYCLES...

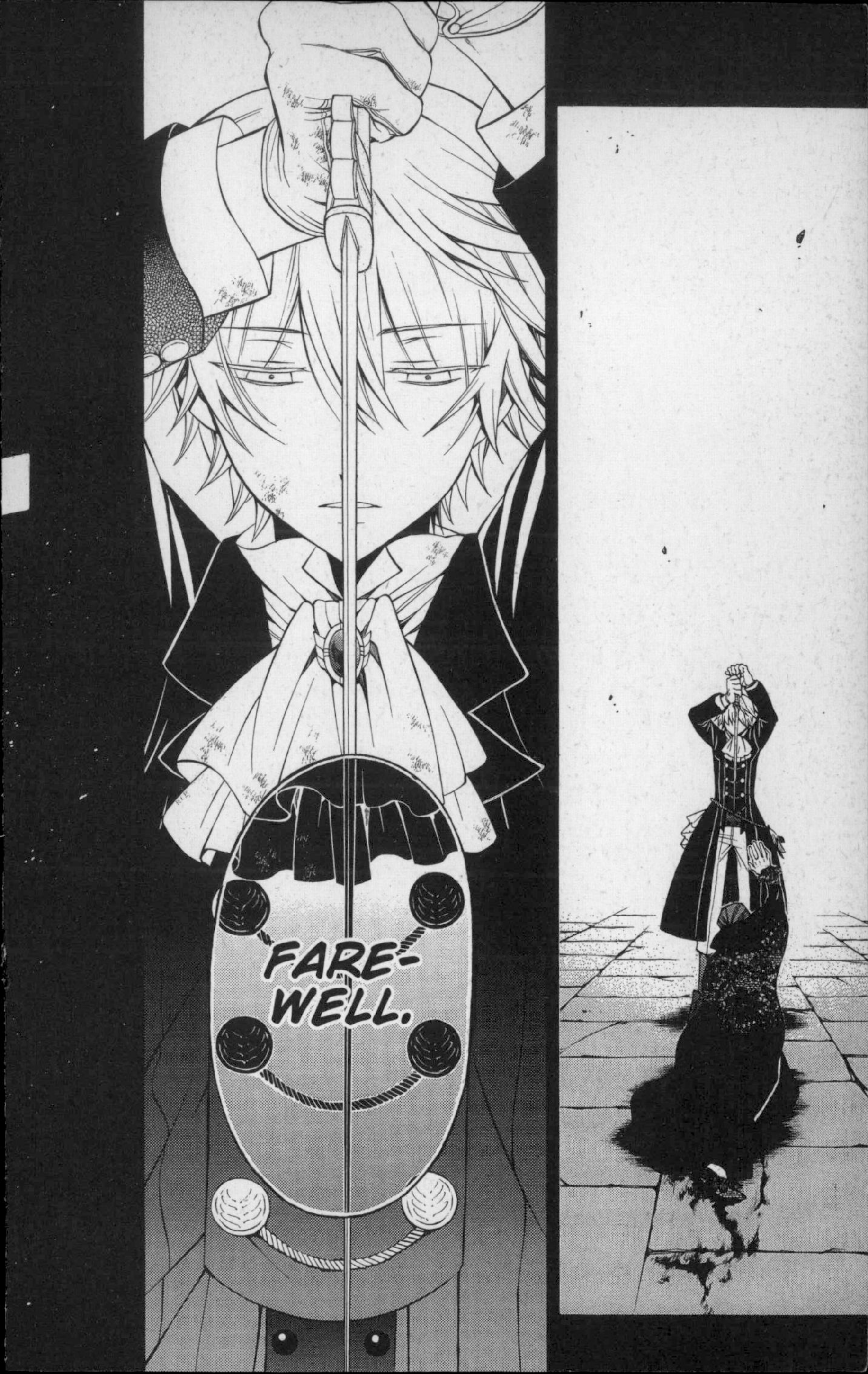
FARE-
WELL.

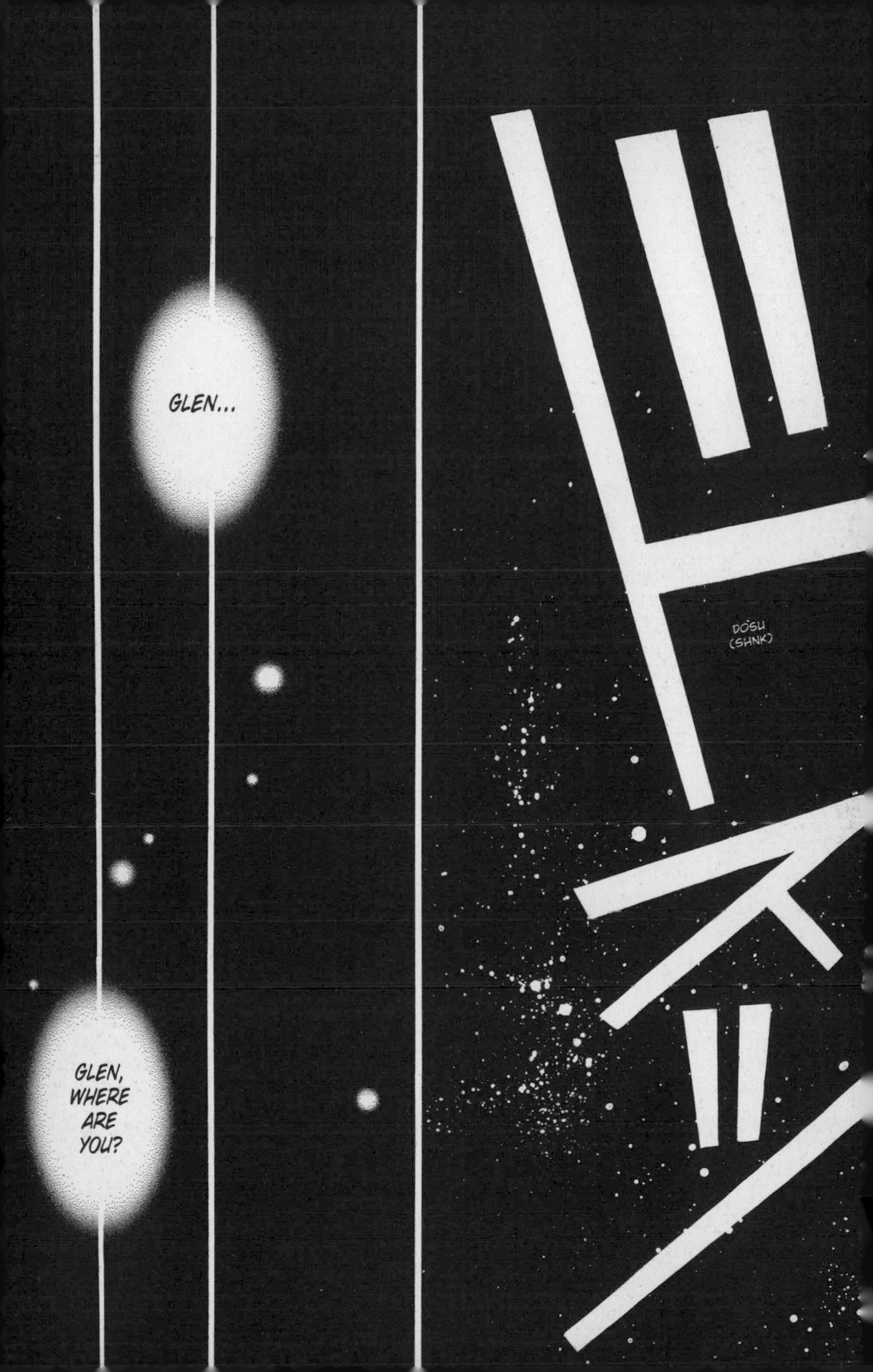
DOSU
(SHNK)
GLEN...
GLEN, WHERE ARE YOU?

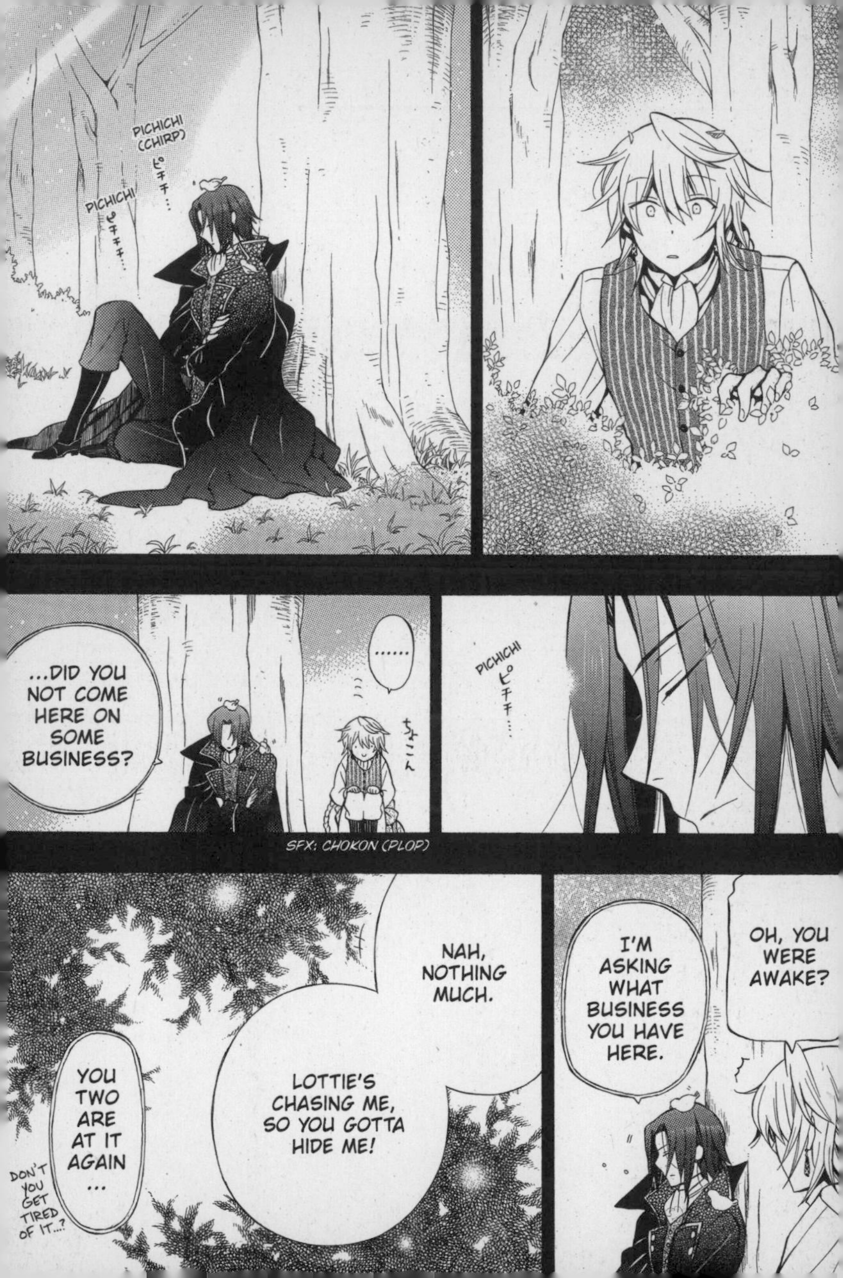
PICHICHI (CHIRP)
ピチチ…
PICHICHI
ピチチチ…
PICHICHI
ピチチ…
......
...DID YOU NOT COME HERE ON SOME BUSINESS?
ちょこん
SFX: CHOKON (PLOP)
OH, YOU WERE AWAKE?
I'M ASKING WHAT BUSINESS YOU HAVE HERE.
NAH, NOTHING MUCH.
LOTTIE'S CHASING ME, SO YOU GOTTA HIDE ME!
YOU TWO ARE AT IT AGAIN...
DON'T YOU GET TIRED OF IT...?

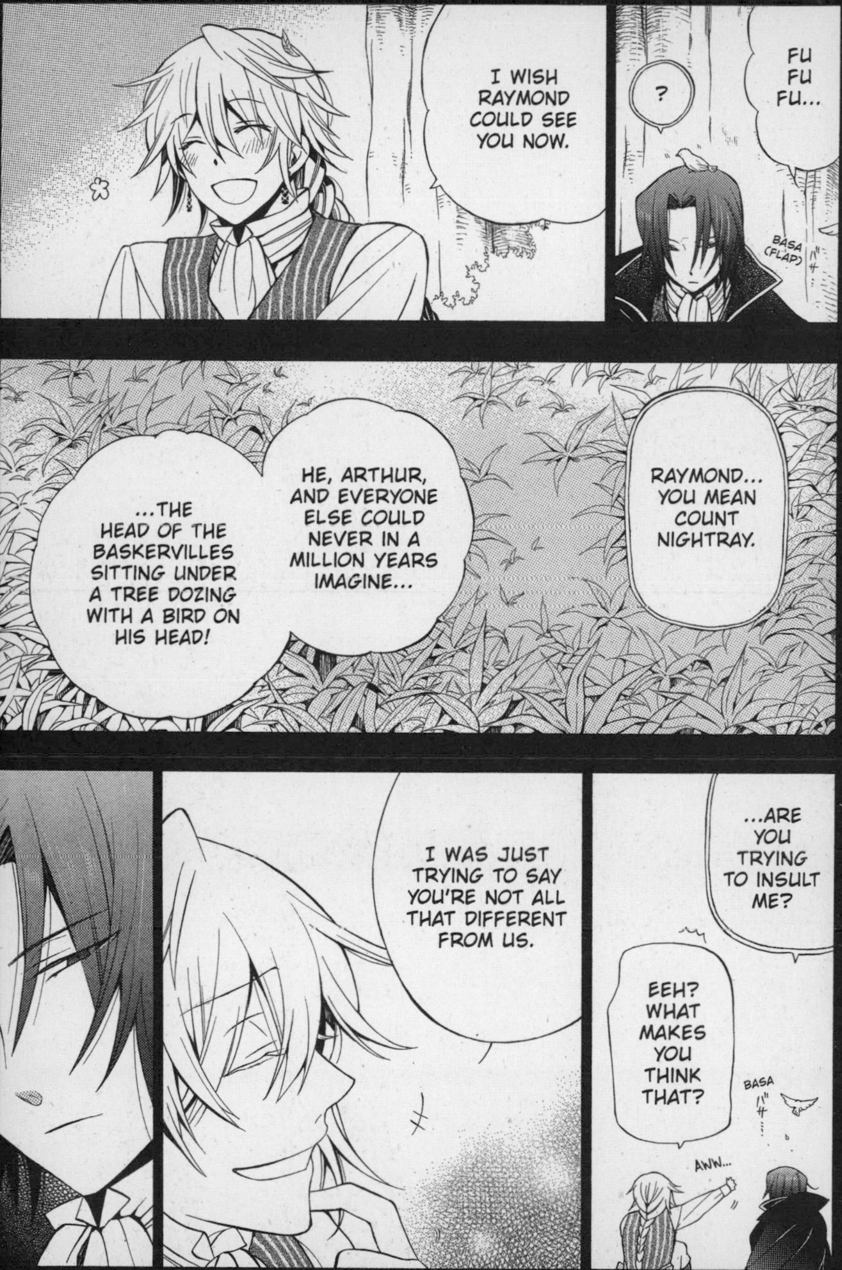
FU FU FU...
?
BASA (FLAP)
I WISH RAYMOND COULD SEE YOU NOW.
RAYMOND... YOU MEAN COUNT NIGHTRAY.
HE, ARTHUR, AND EVERYONE ELSE COULD NEVER IN A MILLION YEARS IMAGINE...
...THE HEAD OF THE BASKERVILLES SITTING UNDER A TREE DOZING WITH A BIRD ON HIS HEAD!
...ARE YOU TRYING TO INSULT ME?
EEH? WHAT MAKES YOU THINK THAT?
BASA
AWW...
I WAS JUST TRYING TO SAY YOU'RE NOT ALL THAT DIFFERENT FROM US.

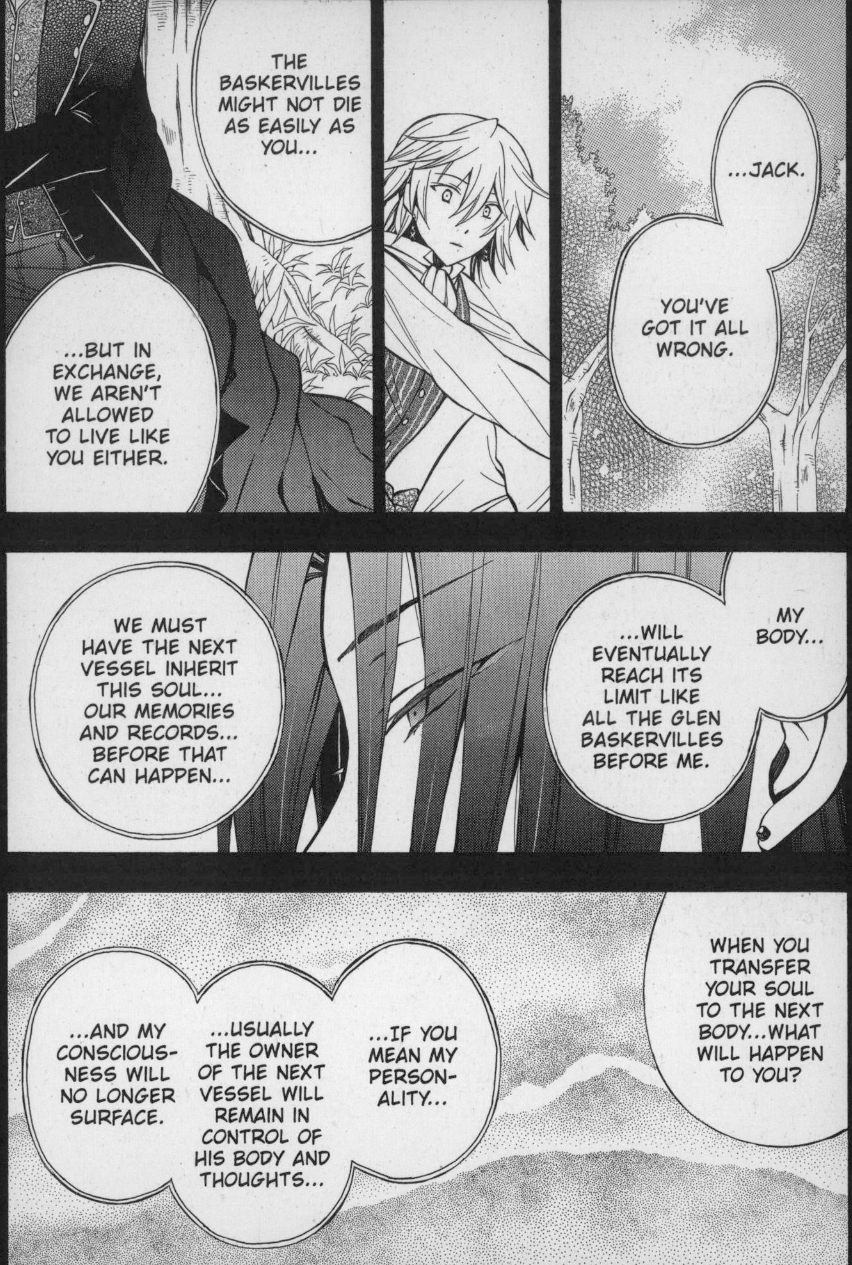
...JACK.
YOU'VE GOT IT ALL WRONG.
THE BASKERVILLES MIGHT NOT DIE AS EASILY AS YOU...
...BUT IN EXCHANGE, WE AREN'T ALLOWED TO LIVE LIKE YOU EITHER.
MY BODY...
...WILL EVENTUALLY REACH ITS LIMIT LIKE ALL THE GLEN BASKERVILLES BEFORE ME.
WE MUST HAVE THE NEXT VESSEL INHERIT THIS SOUL... OUR MEMORIES AND RECORDS... BEFORE THAT CAN HAPPEN...
WHEN YOU TRANSFER YOUR SOUL TO THE NEXT BODY...WHAT WILL HAPPEN TO YOU?
...IF YOU MEAN MY PERSON-ALITY...
...USUALLY THE OWNER OF THE NEXT VESSEL WILL REMAIN IN CONTROL OF HIS BODY AND THOUGHTS...
...AND MY CONSCIOUS-NESS WILL NO LONGER SURFACE.

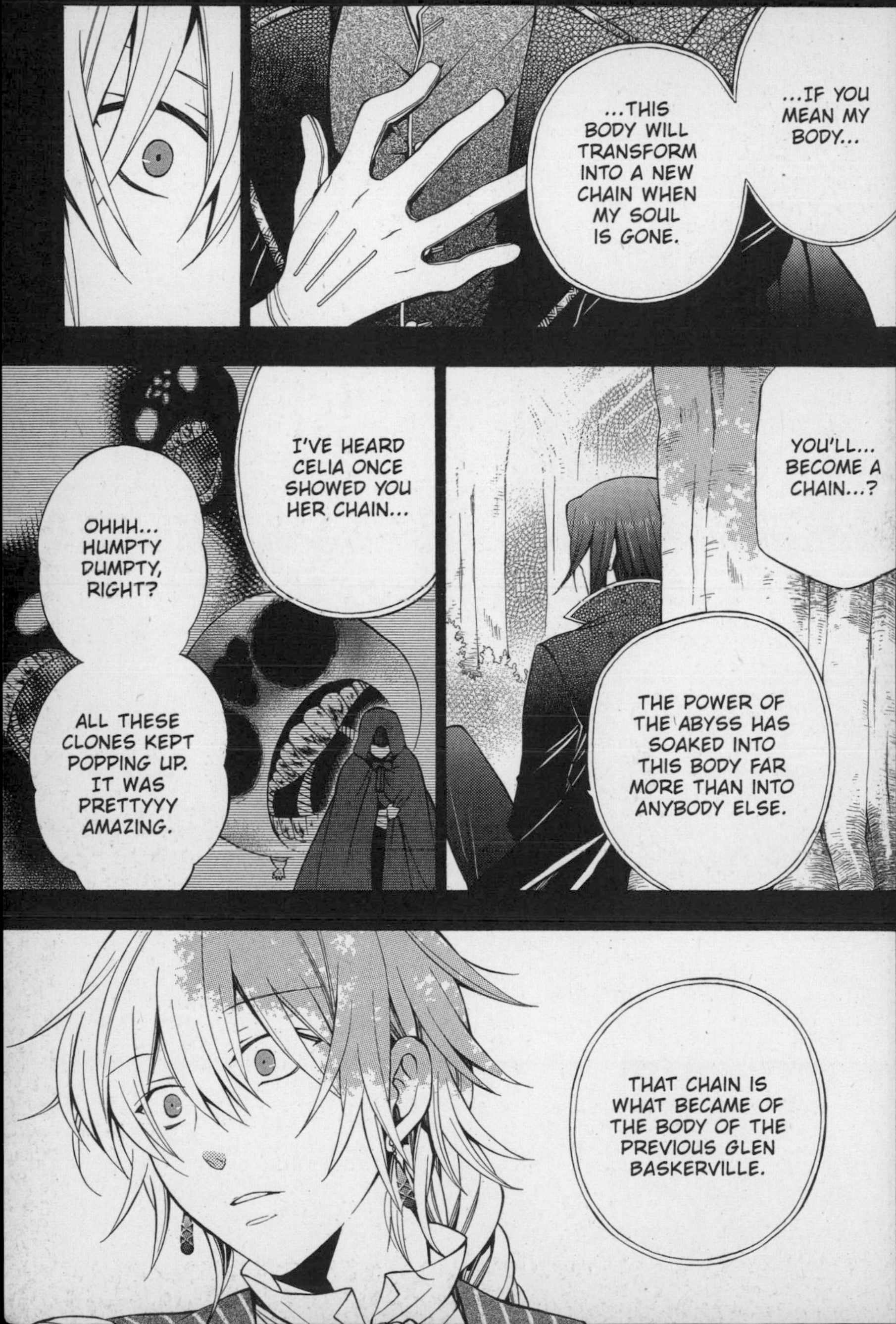
...IF YOU MEAN MY BODY...
...THIS BODY WILL TRANSFORM INTO A NEW CHAIN WHEN MY SOUL IS GONE.
YOU'LL... BECOME A CHAIN...?
THE POWER OF THE ABYSS HAS SOAKED INTO THIS BODY FAR MORE THAN INTO ANYBODY ELSE.
I'VE HEARD CELIA ONCE SHOWED YOU HER CHAIN...
OHHH... HUMPTY DUMPTY, RIGHT?
ALL THESE CLONES KEPT POPPING UP. IT WAS PRETTYYY AMAZING.
THAT CHAIN IS WHAT BECAME OF THE BODY OF THE PREVIOUS GLEN BASKERVILLE.

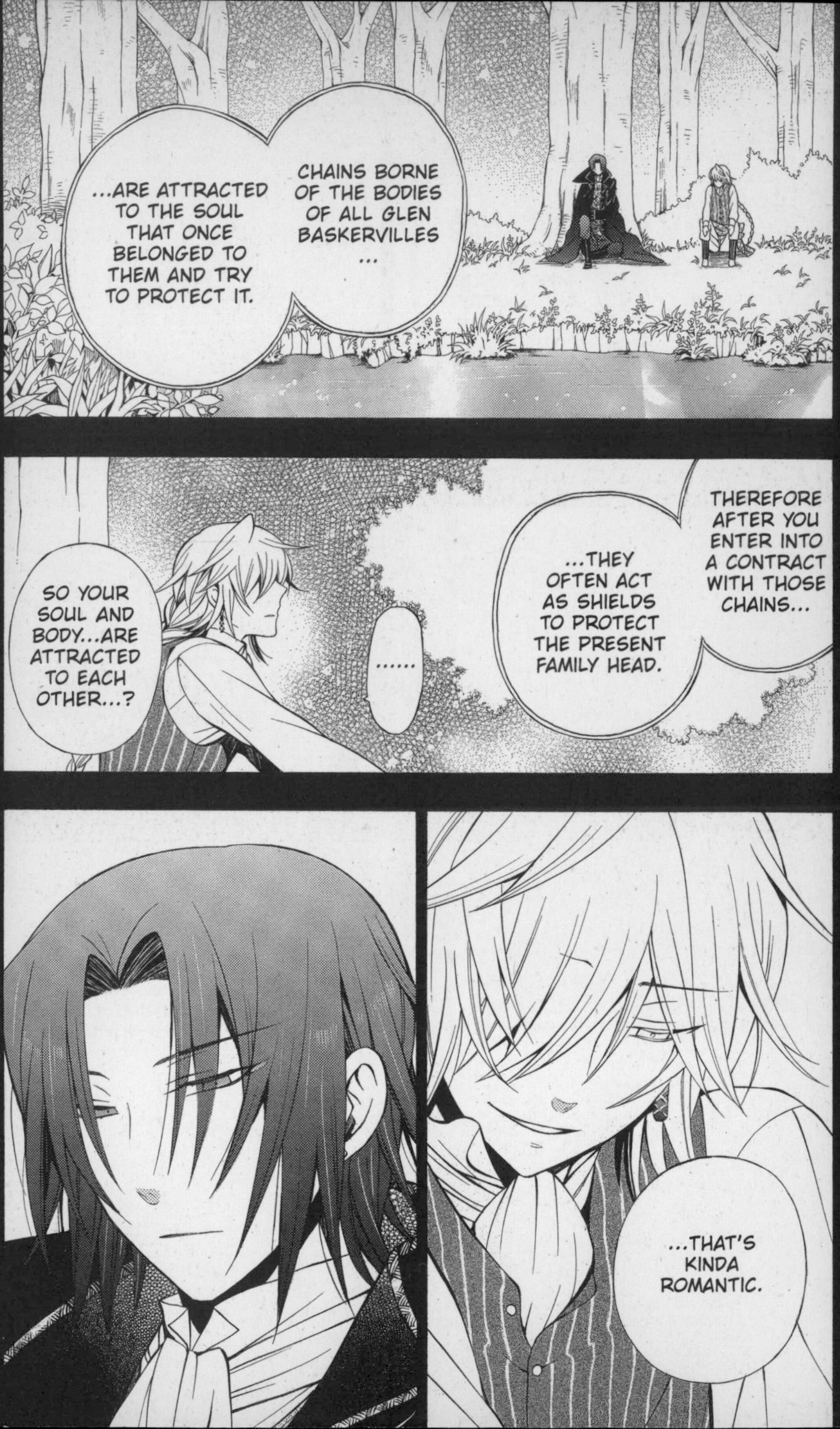
CHAINS BORNE OF THE BODIES OF ALL GLEN BASKERVILLES ...
...ARE ATTRACTED TO THE SOUL THAT ONCE BELONGED TO THEM AND TRY TO PROTECT IT.
THEREFORE AFTER YOU ENTER INTO A CONTRACT WITH THOSE CHAINS...
...THEY OFTEN ACT AS SHIELDS TO PROTECT THE PRESENT FAMILY HEAD.
......
SO YOUR SOUL AND BODY...ARE ATTRACTED TO EACH OTHER...?
...THAT'S KINDA ROMANTIC.

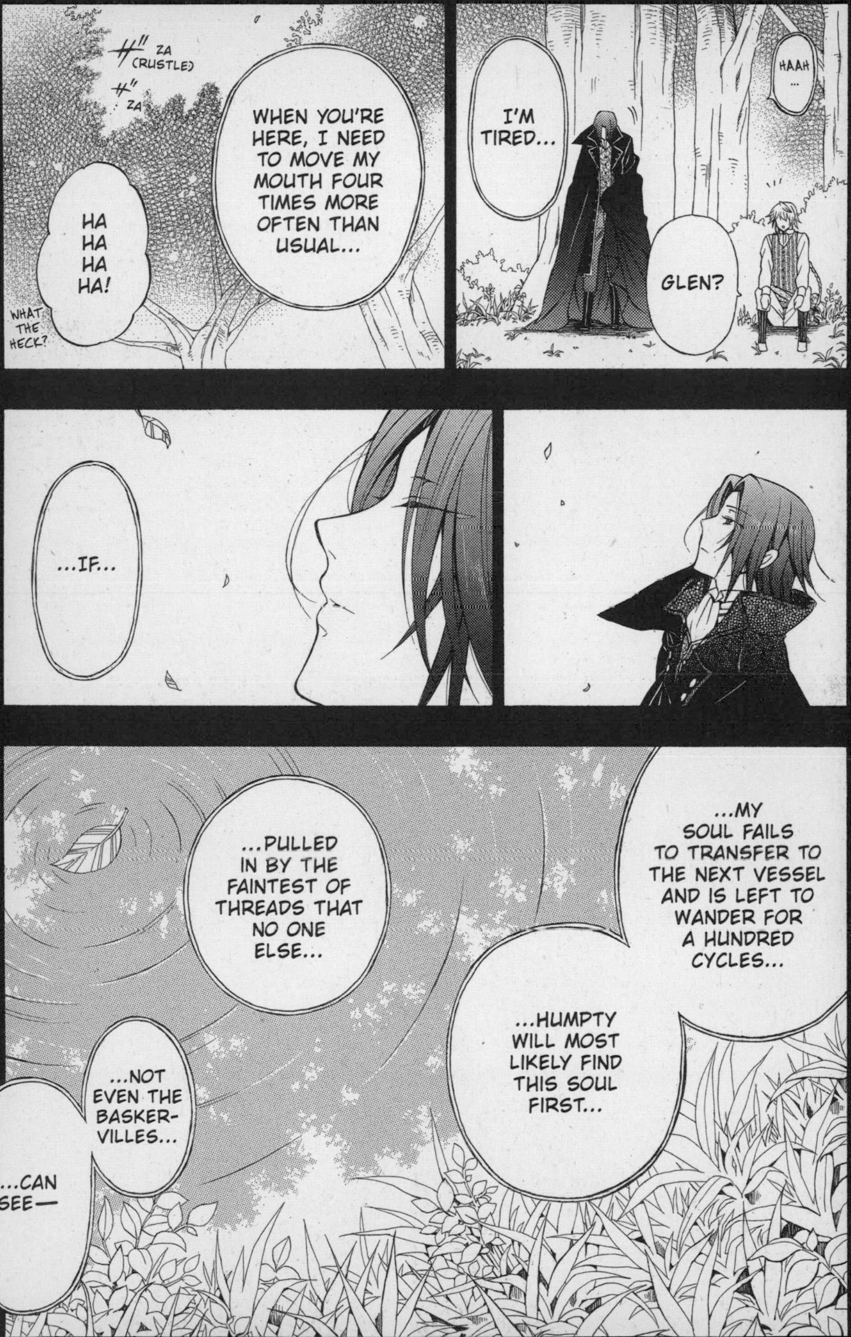
HAAH...
I'M TIRED...
GLEN?
ZA (RUSTLE)
ZA
WHEN YOU'RE HERE, I NEED TO MOVE MY MOUTH FOUR TIMES MORE OFTEN THAN USUAL...
HA HA HA HA!
WHAT THE HECK?
...IF...
...MY SOUL FAILS TO TRANSFER TO THE NEXT VESSEL AND IS LEFT TO WANDER FOR A HUNDRED CYCLES...
...HUMPTY WILL MOST LIKELY FIND THIS SOUL FIRST...
...PULLED IN BY THE FAINTEST OF THREADS THAT NO ONE ELSE...
...NOT EVEN THE BASKERVILLES...
...CAN SEE—

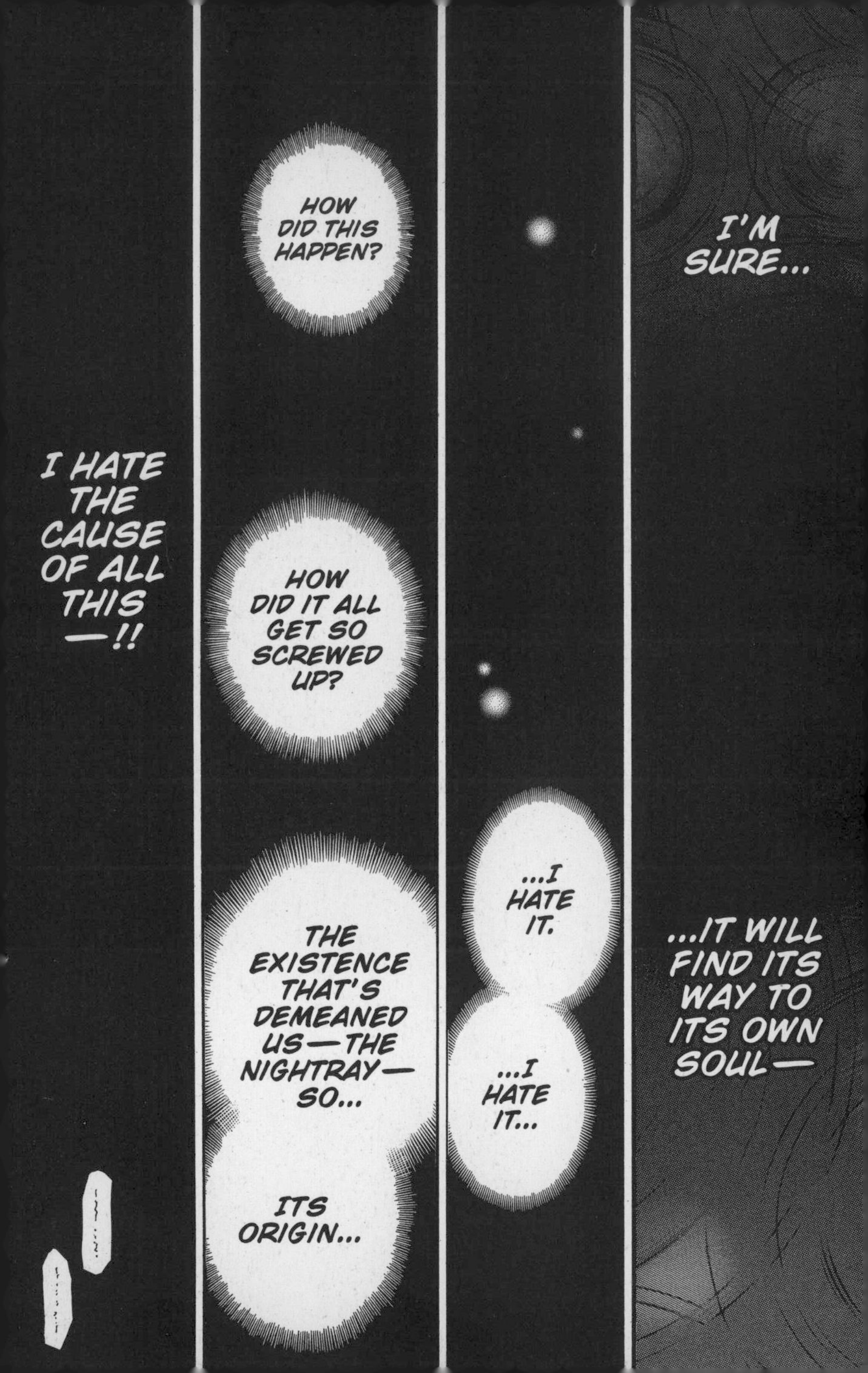
I'M SURE...
...IT WILL FIND ITS WAY TO ITS OWN SOUL—
...I HATE IT.
...I HATE IT...
HOW DID THIS HAPPEN?
HOW DID IT ALL GET SO SCREWED UP?
THE EXISTENCE THAT'S DEMEANED US—THE NIGHTRAY—SO...
ITS ORIGIN...
I HATE THE CAUSE OF ALL THIS—!!

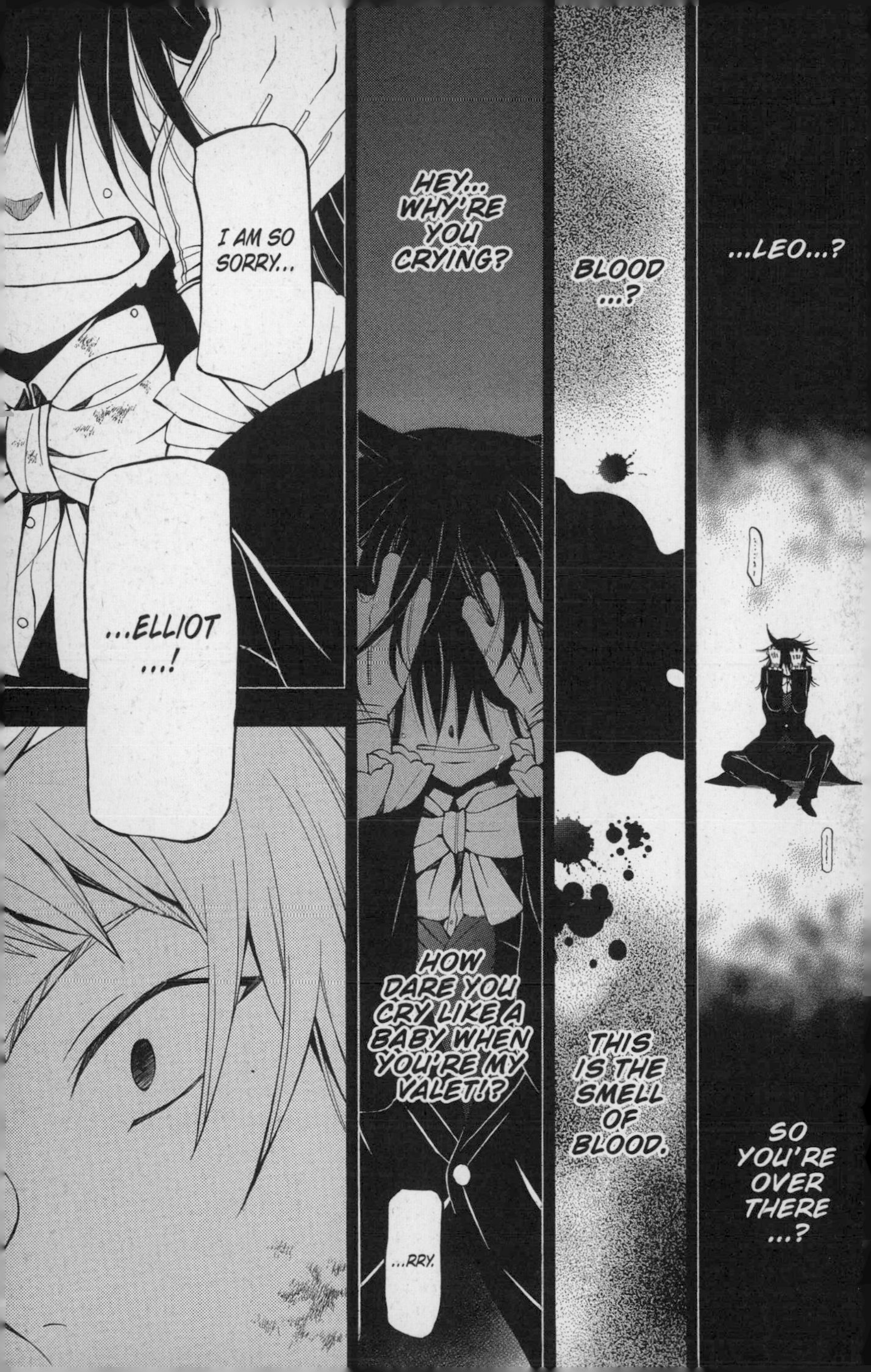
...LEO...?
SO YOU'RE OVER THERE ...?
BLOOD ...?
THIS IS THE SMELL OF BLOOD.
HEY... WHY'RE YOU CRYING?
HOW DARE YOU CRY LIKE A BABY WHEN YOU'RE MY VALET!?
...RRY.
I AM SO SORRY...
...ELLIOT ...!

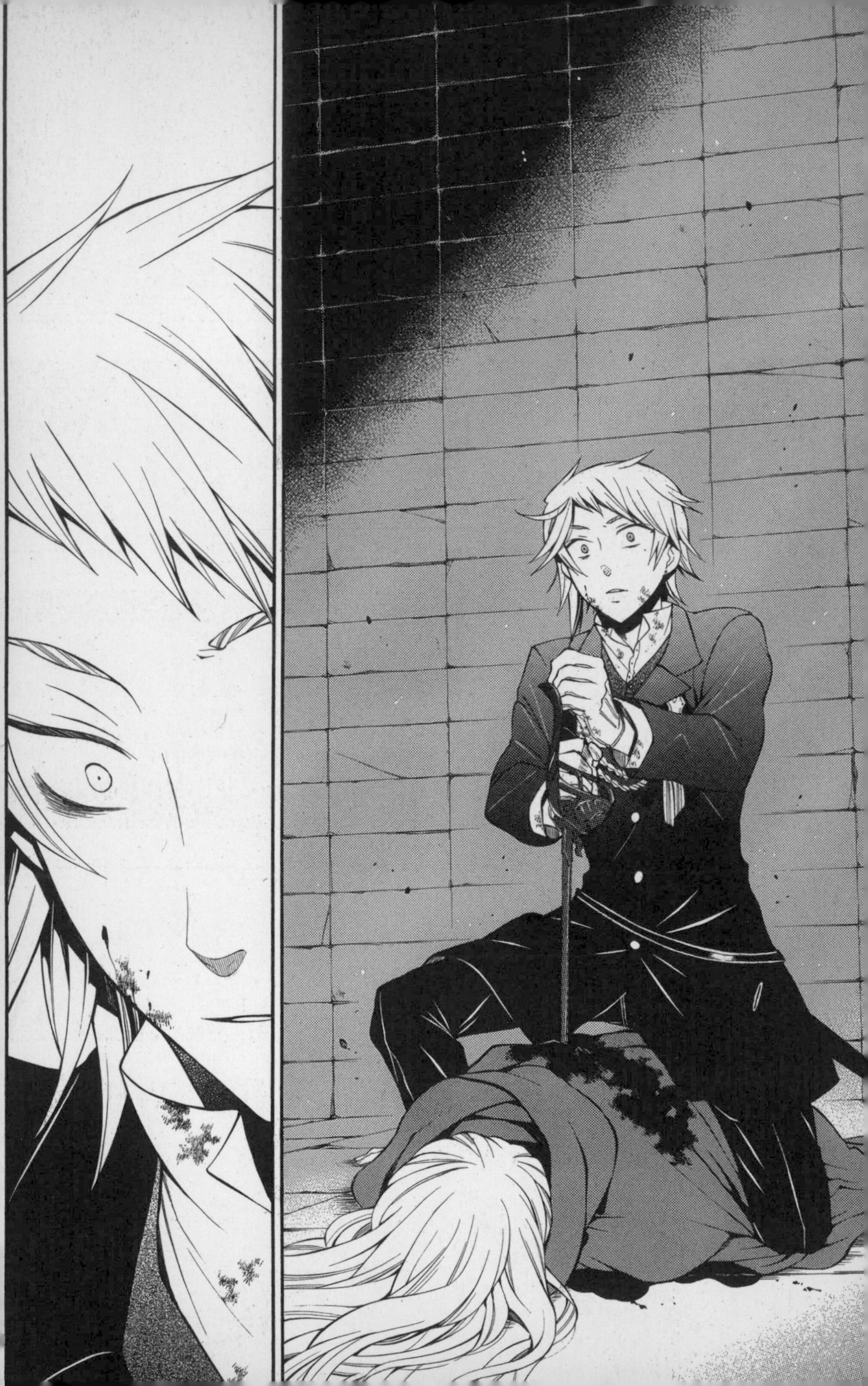

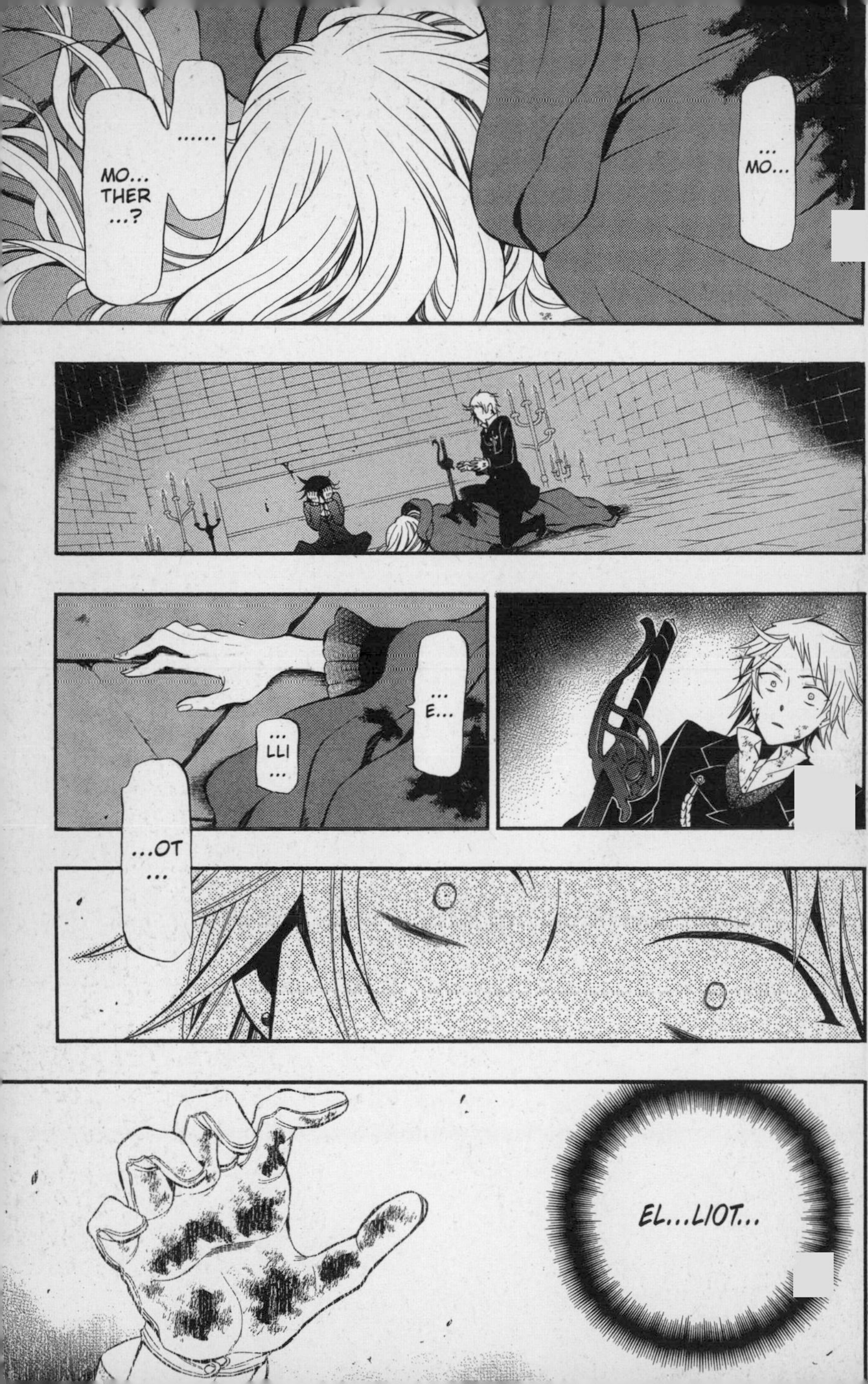
... MO...
......
MO... THER ...?
... E...
... LLI ...
...OT ...
EL...LIOT...

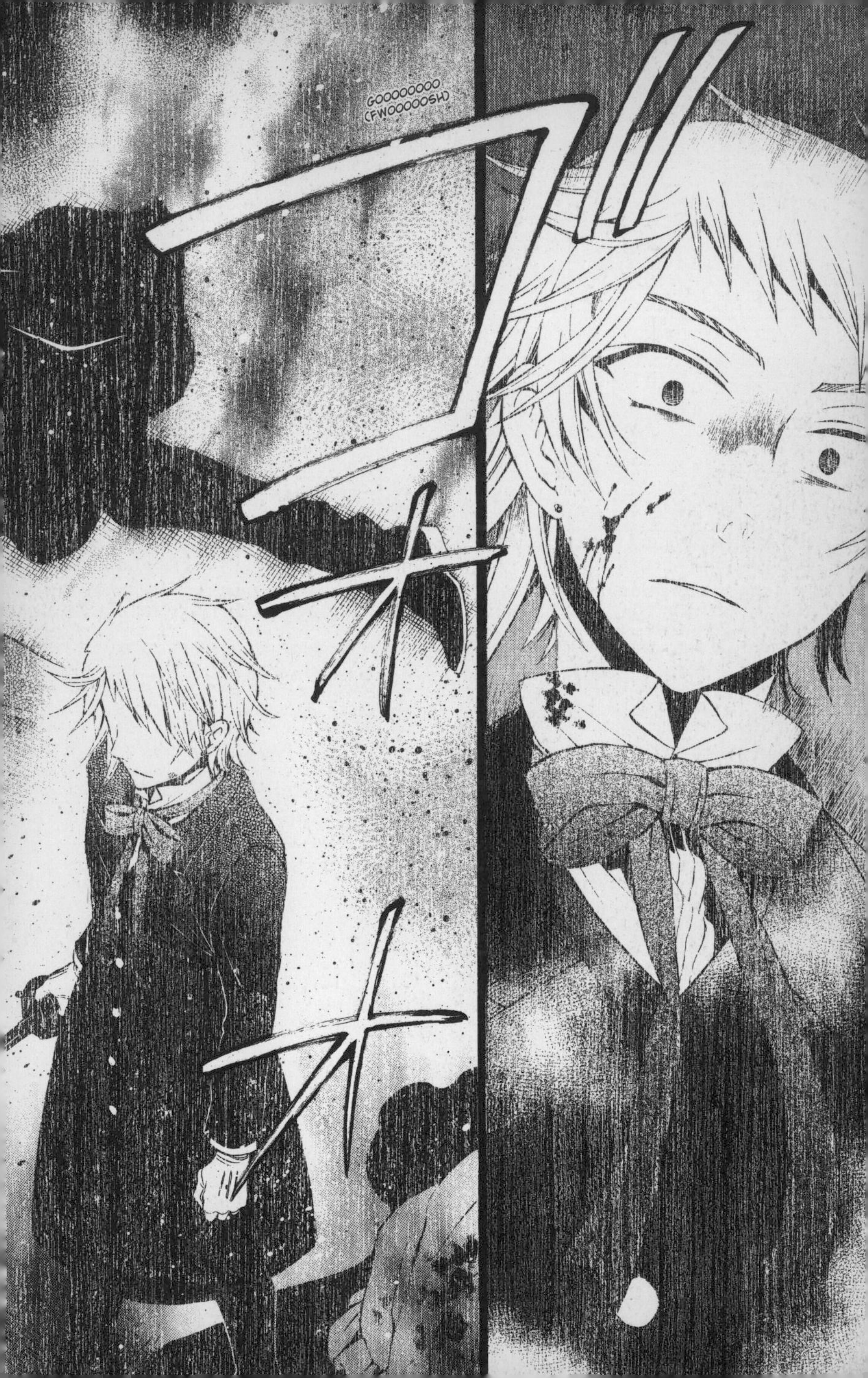
GOOOOOOOO
(FWOOOOOSH)

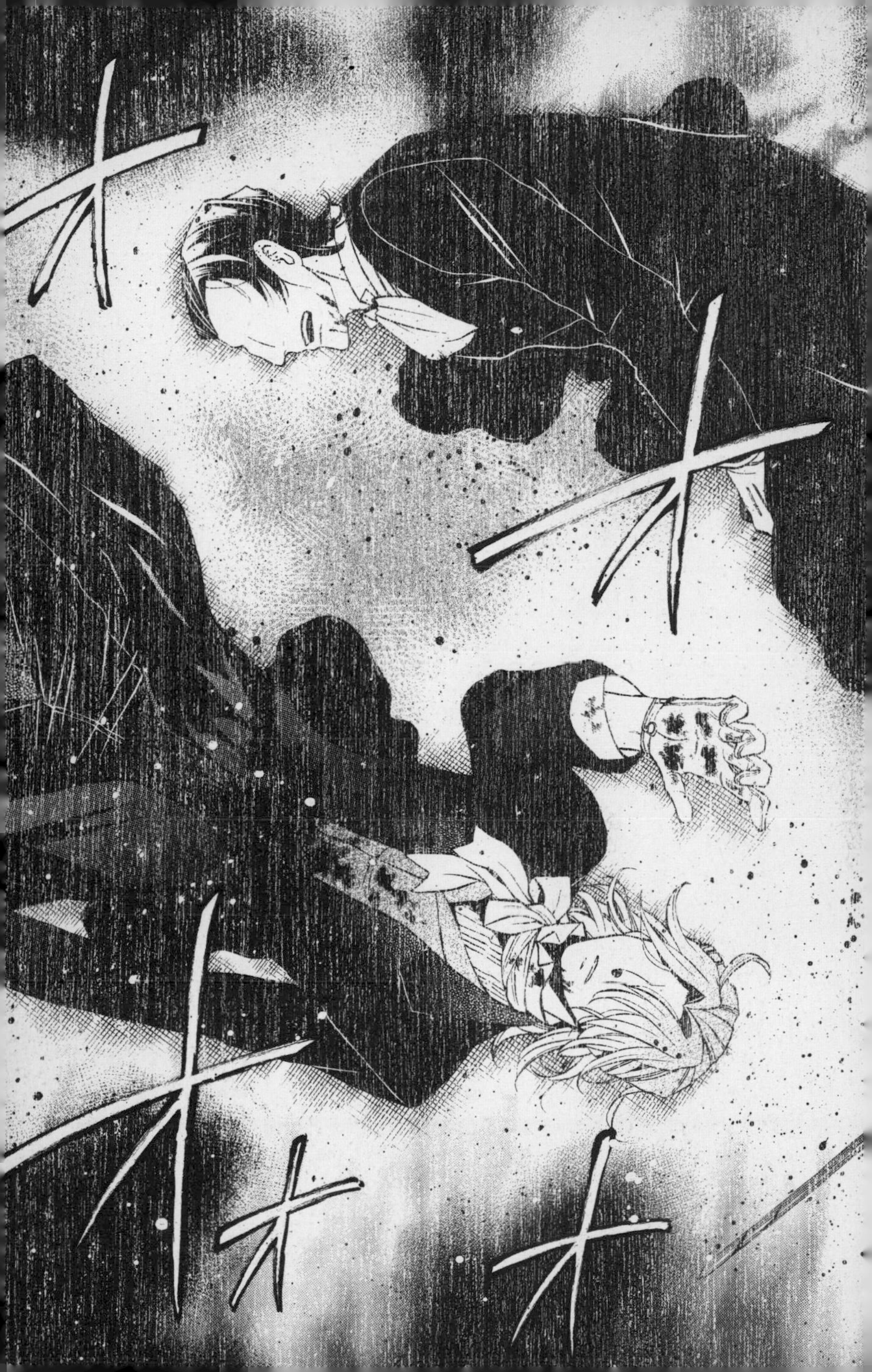

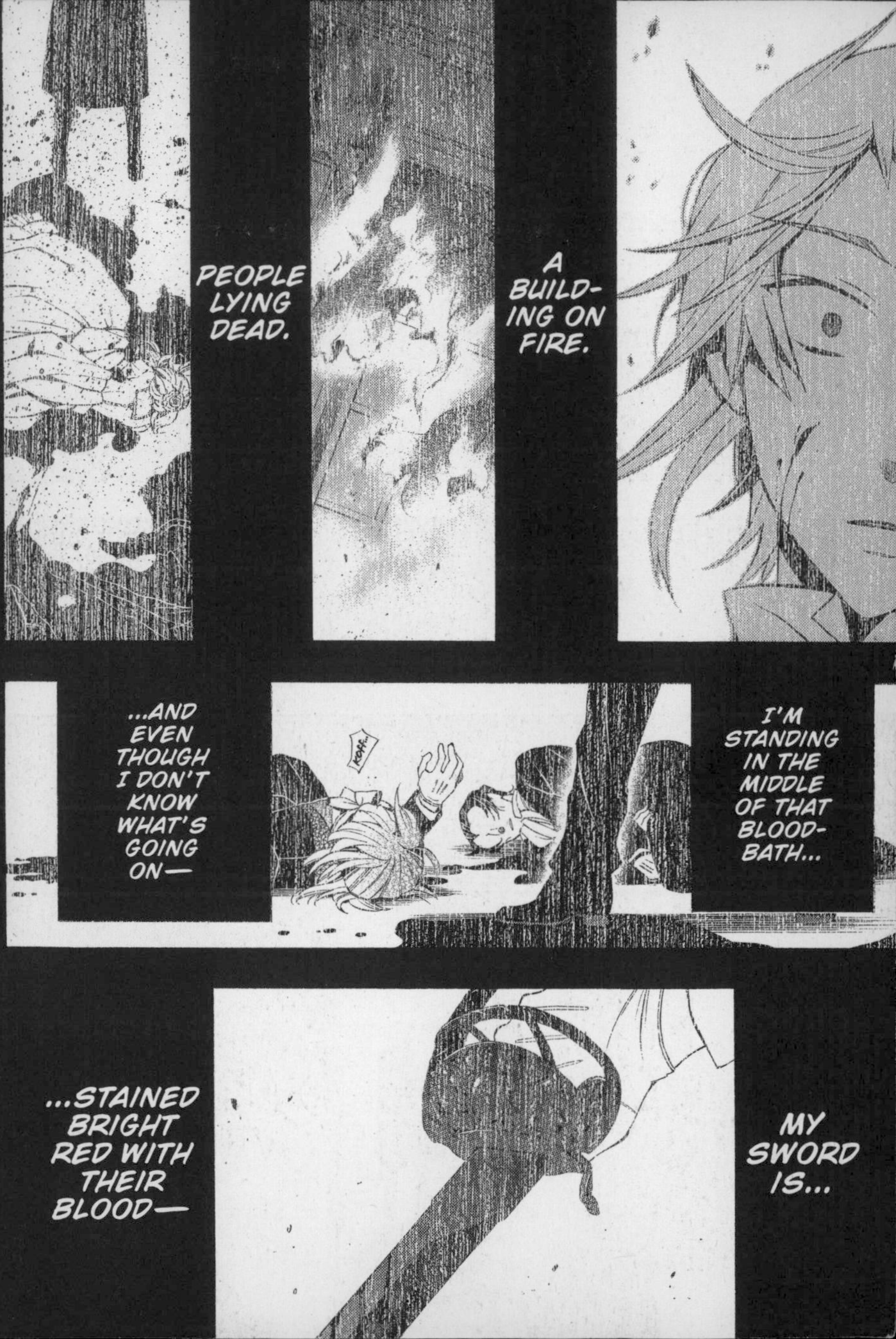
A BUILD-ING ON FIRE.
PEOPLE LYING DEAD.
I'M STANDING IN THE MIDDLE OF THAT BLOOD-BATH...
KOFF...
...AND EVEN THOUGH I DON'T KNOW WHAT'S GOING ON—
MY SWORD IS...
...STAINED BRIGHT RED WITH THEIR BLOOD—

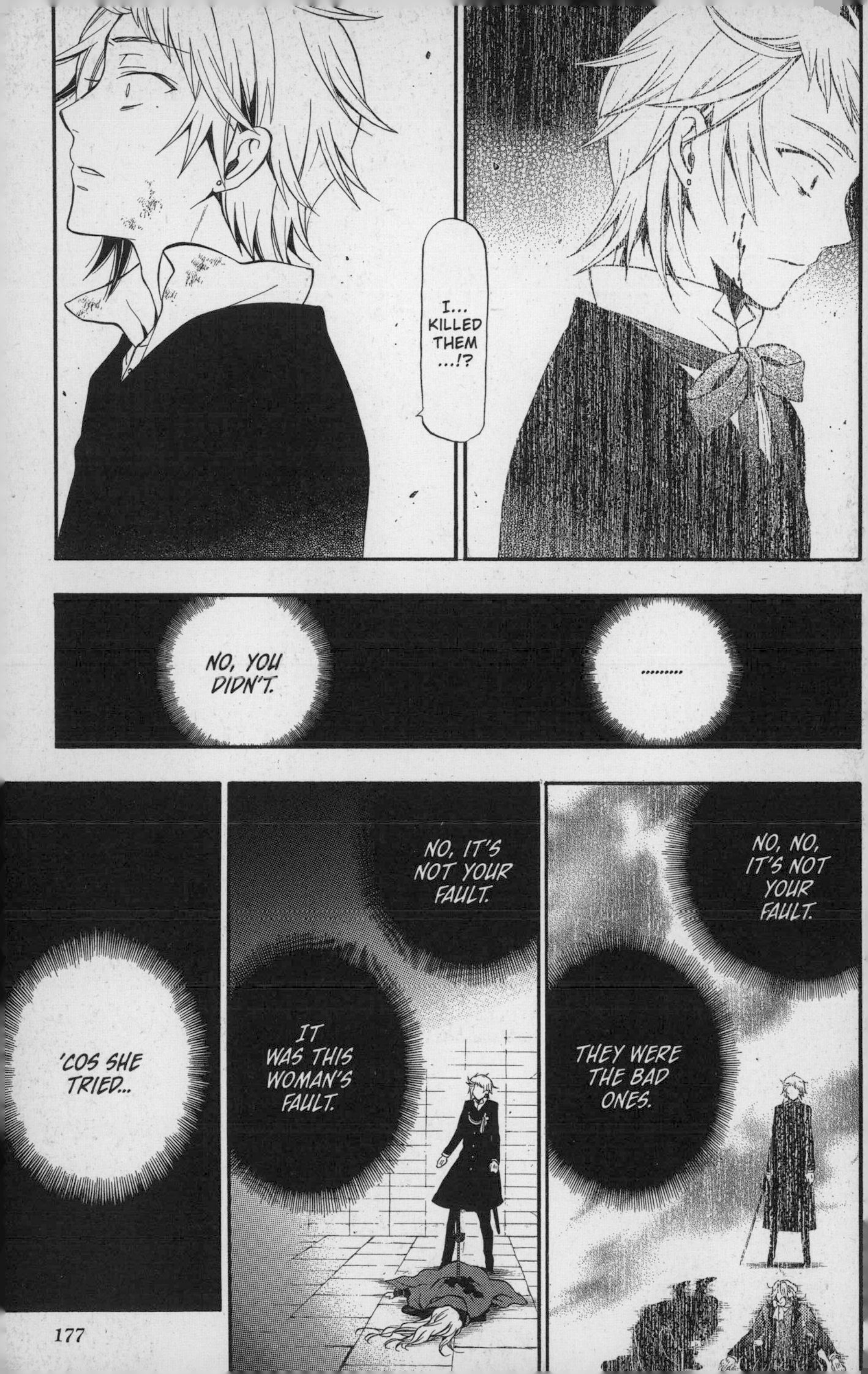
I... KILLED THEM ...!?
....
NO, YOU DIDN'T.
NO, NO, IT'S NOT YOUR FAULT.
THEY WERE THE BAD ONES.
NO, IT'S NOT YOUR FAULT.
IT WAS THIS WOMAN'S FAULT.
'COS SHE TRIED...

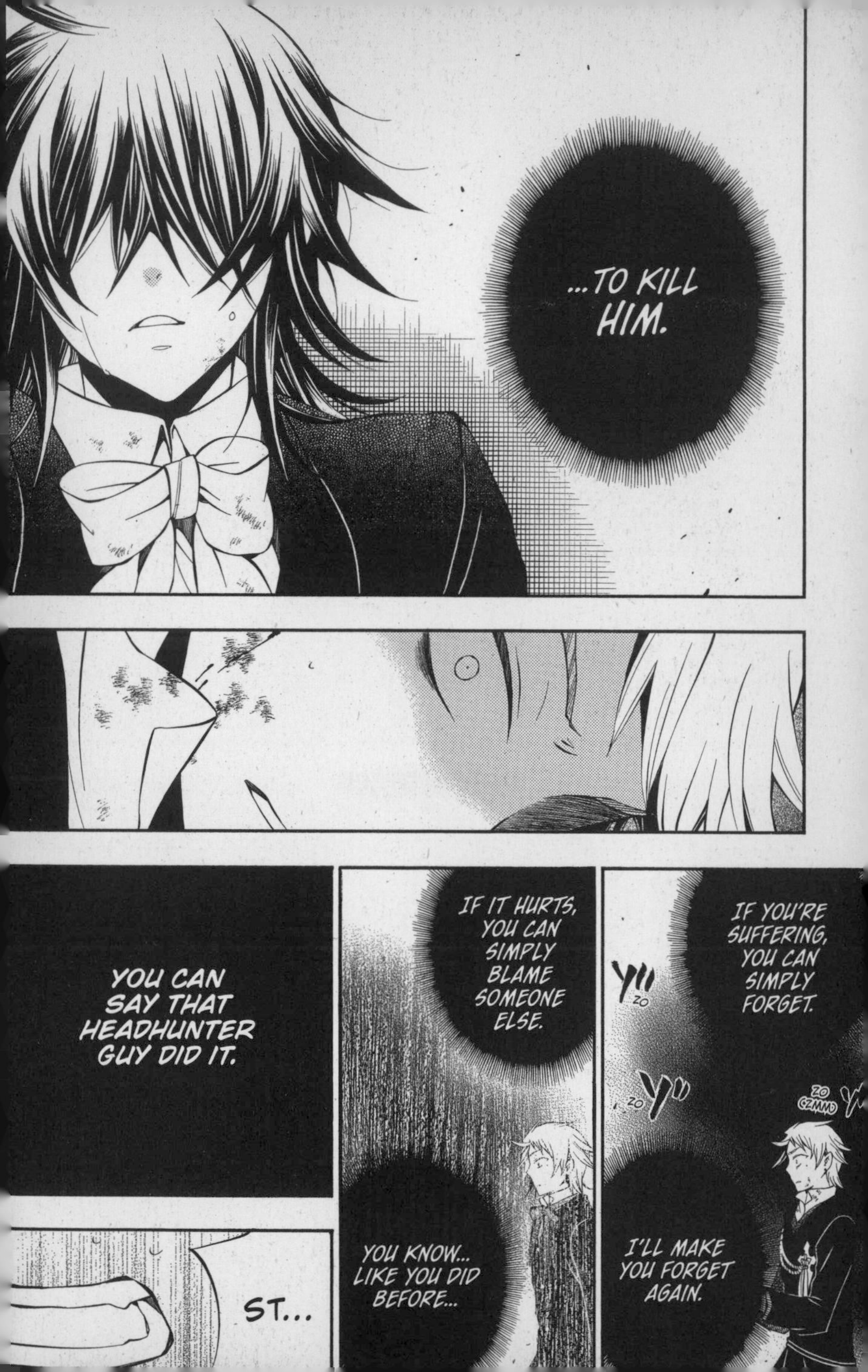
...TO KILL HIM.
IF YOU'RE SUFFERING, YOU CAN SIMPLY FORGET.
ZO
ZO
ZO
I'LL MAKE YOU FORGET AGAIN.
IF IT HURTS, YOU CAN SIMPLY BLAME SOMEONE ELSE.
YOU KNOW... LIKE YOU DID BEFORE...
YOU CAN SAY THAT HEADHUNTER GUY DID IT.
ST...

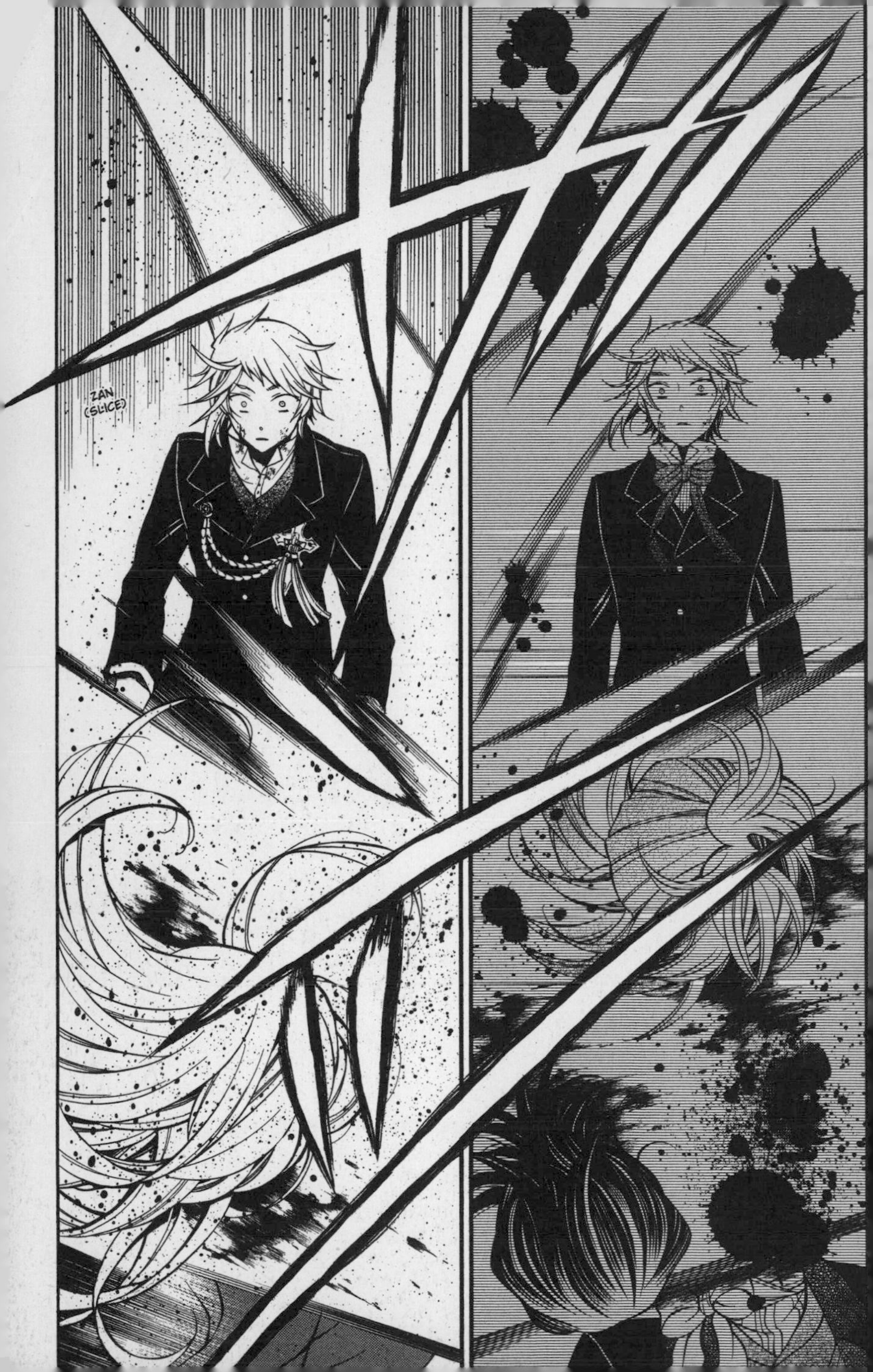
ZAN
(SLICE)

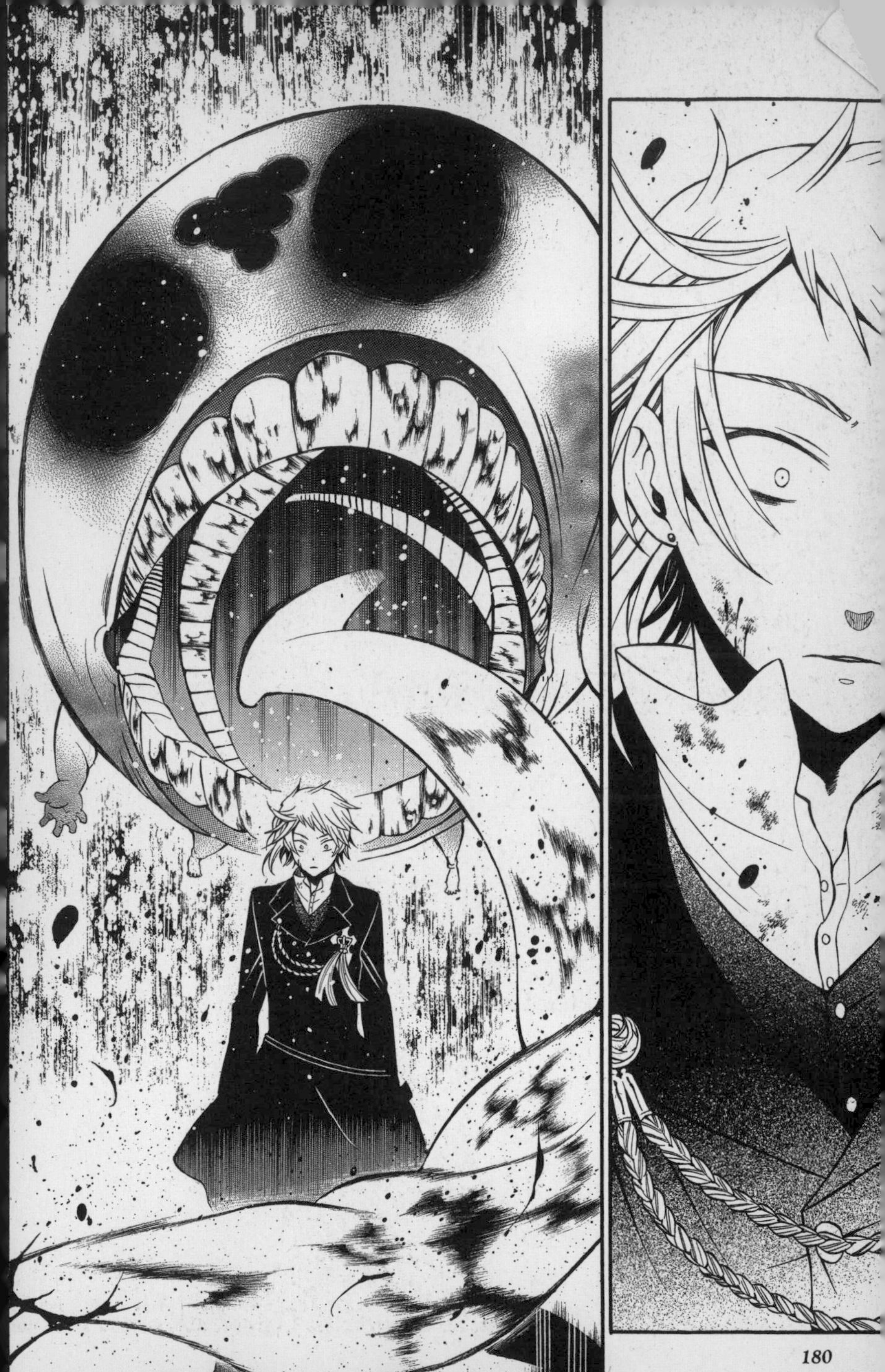

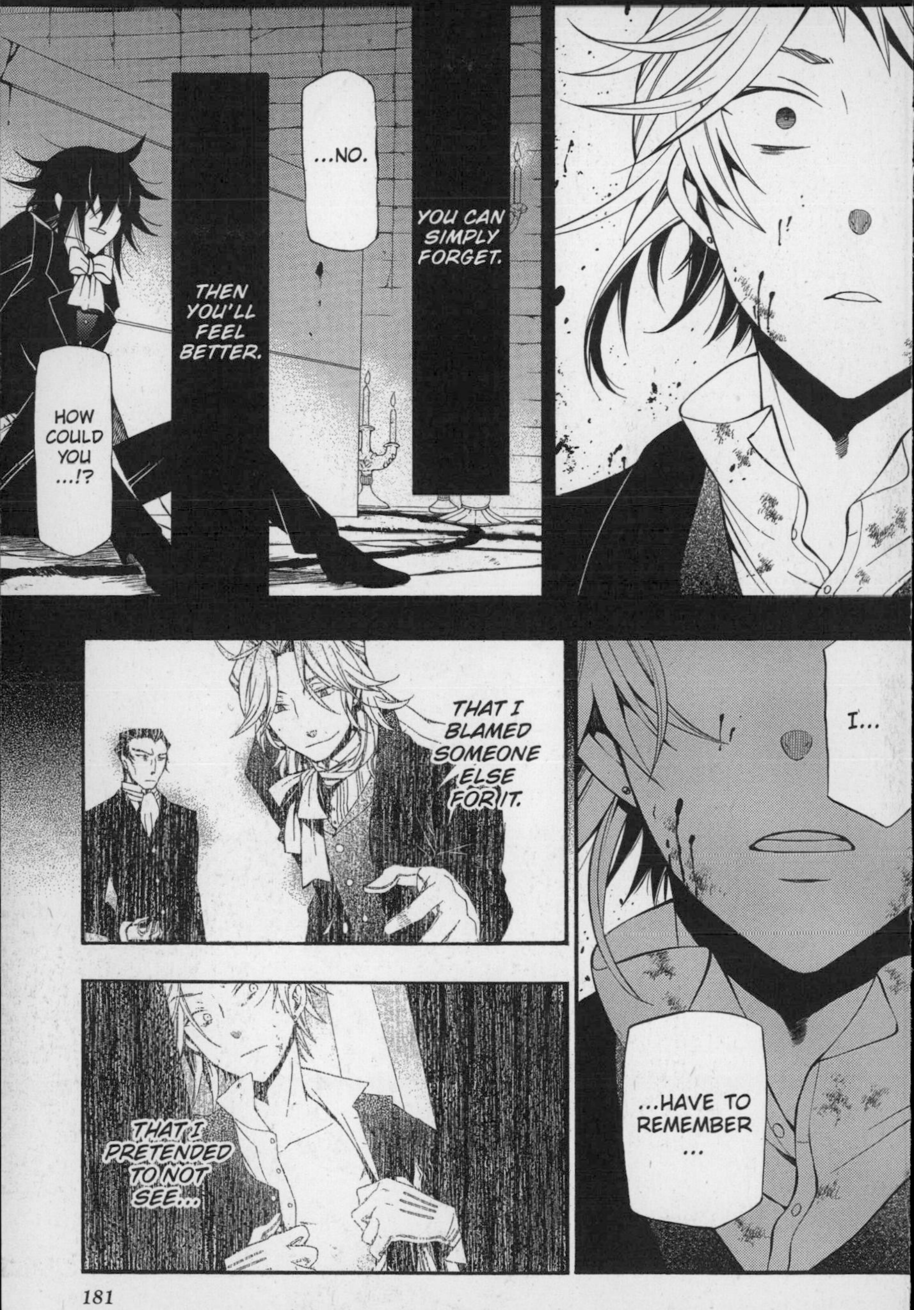
YOU CAN SIMPLY FORGET.
THEN YOU'LL FEEL BETTER.
HOW COULD YOU ...!?
...NO.
I...
...HAVE TO REMEMBER ...
THAT I BLAMED SOMEONE ELSE FOR IT.
THAT I PRETENDED TO NOT SEE...

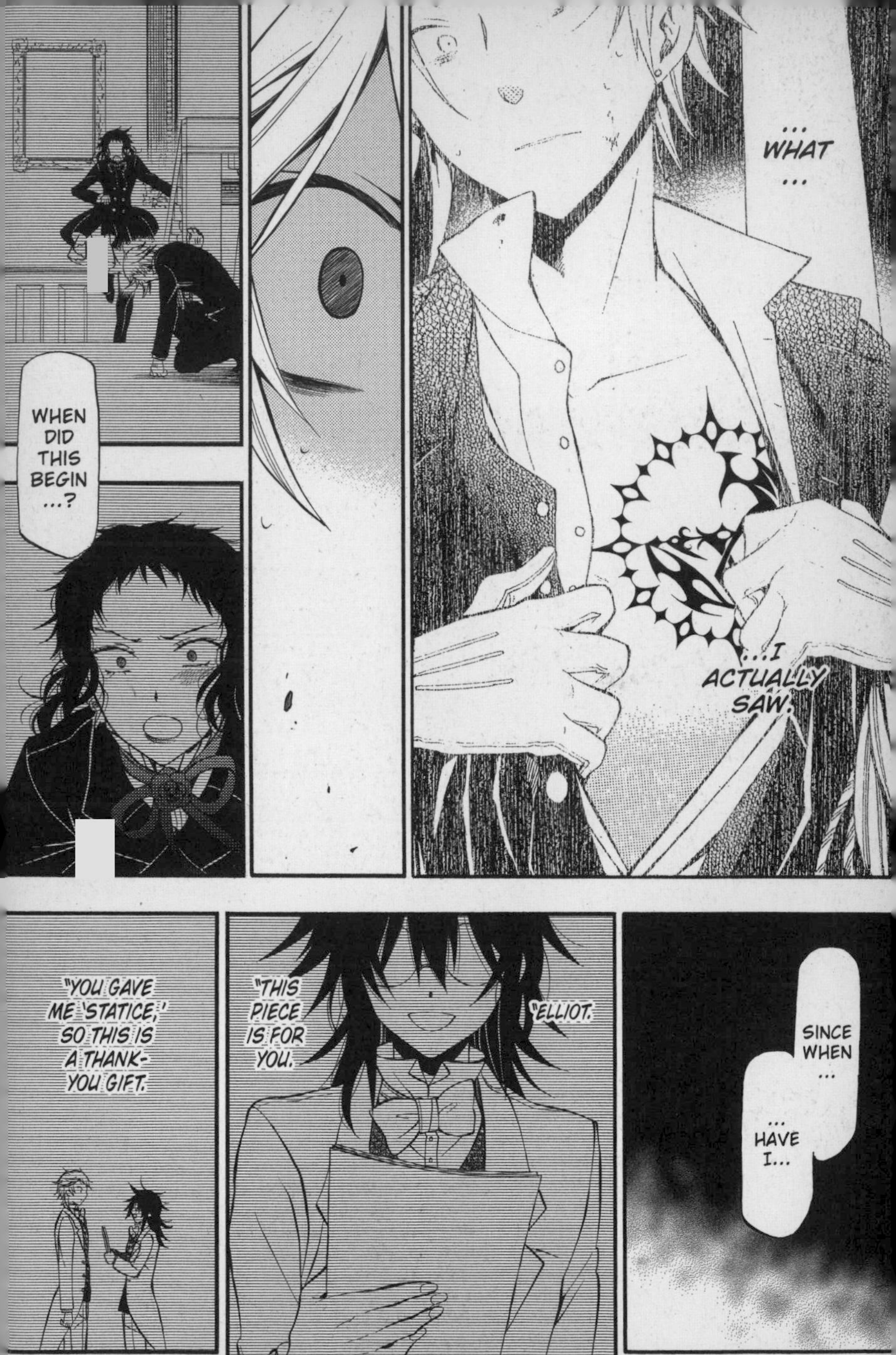
...WHAT...
...I ACTUALLY SAW.
WHEN DID THIS BEGIN...?
SINCE WHEN...
...HAVE I...
"ELLIOT.
"THIS PIECE IS FOR YOU.
"YOU GAVE ME 'STATICE,' SO THIS IS A THANK-YOU GIFT.

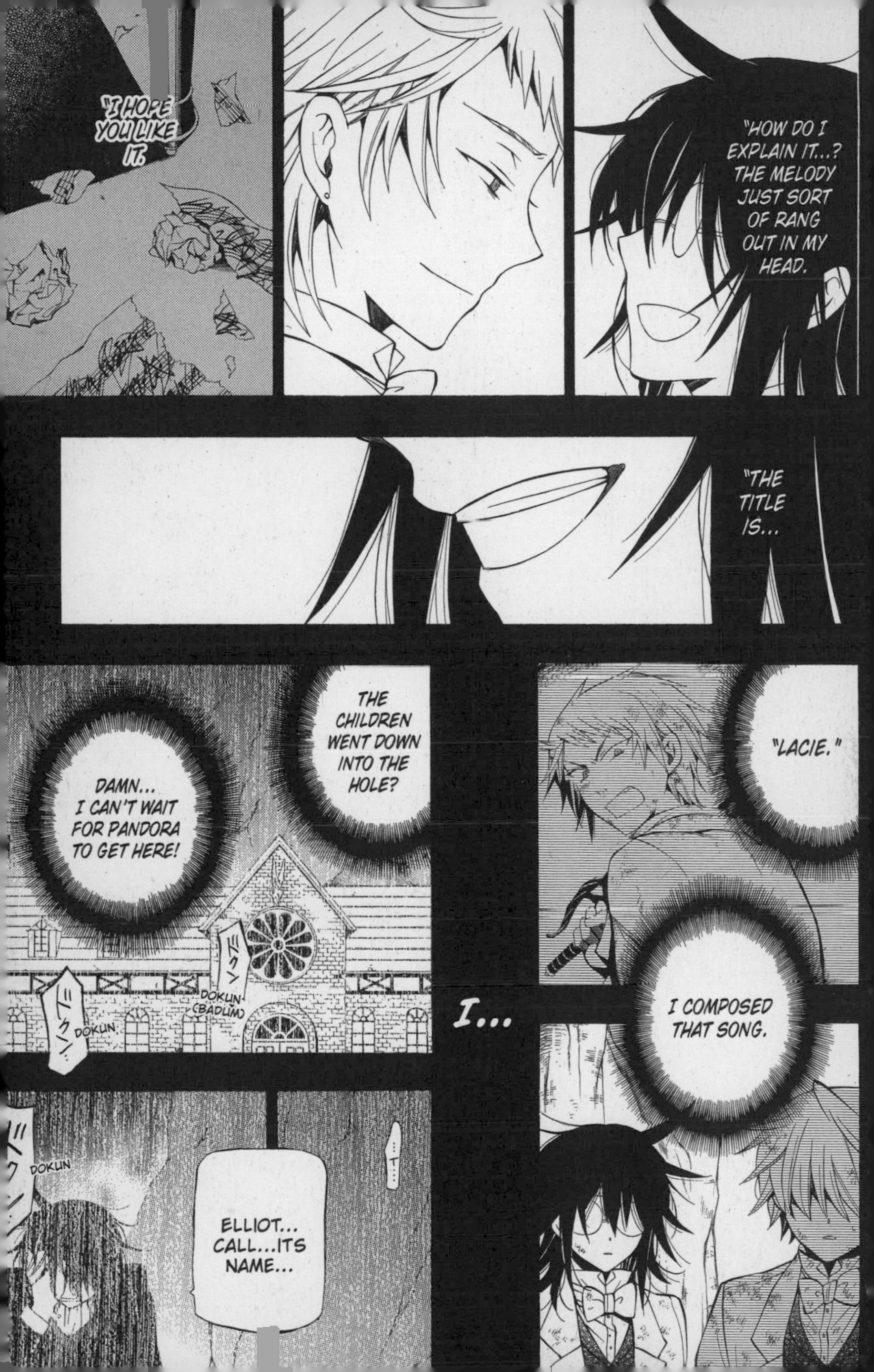
"HOW DO I EXPLAIN IT...? THE MELODY JUST SORT OF RANG OUT IN MY HEAD.
"I HOPE YOU LIKE IT.
"THE TITLE IS...
"LACIE."
THE CHILDREN WENT DOWN INTO THE HOLE?
DAMN... I CAN'T WAIT FOR PANDORA TO GET HERE!
DOKUN (BADUM)
DOKUN
I...
I COMPOSED THAT SONG.
...T...
ELLIOT... CALL...ITS NAME...
DOKUN

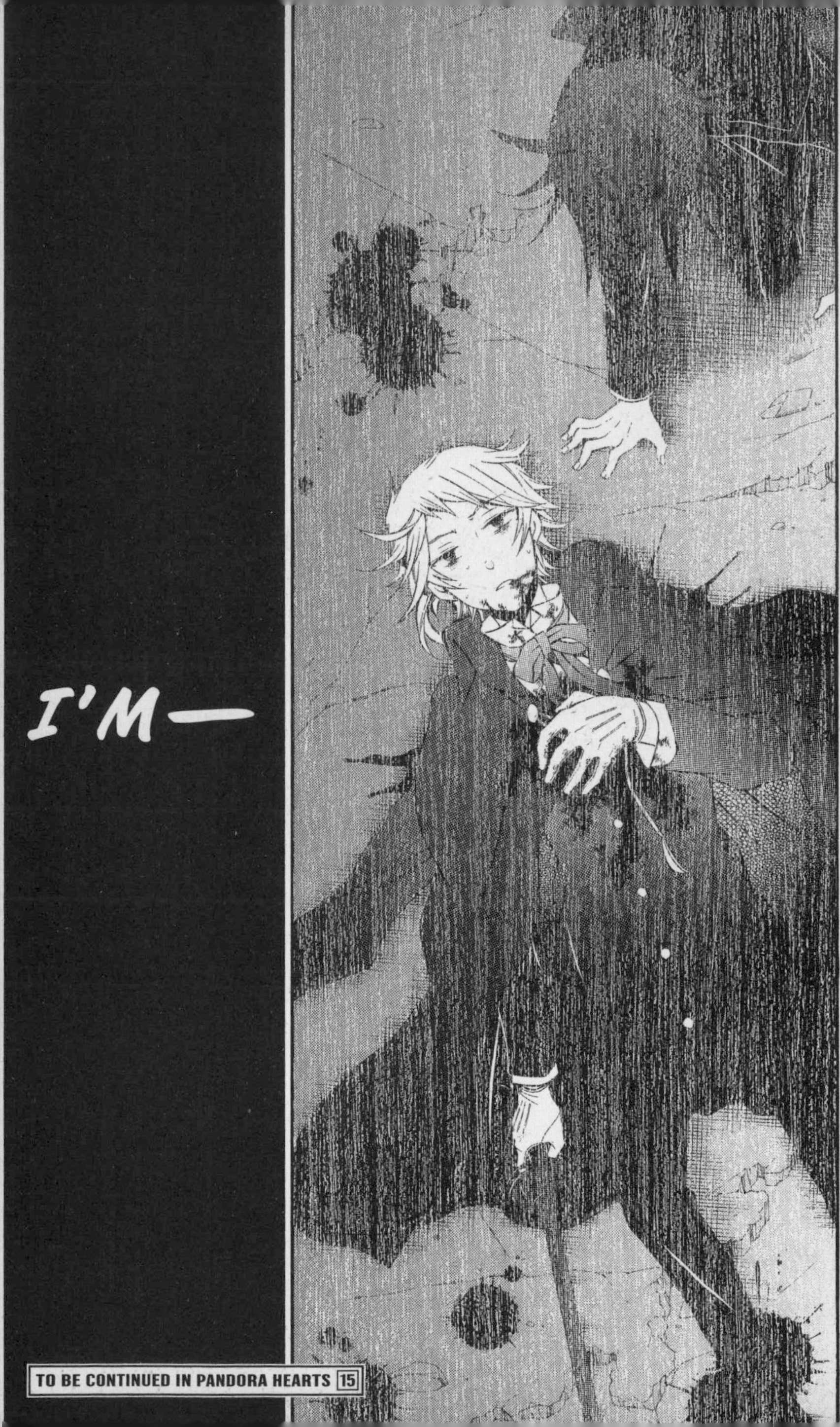
I'M—
TO BE CONTINUED IN PANDORA HEARTS 15

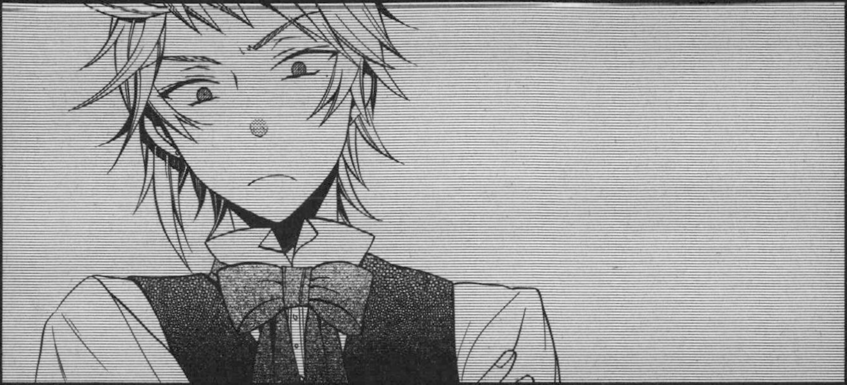

Special Thanks!

FUMITO YAMAZAKI
· MANAGES JUN MOCHIZUKI
· CHIEF ASSISTANT
· LOVES ROCK BANDS

SEIRA MINAMI-SAN
COOOME BACK
Q-U-I-C-K! ♪

SAEKO TAKIGAWA YEAH
LOVES VEGGIES
VEGETARIYAAA!

KANATA MINAZUKI MEOW
SHE LEARNED "FIGHT-OOO!"!!
TA-TA-TAAA-TAA-
TAA-TARU-TA-TAA! ♪

MIDORI ENDO-BIN
NEGATIVE IN A POSITIVE WAY.

YUKINO-TADA
UNDERSTANDS MOST OF
WHAT I MENTION ABOUT
ANIME, SO I'M HAPPY.

RYO-CHAN YEAH
RABBITS! RABBITS! YEAH!

YAJI-SENSEE!
DON'T LEAVE
YEEEET!

ASAGI-NYOON
I GUESS IT'S TIME YOU
STARTED USING PENS.
U-FU-FU-FU-FU.

YUMI NASHIGASA-CHOON
HAS BEAUTIFUL LEGS AS USUAL.
STILL A NATURAL AIRHEAD.
A-AMAZING.

MIZU KING HEH HEH
NOW...SHOW ME
MORE OF WHAT'S
IN YOUR HEART.

BIG BROTHER
& YUKKO-SAN
FATHER, MOTHER,
BIG SIS, BIG BRO

YUKAKO

MY EDITOR
TAKEGASA-SAMA

GESHI
(STOMP)
GESHI

BOKO
BOKO
(PUNCH)

AND YOU !!!

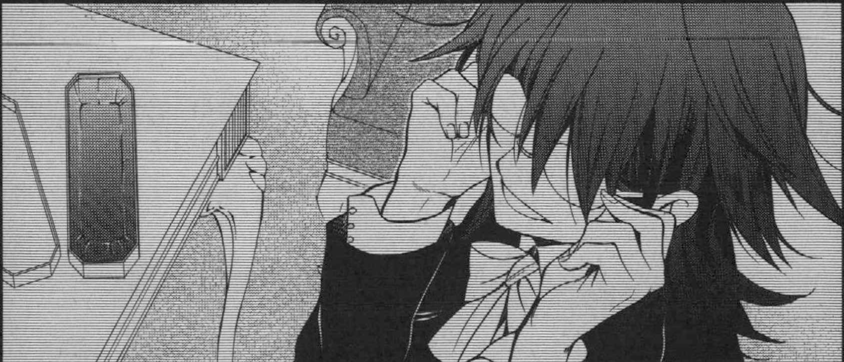

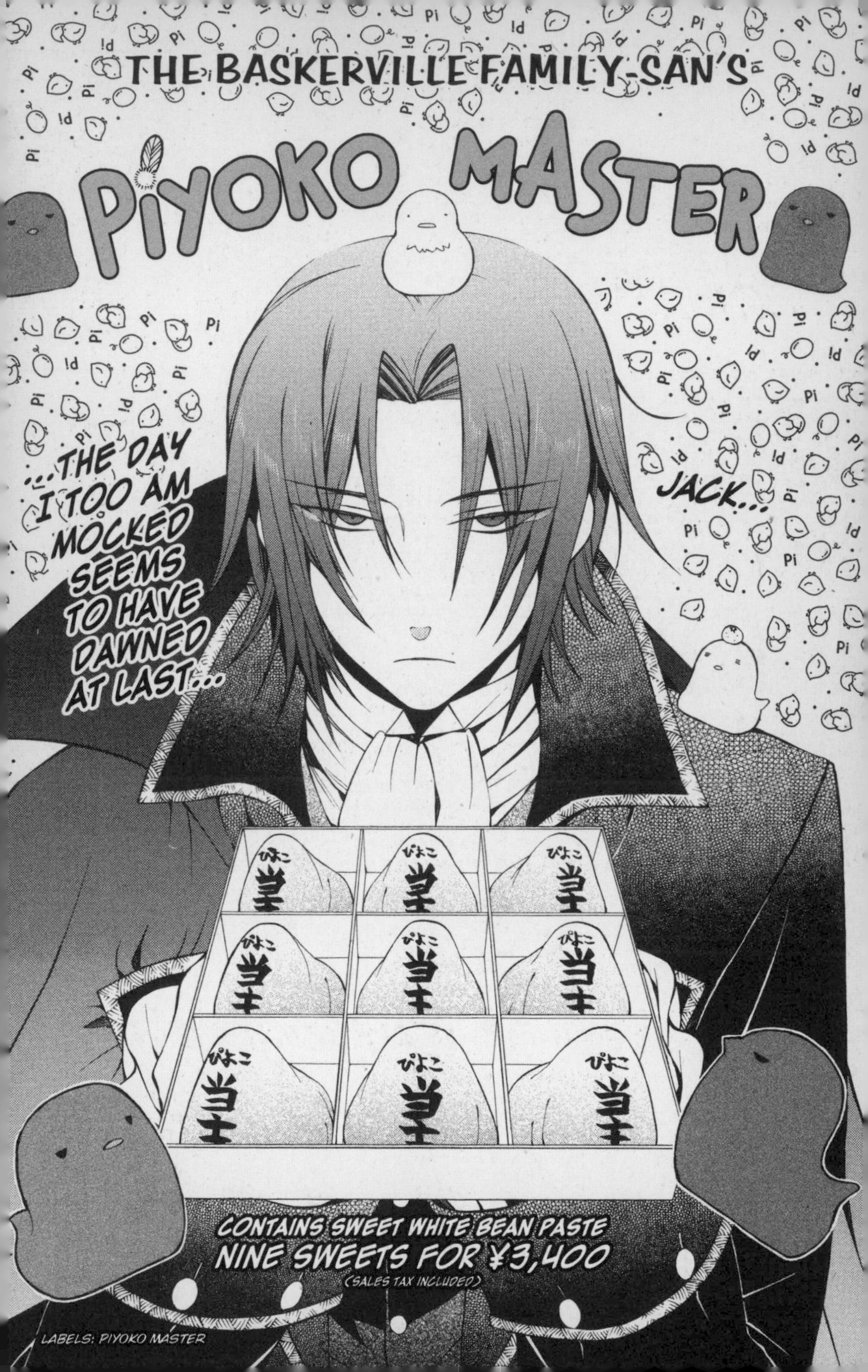
THE BASKERVILLE FAMILY-SAN'S
PIYOKO MASTER
Pi
JACK...
...THE DAY I TOO AM MOCKED SEEMS TO HAVE DAWNED AT LAST...
ぴよこ 当主
CONTAINS SWEET WHITE BEAN PASTE
NINE SWEETS FOR ¥3,400
(SALES TAX INCLUDED)
LABELS: PIYOKO MASTER

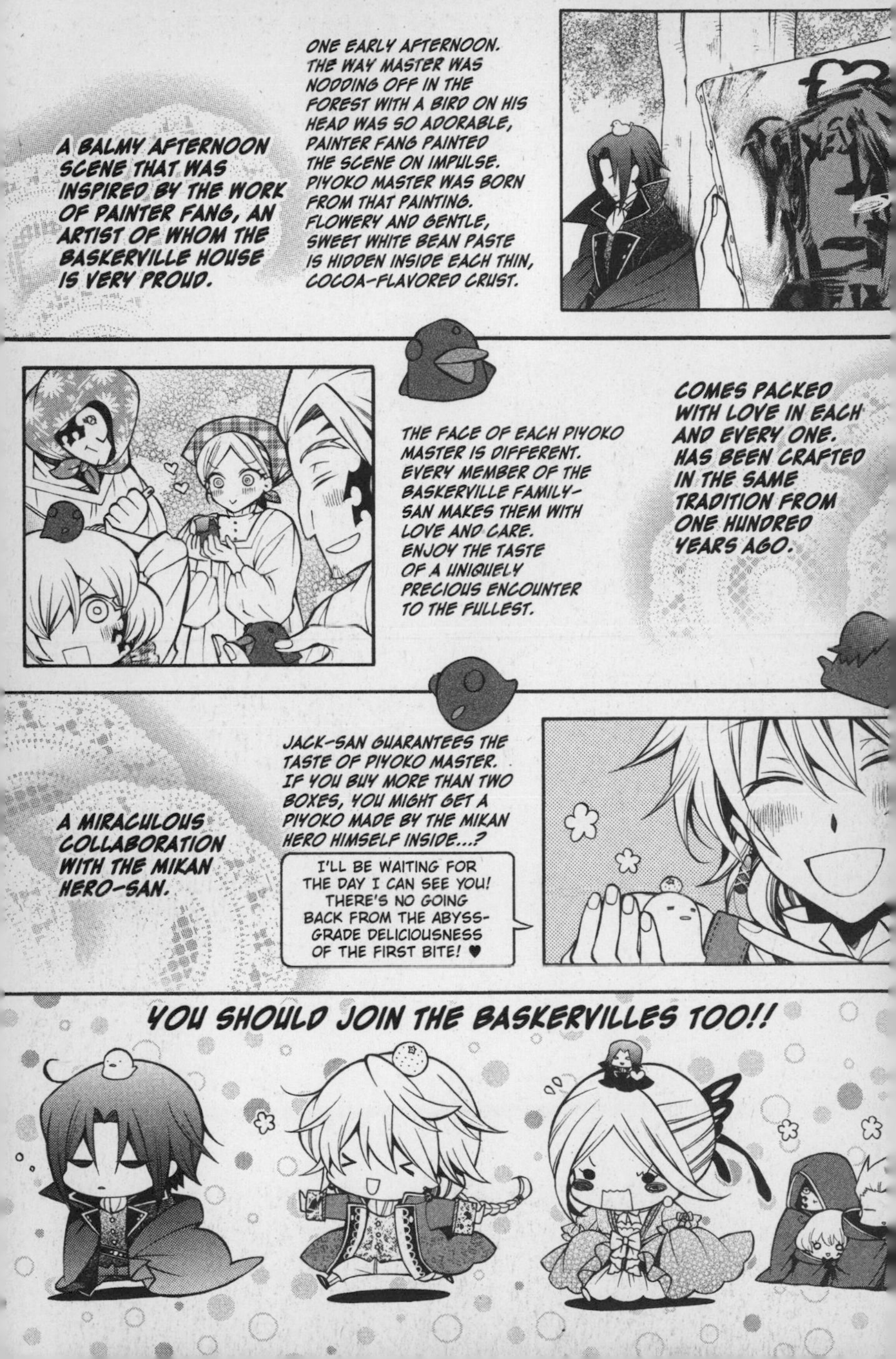

ONE EARLY AFTERNOON. THE WAY MASTER WAS NODDING OFF IN THE FOREST WITH A BIRD ON HIS HEAD WAS SO ADORABLE, PAINTER FANG PAINTED THE SCENE ON IMPULSE. PIYOKO MASTER WAS BORN FROM THAT PAINTING. FLOWERY AND GENTLE, SWEET WHITE BEAN PASTE IS HIDDEN INSIDE EACH THIN, COCOA-FLAVORED CRUST.
A BALMY AFTERNOON SCENE THAT WAS INSPIRED BY THE WORK OF PAINTER FANG, AN ARTIST OF WHOM THE BASKERVILLE HOUSE IS VERY PROUD.
COMES PACKED WITH LOVE IN EACH AND EVERY ONE. HAS BEEN CRAFTED IN THE SAME TRADITION FROM ONE HUNDRED YEARS AGO.
THE FACE OF EACH PIYOKO MASTER IS DIFFERENT. EVERY MEMBER OF THE BASKERVILLE FAMILY-SAN MAKES THEM WITH LOVE AND CARE. ENJOY THE TASTE OF A UNIQUELY PRECIOUS ENCOUNTER TO THE FULLEST.
I'LL BE WAITING FOR THE DAY I CAN SEE YOU! THERE'S NO GOING BACK FROM THE ABYSS-GRADE DELICIOUSNESS OF THE FIRST BITE! ♥
JACK-SAN GUARANTEES THE TASTE OF PIYOKO MASTER. IF YOU BUY MORE THAN TWO BOXES, YOU MIGHT GET A PIYOKO MADE BY THE MIKAN HERO HIMSELF INSIDE...?
A MIRACULOUS COLLABORATION WITH THE MIKAN HERO-SAN.
YOU SHOULD JOIN THE BASKERVILLES TOO!!

COMMON HONORIFICS

no honorific: Indicates familiarity or closeness; if used without permission or reason, addressing someone in this manner would constitute an insult.

-san: The Japanese equivalent of Mr./Mrs./Miss. If a situation calls for politeness, this is the fail-safe honorific.

-sama: Conveys great respect; may also indicate that the social status of the speaker is lower than that of the addressee.

-kun: Used most often when referring to boys (though it can be applied to girls as well), this indicates affection or familiarity. Occasionally used by older men among their peers, but it may also be used by anyone referring to a person of lower standing.

-chan: An affectionate honorific indicating familiarity used mostly in reference to girls; also used in reference to cute persons or animals of either gender.

Tove   page 67

A fictional creature that appears in Lewis Carroll's famous poem "Jabberwocky." The lithe and slippery tove was a kind of badger, with long hind legs, white fur, and short horns, according to Carroll.

Piyoko Master   page 186

A parody of a Japanese confection called Hiyoko (which means "chick"), which are little chick-shaped cake buns with red bean filling and come in a box just like the one Glen is holding.

PandoraHearts

I like clocks. I definitely prefer analog to digital. I love the antique ones even more. My heart flutters at the sight of a windup clock. I love the selfishness of it, the clock being a capable child that automatically stops and pouts when I don't pay attention to it (at least that's how it looks to me). And the winding sound really is lovely, don't you agree?

MOCHIZUKI'S MUSINGS

VOLUME 14

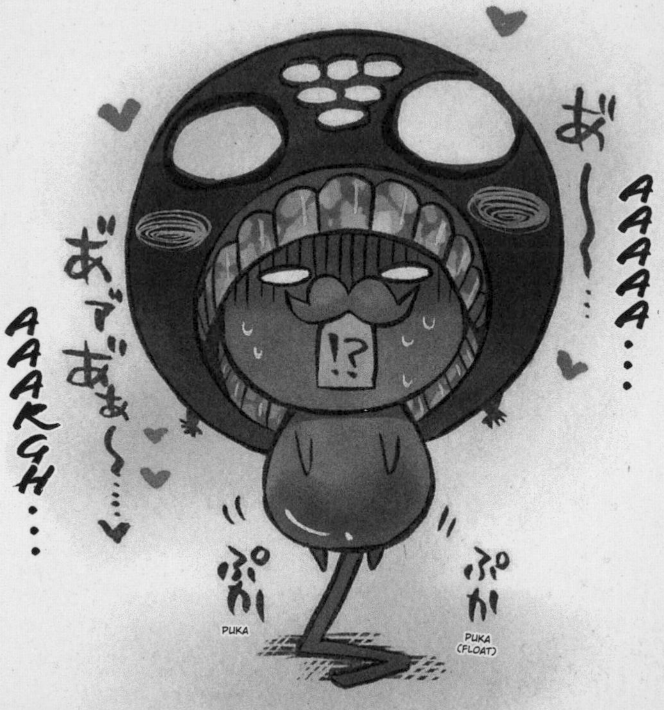
あ゛〜…
AAAAA…
あ゛ア゛あ゛あ〜…
AAAARGH…
ぷか
PUKA (FLOAT)
ぷか
PUKA

PandoraHearts

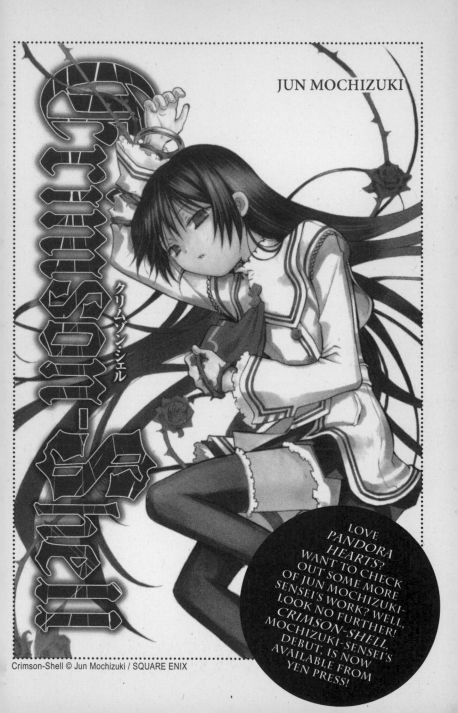

JUN MOCHIZUKI

Crimson-Shell

クリムゾン・シェル

LOVE *PANDORA HEARTS*? WANT TO CHECK OUT SOME MORE OF JUN MOCHIZUKI-SENSEI'S WORK? WELL, LOOK NO FURTHER! *CRIMSON-SHELL*, MOCHIZUKI-SENSEI'S DEBUT, IS NOW AVAILABLE FROM YEN PRESS!

Crimson-Shell © Jun Mochizuki / SQUARE ENIX

PandoraHearts

PANDORA HEARTS ⑭

JUN MOCHIZUKI

Translation: Tomo Kimura • Lettering: Alexis Eckerman

This book is a work of fiction. Names, characters, places, and incidents are the product of the author's imagination or are used fictitiously. Any resemblance to actual events, locales, or persons, living or dead, is coincidental.

PANDORA HEARTS Vol. 14 © 2011 Jun Mochizuki / SQUARE ENIX CO., LTD. All rights reserved. First published in Japan in 2011 by SQUARE ENIX CO., LTD. English translation rights arranged with SQUARE ENIX CO., LTD. and Hachette Book Group through Tuttle-Mori Agency, Inc.

Translation © 2013 by SQUARE ENIX CO., LTD.

All rights reserved. In accordance with the U.S. Copyright Act of 1976, the scanning, uploading, and electronic sharing of any part of this book without the permission of the publisher is unlawful piracy and theft of the author's intellectual property. If you would like to use material from the book (other than for review purposes), prior written permission must be obtained by contacting the publisher at permissions@hbgusa.com. Thank you for your support of the author's rights.

Yen Press
Hachette Book Group
237 Park Avenue, New York, NY 10017

www.HachetteBookGroup.com
www.YenPress.com

Yen Press is an imprint of Hachette Book Group, Inc. The Yen Press name and logo are trademarks of Hachette Book Group, Inc.

First Yen Press Edition: February 2013

ISBN: 978-0-316-22536-6

10 9 8 7 6 5 4 3 2 1

BVG

Printed in the United States of America